Cuba

Managing editor: Liz Coghill
English translation: Atlas Translations, Florence Brutton, Penny Langton
Editor: Maria Morgan
Proofreader: Hilary Hughes

Additional research and assistance: Michael Hutchinson, Sofi Mogensen, Kate Williams, Michael Summers
Index: Dorothy Frame

Series director: Philippe Gloaguen
Series creators: Philippe Gloaguen, Michel Duval
Chief editor: Pierre Josse
Assistant chief editor: Benoît Lucchini
Coordination director: Florence Charmetant

Editorial team: Yves Couprie, Olivier Page, Véronique de Chardon, Amanda Keravel, Isabelle Al Subaihi, Anne-Caroline Dumas, Carole Bordes, Bénédicte Bazaille, André Poncelet, Jérôme de Gubernatis, Marie Burin des Roziers and Thierry Brouard.

Our guides provide independent advice. The authors and compilers do not accept any remuneration for the inclusion of addresses in this guide. Please note that we cannot accept any responsibility for any loss, injury or inconvenience sustained by anyone as a result of any information or advice contained in this guide.

Feedback

We have done our best to ensure the accuracy of the information contained in this guide. However, addresses, phone numbers, opening times etc. do invariably change from time to time, so if you find a discrepancy please do let us know and help us update the guides. As prices may change so may other circumstances – a restaurant may change hands or the standard of service at a hotel may deteriorate since our researchers made their visit. Again, we do our best to ensure information is accurate, but if you notice any discrepancy, please let us know. You can contact us at: hachetteuk@orionbooks.co.uk or write to us at Cassell & Co, address below.

Price guide

Because of rapid inflation in many countries, it is impossible to give an accurate indication of prices in hotels and restaurants. Prices can change enormously from one year to the next. As a result we have adopted a system of categories for the prices in the guides: 'Budget', 'Moderate', 'Chic' and 'Très Chic' (in the guides to France), otherwise 'Expensive' and 'Splash Out' in the others.

First published in the United Kingdom in 2002 by Cassell & Co
© English Translation Cassell & Co 2002
© Hachette Livre (Hachette Tourisme) 2001
© Cartography Hachette Tourisme

Distributed in the United States of America by Sterling Publishing Co., Inc.
387 Park Avenue South, New York, NY 10016-8810.

A CIP catalogue for this book is available from the British Library.

ISBN 1 84202 062 5

Typeset at The Spartan Press Ltd, Lymington, Hants.
Printed and bound by Aubin, France. E-mail: sales@aubin-imprimeur.fr

Cover design by Emmanuel Le Vallois (Hachette Livre) and Paul Cooper.
Cover photo © Getty Images/Stone. Back cover photo © The Travel Library/Stuart Black.

Cassell & Co, Wellington House, 125 Strand, London WC2R 0BB

routard

Cuba

**The ultimate
food, drink and
accommodation guide**

HACHETTE

Contents

Just Exactly Who or What is a Routard?

You are. Yes, you! The fact that you are reading this book means that you are a Routard. You are probably still none the wiser, so to explain we will take you back to the origin of the guides. Routard was the brainchild of a Frenchman named Philippe Gloaguen, who compiled the first guide some 25 years ago with his friend Michel Duval. They simply could not find the kind of guide book they wanted and so the solution was clear – they would just have to write it themselves. When it came to naming the guide, Philippe came up with the term Routard, which at the time did not exist as a bona fide word – at least, not in conventional dictionary terms. Today, if you look the word up in a French-English dictionary you will find that it means 'traveller' or 'globetrotter' – so there you have it, that's what you are!

From this humble beginning has grown a vast collection of some 100 titles to destinations all over the world. Routard is now the bestselling guide book series in France. The guides have been translated into five different languages, so keep an eye out for fellow Routard readers on your travels.

What exactly do the guides do?
The short answer is that they provide all the information you need to enable you to have a successful holiday or trip. Routards' great strength however, lies in their listings. The guides provide comprehensive listings for accommodation, eating and drinking – ranging from campsites and youth hostels through to four star hotels – and from bars, clubs and greasy spoons to tearooms, cafés and restaurants. Each entry is accompanied by a detailed and frank appraisal of the address, rather like a friend coming back from holiday who is recommending all the good places to go (or even the places to avoid!). The guides aim to help you find the best addresses and the best value for money within your price range, whilst giving you invaluable insider advice at the same time.

Anything else?
Routard also provides oceans of practical advice on how to get along in the country or city you are visiting plus an insight into the character and customs of the people. How do you negotiate your way around the transport system? Will you offend if you bare your knees in the temple? And so on. In addition, you will find plenty of sightseeing information, backed up by historical and cultural detail, interesting facts and figures, addresses and opening times. The humanitarian aspect is also of great importance, with the guides commenting freely and often pithily, and most titles contain a section on human rights.

Routard are truly useful guides that are convivial, irreverent, down-to-earth and honest. We very much hope you enjoy them and that they will serve you well during your stay.

Happy travelling.

Map List

Symbols Used in the Guide

Please note that not all the symbols below appear in every guide.

- ■ Useful addresses
- ⬛ Tourist office
- ✉ Post office
- ☎ Telephone
- 🚆 Railway station
- 🚌 Bus station
- 🚖 Shared taxi
- 🚊 Tram
- River transport
- Sea transport
- ✈ Airport
- Where to stay

- ✕ Where to eat
- ▼ Where to go for a drink
- ♪ Where to listen to music
- Where to go for an ice-cream
- ★ To see
- Shopping
- • 'Other'
- ▣ Parking
- ✕ Castle
- Ruins

- Diving site
- Shelter
- ✕ Campsite
- ▲ Peak
- ● Site
- ○ Town
- ✕ Hill
- Abbey, chapel
- ← Lookout
- Beach
- ✖ Lighthouse

Getting There

By Air

FROM BRITAIN

At the time of writing, the national carrier **Cubana** had ceased scheduled flights to Havana and **British Airways** had announced that their flights to Havana would cease in spring 2002. However, in May 2002, **Kuoni** will begin weekly Friday charter flights to Havana from London Gatwick until October, when the flights will depart on Mondays. The alternative is to fly to Havana on a scheduled flight via Madrid, Paris or Amsterdam, with **Iberia**, **Air France** or **KLM**. Travel via Europe is quicker, and works out cheaper, than travelling via Mexico on **Mexicana** or the Caribbean with **Air Jamaica**.

Unlike flights to Havana, travellers will find that there are regular charter flights to the beach resort of Varadero and some to Holguín. Direct flights to Varadero take about 10 hours. Journey time by road from Varadero to Havana is about 2 hours 30 minutes.

Charter flights to Cuba are usually sold as part of a package, although high street and specialist travel agents will sell reasonably priced flight-only deals to Camagüey, Holguín and Varadero. Flights on the charter airline **Airtours** can be booked direct with the company. Charter flights are aimed at holidaymakers wishing for one or two weeks in the sun. The price will increase dramatically if you wish to stay longer than 14 days. Charter flights cannot be purchased on an 'open jaw' basis – you must arrive and depart at the same airport.

Many people visit Cuba as part of a package holiday, usually to Varadero, the destination for the majority of package holidays. Packages in hotels on Varadero are usually sold on an 'all-inclusive' basis where drinks, food and activities are included in the price. Prices for an all-inclusive fortnight in a Varadero resort start at around £800 per person. Room only deals begin at around £450 per person.

Travel agents are increasingly receptive to visitors who wish to see more of Cuba than the beach, and there are more and more options for fly-drive, special interest holidays and tailor-made itineraries. Many of the travel agents listed below offer cultural and historical tours, tailor-made itineraries, and packages that combine a tour of Havana, and surrounding regions, with a beach holiday in Varadero. Cuba can be hard to get around and even those who would normally backpack on holiday might consider contacting a travel agent for assistance in arranging flights, car hire and accommodation for the first few days of the holiday.

If you are staying in Havana with a package operator, try to check the whereabouts of your hotel as many companies use hotels in suburbs of Havana such as Miramar, which are far from the city centre.

The best time to visit Cuba is between December and April, which is, however, when flights and packages are at their most expensive. Prices are highest for departures in the Christmas and New Year period.

Cuba is a popular destination for packages and there is plenty of hotel accommodation. Travellers can find good deals, especially if travelling outside the main holiday seasons. Hunting grounds for package or air ticket bargains include the travel pages of the weekend broadsheet newspapers, teletext and websites such as www.cheapflights.com, www.expedia.com and www.lastminute.com. Always ensure that any airline or travel agent you book with is ABTA endorsed. Contact the **Air Travel Advisory Bureau** for advice on airlines and prices.

⊕**Airtours**: Wavell House, Holcombe Road, Helmshore BR4 4ND. ☎ (0870) 400 1200. Website: www.airtours.co.uk

⊕**Air France**: 10 Warwick Street, First Floor, London WR1 5RA. ☎ (0845) 084 5111. Website: www.airfrance.com

⊕**Air Jamaica**: Central House, Lampton Road, Hounslow TW3 1HY. ☎ (020) 8857 0917. Website: www.airjamaica.com

⊕**British Airways**: Waterside, PO Box 365, Harmondsworth UB7 0GB. ☎ (0845) 773 3377. Website: www.britishairways.com

⊕**Cubana**: 49 Conduit Street, London W1R 9FB. ☎ (020) 7734 1165. Email: cubana@corona.freeserve. Website: www.cubana.cu

⊕**Iberia**: Iberia House, 10 Hammersmith Broadway, London W6 7AL. ☎ (0845) 601 2854. Website: www.iberia.com

⊕**KLM**: Terminal Four, Heathrow Airport, Hounslow TW6 3XQ. ☎ (020) 8750 9200. Website: www.klm.com

⊕**Kuoni**: Kuoni House, Dorking RH5 4AZ. ☎ (01306) 747002. Website: www.kuoni.co.uk

⊕**Mexicana de Avacion**: 75 St Margaret's Avenue, Whetstone, London N20 9LD. ☎ (020) 8849 2000. Email: sales@mextours.co.uk. Website: www.mexicana.com

⊕**The Air Travel Advisory Bureau**: Columbus House, 28 Charles Square, London N1 6HT. ☎ (020) 7635 5000. Website: www.atab.co.uk

TRAVEL AGENTS

■ **Airline Network** (discount flights by phone only): ☎ (0870) 241 0019.

■ **Bridge the World** (discount flights and packages): 47 Chalk Farm Road, London NW1 8AJ. ☎ (0870) 444 7474. Website: www.bridgetheworld.com

■ **Flightbookers** (discount flights and packages): 177–178 Tottenham Court Road, London W1P OLX. ☎ (0870) 010 7000. Website: www.ebookers.com

■ **STA Travel** (students and those under 26): 86 Old Brompton Road, London SW7 3LQ. ☎ (020) 7851 4132. Website: www.statravel.co.uk

■ **Thomas Cook** (flights and packages): branches nationwide. ☎ (0990) 666 222. Website: www.thomascook.com

■ **Trailfinders** (discounts and specialist itineraries): 194 Kensington High Street, London W8 7RG. ☎ (020) 7938 3939. Website: www.trailfinders.com

■ **USIT Campus Travel** (students and those under 26): 52 Grosvenor Gardens, London SW1 OAG. ☎ (0870) 240 1010. Website: www.usit campus.co.uk

Specialist Travel Agents

The following are just a selection of the many travel companies in Britain that can arrange specialist packages and tailor-made holidays to Cuba.

■ **Captivating Cuba** (packages, resorts and self-drive): Centre London West, 43–57 London Road, Twickenham TW1 3SZ. ☎ (0870) 887 0123. Website: www.captivating-cuba.co.uk

■ **Cubanacan** (packages): Unit 49, Limeharbour, Docklands, London E14 9TS. ☎ (020) 7537 7909. Email: tai09@dial-pipex.com

■ **Gane and Marshall** (expensive packages and tours): 98 Crescent Road, New Barnet EN4 9RJ. ☎ (020) 8441 9592. Website: www.ganeand marshall.co.uk

■ **Havanatour UK** (Cuban state-run company. Packages, flights and arrangements for independent travel): 3 Wyllyots Place, Potters Bar EN6 2HN. ☎ (01707) 646463. Email: sales@havanatour.co.uk

■ **Interchange** (specialist): 27 Stafford Road, Croydon CR0 4NG. ☎ (020) 8681 3612. Website: www.interchange.uk.com

■ **Journey Latin America** (specialist itineraries and tours): 12–13 Heathfield Terrace, Chiswick W4 4JE. ☎ (020) 8747 3108. Website: www.journeylatin america.co.uk

■ **Progressive Tours** (specialist tours including salsa): 12 Porchester Place, Marble Arch, London W2 2BS. ☎ (020) 7262 1676.

■ **Regal Dive** (dive packages to Cuba): 22 High Street, Sutton, Ely CB6 2RB. ☎ (01353) 778096. Website: www.regal-diving.co.uk

■ **Regent Holidays** (itinerary and specialist): 15 John Street, Bristol BS1 2HR. ☎ (0117) 921 1171. Website: www.regent-holidays.co.uk

■ **South American Experience** (flights, itineraries and specialist): 47 Causton Street, Pimlico, London SW1 4AT. ☎ (020) 7976 6908. Website: www.southamericanexperience.co.uk

■ **Special Places** (itineraries and packages): Brock Travel Ltd, 4 The White House, Beacon Road, Crowborough TN6 1AB. ☎ (01892) 661157. Website: www.specialplaces.co.uk

For a comprehensive list of tour operators and travel agents, contact:

■ **Cuba Tourist Board**: 154 Shaftesbury Avenue, London WC2H 8JT. ☎ (020) 7240 6655. Email: cubatouristboard.london@virgin.net. Website: www.cubatravel.cu

FROM IRELAND

There are no direct flights from Ireland to Cuba. **Air France** flies twice a day from Dublin to Havana, via Paris. **Iberia** also flies to Havana from Dublin, via Madrid. Flight time is about 11 hours.

Charter flights to Cuba (Camagüey, Holguín, Havana and Varadero) are usually sold as part of a package, although flight-only deals are available. Charter flights to Cuba usually travel via London or other European cities, so it is often worthwhile travelling to London with an airline such as **Aer Lingus** or **British Airways** and joining a charter flight or package from there. From spring 2002, there will be no direct scheduled flights from Britain to Havana, and travellers will have to fly via Madrid or Paris with Iberia or Air France.

Cuba is a popular package destination, especially for resort-based and all-inclusive packages, and many travel agents in Britain can sell you this type of deal. For more details on packages and tailor-made holidays, *see* 'Getting There by Air from Britain'.

✛ **Air France**: Dublin Airport, Dublin. ☎ (01) 605 0383. Website: www. airfrance.com

✛ **Aer Lingus**: 40–41 Upper O'Connell Street, Dublin 1. ☎ (01) 886 8888. Website: www.flyaerlingus.com

✛ **British Airways**: 13 St Stephen's Green, Dublin 1. ☎ 1-800-626-747. For enquiries from Northern Ireland ☎ (0345) 222 111. Website: www.british airways.com

✛ **Iberia**: 54 Dawson Street, Dublin 2. ☎ (01) 407 3018. Website: www. iberia.com

TRAVEL AGENTS

■ **American Express Travel**: 116 Grafton Street, Dublin 2. ☎ (01) 677 2874.

■ **Budget Travel**: 134 Lower Baggot Street, Dublin 2. ☎ (01) 661 3122.

■ **Budget Travel Shops**: 63 Main Street, Finglas 11, Dublin. ☎ (01) 834 0637.

■ **Thomas Cook**: 11 Donegall Place, Belfast BT1 6ET. ☎ (01232) 554 455. 118 Grafton Street, Dublin. ☎ (01) 677 1721. Website: www.thomascook. com

■ **Trailfinders**: 4–5 Dawson Street, Dublin 2. ☎ (01) 677 7888. Website: www.trailfinders.com

■ **USIT NOW**: 19–21 Aston Quay, O'Donnell Bridge, Dublin. ☎ (01) 602 1700. 13B Fountain Centre, College Street, Belfast BT61 6ET. ☎ (01232) 324 4073. Website: www.usitnow.ie

Specialist Travel Agents

■ **Cubatravel** (resorts and independent packages): 11 South Anne's Street, Dublin 2. ☎ (01) 671 3422.

■ **Exodus** (adventure holidays): Colette Pearson Travel, 64 South William Street, Dublin 2. ☎ (01) 677 1029. Email: cptravel@indigo.ie. Website: www.exodus.co.uk

Most travel agents in Britain can also arrange travel to Cuba for travellers from Ireland. For more details, *see* 'Specialist Travel Agents in Britain'.

FROM THE UNITED STATES

LICENSED TRAVEL

Citizens of the United States may visit Cuba only if licensed to do so by the State Department. Technically, United States citizens are prohibited from spending money related to Cuban travel, unless they possess a license. Visiting Cuba without a government license is still classed as **illegal** and you are liable to a fine or imprisonment if you are caught doing so.

Journalists on assignment, academics specializing in Cuba, government officials, diplomats and those with relatives in Cuba have traditionally been licensed to visit the country. Nowadays, increasing numbers of United States citizens wishing to study or engage in humanitarian work are permitted to visit Cuba. If you are visiting Cuba for reasons of study, business or aid work, apply to the United States Government **Licensing Division**.

Those United States citizens who are granted a licence to visit Cuba can book tickets on special charter flights from Miami to Havana or Camagüey, through one of the two official United States travel agents, **Marazul Tours** and **Tico Travel**. These flights are not shown on the electronic departures or arrivals board at Miami airport and leave from an obscure departure gate. Marazul can also book charter flights from Nassau, Bahamas, or Cancun, Mexico, to Havana. Direct flights from Miami to Havana start at around US$300 return and direct flights from Miami to Camagüey start at around US$349 return, plus tax. Flights via Nassau or Cancun are usually slightly cheaper, beginning at US$220, plus tax.

Marazul and Tico can also make hotel reservations for you throughout Cuba. Due to government restrictions, land arrangements cannot cost over US$100 per person per day. Marazul also arranges special interest tours, which explore cultural and environmental issues. The **Center for Cuban Studies** runs special interest tours to Cuba, concentrating on environmental, cultural and humanitarian issues. Prices begin at around US$900 for one week, flights, accommodation and transport included. **Global Exchange** leads short non-profit making 'reality tours' that aim at cultural understanding. Prices begin at around US$1000 for a week of travel.

All travellers, licensed or not, should remember that insurance policies, travellers' checks and credit cards that have been issued in the United States are not valid in Cuba. Citizens of countries other than the United States who live in America do not have to seek a license for Cuban travel. They can obtain tourist cards from the Cuban consulate office in Washington DC.

To obtain a license, contact:

■ **United States Licensing Department**: Steven Pinter, Chief of Licensing, Office of Foreign Assets Control, United States Department of the Treasury, 1500 Pennsylvania Avenue, North West Washington DC 20220. ☎ (202) 622 2520. Miami ☎ (305) 810 5140. Website: www.treas.gov/ofac

■ **Center for Cuban Studies**: 124 West 23rd Street, New York, New York 10011. ☎ (212) 242 0559. Website: www.cubaupdate.org

■ **Global Exchange**: 2017 Mission Street, Room 303, San Francisco, California 94110. ☎ (415) 255 7296 or 1-800-497-1994. Website: www. globalexchange.org

■ **Marazul Tours**: Tower Plaza, 4100 Park Avenue, Weehawken, New Jersey 07087. ☎ (201) 319 9670 or 1-800-223-5334. Website: www. marazultours.com.

■ **Tico Travel**: 161 East Commercial Boulevard, Fort Lauderdale, Florida 33334. ☎ (954) 493 8426. Website: www.destinationcuba.com

UNLICENSED TRAVEL

Many United States citizens visit Cuba without a license by travelling via Mexico, the Caribbean or Canada. Travellers should be aware that visiting Cuba without a license is still **illegal**. Those caught doing so are liable for fines of up to $250,000 or a jail sentence. For this reason, many travellers dispose of their tourist card and airline ticket before boarding their return flight to the United States.

Various airlines fly from Canada, the Caribbean and Latin America to destinations in Cuba. The United States offices of these airlines cannot book you places on flights to Cuba. You must work through their offices abroad, or use travel agents overseas. Travel agents in Cancun, Mexico City, Montreal, Nassau and Toronto are particularly experienced in booking trips for United States citizens to Cuba and can arrange flights, hotels and the purchase of your tourist card. Do not ask these travel agents to book your flight from the United States to the foreign city, as you could have embargo-related problems. Book the United States leg of your trip separately with a home travel agent and don't mention that you are continuing to Cuba.

FROM MEXICO AND THE CARIBBEAN

Most travellers from the western United States travel to Cuba via Mexico. Unlike services from Canada, most flights from Mexico are direct to Cuba. Cancun, particularly, is easily accessible on a cheap charter flight. **Cubana** flies daily from Cancun to Havana. **Aerocaribe**, Mexico's regional airline, flies twice a day from Cancun to Havana. Aerocaribe flights to Cuba connect with **Mexicana** flights from across the United States. You can buy tickets on Aerocaribe or Mexicana from their offices in Mexico, via local travel agents or from their desks at Cancun airport. Most Mexicana offices also sell Aerocaribe tickets.

Mexicana also flies daily to Havana from Mexico City and twice weekly from Mérida. Fares from Mexico City to Havana begin at around US$330 single and US$500 return, plus tax. Fares to Camagüey are less, at US$170 for a single and US$260 for a return, plus tax. Mexicana offices in the United States cannot book flights from Mexico to Cuba. Contact their offices in Mexico City or Cancun. Cubana fares are usually cheaper than both Mexicana and Aerocaribe, however Cubana attracts complaints from travellers about the standard of service. Travellers on any of these airlines should check in well in advance, as there are sometimes problems with overbooking.

Many Mexican travel agents sell tours to Havana and beyond, or package deals to the beach. If you are staying in Havana, ensure that your hotel is not in Miramar or Mariel Hemingway, unless you would prefer to stay in the suburbs. Check that your tourist card is included in the price and, if not, agree the price that you will pay for it.

✈ **Aerocaribe**: Xola Número 535, Piso 28, Colonia del Valle-Mexico, Mexico City. ☎ 54 48 30 00, ext. 3874. Email: info@aerocaribe.com

Cancun: Avenida Coba, Numero Cinco, Plaza America, Cancun. ☎ 99 84 20 00. Merida: Paseo de Montejo, Número 500B, Merida. ☎ 99 28 67 90. Website: www.aerocaribe.com

✈ **Cubana**: Temistocles 246 esquina, Homero, Colonia Polanco, CP 11560, Delegacion Miguel Hidalgo, Mexico City. ☎ 52 50 63 35. Fax: 52 55 08 35. Email: idalia@mpsnet.com.mx. Cancun: Avenida Yaxchilan Número 23, Cancun. ☎ 99 87 73 73. Email: solyson@mpsnet.com.mx. Website: www.cubana.cu

✈ **Mexicana de Avacion**: Aeropuerto Internacional, Sala C, CP 155520, Mexico City. ☎ 55 71 28 57. Cancun: Avenida Pedro Joaquin Coldwell, Numero 70-A, Cancun. Mérida: Calle 56, Numero 493, Paseo Montejo, Mérida. Website: www.mexicana.com

■ **Taino Tours** (flights and travel arrangements): Avenida Coyocan Numero 1035, Sudeman 226, Colonida del Valle CP 01300, Mexico City. ☎ 52 59 39 07. Paseo de Montejo, Numero 496, Mérida. ☎ 99 23 05 48. Website: www.pceditores.com/taino

■ **Cuba Tourist Board**: Goethe 16, 3er Piso, Colonia Anzures, Mexico City, Mexico. ☎ 52 50 79 74. Email: otcumex@mail.internet.com.mx. Website: www.cubatravel.cu

From the Caribbean, **Cubana** flies daily from Nassau to Havana. Cubana also flies from Curaçao, Fort de France, Kingston, Montego Bay, Pointe a Pitre, Santo Domingo and St Martin to Havana. There is also a weekly Cubana flight from Santo Domingo to Santiago de Cuba. **Air Jamaica**, highly recommended by travellers, flies from Montego Bay to Havana three times a week. This service connects with Air Jamaica flights that arrive in Montego Bay from the United States. Air Jamaica also flies regularly from Kingston, Santo Domingo and Grenada to Havana.

Prices to Cuba from the Caribbean vary according to your departure airport and the airline you choose. Fares on Cubana from Nassau to Havana start at about US$190 for a return ticket, plus tax.

Travellers who choose the Caribbean route to Cuba should remember that many travel agencies will not take credit cards, so they will have to wire money, or send the funds by cheque.

✪ **Air Jamaica**: 4 St Lucia Avenue, Kingston 5. ☎ (876) 922 3460 or 1-888-FLYAIRJ. Website: www.airjamaica.com

✪ **Cubana**: 22 Trafalgar Road, Second Floor, Suite 11, Kingston 10. ☎ (978) 3410. Email: cubana@cwjamaica.com. Hotel British Colonial Beach Resort, Hab. 239, Nassau, Bahamas. ☎ (242) 322 2322. Website: www.cubana.cu

■ **Havanatour Bahamas**: PO EE 16319, Nassau, Bahamas ☎ (242) 394 7195. Fax: (242) 356 2733.

■ **Majestic Holidays**: Hillside Manor, Cumberland Street, PO Box N-1401, Nassau, Bahamas. ☎ (242) 322 2322. Email: holidays@bahamas.net.bs. Website: www.majesticholidays.com

For travel to Cuba via Canada, *see* 'Getting There from Canada'. United States travel agents can only arrange tickets to Canada and cannot sell you travel to Cuba. You should not ask them to do so, or mention that you plan to travel to Cuba. The United States offices of airlines flying between Cuba and Canada cannot sell you tickets on these flights. You should contact the Canadian office of the airline or a Canadian travel agent.

FROM THE UNITED STATES TO MEXICO, THE CARIBBEAN AND CANADA

Mexico and Latin America, the Caribbean and Canada are easy to reach from the United States on cheap charter flights or scheduled flight air deals. The travel sections of Sunday broadsheet newspapers are good for hunting for bargain flights to Mexico, Latin America, the Caribbean and Canada, as are internet travel sites such as www.cheaptickets.com, www.lowestfare.com, www.priceline.com and www.previewtravel.com. Check the prices offered by discount travel agents, which sell tickets offloaded by airlines, often on an 'open jaw' basis that allow arrival in one city and departure from another. Always ensure that your travel agent is endorsed by ASTA. Airlines themselves can often be as competitive as agencies, especially if booking APEX (Advanced Purchase Excursion) tickets or winter Super APEX tickets.

✪ **Air Jamaica**: 8300 North West 33rd Street, Suite 440, Miami, Florida 33122. ☎ (305) 670 3222 or 1-800-523-5585. Website: www.airjamaica. com

✪ **Mexicana de Avacion**: 7205 North West 19th Street, Miami, Florida 33126. ☎ (305) 599 9210. Website: www.mexicana.com. Also takes bookings for **Aerocaribe** on ☎ 1-800-531-7921. Website: www.aerocaribe.com

✪ **Air Canada**: Satellite Airline Terminal, 125 Park Avenue, New York, New York 10017. ☎ 1-888-247-2262. Website: www.aircanada.com

⊕American Airlines: 4200 Amon Carter, PD 2400, Fort Worth, Texas. ☎ 1-800-433-7300. Website: www.aa.com

⊕Continental Airlines: 2929 Alan Parkway, PO Box 4607, Houston, Texas. ☎ 1-800-525-0280. Website: www.continental.com

⊕Delta Airlines: Atlanta International Airport, Atlanta, Georgia 30320. ☎ 1-800-221-1212. Website: www.delta.com

⊕Northwest Airlines / KLM: 100 East 42nd Street, Second Floor, New York, New York 10017. ☎ 1-800-447-4747. Website: www.nwa.com / www.klm.com

⊕TWA: 650 Anton Boulevard, Suite F, Costa Mesa, California 91364. ☎ 1-800-982-4141. Website: www.twa.com

⊕United Airlines: ☎ 1-800-241-6522. Website: www.ual.com.

⊕US Air: 10 Eyck Plaza, 40 North Pearl Street, Albany, New York 12207. ☎ 1-800-428-432. Website: www.usairways.com

Travel Agents in the United States

■ **Air Courier Association**: 191 University Boulevard, Suite 300, Denver, Colorado 80206. ☎ (303) 278 8810 or 1-800-282-1202. Website: www.air courier.org

■ **Last Minute Travel Club** (standby deals): 132 Brookline Avenue, Boston, Massachusetts 02215. ☎ 1-800-LAST MIN.

■ **STA Travel** (students and those under 26. Branches nationwide): 48 East 11th Street, New York, New York 10003. ☎ 1-800-781-4040. Website: www.statravel.com

■ **USIT (Council Travel) USA** (students and those under 26. Over 60 branches nationwide): 931 Westwood Boulevard, Westwood, Los Angeles California 90024. ☎ 1-800-226-8624. Website: www.counciltravel.com

FROM CANADA

Air Canada, **Cubana** and **Lacsa** offer scheduled flights from Canada to Cuba. Cubana flies twice a week from Montreal to Havana and Varadero throughout the year. Some Havana flights stop at Cienfuegos. The Costa Rican airline, Lacsa, flies from Toronto to Havana twice a week throughout the year. Fares with Lacsa can be very expensive. Air Canada flies from Toronto, Montreal and Vancouver to Varadero and Holguín. Return tickets on Air Canada and Cubana cost from around CAN$1000, plus tax.

The main charter airlines between Canada and Cuba are **Air Transat** and **Sky Service**. Travellers should find that fares on the charter airlines are cheaper than fares on scheduled flights. There are frequent charter flights from Toronto and Montreal to Cuba, particularly during the winter season from mid-December to April. During winter, charter flights usually also run from Vancouver, Edmonton and Halifax to Cuba. Air Transat and Sky Service fly from Toronto and Montreal to most Cuban airports that receive inter-national flights. Charter fares from Toronto to Havana begin at around

CAN$500 for a return, plus CAN$46 for tax and tourist card. Fares are higher for departures at Christmas, New Year, Easter and weekends. Most charter flights leave or arrive in the middle of the night and stop at two destinations, such as Varadero and Santiago or Cienfuegos and Holguín. Charter tickets cannot be bought on an 'open jaw' basis and if you wish to stay longer than 14 nights, the price of the fare will increase significantly. Contact your travel agent for assistance in booking charter flight-only deals. For deals on scheduled flights, check the websites, try discount travel agents, and look at the travel sections of the weekend broadsheet newspapers.

Many Canadians visit Cuba as part of a package deal to Varadero or another beach resort. These beach packages are largely sold on an 'all inclusive' basis, where drinks, food and activities are included in the price, and there is little incentive to leave the resort. One week at an all-inclusive Varadero resort out of high season starts at around CAN$750. If you're travelling to Havana on a package, try to check where you will be staying. Many hotels booked as part of package tour are not situated as close to Havana proper as your agent might claim.

✪ Air Canada: Royal York Hotel, 100 Front Street, West Arcade Level, Toronto M5K 1GD. ☎ 1-888-247-2262. Website: www.aircanada.ca

✪ Air Jamaica: 4141 Yonge Street, Suite 104, Willowdale, Toronto M2P 2A8. ☎ (416) 229 6024. Website: www.airjamaica.com

✪ Air Transat: Lester B Pearson International Airport, Toronto. ☎ 1-866-847-1112. Website: www.airtransat.com

✪ Cubana: 4 Place Ville Marie, Suite 405, Montreal H3B 3N6. ☎ 1-800-871-1222. Email: cubana@qc.aira.com. Website: www.cubana.cu

✪ Lacsa: Lester B Pearson International Airport, Toronto. ☎ 1-800-225-2272. Website: www.centralamerica.com/cr/lacsa

✪ Sky Service: Lester B Pearson International Airport, Toronto. ☎ 1-877-485-6060. Website: www.skyservice.com

TRAVEL AGENTS

■ **Collacutt Travel** (general travel services): The Bayview Village Centre, 2901 Bayview Avenue, Toronto M2K 1E6. ☎ 1-888-225-9811. Website: www.collacutt-travel.com

■ **New Frontiers/Nouvelles Frontières**: 1001 Sherbrook Street East, Suite 720, Montreal H21 1L3. ☎ (514) 526 8444.

■ **Sears Travel** (general services. 81 offices throughout Canada): ☎ 1-888-884-2539. Website: www.sears.ca

■ **Travel Cuts** (student travel. Branches countrywide): 187 College Street, Toronto M5T 1P7. ☎ (416) 979 2406 or 1-800-667-2887. Website: www.travelcuts.com

■ **Travel House** (tours, packages, discount travel. Branches countrywide): 1491 Yonge Street, Suite 401, Toronto M4T 1ZR. ☎ (416) 925 6322. Website: www.travel-house.com

Specialist Travel Agents

■ **Alba Tours** (package deals): 130 Merton Street, Toronto M4S 1A4. ☎ (416) 485 6060. Website: www.albatours.com

■ **Bel Air Travel** (discount travel agency selling package deals): 93 Skyway Avenue, Suite 101, Toronto M9W 6N6. ☎ 1-877-675-7705. Website: www.belairtravel.com

■ **Hola Sun** (packages, flights, hotels and car hire): 146 Beaver Creek Road, Unit Eight, Richmond Hill L4B 1C2. Website: www.holasunholidays.com

■ **Scubacan** (scuba dive packages in Cuba): 1365 Yonge Street, Suite 208, Toronto M4T 2P7. ☎ (416) 927 1257 or 1-888-799-2822. Website: www.scubacan.com

■ **Signature Vacations** (packages and flights): 160 Bloor Street East, Suite 400, Toronto M4W 1B9. ☎ 1-866-324-2883. Website: www.signature vacations.com

■ **Sun Holidays** (packages and hotels): 77 Bloor Street West, Suite 1903, Toronto M5S 1M2. ☎ (416) 323 1960 or 1-888-201-5019. Website: www.sunholidays.ca

■ **World of Vacations** (package deals): 191 The West Mall, Suite 600, Etiobicoke M9C 5K8. ☎ (416) 620 8050. Website: www.worldofvacations. com

■ **Worldwide Adventures** (adventure travel to Cuba, especially biking, also independent itineraries): 1170 Sheppard Avenue West, Suite 45, Toronto M3K 2A3. ☎ (416) 633 5666 or 1-800-387-1483. Website: www.worldwide quest.com

■ **Vacations-Culture in Cuba** (cultural, educational and sports tours and itineraries): 5059 Saint-Denis, Montreal H25 2L9. ☎ (514) 982 3330 or 1-888-691-0101. Website: www.culturecuba.com

For a comprehensive list of tour operators and travel agents, contact:

■ **Cuba Tourist Board**: 55 Queen Street East, Suite 705, Toronto MC5 1R6. ☎ (416) 362 0700. Website: cuba.tbtor@sympatico.ca. Montreal: (514) 875 8006. Email: mintur@generation.net. Website: www.cubatravel.cu

FROM AUSTRALIA AND NEW ZEALAND

There are no direct flights from Australia and New Zealand to Cuba. Travellers to Cuba will have to fly via Europe, Canada or the Caribbean.

The most direct route to Cuba from Australia is via Tokyo to Mexico City, from where there are direct flights to Havana and Varadero. **JAL Japan Airlines** flies from Sydney or Melbourne to Tokyo, Mexico City, and then to Havana. Prices start at AUD$2600. **Air Canada** flies from Sydney or Melbourne to Vancouver, Toronto, Mexico City and Havana from AUD$3500. From New Zealand, **Qantas**, in partnership with **Lan Chile**, flies to Havana via Mexico City, and other stops, for upwards of NZ$4000. If your route takes you via the United States to Mexico, you should ensure that any Mexico–Cuba ticket issued in Australia or New Zealand is separate to your main ticket. Otherwise it is possible that the United States authorities at immigration will confiscate the whole ticket, as it violates the United States embargo of Cuba.

Travellers from Australia and New Zealand may find it cheaper to fly first to Europe. There are direct scheduled flights to Havana from cities in Europe, including Madrid and Paris. There are regular charter flights from major European cities to Havana, Varadero, Camagüey and Holguín.

Package holiday deals to Cuba are particularly affordable from Europe, especially if bought in London. Varadero is the main destination for package deals, many of which are sold on an 'all inclusive' basis, where drinks, food and activities are included in the price. For more details on onward travel to Cuba from Europe, *see* 'Getting There from Britain'.

There are direct flights to cities in Europe from the major cities in Australia and New Zealand. These flights will usually include a stopover in an Asian city and flight times vary from 19 to 25 hours.

The cheapest fares to Europe are frequently with Asian airlines such as **Garuda** or **Malaysia Airways**. **British Airways** and **Qantas** make the most frequent flights to Europe. Travellers should expect to pay around AUD$1500 and AUD$2000 for a return fare in low season. Return tickets increase by between AUD$500 and AUD$1000 in high season. Return flights from New Zealand begin at around NZ$2200 in low season.

✚ **Air New Zealand**: 5 Elizabeth Street, Sydney 2000. ☎ 13 24 76. Air New Zealand House, 72 Oxford Terrace, Christchurch. ☎ 0800-737-000. Website: www.airnz.co.nz

✚ **British Airways**: Chifley Square, 70 Hunter Street, Sydney 2000. ☎ (02) 9258-3300. Auckland International Airport, Auckland. ☎ (09) 356-8690. Website: www.britishairways.com

✚ **Cathay Pacific**: 3/F International Terminal, Sydney International Airport, Mascot, Sydney 2020. ☎ 13 26 27. 11th Floor, Arthur Andersen Tower, 205–209 Queen Street, PO Box 1313, Auckland. ☎ (09) 379-0861. Website: www.cathaypacific.com

✚ **Air Canada**: Comaltech House, Level One, Sydney 2000. ☎ (02) 286-8900. 18 Shortland Street, Sixth Floor, Auckland 1. ☎ (09) 379-3371. Website: www.aircanada.com

✚ **JAL Japan Airlines**: Darling Park, 14th Floor, 201 Sussex Street, Sydney 2000. ☎ (02) 972-2111. Westpac Tower, 12th Floor, 120 Albert Street, Auckland 1. ☎ (09) 379-9906. Website: www.jal.com

✚ **KLM / Alitalia**: 115 Pitt Street, Level 13, Sydney 2000. ☎ (02) 9922-1555. Second Floor, Salvation Army Building, 369 Queen Street, Auckland 1. ☎ (09) 309-1782. Website: www.klm.com

✚ **Malaysia Airlines**: MAS, 16th Spring Street, Sydney 2000. ☎ (02) 913-2627. MAS, 12th Floor, The Swanson Centre, 12–26 Swanson Street, Auckland, PO Box 3729. Auckland. ☎ (09) 373-2741. Website: www.malaysiaairlines.com

✚ **Mexicana de Aviación**: 24 Albert Road, Seventh Floor, South Melbourne 3205. ☎ (09) 9699-9355. 18 Shortland Street, Auckland 1001. ☎ (09) 914-2573. Website: www.mexicana.com

✈ **Qantas**: Qantas Centre, 203 Coward Street, Mascot, Sydney 2020. ☎ (13) 1211 or (02) 9691-3636. 191 Queen Street, Auckland 1. ☎ (09) 357-8900 or 0800-808-967. Website: www.qantas.com

✈ **Singapore Airlines**: Singapore Airlines House, 17–19 Bridge Street, Sydney 2000. ☎ (02) 9350-0100. Tenth Floor, West Plaza Building, Corner Albert and Fanshawe Streets, Auckland 1. ☎ 0800-808-909. Website: www.singaporeair.com.

TRAVEL AGENTS

■ **Flight Centres**: Level 13, 33 Berry Street, North Sydney 2060. ☎ (02) 924-2422. 205 Queen Street, Auckland 1. ☎ (09) 309-6171. ☎ 1-1300-131-600 for nearest branch.

■ **STA Travel**: 855 George Street, Sydney 2000. ☎ (02) 9212-1255 (72 branches). 90 Cashel Street, Christchurch, New Zealand. ☎ (03) 379-9098 (13 branches). For nearest branch ☎ 13 17 76. Website: www.statravel.com.au

■ **Thomas Cook**: 175 Pitt Street, Sydney 2000. ☎ 1-300-728-748 (branches nationwide). 96 Anzac Avenue, Auckland. ☎ 0800-500-600 (branches nationwide).

■ **Trailfinders**: 91 Elizabeth Street, Brisbane, Queensland 4000. ☎ (07) 3229-0887. Website: www.trailfinder.com/australia

Specialist Travel Agents

The following is a selection of the travel agents that can arrange travel to Cuba. For example, **Caribbean Destinations** offer one-week packages, including airfares, to Havana, beginning at AUD$3500 or NZ$4500.

■ **Adventure World**: 73 Walker Street, Sydney 2000. ☎ (02) 9956-7766. Website: www.adventureworld.com

■ **Caribbean Destinations**: Rialto Tower, Level One, 525 Collins Street, Melbourne. ☎ (03) 9618-1128. Website: www.aerolinas.com.au

■ **Contours Travel**: 84 William Street, Level One, Melbourne. ☎ (03) 9670-6900. Website: www.caribbeanislands.com.au

There is no branch of the Cuban Tourist Office in Australia or New Zealand. Check the website on www.cubatravel.cu for general information.

FROM SOUTH AFRICA

There are no direct flights from South Africa to Cuba. Travellers should fly first to Europe, Canada, Mexico or the Caribbean, from where they can connect to a flight to Cuba. Europe and Canada are frequent destinations for flights leaving South Africa, and competition can decrease prices, particularly on flights to London.

Air Canada and **British Airways** fly frequently from Johannesburg and Cape Town to Cuba, via (usually long) stops in Canada and London. **Air France** also flies to Cuba via Paris. **South African Airways** flies regularly to cities in Europe. Standard return tickets should cost between R3300 and R5000, depending on the season.

✚ Air Canada: Sandton Terrace, 137C 11th Street, Parkmore, Benmore 2010. ☎ (011) 884-7788. Website: www.aircanada.com

✚ Air France: Oxford Manor, First Floor, Oxford Road, Ilovo 2196. ☎ (0860) 340 340. Website: www.airfrance.com

✚ British Airways: Grovesnor Court, 195 Grovesnor Corner, Rosebank, Johannesburg 2196. ☎ 0860-011-747 or (011) 441-8600. Website: www.britishairways.com

✚ Mexicana: c/o Lu Dowell Representations, 21 Gleneagles Road, Hurlingham, Sandton, Johannesburg 2196. ☎ (011) 784-0985. Email: ludowell@mweb.co.za. Website: www.mexicana.com

✚ South African Airways: Airways Park, Jones Road, Johannesburg International Airport, Johannesburg 1627. ☎ (011) 978-1763. Website: www.saa.co.za

TRAVEL AGENTS

■ **STA Travel**: Level Three, Leslie Social Sciences Building, University of Cape Town, Rondebosch 7700, Cape Town. ☎ (021) 685-1808. Website: www.statravel.co.za

■ **USIT Adventures**: Rondebosch Shopping Centre, Rondebosch Main Road, Rondebosch, Cape Town. ☎ (021) 685-2226.

There is no branch of the Cuban Tourist Office in South Africa. Check the website on www.cubatravel.cu for general information.

General Information

Things change more rapidly in Cuba than in most other countries. Since it opened itself up to tourism, which is now officially a 'national priority', Cuba altered more in a few short months than it had in the previous 20 years. A new 'revolution' is gradually taking place: privatization is on the increase and, with the arrival of foreign capital, tourist areas are multiplying. Any tourist-related income goes directly into the state coffers. Cubans, removed from this process, reap little benefit from it as a result. As some places close down, others are moving or under restoration, and new hotels and restaurants open on what seems like a daily basis. Inevitably, customs and attitudes are changing as a result.

ACCOMMODATION

CAMPING

To avoid any misunderstandings, Cuban 'campsites' are completely unlike their European counterparts. In Cuba, a 'campsite' is a tourist complex with basic chalets sleeping several to a room.

The country offers little for anyone looking to pitch a tent. Camping on undesignated land is still prohibited and the only campsites (in the European sense) were converted into hotels a few years ago.

HOTELS

Hotels are found virtually everywhere, but there are still too few, given the recent expansion of the tourism industry, and their tariffs also tend to be rather high. During the school holidays, the hotels in Havana and Varadero are often full. Book at least three weeks in advance in summer and at Christmas, otherwise you will need to take a room in a private home.

There are five major hotel chains in Cuba: Izlazul, Horizontes, Gran Caribe (luxury hotels), Gaviota (army-sponsored) and Cubanacan. Officially, they are all state-owned, although in fact they are financed by foreign groups. The hotels aren't much to write home about, but are comfortable and well kept. Most rooms have a shower. You will sometimes find that they also have a nightclub, restaurant, shop and other facilities such as a car rental agency or tourist information desk. Most do a self-service buffet for breakfast. Bear in mind when preparing your itinerary that hotels outside Havana are much cheaper.

NB: Cubans are in principle not allowed into hotel rooms reserved for tourists.

CASAS PARTICULARES (PRIVATE LODGINGS)

Until now, the government has allowed foreigners to stay with Cubans in their homes. This offered something to suit every taste and budget, from a bleak suburban tower block to a grand colonial estate or baroque palace.

This type of accommodation is now regulated. Since 15 July 1997, and new laws in January 1999, any Cuban offering private lodgings to foreigners has had to pay an additional tax. The draconian conditions dissuaded many from continuing this practice and only the most luxurious homes have survived. This accommodation is already relatively expensive, at around $25, and prices are likely to go up even more. It's probably not the ideal solution any more if you're travelling on a shoestring, but it's a unique way of getting to know Cuban people.

BUDGET

For nearly 40 years, Cubans have been issued with ration cards, but living conditions are still difficult, with rations being tiny, and wages low.

For tourists paying with dollars, life in Cuba is increasingly expensive, especially compared with South American countries. For travellers on a budget, the best thing to do is to try to live Cuban-style, by eating and living in a private home. You will still have to pay in dollars, but it will be cheaper. Bear in mind that everything costs more in Havana than elsewhere in Cuba.

As a guideline, the following is an idea of average prices, to help you work out a budget. Note that all dollar prices given in this guide refer to US dollars unless stated otherwise.

ACCOMMODATION

Hotel prices are per night, based on two people sharing a double room. Breakfast is often extra.

Budget: less than $20, except in large towns and cities

Moderate: $20–60

Expensive: $60–80

Splash Out: over $80

Casas particulares (private lodgings): $15–25 for a night in a double room. In Havana the average is $25.

EATING OUT

Inexpensive: less than $5

Moderate: $5–15

Expensive: over $15

Paladares (private restaurants): prices vary, but a meal starts from $5 or 6, with the average $7–9. The most expensive *paladares* cost $10–15 per person and these are quite common.

MISCELLANEOUS PRICES

– Museum entry: usually $1–3 per person

– Nightclub entry for tourists: $10

– Rum-based cocktail: $2–4

– Car rental: a small car costs around $40 a day, plus $10 per day for compulsory comprehensive insurance.

– Hiring a **private car** with a local driver costs around $20 a day after a bit of bargaining.

– Petrol: around $1 per litre, and 50 cents on the black market but there's no guarantee of quality.

INTERNATIONAL STUDENT CARD

The ISIC card offers students the same advantages as they would get in their own country, such as discounted fares, reduced admission to museums, discounts on accommodation and so on. You can get more information on the advantages of the ISIC card by visiting the organization's international website at www.istc.org.

CLIMATE

Cuba has a tropical climate with just two separate seasons: a dry season in winter and a wet season in summer. The former is generally from November to May, the latter from June to October. The wet season is characterized by short, violent rainstorms and slightly higher temperatures – on average 27°C (80°F), compared with 22–26°C (72–79°F) in winter. Though it's hot all year round, the sky is usually clearer in winter and the heat less stiflingly humid. This is the ideal time to go, but naturally it's also the busiest. Having said that, in inland areas temperatures can fall to just 4°C (39.2°F).

The average water temperature is high, at 30°C (86°F) in summer and 24°C (75.2°F) in winter.

CLOTHING

Confine your packing to light clothing: shorts, T-shirts, short-sleeved shirts and, of course, swimsuits. Any spare clothes to give to people in villages will be welcome. Waterproofs are handy in the wet season, and you may need a sweater if you're staying in an air-conditioned hotel or in an inland region such as Topaste (which actually means 'cover up').

GENERAL
INFORMATION

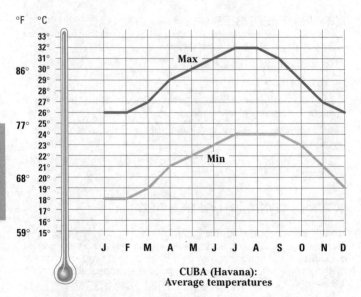

CUBA (Havana):
Average temperatures

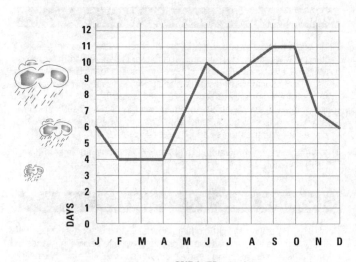

CUBA (Havana):
Number of rainy days

CONVERSION TABLES

Men's sizes

Shirts

UK	USA	EUROPE
14	14	36
14$^1/_2$	14$^1/_2$	37
15	15	38
15$^1/_2$	15$^1/_2$	39
16	16	41
16$^1/_2$	16$^1/_2$	42
17	17	43
17$^1/_2$	17$^1/_2$	44
18	18	46

Suits

UK	USA	EUROPE
36	36	46
38	38	48
40	40	50
42	42	52
44	44	54
46	46	56

Shoes

UK	USA	EUROPE
8	9	42
9	10	43
10	11	44
11	12	46
12	13	47

Women's sizes

Shirts/dresses

UK	USA	EUROPE
8	6	36
10	8	38
12	10	40
14	12	42
16	14	44
18	16	46
20	18	48

Sweaters

UK	USA	EUROPE
8	6	44
10	8	46
12	10	48
14	12	50
16	14	52
18	16	54
20	18	56

Shoes

UK	USA	EUROPE
3	5	36
4	6	37
5	7	38
6	8	39
7	9	40
8	10	42

Temperature

- To convert °C to °F, multiply by 1.8 and add 32.
- To convert °F to °C, subtract 32 and multiply by 5/9 (0.55). 0°C=32°F

US weights and measures

1 centimetre	0.39 inches	1 inch	2.54 centimetres
1 metre	3.28 feet	1 foot	0.30 metres
1 metre	1.09 yards	1 yard	0.91 metres
1 kilometre	0.62 miles	1 mile	1.61 kilometres
1 hectare	2.47 acres	1 acre	0.40 hectares
1 litre	1.76 pints	1 pint	0.57 litres
1 litre	0.26 gallons	1 gallon	3.79 litres
1 gram	0.035 ounces	1 ounce	28.35 grams
1 kilogram	2.2 pounds	1 pound	0.45 kilograms

GENERAL INFORMATION

DRUGS

The use and possession of drugs of any kind are strictly prohibited in Cuba and incur heavy prison sentences. In spite of this, trafficking seems to have intensified with the increase in tourism. The *jineteros* ('escorts') offer drugs such as marijuana and cocaine discreetly to foreigners, particularly in Havana and Varadero. Note: the government is actively cracking down on drugs, so if you want to smoke, settle for a decent Havana.

ELECTRICITY

– As in the USA and Japan, the **voltage** in Cuba is 110V. Some hotels have 110V and 220V sockets. Apart from some of the larger hotels, where European round two-pin plugs may be used, most places use American-style flat two-pin plugs. So, generally, it's best to bring an adaptor.

– **Power cuts** are common in Cuba, particularly at night, and usually last from two to four hours, depending upon the day and location. They are always planned. For the government, this is a good way of saving energy. So is the dim street lighting in the towns. However, the power is never cut while the soap operas are on, for fear of a riot!

EMBASSIES AND CONSULATES

IN CUBA

British Embassy: calle 34, No. 702/704 on the corner of avenida 7, Miramar, Havana. ☎ 24-17-71 and 24-17-72. Fax: (53 7) 24-8104. Email: embrit@ceniai.inf.cu

United States Interests Section: calle Calzada, between L and M, Vedado, Havana. ☎ 33-35-51–59 and 33-35-43–47. Fax: 66-20-95.

South African Embassy: avenida 5, No. 4201 on the corner of 42, Miramar, Havana. ☎ 24-96-71–76. Fax: 24-11-01.

CUBAN EMBASSIES ABROAD

UK: Embassy of the Republic of Cuba, 167 High Holborn, London, WC1V 6PA. ☎ 020 7240 2488. Fax: 020 7836 2602. Email: embacuba.lnd@virgin.net

USA: Cuba Interests Section, 2630 16th Street NW, Washington DC, 20009. ☎ (202) 797 8518. Fax: (202) 797 8521.

Australia: Consulate-General of the Republic of Cuba, 18 Manwaring Avenue, Maroubra, New South Wales 2035. ☎ 61-2 9311 4611. Fax: 61-2 9311 5512. Email: consulcu@prg.apc.org

South Africa: Embassy of the Republic of Cuba, 45 Mackenzie Street, Brooklyn 0181, Pretoria, PO Box 11605, Hatfield 0028. ☎ (2712) 364 2215. Fax: (2712) 346 2216. Email: sudafri@iafrica.com

EMERGENCY TELEPHONE NUMBERS

☎ 110 Operator

☎ 113 General information (business hours only)

☎ 114 Telephone repairs

☎ 115 Fire brigade

☎ 116 Police

☎ 118 Ambulance

These numbers apply throughout Cuba, but don't reply on the person on the other end speaking English. Remember that most public telephones in Cuba are out of order: you are most likely to come across one that works in a hotel.

ENTRY FORMALITIES

– No **vaccinations** are currently required for entry into Cuba, but a few precautions would be wise (*see* 'Health').

– You must have a valid **passport**. Nowadays, most foreign visitors will just need to get a tourist card; you will only need a visa if you are going to Cuba for professional reasons.

– The **tourist card**: should be available via your local travel agency. It costs about $20 (payable by cash, cheque or credit card). To get a tourist card (which replaces the visa), you will need to present your passport together with a certificate from the airline or travel agency showing the outward and return dates of your plane journey. This certificate should also certify that hotel accommodation has been booked for the first two nights of your stay in Cuba (*see* 'Customs'). In general, travellers should ask their travel agency to complete this formality for them. Tourist cards are sometimes available at the check-in desk on departure in Europe. The card, valid for six months from the issue date, is only valid for one month after arrival in the country. Anyone staying for more than one month can renew the card by taking their passport and $80 to the immigration office at calle K 19–21, Vedado. Much simpler, from the administration point of view, is to take a trip to Mexico and then come back. Note that tourist cards are only renewable once.

– **Professional visa**: this is compulsory for professional visits to the country, or if you are staying with a Cuban family or with friends. It costs about $60. Contact the Cuban consulate for further information.

CUSTOMS

– On arrival, customs officers will ask for your passport and tourist card or visa. They sometimes also ask for confirmation of **two nights' accommodation in a hotel**. In most cases, this is shown on the tourist card, so they will only ask for the name of the hotel. If all this is in order, you should be allowed through customs without any problem.

However, if you booked a room in a hotel or private house before you left home, you will need to provide some kind of proof of this reservation, such as a voucher, fax or letter of confirmation from the hotel or landlord. Even without a reservation, some people just seem to sail through customs, so the rule seems to apply in some cases but not in others. Do remember though, that officials can force you to book a two-night stay in a hotel and pay for everything (in dollars) at the airport. Backhanders to customs officers in this case will not work, and may even make matters worse. So, plan ahead, and make sure you are carrying proof of your reservation.

– **When leaving Cuba**: a tourist tax of $20 is payable at any of the island's airports before departure.

What Not to Bring into Cuba

Don't try to get offensive weapons, drugs or pornographic material past Cuban customs – officials are becoming increasingly wise to the use drug traffickers are making of Cuba as a transit country for narcotics on their way to Europe. If you get caught smuggling drugs into Cuba you could be facing a very long jail sentence – up to 20 years – or even the death penalty. Check with the Cuban embassy if you need to take drug substitutes with you, and if you're on medication that's slightly unusual you should get a doctor's certificate.

Since the outbreak of Foot and Mouth Disease in Britain the import of all meat and dairy products to Cuba from the UK and some other European countries has been banned.

You might have trouble bringing video cassette recorders into Cuba, especially if customs officials think you've come from the USA.

There are also restrictions on the import of telecommunications devices, especially those incorporating the Global Positioning System (GPS) technology, so get authoritative advice if you're taking your mobile phone with you.

Customs Allowances On Leaving Cuba

You can take home up to 50 cigars and as much rum as you want with a clear conscience! Moreover, you can export cigars up to a value of 2000 Cuban pesos if you have a receipt from a retailer recognized by the authorities, and you get clearance in advance from Cuban customs. However, don't go overboard with the rum: large amounts will not be allowed out of the country if customs officers think it forms part of a commercial enterprise.

The export of items regarded by the Ministry of Culture as being part of Cuba's cultural heritage is banned, as the value of this heritage to the tourist economy becomes increasingly clear. If you arrive with anything that might be regarded as a work of art, get it certified so that you won't have any problems when you leave. The same goes for large amounts of cash:

anything above US$5000 should be declared on arrival so that you can go home with the same amount.

For up-to-date information check: www.dtcuba.com/eng/datos_raduana.asp

FESTIVALS AND PUBLIC HOLIDAYS

It is highly likely that your stay will coincide with one of Cuba's many feast days, held to commemorate a variety of events. These range from the birth of José Martí (28 February) to the anniversary of the death of Camilo Cienfuegos (28 October), not to mention International Women's Day (8 March), the victory of the Bay of Pigs (Playa Girón, 19 April) and the death of Che Guevara (8 October).

Cubans also love to party, and, despite the economic hardship, fiestas are common. You'll find this out while you're in the country, and when you leave; farewell parties are called *despedidas*.

In addition, an increasing number of festivals are being organized, mainly in Havana, Santiago and Varadero. These range from festivals of culture to music, jazz and even water festivals. Try to find out what's on as soon as you get there (or before you go) as dates may change. The most prestigious event is the international festival of Latin American cinema, which takes place in December. The National Festival of Theatre, which takes place in February, is also renowned, as is the International Festival of Theatre, held in Havana in September.

Even more spectacular are the carnivals, which were reinstated after being banned at the beginning of the *periodo especial* (*see* 'History'). There is a three-week long carnival in Old Havana in August, and for one week at the end of July there is the famous and unmissable carnival of Santiago, which is gradually recovering its former pomp and splendour.

Official Public Holidays

1 January: Liberation Day

1 May: Labour Day

25, 26 and 27 July: Anniversary of the Revolution

10 October: Beginning of the Wars of Independence

HEALTH

Cuba's health system seems to be one of the great successes of socialism. There are many hospitals here, with highly skilled doctors. Although, with the shortages that have hit Cuba since the fall of the Berlin Wall, these hospitals are now poorly equipped, and lack the necessary medicines, visitors who experience a health problem while in Cuba need not worry. Everything will be done to help them. Health care is free for Cubans, but tourists have to pay; this money is used to subsidize the national health system. As for medicines, you should be able to find what you need at pharmacies (*farmacias*), which are plentiful, if somewhat poorly stocked. If you have a problem, you can get drugs and treatment at the Clínica Central Cira García (*see* 'Havana: Useful Addresses').

There are few statistics on the exact state of the Cuban health system, but official health propaganda can usually be ignored. Cuba is regularly the victim of curious epidemics. A few years ago, a disease of the optic nerve affected tens of thousands of people; its cause was never clearly identified. In 1981, a huge epidemic of dengue affected 350,000 people – and officially caused just 158 deaths; a few years later, the Cuban authorities announced that the disease had been eradicated, yet, in June 1997, there was a repeat outbreak (200,000 cases).

Vaccinations

There are no compulsory vaccinations needed for visitors to Cuba from the northern hemisphere, but it's a good idea to have a few basic ones, regardless of where you are travelling from:

– Make sure your tetanus, polio, diphtheria and hepatitis B are up to date.

– It's unwise to go to Cuba without being protected against typhoid and hepatitis A. Make sure you have these vaccinations, even if you're planning to travel in excellent conditions.

– Yellow fever has been eradicated from Cuba, so there's no need for this vaccination unless you're travelling onwards to south of the Panama Canal.

Advice and Prevention

– There is no malaria in Cuba, but the abundant and aggressive mosquitoes may carry other diseases, such as dengue. As soon as it starts to get dark, cover up as much as possible. On areas of skin that are exposed, apply strong insect repellent containing 50 per cent DEET or 25 per cent 35/35. Finally, it is a good idea to sleep beneath a mosquito net impregnated with insecticide.

– Even when it is cloudy in the tropics, the sun can be quite strong. Make sure you are wearing sun cream from the moment you arrive, and don't forget to cover your head.

– Finally, be careful about becoming sexually involved with Cubans. The official line is that cases of AIDS are rare, but this may not necessarily be true. Cubans who are HIV positive are sent to a special centre called 'Los Cocos', where they undergo rigorous psychological testing to see if they are fit to live in society. No one knows the exact number of cases. With the expansion of tourism and prostitution, the risks have become very real. It's best to carry your own condoms, but if you need to buy any in Cuba, remember the word *condones*.

Food Hygiene

Officially, the water and food in Cuba are safe. However, you would be well advised to observe the following basic guidelines:

– only eat fruit and vegetables if they've been peeled, washed thoroughly or cooked;

– ask for meat to be well done;

– fish in restaurants is safe, but don't eat any by-products due to the risk of poisoning (*ciguatera*);

– indulge to your heart's content in Cuban rock lobster and other members of the lobster family, but steer clear of shellfish;

– milk and dairy products are OK, provided they are from an official source.

Water

Avoid drinking the tap water wherever you are in Cuba (even in up-market hotels in Havana). Officially, the water is drinkable but it tastes horrible. Take disinfecting tablets or a special anti-bacterial water filter with you.

The problem is with water distribution. Although there is no shortage of water in hotels, private homes often have to do without. Often, in Havana in particular, inhabitants are without water for part of the day, especially in the older parts of town with ancient plumbing. They only get by if they've managed to fill the reserve tanks that are specially installed in their homes for this purpose. Don't be surprised, therefore, if the water gets cut off, especially while you're staying in a *casa particular*.

LANGUAGE

The national language of Cuba is Spanish. Although it's similar to the Spanish spoken in Spain, the accent may be harder to understand at first. Cubans who can speak English are still few and far between, so learn a bit of Spanish before you go and don't forget to carry a small phrasebook. Make the most of such a friendly population, and take some time to try to communicate with them.

Pronunciation

Words are pronounced as they are written; bear in mind the following pronunciation rules:

– *u* – always pronounced 'oo'.

– *j* – rota, a guttural sound, pronounced like the Scottish 'ch' in 'loch'.

– *ll* – pronounced 'ye'.

– *r* – a rolled r.

– *rr* – an exaggeratedly rolled r.

– Cubans don't always pronounce the 's' at the end of sentences, for example, *más* is 'ma'.

Accents

In Spanish, one syllable is emphasized more than the others. This is the penultimate syllable when the word ends in 's', 'n' or a vowel. The emphasis is on the last syllable when the word ends in any other consonant. The word is accented only where there is an exception to either of these rules.

– Examples:

por favor is pronounced por faVOR

Inglaterra is pronounced InglaTErra, but inglés is pronounced ingLES

turístico is pronounced tuRIStico (and not turisTIco)

A BASIC VOCABULARY

Civilities

Yes	*sí*
No	*no*
Please	*por favor*
Thank you	*gracias*
Sorry/excuse me	*disculpe*
Hi	*hola*
Good morning/good day	*buenos días*
Good afternoon, evening	*buenas tardes*
Good night	*buenas noches*
Goodbye	*adiós*
I like you	*me gustas*
I love you	*te quiero*

Frequently Used Expressions

Where are you from?	*¿de dónde viene?*
I'm British	*soy británico(a)*
What's your name?	*¿cómo te llamas?*
How do you say . . .?	*¿cómo se dice . . . ?*
I don't understand	*no entiendo*
I want . . .	*quiero . . .*
Do you know . . . ?	*¿conoce . . .?*
Watch out!	*¡cuidado!*
With	*con*
Without	*sin*
More	*más*
More or less	*más o menos*

Daily Life

Ashtray	*cenicero*
Bank	*banco*
Centre	*centro*
Entrance	*entrada*
Exit	*salida*
Letter	*carta*

Matches	*fósforos*
Police	*policía*
Post office	*correos*
Stamp	*sello*
Timetable	*horarios*
To telephone	*llamar por teléfono*
Tourist office	*oficina de turismo*
Town	*ciudad*

Transport

Car	*carro* (or *auto*)
Motorway	*autopista*
Train station	*estación (de ferrocarriles)*
Return ticket	*ida-vuelta*
I would like a . . .	*quisiera . . .*
train ticket for . . .	*un billete de tren para . . .*
bus ticket for . . .	*un billete de omnibus para . . .*
When does the train to . . . leave?	*¿cuándo sale el tren para . . . ?*

Money

The bill	*la cuenta*
Cash	*efectivo*
Cheap	*barato*
Do you take Visa?	*¿toma la tarjeta Visa?*
Expensive	*caro*
How much is . . . ?	*¿cuánto vale . . . ?*
Money	*dinero*
To pay	*pagar*
Price	*precio*
Receipt/invoice	*comprobante de ventas, factura, recibo*
Present	*regalo*

At the Hotel

(Double) bed	*cama (matrimonial)*
Blanket	*manta*
Can I see the room?	*¿puedo ver la habitación?*
Hot, cold water	*agua caliente, fría*
Hotel	*hotel, hostal*
Private lodging	*casa particular*
Reception, foyer	*carpeta*
Room (single, double)	*habitación (sencilla, doble)*
Sheets	*sábana*
Soap	*jabón*
Toilets/bathroom	*los servicios/baños*

Eating Out

Beef	*res*
Bread	*pan*
Breakfast	*desayuno*

Butter	*mantequilla*
Cheese	*queso*
Chicken	*pollo*
Chilli	*picante*
Crab	*cangrejo*
Dessert	*postre*
Egg	*huevo*
Fish	*pescado*
Food	*comida*
Fork	*tenedor*
Grilled	*a la plancha*
Knife	*cuchillo*
Liver	*higado*
Lobster	*la langouste de Cuba*
Meal	*almuerzo* (lunchtime), *comida* (evenings)
Meat	*carne*
Pepper	*pimienta*
Pork	*cerdo*
Salads	*ensaladas*
Salt	*sal*
Seafood	*mariscos*
Spoon	*cuchara*
Still water	*agua natural*
To drink	*beber*
To eat	*comer*
Vegetables	*verduras*
Water (sparkling)	*agua mineral (con gas)*
Wine (red, white)	*vino (tinto, blanco)*

Days of the Week

Monday	*lunes*
Tuesday	*martes*
Wednesday	*miércoles*
Thursday	*jueves*
Friday	*viernes*
Saturday	*sábado*
Sunday	*domingo*

Numbers

1 *uno*	11 *once*	30 *treinta*
2 *dos*	12 *doce*	40 *cuarenta*
3 *tres*	13 *trece*	50 *cincuenta*
4 *cuatro*	14 *catorce*	60 *sesenta*
5 *cinco*	15 *quince*	70 *setenta*
6 *seis*	16 *dieciseis*	80 *ochenta*
7 *siete*	17 *diecisiete*	90 *noventa*
8 *ocho*	18 *dieciocho*	100 *cien* (or *ciento*)
9 *nueve*	19 *diecinueve*	500 *quinientos*
10 *diez*	20 *veinte*	1,000 *mil*

MEDIA

NEWSPAPERS AND MAGAZINES

There is only one daily newspaper worth reading in Cuba: *Granma*. Behind the gentle and innocuous-sounding title lies the official organ of the Cuban Communist Party. This was also the name of the boat on which Fidel Castro and Che Guevara arrived in Cuba. Castro himself contributes regularly to the newspaper, although never under his own by-line. Granma is translated into several languages, and the English version is found in most hotels. Alternatively, lots of news vendors sell the Spanish version.

Kiosks in Havana sell foreign newspapers and magazines, although they are normally a week behind. Alternatively, some of the larger hotels may sell British newspapers, although these too may be out-of-date by the time they reach the island.

RADIO

Cuba has come a long way since Cubans searched feverishly for the frequency of Radio Rebelde, the revolutionary station launched by Che Guevara. Today, young people mainly tune into American rock stations broadcast from Florida. Radio Taïno is also popular. Originally intended for tourists, it has won a large audience among Cubans and plays nothing but Cuban Salsa music from 5 to 7pm. It announces all the forthcoming festivals, as well as concerts and tourist activities. Broadcasts are in English and Spanish. Taxi drivers will expose you to other music stations on the island. They are ideal for getting into the mood, and for listening to the latest salsas.

TELEVISION

This is undisputedly the favourite pastime of Cubans, together with sex and dominoes, however, there are only two national channels (Canal 2 and Canal 6), on air between 2pm and midnight. There is also a tourist channel (Canal 11), which broadcasts English and Spanish programmes but only in hotels, and a local channel in Santiago. In the larger hotels, you can tune into US stations (such as CNN) and Mexican stations.

To get a better feel for the Cuban mindset, don't miss the soap operas (*novelas*), which have been a staggering success. No one misses a single episode. Also popular are sports programmes and Hollywood films. One of the most popular actors in Cuba at the moment is Pierre Richard, a Frenchman, nicknamed *el rubio con el zapato negro* ('the tall blond-haired man with a black shoe').

MONEY

CURRENCY

The national currency is the **peso cubano**, divided into **centavos**. In the major towns most consumer goods are bought with US dollars, or a peso convertible, which is, in fact, a dollar in disguise. You can get peso convertible notes equivalent to $1, 5, 10, 20 and 50 bills.

It is best to take US dollars with you, in small denominations ($5, 10 or 20) if possible, otherwise you'll have a hard job getting change. With greenbacks you'll have few problems changing money. You'll rarely see a Cuban refuse dollars, unless you are in a restaurant frequented only by locals, which only accepts pesos cubanos.

– A word of advice: in spite of the all-pervading influence of the dollar, it is a good idea to keep a few pesos on you for the rare occasions when you do need them. Although the currency has been completely devalued and is virtually useless in the major towns, pesos are essential to buy a range of local goods, including a snack at lunchtime. In a few non-touristy areas of Havana and in the provinces, there are some restaurants, groceries, small businesses, village cafés, that only accept payment in the national currency. In practice however, such places are few and far between and any foreigner who doesn't speak a word of Spanish is more likely to end up with too many pesos than too many dollars.

– Look out for the sign in every shop displaying the currency accepted: if it's crossed with blue it accepts dollars, if crossed with yellow it accepts only pesos.

BANKS

The major banks (Banco Nacional de Cuba, Banco Financiero Internacional, Banco Internacional de Comercio, Banco Popular de Ahorro) are usually open from 8.30am to 3pm Monday to Friday. Some banks (the Cadeca in Santiago de Cuba, for example) are open Saturday mornings and sometimes even Sunday mornings. When everything else is closed in Havana, you can still change currency at the Habana Libre hotel.

CREDIT CARDS

International Visa, Eurocard and MasterCard are accepted all over Cuba, provided that they aren't issued by a US bank (due to the trade embargo). Therefore, American Express credit cards and traveller's cheques are not accepted in Cuba.

Bear in mind, though, that you can get away without having a credit card in Cuba. It all depends on your budget and requirements. For example, if you hire a car in Havana or Varadero, let's say, you will need a credit card (Visa or MasterCard) as a deposit (*deposito*) when you sign the contract. You will also need it to arrange additional insurance for the car, unless you make arrangements before you leave home.

You should be able to pay by credit card in most of the major hotels, although rarely in restaurants, and almost never in the *paladares* (private restaurants). CUPET petrol stations sometimes (but not always) accept credit cards, as do many tourist stores.

– Visa and MasterCard have an office in Havana at avenida 23, between calle L and M, Vedado. ☎ (537) 34-44-44. Fax: (537) 33-40-01.

– The Eurocard MasterCard provides the bearer (and family if travelling as a family) with repatriation assistance in case of a medical emergency. In case of a problem, dial the following number immediately: ☎ 0-800-22-22-11.

If your Visa card is stolen, call the number provided by your bank. The International Visa is accepted in the more touristy parts of Cuba, and often in the more expensive places, such as top-of-the-range hotels, car rental agencies and certain boutiques.

– **Withdrawing money using a credit card**: cash machines are starting to appear in Havana but it's a slow process. Tourists can more easily obtain dollars at a bank using a Visa credit card or MasterCard. These days, most banks will let you make a cash transaction – simply look for the traditional sticker. Try the Banco Financiero International (BFI), the Banco Nacional de Cuba (BNC), or even the Cadeca (Casa de Cambio) or the Banco de Credito y Comercio (Vedado, Havana). You will have to show your passport whenever you withdraw cash. Check your credit limit before you go. The minimum withdrawal is $100 and the authorized maximum (in theory, as Cuba tries to limit outgoings) is $500. Ask for small denominations; $10 bills are more practical than $50 or $100 bills.

You will be able to withdraw cash in the following towns: Havana, Pinar del Río, Sancti Spiritus, Guanabo (Playas del Este), Matanzas, Varadero, Cienfuegos, Ciego de Avila, Camagüey, Holguín, Bayamo and Santiago de Cuba.

TRAVELLER'S CHEQUES

Be careful with traveller's cheques: Cuba only accepts those issued by non-US banks, so opt for those issued by Visa or Thomas Cook, not American Express. Very few shops accept them, so you will have to change them at your hotel, or in the Cadeca, for cash. Take them with you as a precaution, just in case you are unlucky enough to have your money stolen. Commission on traveller's cheques ranges from 2.5 to 3 per cent, whereas there's no commission on currency.

TAKE CARE OF YOUR CASH

– In guesthouses and hotels: if you are staying in a private home, make sure the house is secure and check the state of the doors to the rooms before accepting the room. If you leave money in your room, make sure you hide it right at the bottom of your bag, and lock this with a small padlock. Avoid tempting thieves. In many moderate and top-of-the-range hotels, there are safety deposit boxes in reception, as well as small, computerized safety deposit boxes in the rooms.

– In the street: when walking around, only carry as much money as you need. Avoid external bumbags and don't keep your money in a rucksack. You might find it reassuring to know that there's a police presence on every street corner.

– In shops: count your change, ask for a receipt (*comprobante de venta*) and make sure you aren't being ripped off.

PHOTOGRAPHY

Cuba is a great place to take photos – old strawberry-coloured American cars cruising against a backdrop of crumbling colonial buildings; children playing; leather-faced old men; beautiful girls; families taking their evening stroll; rustic Creole houses. This society offers a wealth of wonderful photo opportunities. The people are usually happy to be photographed, but out of courtesy you should always ask their permission before you start snapping. They are unlikely to object if you are polite and smile.

You might not be able to get your preferred type of film once you get to Cuba, so stock up before you go. Fuji or Kodak films are usually on sale in *tiendas* (stores) and the larger hotels. Kodak Élite slide film is sold in the government Photo Service shops in the larger towns – in return for dollars. If you prefer using black and white film, bring your own supply.

POST

Post offices are hard to come by and, in principle, are reserved for Cubans. However, in Plaza Francisco-de-Asís in Old Havana, a large, modern post office has been opened for Cubans and tourists. You will also find stamps and letterboxes in hotels. Letters and cards collected from hotels arrive more quickly than collections from Cuban post offices, which tend to be disorganized and bureaucratic. Mail may take three weeks to a month to get to Europe, sometimes longer.

SENDING POST TO CUBA

– **Letters** will probably reach their destination, but are often opened by the Cuban post office, so don't include anything compromising, and don't send money.

– **Parcels** do not always reach the recipient, as they are automatically opened by post-office workers to check their contents. If they are of value, the contents may be stolen. Use a courier firm such as DHL. Although it will cost more, at least the parcels are sure to find their way to the recipient.

– **Humanitarian aid** for Cubans: you can send medicines, soap, shampoo, pencils, pens and books by priority mail. The best thing to do is to contact an association that organizes aid and distributes the gifts when they arrive.

RESTAURANTS AND *PALADARES*

Cuba has four very different types of restaurant:

– **Official tourist restaurants**: these only accept dollars and are frequented almost exclusively by foreigners. The menu is invariably the same (*criollo*, or creole, or sometimes international cuisine), but the prices range from double to three times what you would normally expect to pay, depending upon the comfort and reputation of the place. Usually, the best food is found in this kind of restaurant, and there is no problem with hygiene and the quality of the produce. However, this is a long way from Cuban reality. Note that the best restaurants add 10 per cent tax to the bill.

– *Paladares*: are restaurants in private houses, which opened some years ago and are recognized by the government.

The word *paladar* comes from a *novela*, a Brazilian soap opera that is very popular in Cuba. It tells the story of a mother who, ruined by her spiteful daughter, starts a new life by selling sandwiches on the beach. Eventually, she ends up setting up a little restaurant called Paladar.

Anyone displaying a sign outside is licensed to operate a *paladar* but these establishments are increasingly crippled by high taxes and many of them have gone out of business. In fact, as is the case with rooms to let in private houses (*casas particulares*) the owners of *paladares* are only entitled to serve 12 guests, subject to government taxes, which in some regions can amount to several hundred dollars.

Most of the *paladares* are in charming old houses, and it is usually possible to eat well in them at more attractive prices than in official restaurants (except in Havana where they tend to be quite expensive). Payment is required in dollars, however, so you won't meet many Cubans eating in *paladares*, except on very special occasions.

– **Restaurants for Cubans**: these only accept Cuban pesos (*moneda nacional*) and so may only interest independent travellers on a shoestring budget. Unfortunately, the food in these is poor, consisting of boiled vegetables, a limited choice of poor quality meat and stale bread. Portions are usually pretty meagre. Go once to see for yourself, even if it's only to get a feel for the kinds of difficulties faced by local people, and to appreciate the everyday Cuban reality of deprivation.

The menus are reminiscent of Russian restaurants – the lack of ingredients (ham, ham or ham) means that the cooks are forced to concoct different dishes with the bare minimum. Some of these restaurants are not open to tourists in the hope that they will be forced to eat in the (more expensive) tourist restaurants.

– **Large hotels**: cafeterias in the bigger hotels serve meals at reasonable prices, but don't offer a very varied menu. They are often clean, air-conditioned and pleasant, but not the place to meet Cubans.

SAFETY

Before the arrival of mass tourism, Cuba experienced virtually no instances of theft, especially since all petty criminals were expelled by Fidel to Miami. However, things have changed and, sadly, thefts are now increasingly common. Your dollars will be of considerable interest to the younger generation, starting with the *jineteros* (*see* 'Background'). On the whole, Cubans are honest, but they also have real material problems and are irresistibly tempted by the way some foreigners behave.

Avoid ostentatious displays of wealth (for example, avoid wearing large items of jewellery), don't take wads of money out in the street, and always keep your things close to you.

PRECAUTIONS

While there is a risk of petty theft, assaults are rare, and only likely to occur in the larger towns such as Havana and Santiago. By taking a few sensible precautions, you should be able to avoid being robbed:

– Leave your plane tickets, passport and large sums of money in the hotel, and only carry around with you as much as you need.

– Always carry a photocopy of your passport with you, rather than the original. Unfortunately, many thefts happen in hotels, so a padlock on your suitcase isn't really going to help.

– Bike theft is also commonplace, so if you are planning on hiring one, consider bringing a bicycle lock with you.

– If you hire a car, always lock doors and close windows, and try not to leave it unattended (locals may offer to watch it for you in return for a small fee).

– If you feel as though you're being mobbed by people trying to sell you something, just smile and refuse politely if you aren't interested. Don't let paranoia put you off getting to know the locals.

PASSPORT THEFT

If your passport is stolen, you need to report it to the local police. Given the snail-like speed of Cuban bureaucracy, this could take between one and three hours. The police will issue you with a certificate. The next stage is to validate the certificate by buying excise stamps which cost $25–35 from a special bank (follow the directions of the police). Next, go to the local immigration bureau. There, you will be given an official document to replace your stolen visa. This will allow you to remain legally in Cuba until the end of your stay. Get passport photos taken as soon as possible – everything takes twice as long in Cuba than in Europe (48 hours in Santiago). You might consider bringing these with you.

The final stage is to telephone your embassy as soon as possible to inform them of the theft and to arrange to go in to collect a temporary passport. This procedure shouldn't take more than a couple of hours. However, you need to have the right documents on you, and you will have to pay around 40 pesos.

TELEPHONES

The Cuban phone system is inefficient, to say the least. It can sometimes be easier to ring Cuba from abroad than from within the island itself. To complicate matters, several numbers are often allocated to one address, and you never know which is the right one. Be patient however as someone is bound to answer eventually. Ten-dollar telephone cards come in very handy, and are sold in ECTESA outlets, various places in town, some post offices and CUPET stations.

– **Calling Cuba**: dial 00 + 53 + the regional dialling code of the town + the number of the person you are trying to call.

– **Calling the UK** from Cuba: dial 119 + 44 + the STD code (without the initial zero) + the number of the called party. Calls are expensive, at around $8 a minute.

International Dialling Codes

– To Great Britain: +44

– To Ireland: +353

– To the USA and Canada: +1

– To Australia: +61

– To New Zealand: +64

– To South Africa: +27

Regional Dialling Codes

Baracoa 21	Guantánamo 21	Sancti Spiritus 41
Bayamo 23	Holguín 24	Santa Clara 422
Camagüey 322	Isla de la Juventud 61	Santiago de Cuba 226
Ciego de Avila 33	Havana 7	Trinidad 419
Cienfuegos 432	Matanzas 52	Varadero 5
Girón 59	Pinar del Río 82	

TIME DIFFERENCE

Cuba is five hours behind Britain (GMT-5); when it is noon in London, it is 7am in Havana.

TIPPING AND BARGAINING

Tipping is now quite common in Cuba. It has re-emerged in very touristy areas such as Varadero where, if you don't leave a tip, people will make pointed remarks such as 'the Spanish are more generous than that' or 'Mexicans aren't that mean'! The size of the tip is up to you, depending on your view of the service you've received.

Bargaining is also acceptable, especially in tourist areas. Remember that most Cubans have only a vague idea of the value of dollars and, in any case, it's always more than they earn. Bargain with them when you're buying souvenirs or taking a private cab anywhere, or booking a room in a hotel, particularly out of season. If your attempt at haggling isn't getting you anywhere, don't push it, and do remember that Cubans have to make a living like anyone else.

TRANSPORT

Public transport is one of Cuba's main problems. Because of the shortage of petrol, cars are few and far between. Trains are rare and the buses are nearly always jam-packed. As a result, Cubans spend a lot of time walking, hitchhiking or standing in queues in bus or train stations. But everyone gets by the best they can. People ride horses, donkeys (or buffaloes), they bring out their old *barouches* (horse-drawn carriages) – as in Pinar des Rio or Cardenas – 'borrow' rickety old bikes that are lying around, learn to roller skate, pile onto old tractors and so on. Of course, some do better than others; attractive young women, for example, seem to have no trouble in hitching a lift, and many employ irresistible methods to appeal to truck drivers.

On the other hand, independent travellers on a shoestring should be prepared for a certain amount of hassle. Living Cuban-style – that is, getting by on just a few pesos – involves being very patient and making the best of the means at your disposal. Anyone who can speak Spanish or who has Cuban friends will be at an advantage.

AIR TRAVEL

There are regular flights between the major towns on the island. This is a good way of getting around without wasting too much time, and air fares are reasonable. For example, a flight from Havana to Santiago will save 18 hours of train travel. Travelling by air is sometimes the only way of getting to certain places, such as Cayo Largo, Cayo Coco and Cayo Guillermo. Recently, there has been an upsurge in the number of private air charter firms and aerotaxis (old family-owned, prop-driven monoplanes).

BUSES

Buses in Cuba are very cheap, sometimes costing only pesos. The drawback is that they are old, slow and often break down, rarely arrive at their destination on time, and are also always packed. However, a certain number of seats are allocated to tourists paying in dollars, who may easily make a reservation.

Long-distance buses are more efficient than the local buses in Havana, where the queues are often long. The Astro and Viaje Azul companies divide the long-distance market between them. The former is mainly used by locals, and the latter by tourists, even though it's much more expensive and connections aren't nearly as good.

– The *guagua* (pronounced 'wa-wa'): these single-deck buses are a good way of getting around the larger towns and are still the least hassle when it comes to transport in Cuba. However, you often have to queue, and people are crammed into them like sardines. In Havana, there are also *camelos* (camels) – lorry cabs pulling a kind of long bus with two humps.

DRIVING

Since the petrol shortages, and because of the shortcomings of public transport, car rental is the best solution for exploring Cuba. However, it is expensive, costing between $500 and $700 a week, so you should try to share the cost between a few people.

– **Car rental**: The car rental fleet is still quite limited in Cuba, so make sure you book well in advance through a travel agency. In general, the vehicles are usually in fairly decent condition, sometimes even brand new depending on the company. Be aware that the Oriente region is (and will probably remain for some time) the down-market end of Cuban tourism and this has an effect on the state of the vehicles for hire here. You should therefore check the car thoroughly in the presence of a member of staff from the rental agency. Some hire companies rent out cars that are shortly due for a service. Make sure it has a spare tyre and a jack and that the brake pads and petrol cap are intact. Also check the petrol level.

Note: car rental agencies often 'forget' bookings, and a reservation (even through an established agency) does not always guarantee a car for you on arrival. In this case, your only option is to contact the head office of the rental agency and to insist that they find you a car as quickly as possible. Don't accept a car that is more expensive than the one you reserved.

It may not be possible to return your hire car to a different place from the one where you collected the car, but rental firms should allow you to do this if you insist.

– The Havanautos agency charges for a full tank when you hire the car, and you are not reimbursed if you return the car with petrol left in the tank. Always check whether the car has to be returned with a full or an empty tank (this varies with the company). The small print on the contract – that most people don't bother to read – indicates what you have to pay if you exceed the stated mileage. Don't expect the hirer to draw your attention to this until you return and he charges you for the extra.

– **Petrol**: If you're careful, there shouldn't be a problem with fuel. In all the major towns you will find CUPET (Cubana de Petroleo) petrol stations, which only take dollars. The official price is 90 cents for a litre (0.2 gallons) of *especial* petrol, which is recommended for most cars. Be careful that the pump attendant doesn't overcharge you, or make a mistake when calculating the total. Petrol station shops open 24 hours a day and sell virtually everything (cold drinks, food, coffee, batteries, cigarettes and so on) for dollars.

There is a flourishing black market in petrol. By asking at private homes or supervized car-parks you can get petrol for 50 cents a litre. This is worth bearing in mind in case of emergency or if you break down, but you can never be sure of the quality until it's too late. First agree on the quantity you need and then make the exchange somewhere discreet.

Car Theft

Car theft is common, but you can pay $1 or $2 to have a car looked after all night in an official supervized car park or a private garage. Alternatively, you can engage a young man to sleep in the car.

If parts of the car (wing mirror, windscreen wiper, bumpers) are stolen, report the theft to the police and ask for a copy of the report. If not, the car rental firm will charge you excessively for the damage. Be wary of insurance policies that don't cover you for 'partial theft' (*robo parcial*). Insurance has to be paid for on the spot, since it is unlikely to be included in a voucher from a travel agency.

Road Safety

Cuban roads are often crowded with walkers, hitchhikers and all kinds of animals. This is dangerous at night, since often there are no streetlights and the roads are poorly maintained. Watch out for potholes (some of them very deep), which are particularly tricky to see at night. Watch out too for bicycles suddenly swerving into the road to avoid potholes, or hitchhikers throwing themselves onto the car to attract attention. At night, none of the bikes has lights, the lorries only have one and car lights are fairly theoretical. When overtaking, particularly a truck, it's a good idea to sound the horn. The thick black smoke that comes gushing out of trucks can make it impossible for the driver to see anything.

Breakdowns

If you break down, inform the rental agency immediately so that they can take care of you. Don't expect too much though. They might offer to call out a breakdown recovery firm, which is unlikely to arrive very quickly. Try to get the problem fixed on the spot if you break down in a built-up area. Many Cubans are brilliant car mechanics and will know what is wrong with the car and how to fix it. An accelerator cable or fan belt can be repaired for $20–30. It's up to you to decide whether to waste 24 hours of your holiday waiting for the official breakdown recovery service (and then the time to repair the vehicle) or to fork out and get the job done with the minimum hassle and disruption. If you do get a puncture (*poncho*) you can get it repaired at most CUPETs. Otherwise there are people in most of the little towns who will repair it for you as a way of making a bit extra. Look for the small (discreet) signs saying '*Ponchera*'. Some specialize only in bike inner tubes, others in car tyres.

HITCHHIKING

This is known as *botellas* in Cuba. It is the most popular means of getting around, and competition for lifts can be fierce. Foreigners have little trouble in getting cars to stop, since most Cuban drivers will expect to be paid a few dollars in return. You will also find Cubans who are genuinely delighted to meet tourists and who will pick you up simply as a favour. Conversely, if you drive a car, you could find yourself acting as a chauffeur yourself. Cubans are relying increasingly on tourist cars, which are easily recognizable by their 'TUR' number plates. Actually, after the first couple of times, you feel almost morally obliged to offer people a lift. What's more, it's a great way of meeting local people. In the east of Cuba and the suburbs, take care not to get ripped off by hitchhikers. Play safe and avoid giving people a lift at night.

Occasionally, at major junctions as you leave some of the big towns, you might see men in yellow uniforms. These are officials in charge of a sort of state-controlled system of hitchhiking. Their job is to wave down passing administrative vehicles so that they can give a lift to people waiting interminably for a bus.

In most private vehicles there is a CD hanging from the inside rear mirror. This may seem an odd place to put a CD but the Cubans swear it interferes with police radar systems.

Maps and Atlases

Consider buying a road map before you leave home as the road maps on sale in Cuba are often poor quality. However, the pocket road atlas *Guía de Carreteras de Cuba* is excellent and on sale in some car rental agencies and CUPET stations. Published in colour (in Mexico), it is very detailed, reasonably priced and shows main routes and small country roads. It is essential since there are practically no signposts in Cuba.

– In Havana, one of the best places to buy town plans and road maps is the Tienda El Navegante, calle Mercaderes 115 (Habana Vieja), between Obispo and Obrapía. Open Monday to Saturday 8am–5pm.

– Another place to try is Geotech, calle 13, 409, at the corner of calle F, Vedado. Open Monday to Friday 9am–5pm, it sells maps, guides and atlases of particular interest to walkers.

TAXIS

If you don't fancy your chances on a train or bus, you can take a taxi (official or otherwise), provided that you pay in dollars. Official companies are in all the tourist spots and offer a good service.

– **Private**: *taxis particulares* are no cheaper than official, metered taxis. However, they aren't allowed to pick up fares from hotels and the airport, although they can deliver fares there. The state of private taxis can be deplorable, and they often break down, so they aren't always the best idea if you have a plane to catch.

With *taxis particulares* always negotiate directly with the driver and not with a tout (who gets commission). One way of finding out about fares is to take a metered taxi. That will give you an idea of how much you should be prepared to pay a private taxi.

– **Bike-taxis**: These are a bit like Asian rickshaws. Economical, ecological and quite fast around town centres, bike-taxis are found in a variety of forms. In Havana the passenger is protected from the rain by a cover or sort of metal hood. In Camagüey there are two seats at the back and the driver sits between them. In Holguín the passenger sits on one side. These are cheaper than taxis and much more fun. Fares vary depending on how far you're going; for the trip from Old Havana to the Vedado quarter, expect to pay $1 or $2; the same journey by taxi costs $5.

TRAINS

The rail network links Havana to all the main towns in the country. While the system improves year on year, the trains are still archaic, slow and never on time. They are also packed and overbooked.

There is no buffet service on board the trains (except the service between Havana and Santiago), so don't forget to bring refreshments and water with you. However, there are often itinerant vendors at each station stop selling sandwiches, fresh fruit or Cuban-style beverages.

Even if you are travelling first class, the comfort is minimal (with worn, sunken seats), so remember to bring socks, a sweater and a pocket torch with you: the carriages are rarely air-conditioned, and power cuts and broken bulbs are common. The toilets are often basic too – just two holes giving on to the road without a flush (or even a door, sometimes). Note that the train doors often don't close properly, and may bang loudly, which doesn't help much when you want to get a bit of sleep. The corridors between the carriages are sometimes riddled with gaping holes, so be careful when passing from one carriage to the next. Another joy of the Cuban rail system is that the train shakes around a lot and you sometimes find yourself gripping the armrest for support.

DISTANCES IN KM	PINAR DEL RIO	LA HAVANE	MATANZAS	CIENFUEGOS	SANTA CLARA	SANCTI SPIRITUS	CIEGO DE AVILA	CAMAGÜEY	HOLGUÍN	SANTIAGO DE CUBA	GUANTANAMO
GUANTANAMO	1074	910	847	702	648	563	488	378	182	86	
SANTIAGO DE CUBA	1024	860	797	658	598	513	438	328	134		86
HOLGUÍN	899	734	671	532	472	387	312	202		134	182
CAMAGÜEY	698	533	469	330	270	186	170		202	328	378
CIEGO DE AVILA	588	423	359	220	160	75		170	312	438	488
SANCTI SPIRITUS	513	348	284	145	85		75	186	387	513	563
SANTA CLARA	435	270	199	61		85	160	270	472	598	648
CIENFUEGOS	421	256	241		61	145	220	330	532	658	702
MATANZAS	264	98		241	199	284	359	469	671	797	847
LA HAVANE	147		98	256	270	348	423	533	734	860	910
PINAR DEL RIO		147	264	421	435	513	588	698	899	1024	1074

GENERAL INFORMATION

Distances between the principal towns (in kilometres)

Background

Cuba, the largest of the Caribbean islands, looks rather like a huge crocodile, and yet it is constantly being compared to a pearl. Its heady culture and thousands of miles of irresistible beaches add up to an unforgettable experience for those who visit its shores. Spanish and African traditions are fused here in a fabulous mix that invites discovery. The people are gifted with a rare sense of hospitality, laced with humour, smiles, naturalness and a sense of occasion. Add to this the delights of the island's half-Spanish half-colonial architecture, and you can see the appeal of the place.

On the other hand, the people of Cuba are desperately impoverished, with an average monthly income of just $10. And yet, these are people who have built, out of nothing, an empire – or 'Socialist Eldorado' – at least as far as tourists are concerned. These days, individual initiative on the part of the local populace often comes to nothing. The regime of Fidel Castro, who came to power in 1959, is a sort of 'velvet dictatorship', which prevents Cubans from being truly liberated. Young people born after the Revolution want something more, but there's nothing on the horizon (*see* 'La Revolución!').

The typical Cuban response is '*Hay que luchar*' ('We must fight'), obsessed as they are by hardship, and crushed beneath the weight of everyday problems. For once, the enemy, poverty, is within: the product of an obsolete system and a US embargo that is becoming increasingly difficult to justify.

Living from hand to mouth, Cubans expect little from the official economy (which is paralyzed by bureaucracy) and a great deal from the 'parallel' economy, which can bring them vital additional income. Everyone does what he or she can to get by, whether this be moonlighting, trafficking or the odd bit of illegal work. *Lucha* is the term used to designate this crazy obsession with dollars (*see* 'Economy'). *Lucha* is the only means of survival in a country where most of the consumer goods are sold in return for dollars, even though 95 per cent of the workforce is paid in pesos, the national currency.

This island may seem to be a sort of paradise to outsiders, but the daily life of the Cuban people is sometimes more like hell. The simplest needs – such as getting hold of sugar, milk for children, soap, cooking fuel, lard to fry bananas, spare parts for the Lada or petrol for the old Buick – take on Kafkaesque proportions. Here, the spur of necessity is the driving force behind an entire society.

VITAL STATISTICS

Surface area: 110,861 square kilometres (42,820 square miles)

Population: 11 million, with 99.8 inhabitants per square kilometre (0.39 square miles)

Capital: Havana (2 million inhabitants)

Main towns: Santiago de Cuba, Camagüey, Cienfuegos, Santa Clara and Holguín

Official language: Spanish

Currency: the *moneda nacional* is the Cuban peso. The exchange rate fluctuates frequently, between 17 and 23 pesos to the US dollar. Tourists nearly always pay with US dollars.

Government: Socialist Republic (single Communist Party)

Head of State: Fidel Castro Ruz (Prime Minister 1959–76, President since 1976)

Religion: Catholic, animist and santérist (Afro-Cuban religion)

Literacy rate: 95.7 per cent

Birth rate: 1.5

Average monthly income: $10

GEOGRAPHY

Cuba is the largest island in the Caribbean, an elongated 'green crocodile' that measures around 1,250 kilometres (775 miles) long, and just 200 kilometres (125 miles) at its widest part. Apart from the main island, Cuba also includes a host of smaller islands. One of the most famous is **Isla de la Juventud** (Isle of Youth), but there is also the archipelago of cayos, including **Cayo Largo**, **Cayo Coco** and **Cayo Levisa**.

The main island can be divided roughly in half into west (*oeste*) and east, more commonly referred to as the Oriente. Most of the major towns are situated in the centre of the island.

In addition to its coastline, with 2,600 kilometres (1,615 miles) of beaches, the Cuban landscape features several mountain chains known as sierras, which are riddled with caves.

HISTORY

FROM 1492 TO THE WARS OF INDEPENDENCE

– **Before 1492**: an indigenous people called the Tainos inhabit Cuba.

– **28 October 1492**: Christopher Columbus, a 'mercenary' of the Catholic Monarchs of Spain, and his crew encounter Guanahani (the Bahamas) three months after leaving Spain on board the *Santa María*, the *Niña* and the *Pinta*. The exact spot of his landing in Cuba is still in dispute – at Baracoa (Oriente) or the Bay of Baray, near Gibara. Columbus thinks he has discovered the Kingdom of the Mangi, or South China, and thus the start of the route to India. He is sure that the Straits of Malacca have to be near by, as well as the province of Cipangu (Japan) and the Garden of Eden. Thinking he is in China, Columbus names various flora 'Chinese rhubarb' and 'Chinese cinnamon tree'. He asks indigenous people whether there is gold near by. They reply, 'Yes, in Cubanacan', which Columbus misunderstands as 'Gran Can', or the Grand Khan. He immediately sends his emissaries (an Arab speaker and a sailor known to the kings of Guinea) to what he thinks is Cambaluc, the Mongolian capital. They find a village of around 50 huts inhabited by people who greet them as gods. Although there is no China, no Mongolian capital and no spices, Columbus returns to Spain still convinced he has found China.

– **1493**: Juan de la Cosa, boatswain of the *Santa María*, suggests that the place is an island and not a continent. Columbus insists that his men – on pain of reprisals – back up his Chinese theory. In 1500, although he still isn't 100 per cent sure, Juan de la Cosa draws his remarkable map of the world, on which Cuba appears as an island.

– **1509**: Sebastián de Ocampo concludes that Cuba is an island and not the coastline of a continent, confirming what Juan de la Cosa knew all along: that Columbus was way off the mark.

– **1510**: the conquest of Cuba begins under the leadership of Diego Velázquez, Hernán Cortés and some 300 men who become the first Spanish *conquistadores*.

– **1512**: the first town in Cuba (Asunción de Baracoa, in the southeast corner) is founded.

– **2 February 1512**: first rebel uprising, led by Hatuey, and the legendary victory of Yara.

– **1513**: arrival in Cuba of the first ships from Africa, filled with Congos, Loucoumis, Gangas, Mandingues and Carabalis.

– **1514**: the Spanish believe their conquest is over. The country is declared pacified and the systematic massacre of the native Indians begins. Once Cuba is conquered, the island becomes a base for the *conquistadores*.

– **16 November 1519**: official founding of Havana, which becomes the 'key to the New World'.

– **1524**: the first slaves arrive from Africa.

– **1526**: local administration established for the first time.

– **1576**: the first sugar refinery is founded in El Cerro.

– **1697**: official end to piracy in the Caribbean Sea. The names of Sir Francis Drake and pirate Henry Morgan become legendary.

– **1728**: founding of the University of Havana, the first in Latin America.

– **1762–63**: the English occupy Havana for a year, but then swap it with the Spanish for Florida under the Treaty of Fontainebleau of 6 July 1763.

– **1809**: first major demonstrations against the Spanish occupying forces and in the name of independence.

– **1812**: a liberated slave, carpenter and santería priest, José Antonio Aponte, dreams of leading a slave revolt. Nicknamed the 'Spartacus of Cuba', he is eventually killed.

– **1817**: decree for the abolition of slavery adopted by Britain and Spain. Cuba considers it to be a con, and slavery continues. People are bribed to turn a blind eye to the cargoes of human beings. The slave trade tails off towards the end of the 19th century.

– **1818**: royal decree opens Cuban ports to free international trade.

– **1838**: inauguration of the first railway line, not only in Cuba, but in the whole Spanish empire, including the Spanish mainland.

THE WARS OF INDEPENDENCE

Cuba's modern history starts with the uprising against the Spanish descendants of the *conquistadores*. Independence fever sets in and at the start of the 19th century the new enemy is the 'Yankees' rather than the Spanish.

– **10 October 1868**: the Demajagua uprising of Carlos Manuel de Céspedes marks the beginning of the Wars of Independence. The first war is dubbed the 10-Year War, and the rebels lay down their arms in 1878.

– **Around 1880**: Cuba's trade with the USA is six times greater than with Spain.

– **1895**: the three great early revolutionaries, José Martí, Antonio Maceo and Máximo Gómez join forces to evict the Spanish. Their attempt fails, and the Americans immediately try to re-establish law and order in Cuba under an American system. They begin by inspecting three boats belonging to a rebel Mambís expedition. Although the rebels' fight against the Spanish has already been subdued, the American press assumes the role of warmonger. The Cuba correspondent for the *New York Journal* (owned by the press magnate Randolph Hearst) wants to return home, but is told by his boss, 'Stay there. You provide the descriptions, I'll provide the war.' The lie gains ground. Joseph Pulitzer of *World* magazine publishes misinformation on Cuba. The only real war is the one being waged between rival American newspapers. The public follows the movement in the US and swallows the anti-Spanish propaganda hook, line and sinker.

– **15 February 1898**: the USS *Maine* explodes mysteriously in the Bay of Havana, with the loss of 266 Marines.

– **April 1898**: the US Chamber of Representatives and Senate vote in favour of Cuba's right to independence and demand the withdrawal of the Spanish. This represents a complete U-turn in US policy on Cuba, the first of many. On 19 April, Congress votes for war, and on 25 April the US declares that it is at war with Spain.

– **3 July**: US ships scupper Admiral Cervera's squadron in waters off Santiago de Cuba. On 16 July the town capitulates.

– **10 December 1898**: the Treaty of Paris is signed and Cuba falls into American hands. The US seizes the opportunity to buy Puerto Rico and the Philippines, formerly under Spanish rule. Cuba struggles free from the grip of Spain only to come under the rule of its powerful neighbour to the north. Cuba is to remain under US military occupation for four years.

– **1 January 1899**: Spanish power is officially transferred to the US.

– **5 November 1900**: the first meeting of the Cuban constituent assembly, presided over by the US Governor General Leonard Wood.

BACKGROUND

– **1901**: the Platt Amendment (abolished in 1934) authorizes the US to intervene in Cuban affairs as it sees fit. Tomás Estrada Palma is elected the first President of the Cuban Republic. The first of the puppet governments is established.

– **22 May 1903**: the American plan of action is complete. Guantánamo becomes a US territory. The economic advantages are considerable, especially since the US can now buy Cuban sugar at preferential rates in exchange for low customs duties on US goods.

– **1904**: the first legislative elections are marked by widespread fraud. At the end of the year three parties have been formed: the Conservative Republican Party, the Liberal National Party and the Labour Party – the creation of José Martí – which is to form the basis for the Cuban Communist Party.

AMERICAN CAT'S-PAW

– **1906–7**: various US interventions in Cuba are requested by President Estrada Palma, who is eventually deposed. Lawyer Charles Magoon governs the country for more than two years.

– **1909**: Cuban general José Miguel Gómez is elected president by those in power in the US.

– **1913–20**: term in office of General Mario G. Menocal, another American protégé. He authorizes the first US intervention in a Latin American country, when Marines enter Cuban territory in a show of force.

– **1921**: the Liberal Alfredo Zayas becomes president, followed by Gerardo Machado, a forerunner of the typical Latin American dictator. He is forced to leave the country in August 1933.

– **1921–33**: the opposition gathers strength. On 17 August 1925 the Cuban Communist Party is founded, and the first armed actions of the *Directorio Revolucionario Estudiantil* take place in December 1932.

– **1933**: Colonel Fulgencio Batista (1901–73) overthrows the government of Grau San Martín, which had never been recognized by the US. With open arms, Batista receives American Mafia bosses such as Meyer Lansky, 'Lucky' Luciano, Frank Costello and Bugsy Siegel. Batista asks Lansky, the godfather, to revive businesses 'under military control', the Nacional casino and Oriental Park racecourse, which had been struggling since the Depression. Corruption in the casino and race-fixing are banned. The Las Vegas Mafia imposes its luxurious, elegant style on Havana. Business booms.

– **July 1940**: Batista, now a general, is elected President of the Republic for four years. His National Unionist government includes the Communists, who have two ministers without portfolio. He is ousted by Grau San Martín. The Communist Party becomes the People's Socialist Party (PSP) and joins the opposition.

– **1946**: a young Fidel Castro is elected president of the student union. 'Lucky' Luciano, deported from the US to Italy, ends up in Cuba. Frank Sinatra entertains here. The FBI search for Luciano and the US government asks Batista to expel him from Cuba immediately under penalty of the withdrawal of medical aid.

– **1952**: Batista defeats President Prio Socarras to retake power. Under Batista, the Mafia strengthens its grip on Havana. Relations between Batista and the Cosa Nostra are such that, on his return to power, he makes Meyer Lansky his tourism adviser (a sort of unofficial minister). Lansky stays in the Sevilla Biltmore hotel and controls proceedings at the Montmartre, Nacional and Monseigneur. Shabby and sleazy establishments are cleaned up, yet Havana still has 270 brothels, as well as 'clubs' and hostess bars. It is still a Mecca for prostitution and a paradise for foreign sex tourists, all just a few hours by plane from New York. Vice in all its forms thrives in the heart of the Americanized quarter of the Vedado, which teems with large hotels and modern buildings.

FROM GUERRILLA WARFARE TO THE REVOLUTION

– **26 July 1953**: unsuccessful attack on the Moncada barracks in Santiago de Cuba by lawyer Fidel Castro and some 130 men. Castro is sentenced to 15 years' imprisonment, but 'Castroism' is born.

– **1955**: the Moncada rebels are granted an amnesty. Castro and several others, including his brother Raúl, reach Mexico. They buy a small yacht, the *Granma*, and prepare for the landing that would see them seize power in Cuba.

– **July 1955**: Fidel meets a young Ernesto ('Che') Guevara at a friend's house in Mexico and appoints him commando doctor.

– **2 December 1956**: the *Granma* berths on the east Cuban coast near Playa Las Coloradas, with 82 men on board. Pursued by Batista's troops, Fidel Castro and his men seek refuge in the Sierra Maestra mountains above Santiago. Meanwhile, in Havana, Batista and Lansky lay the foundation stone of the Riviera, the ultimate casino. It opens on 10 December 1957 with a show featuring Ginger Rogers.

– **June 1957**: the Resistance movement in the towns joins the fighting. On 18 December, rebels in Havana seize the great Argentinian motor-racing champion, Juan Manuel Fangio (1911–95), and hold him hostage for 48 hours.

– **1958**: on the eve of the Revolution, the American economic stranglehold on Cuba is stronger than ever. Wall Street controls 90 per cent of the mines, 90 per cent of the plantations, 80 per cent of the public utilities and 50 per cent of the railways. The US indirectly controls the island's economy.

– **5 May 1958**: Fidel Castro becomes leader of the M-26 (Movement of 26 July).

– **9 December**: Che Guevara signs an agreement for unity of action with the *Directorio* and the PSP. Camilo Cienfuegos joins Che's troops at the gates of Santa Clara.

– **January 1959**: the rebels seize Santiago, where Fidel Castro gives his first national speech. The defeated Batista flees to the Dominican Republic. Dr Manuel Urrutia is nominated Acting President. Castro enters Havana and gives a long speech promoting revolutionary unity.

KEY DATES OF THE REVOLUTION

– **13 February 1959**: Fidel Castro becomes Prime Minister.

– **18 July**: Osvaldo Dorticos is named President of the Republic.

– **29 October**: Camilo Cienfuegos dies in a plane crash.

– **26 November**: Che Guevara is named director of the national bank. He becomes Minister of Industry on 23 February 1961.

– **4 March 1960**: the French boat *La Coubre* explodes in Havana, killing 70. Cuba accuses the CIA. As the victims are buried, Castro launches Cuba's new slogan, '*Patria o muerte!*' ('Homeland or death!').

– **8 May**: Cuba and the USSR enter into diplomatic relations.

– **5–9 July**: the first sugar crisis between Cuba and the USA.

– **6 August**: first wave of nationalization.

– **19 October**: the USA declares a trade embargo that becomes total on 25 April 1961. On 3 January 1961 it breaks off diplomatic relations with Cuba.

– **1961**: concerted literacy campaign in Cuba.

– **15 April 1961**: the first bombardments of Cuba before the failed landing at the Bay of Pigs.

THE BAY OF PIGS

On the morning of 17 April 1961, some 1,400 heavily armed anti-Castro mercenaries invaded the pretty sandy beach of Playa Girón (the Bay of Pigs) in the south of the island. Their mission (ordered the previous day by President John F. Kennedy, 1917–63) was to overthrow Fidel Castro's regime – but in just a few hours. The mercenaries were trained by the CIA and US Marines in camps in Nicaragua and Guatemala, yet no Americans took part in the offensive. However, the secrecy of the mission had been compromised and Castro had known since 7 April that an invasion was imminent.

Brigade 2506 was routed and the mercenaries driven back, but there were Cuban casualties. The victims were buried on 25 April, when Castro first proclaimed the 'Socialist' nature of the Cuban Revolution.

In less than 48 hours, Fidel had seen off the enemy with eight aircraft and artillery inherited from Batista, and with just one working telephone in the combat zone. More important than equipment was the complete dedication of more than 20,000 civilians and soldiers alike. More than 1,100 mercenaries were held captive until December 1962, when they were released in return for $53 million of medical equipment, drugs and baby food.

The operation had actually been dreamed up and organized by the strategist and former US President Dwight Eisenhower (1890–1969) – Kennedy merely carried it out – yet the US received a major public military humiliation. The Cuban victory (and the victory of Fidel Castro, who proved himself an able strategist and warlord) against imperialism remains a cornerstone of the country's unity.

CUBAN MISSILE CRISIS

In 1962 the world's two superpowers were involved in a stand-off. Moscow objected to the deployment of US missiles in Turkey, not far from Soviet territory. In reply, the Soviet leader Nikita Krushchev (1894–1971) arranged the secret installation in Cuba of medium-range nuclear missiles. Also known as the October Crisis, the ensuing conflict was the most serious international incident since World War II, and led the international community to the brink of nuclear war.

In a letter to Krushchev, a determined Fidel Castro said that if the Americans decided to invade Cuba, it would be the opportune time to eliminate such a danger permanently through an act of legitimate defence, as hard and terrible as such a solution might seem. In other words, he was asking Krushchev to deploy nuclear weapons in case of an American attack.

However, after American spy planes detected the Soviet installations, Kennedy addressed a 'message to the nation' and a naval blockade was put into place. It was lifted in November, when the US was sure that the launchers and missiles had been removed. Krushchev finally reached an agreement with Kennedy in return for the removal of the US missiles in Turkey.

The crisis lasted only a few days, but the whole world feared the worst. Fidel Castro, who by this time had been excluded from talks, made it clear that he did not agree with the conclusions of the two superpowers. The US had pledged not to attack Cuba but, in his eyes, this clause was inadequate.

Following the Cuban Missile Crisis, relations between Havana and Moscow became temporarily bitter. Paradoxically, it was during the October Crisis that Castro's regime became unified and consolidated. In global terms, it was the period of détente.

FIDEL CASTRO

'Fidel will always be Fidel', according to his friends, his entourage and to most Cubans on the island. His opponents, in exile or otherwise, can also be heard bemoaning this fact. In any case, everyone always refers to him simply by his first name.

According to Western observers Fidel Castro has changed over the years. There is no statue, official photo or organized personality cult of him as guerrilla leader, romantic and mythical figure and leader of the Third World. So these have nothing to do with his dominant status today – his image as a 'tired old man' and 'dictator', which are some of the more complimentary descriptions of him. Fidel is not a bloody tyrant, but neither is he the world's greatest democrat. He says himself that history will decide who the Líder Máximo is, or was. In 1953, faced with judges who were about to sentence him to 12 years in prison, he shouted at the court, 'History will acquit me!'

There are no modern history books in Cuba, and still fewer on Fidel Castro himself. Fidel has never allowed his portrait to be done. His great Nobel Prize-winning friend, the Colombian writer Gabriel García Márquez, said of him that 'his personality is so complex that different people can leave the same interview with him each with a completely different impression'.

Fidel Alejandro Castro Ruz is the eldest son of an immigrant landowner from a modest background in Galicia in Spain. He was born on 13 August 1927, received a Catholic education, then studied under the Jesuits. His teachers wrote of him, 'He is made of good stuff and is a man of action'. Later on he would earn the reputation as a pugnacious student and a rebel. The young Fidel was already a leader of men, able to articulate his ideas well, intransigent (sometimes to the point of brutality), self-assured, fanatical about politics, radical, independent, a man of action, patriotic, able, vindictive and headstrong.

His epic period in the Sierra Maestra, his triumphant arrival in Havana, his idealist politics at the beginning of the Revolution and the hope that he represented for the developing world, would earn him praise and make him the subject of numerous writings, flattering to the point of being bombastic. However, since the installation of the Castroist Communist regime, and in the light of his never-ending power and resistance to international condemnation, Fidel's every action, gesture and speech has been judged gravely. Fidel is a rare politician in being able to inspire judgements on his person that are diametrically opposed, to the point of being commonplace and preconceived.

It seems that Fidel has always been there. His long political life is due in part to a series of lucky escapes. First, he managed to avoid being committed to a psychiatric hospital, where his parents wanted him to receive treatment. Then, in the 1940s, he escaped from prison several times and dodged the bullets of Fulgencio Batista's troops. In 1947, he was spared from shark attacks as he swam for several kilometres across a bay near Santo Domingo. In July 1953, his life was saved by one of Batista's soldiers, Pedro Sarria, when he was arrested for attacking the Moncada de Santiago barracks. In 1955, he was released, and granted an amnesty. He announced to all that he was leaving for Mexico and that he would come back, armed, to liberate the country. During the guerrilla warfare period, he succeeded in passing through Batista's lines and, once in power, the CIA never managed to get rid of him, despite several alleged attempts.

The austerity of Fidel Castro is undisputed, and anyone who comes into close contact with him claims that he continues to live in simple and unostentatious conditions (although some claim that he has a Swiss bank account and numerous residences and that he eats better than his people). Fidel was never seen wearing anything other than his legendary battledress, an olive-green military uniform, and his peaked comandante's cap. Then, in 1994, during a Latino summit in Colombia, he appeared bareheaded for the first time in public, wearing a traditional guayabera shirt. The photo hit the headlines all over the world. The following year, he appeared in a dark suit, white shirt and tie during a series of diplomatic talks held overseas.

Castro has never spoken publicly of his private life, and yet Cubans know virtually everything about him – his personal life, his family situation, his preference for French cheese, a predilection for a certain whisky, his favourite reading material and so on, down to the finest detail.

It is likely that Fidel will remain as Líder Máximo for as long as he has energy to fight. He has always liked fighting battles, and seems nostalgic for the era of guerrilla warfare. He is never more comfortable than at the centre of a storm. Once the US embargo is lifted, Fidel may decide that it is time to relinquish power, but he shows no signs of doing so for the time being.

THE CASTRO YEARS

– **27 April 1963**: Fidel Castro arrives in Moscow on his first trip to the USSR.

– **20 February 1965**: Che Guevara gives his last public address in Algiers.

– **Until September 1965**: mass exodus of Cubans.

– **8 October 1967**: arrested in Bolivia, Che is executed on the orders of the CIA.

– **13 March 1968**: trade and private corporations nationalized.

– **23 August**: Cuba 'approves' of Russian intervention in Czechoslovakia.

– **Summer 1970**: sugar crop fails, leading to the 'zafra of the 10 million' affair.

– **1972**: Cuba joins COMECON, the common market of the Communist Bloc. (The first five-year trade agreement with the USSR is signed in 1976.) Soviet pressure is strengthened.

– **1974**: first elections in Cuba (People's Power organizations). The National Assembly is inaugurated on 2 December 1976, at the same time as the Council of State.

– **November 1975**: military engagement of Cuba in Angola to safeguard the country's independence at the behest of President Neto (withdrawal does not begin until 1988). Cuba also later establishes a presence in Ethiopia.

– **17 December**: first congress of the PCC held; the first five-year plan is decided.

– **24 February 1976**: the Socialist Constitution of the Republic of Cuba is proclaimed.

– **1979**: sixth summit in Havana of non-aligned countries.

– **Early 1980**: second mass exodus of Cubans (named the Mariel Crisis, after the port in Havana from which the exiles depart).

– **1986**: launch of the 'rectification of mistakes and negative tendencies' campaign. Castro adds, 'We have to acquire currency'.

– **March 1986**: Fidel Castro meets Mikhail Gorbachev in Moscow.

– **1987**: the first arrival of significant numbers of foreign tourists. Fidel makes his final trip to the USSR.

– **1988**: with Fidel Castro's consent, the first international human rights' committees arrive in Cuba.

– **2 April 1989**: Gorbachev visits Cuba. Castro refuses to acknowledge *perestroika*.

– **June 1989**: General Arnoldo Ochoa is arrested for drug trafficking, tried and executed. The fall from grace of this national hero (a former leader of the Cuban expeditionary corps in Angola) shocks the country.

– **November 1989**: fall of the Berlin wall.

– **1 September 1990**: after being dropped by the USSR and the declaration of bankruptcy of the Eastern Bloc, Cuba finds itself isolated. Economic recession prompts the government to call a *periodo especial* ('special period'), and Cubans suffer years of austerity not known since 1959. The Castro regime adopts an emergency programme of restrictions initially intended for wartime (with the issue of ration books, and grave shortages in some areas).

– **May 1991**: the last Cuban soldiers leave Angola.

– **April 1992**: the US Toricelli Act strengthens the embargo.

– **26 July 1993**: possession of US dollars becomes legal.

– **July–August 1994**: third mass exodus, the *balseros* affair and incident on the US Guantánamo base.

– **October 1994**: free trade in agricultural produce is authorized.

– **March 1995**: Fidel Castro visits Europe for the first time.

– **5 September 1995**: foreign investment is authorized, with the promise of 'protection'.

– **Early 1996**: new Cuban-American incident with the affair of the *avionetas*. Washington strengthens the trade embargo with the Helms-Burton Act, to the point where Cuba faces international isolation. In July, President Clinton suspends part of the Helms-Burton Act for six months.

– **1997**: Castro celebrates his 70th birthday (and his tenth US President!).

– **1998**: Cuba receives a visit from Pope John Paul II, and Castro releases almost 300 political prisoners. In April, the US trade embargo is eased. Direct flights between Cuba and the US, as well as monetary transfers and the import of medicines, are authorized. For the first time since 1991, the UN refuses to follow the recommendations of the US and decides not to impose sanctions on Cuba for violation of human rights.

– **November 1999**: Spanish-American summit in Havana. The two key outcomes are first that Castro wins the day in diplomatic terms by demonstrating that, despite the embargo and US policy towards Cuba, the island is certainly not cut off from the international community. Second, despite the regime's sidelining of 'dissidents' during the summit, many foreign heads of state insisted on meeting the leading players in the 'moderate opposition' and Castro put up no objection. As a result of the summit, the world at large and the international press discovered that these so-called 'counter-revolutionaries' and 'American puppets' were often merely groups of intellectuals and independent journalists calling for a few basic liberties and the right to a little free enterprise.

– **End of 1999 to early 2000**: the Elian affair (*see* 'Exile and Emigration') rekindles anti-American hostility and whips up the people against the Cuban members of the NCAF (National Cuban-American Foundation).

POST-REVOLUTIONARY CUBA

The Revolution of 1959 remained stable until the end of the 1980s. But with the disappearance of the Eastern Bloc and the fall of the Berlin Wall, Cuba lost its main economic allies, suppliers and customers virtually overnight.

The impact on the country was terrible. With Moscow out of the picture, the equivalent of almost $5 billion, 10 million tonnes of oil and $6 billion of imports went up in smoke. The problem was further aggravated by the continuation of the US embargo.

Ever since, Cuba has been living in the *periodo especial*, a programme of economic austerity. The 'construction of Socialism' has been suspended, and the sole problem is now how to survive on the country's national resources.

Cuba has been somewhat unfairly portrayed for the past decade, which has been an uncertain and difficult time of living from hand to mouth, during which Cubans have been on the brink of national and individual bankruptcy. The scale of the recession is such that there could soon be a real shortage of essentials like aspirin, electricity, public transport and food staples. The *libreta* (ration card) is being reduced. At the same time, the black market is becoming increasingly widespread. One dollar can be exchanged for up to 130 pesos. Resourcefulness and bartering are the secret to economic survival and, inevitably, petty crime and prostitution are becoming more prolific. The romantic image of the Revolution is taking a hammering.

Yet, since the end of 1995, there have been signs of a change for the better. Cuba must acquire foreign currency, and the bulk of this is likely to come from international tourism. Slowly but surely, the authorities take hesitant steps towards a national and international market economy, something that was unthinkable and inconceivable not that long ago. Cubans watch this movement carefully, since they, like tourists and the business world, stand to benefit. Currency trafficking, the black market and other contrivances are on their way out.

Cuba has implemented a widespread investment policy: dozens of professions have been liberalized and overseas visits are now possible. Spanish and Canadian capital is welcomed. The European Union and most Latin American countries refused to accept pressure from Washington's Helms-Burton Act (*see* 'The Castro Years').

The idea that Castro, Cuba and the Revolution no longer present an ideological or strategic threat to the USA (separated as they are by only 150 kilometres/93 miles of ocean) seems to be filtering through to the American consciousness at last. A 1995 Pentagon report suggested that only under Castro would Cuba remain politically, and therefore socially, stable.

MODERN CUBA

Cuba is reverting to its island status. 'It isn't fair that Cuba should be judged when there are people who are doing everything they can to suffocate it', declared Castro, referring to the US embargo. In Cuba, visitors find two separate countries: the political country, with its traditions and austerity – the

Cuban Communist Party is still the pillar of political life, Western-style pluralism being kept at bay – and the economic and social country, hungry for dollars (*see* 'Economy').

Fidel's old guard is still there, but others are being pushed to the front. Cubans are quick to say that they don't want a return to the US-style capitalism that existed prior to 1959, which could see the disappearance of their social achievements and the transformation of their world by foreign interests.

By using the dollar as a provisional tool to help the Cuban economy back on its feet, Fidel Castro is trying to avoid the terrible famine of 11 million Cubans and to satisfy the country's primary needs as best he can. Castro still has the complete backing of the Cuban people – some 800,000 people gathered in Plaza de la Revolución on 1 May 1996 to pledge their support for him – because the alternative, his permanent departure, is so widely feared.

Like the heroine of Julio Garcia Espinosa's *Reina y Rey*, Cubans are obliged to continue 'waiting and hoping'.

The Hardening of the Regime

From 1996 there had been increasing signs that the regime was about to open up. Then, at the beginning of 1999, there was something of a U-turn by the Cuban government. Although the *periodo especial* is not officially disputed, it is definitely in a bad way.

The authorities are convinced that the 'concessions' made to capitalism have created new injustices and the development of so-called 'negative social conduct'. For hardliners, this change risks weakening the Socialist society in the long term, so the decision was made to toughen legislation. Special laws have been introduced, and an across-the-board ideological offensive launched. A new subject entitled 'value training' has been added to the school curriculum, and at roadsides visitors will see slogans like 'We will never return to capitalism'.

The National Assembly has brutally reinforced its legal arsenal against dissidents and the free press 'for the protection of independence and the economy'. The parliament has enacted a law providing for penalties of up to 20 years' imprisonment and prohibitive fines of 100,000 pesos ($4,400) for anyone who directly or indirectly collaborates with the foreign media.

Tried in March 1999, although imprisoned since July 1997, four members of the support group for internal dissidence who dared to criticize a document produced for the Fifth Congress of the Cuban Communist Party were jailed for between three and a half years and five years for seditious activities. This time round the UN Commission on Human Rights condemned political repression in Cuba.

Fighting petty crime, particularly in the capital, has become an obsession with a regime that expected 2 million tourists in 1999. Several articles of the penal code have been amended, and in Havana there is now a policeman on virtually every street corner. Cubans who solicit trade from tourists are regularly charged by police with *jineterismo* (prostitution) or drug dealing, whereupon they are hauled to police headquarters and fined a few hundred pesos. If they re-offend, they may even be jailed.

The same applies to unofficial taxi drivers and unauthorized *paladares* (private restaurants). 'Private tourism' is on the decline despite the tourist boom. Faithful to its Socialist economic concept, the government still loves tourists who pour money into state coffers. Heads rolled recently following the discovery of corruption in a number of major tourist organizations.

Recently, the most symbolic political manoeuvre was the ousting of Roberto Robaina, the head of the Cuban diplomatic corps and known to be in favour of liberalization. Highly extrovert, the jovial smile of 'Robertico', as the Líder Máximo called him, had managed to breach the island's international isolation, convincing foreign delegates of the regime's desire to embark upon reforms. The appointment of Fidel's own private secretary to this post suggests that Fidel really is in the driving seat when it comes to Cuba's future.

Although the effects of the hardening of the regime are most obvious in Havana, the atmosphere all over Cuba has recently become less cheerful. The third millennium dawned on a distinctly sombre note. There are fewer street musicians and Cubans seem visibly worried. Before, they trusted Fidel not to go back on his word or give way to external pressure; it appears now he might have shattered their illusions, perhaps forever.

One thing is sure – it is harder to travel independently around the island since tourism became a national priority and 'bleeding' the tourist dry became a national pastime. Even contact with the local people is risky – for the Cubans, never the tourists. Whatever happened to the government's cherished ambition, so dear to socialism, of 'forging bonds between peoples'?

CHE GUEVARA

His portrait is everywhere. The most venerated idol in Cuba is not a god, and not even Cuban, but Fidel Castro's famous right arm during the Revolution. He is El Comandante Guevara, nicknamed 'Che' because he punctuated most of his sentences with '*che*', a typical but untranslatable Argentine interjection.

Ernesto Guevara Lynch de La Serna was born on 14 June 1928 in Rosario de la Fé in Argentina. At the age of two, after swimming in a river, he suffered his first asthma attack. From that point on, Ernesto would be condemned to fight against this complaint, which he tried in vain to overcome with heavy doses from a Ventolin inhaler and steroid injections.

Young Ernesto developed a wilful nature that commanded respect. To overcome his illness, he threw himself headlong into sport – football, tennis, golf and pelota – and developed a passion for rugby. Ernesto also became a compulsive reader, and he was already familiar with the writings of Jung, Adler, Marx, Engels and Lenin by the age of 15. He read all the French poetry he could find, and devoured London, Kipling, Dumas and Stevenson. The works he read sowed the seeds of his idealism. At the age of 17, he wrote a philosophical essay inspired by Voltaire. He could have been a writer, but opted instead for medicine. In 1947, he spent his vacation in a leper colony tending the sick, guided, as ever, by altruism.

When he was 23, Ernesto decided to explore South America with his friend Alberto Granado, and on 29 December 1951, they left Argentina on an old Norton motorbike. During the seven months spent crossing Chile, Peru and Colombia, the social and political conscience of the young adventurer, confronted each day with the sight of exploited Indians, began to take shape.

Armed with a wealth of experience, the traveller returned to Buenos Aires to finish his medical studies. No sooner had he graduated than he hit the road again, this time in search of action in the fight against injustice.

The doctor arrived in Guatemala in 1953. It was here, in a tense atmosphere of insurrection, that he contracted Revolution fever, and where he also met his first wife, the Peruvian Hilda Gadéa. On file as activists, the couple was forced to seek exile in Mexico. In July 1955, in Mexico City, Ernesto met a young man called Fidel Castro, a Cuban in revolt against Batista, the dictator ruling his island. Che Guevara offered his services as a doctor to the rebel troops that would eventually liberate Cuba. Castro agreed and Che Guevara boarded the *Granma*. It wasn't long before the doctor exchanged his medical kit for arms. The rest is history.

Once Cuba had been liberated, Guevara travelled the world as itinerant ambassador of the Revolution. On his return to Cuba, on 26 November 1959, he was made head of the central bank, where he would sign banknotes with an ironic and provocative 'Che'.

Guevara was to enjoy six years of power. He developed his theory of the New Man and put the finishing touches to his socio-economic views of an ideal society, but at the same time he gradually lost faith in the USSR, Cuba's main ally. On 24 February 1965, in Algiers, he delivered the famous speech that would isolate him for ever from the political scene. His foresight and frankness gave him the itinerant status of a Don Quixote.

His Cuban idyll over, Che was forced to seek other battles. First there was the Belgian Congo, where he wanted to instigate another Vietnam War. It was a crushing defeat. On 3 November 1966, Comandante Guevara arrived in La Paz in Bolivia. An attempt at bringing Bolivian liberation one step closer would turn into 11 tragic months of fear, rout and betrayal.

On 8 October 1967, Che – with no strength left – was captured by the Bolivian army. Injured in the leg, he was held captive in the village school in La Higuera. It seems that the CIA and other US authorities (including the president) had already decided his fate: that night, at around midnight, the Bolivian government received a formal order from the United States to execute the guerrilla. The next day, CIA agents Mario Terán and Felix Ramos filled Che's body with bullets.

From this assassination was born the finest myth of modern-day Latin America. With his integrity and morality intact, Che became a role model for all revolutionaries. His image is a romantic one – a political man who died for his beliefs. Exacting, a disciplinarian, unwilling to compromise, with a 'fierce saintliness' that served as his armour, no one can deny that he was a man who acted on his beliefs.

In 1964, before a meeting of UN delegates, Che uttered the following lines, which remain a fitting eulogy for the altruistic revolutionary: 'I am at once Cuban and Argentine, and if the illustrious countries of Latin America permit me, I am also a patriot of Latin America as a whole. I will be ready, when the time comes, to give my life for the liberation of a Latin American country, without asking anything of anybody, without requiring anything, without exploiting anyone.'

Che's remains have lain in a mausoleum in Santa Clara, Cuba, since 1997.

LA REVOLUCIÓN!

Judging by the numerous signs, murals, flags, statues, monuments to heroes, commemorative plaques and slogans (such as 'Every Cuban should know how to shoot, and shoot well'), the concept of the Revolution appears to be in the best of health, even after more than 40 years of Castro's regime.

However, the reality is more complex. Some of the murals are fading and losing their fine colours, and an ever-widening gulf is emerging between appearance and reality. Don't imagine that Cuba is undergoing a counter-revolution – far from it. But dissatisfaction is growing and the future seems bleak for young people. Worse still, the older generation has come to the bitter realization that its pro-Fidel arguments hold no weight for a younger generation principally concerned with decent living conditions and hope for the future. Even if they do not admit it, older people feel deprived of their Revolution. Shortages and rationing sap Cuban morale. Three very different classes have emerged – the establishment, the people, and all those who are making a quick buck on the back of tourism or the free market (a cousin in Miami, a job in one of the grand hotels). The differences between them provides stark contrasts. There is a real danger that the Revolution, under-mined from within by a fading of the 'revolutionary conscience', material difficulties and the pull of capitalism, will soon be nothing more than an empty shell.

A GENERATION WITHOUT HOPE

It is the younger generation, those born after the Revolution, who are most fed up. All they know of the Revolution's causes is what they hear from their elders. The sight of Castro, clinging harder and harder to his increasingly threadbare ideals, is not funny any more. They are sick of being asked to look back in time to see how far they have come: what they long for is something to look forward to, some glimmer of hope on the horizon. But all they get from Castro is the same old song, which turns their frustration into bitterness and their spirit of solidarity into a dog-eat-dog mentality.

However, few Cubans would welcome the triumphant return of the Miami emigrants. The emblematic figures of Che Guevara, Camilo Cienfuegos and, to a certain extent, Fidel, have given Cubans their dignity. All three still have an excellent reputation. Che in particular is viewed as a pure idealist who never compromised his beliefs.

BACKGROUND

INTERNAL DISSIDENCE

Fidel's great strength (besides his control of the media) comes from a balance of power between what may be called, in simple terms, the two main forces of opposition: the very radical anti-Castroists in Miami and dissident movements within Cuba itself.

Ever since the Revolution, the anti-Castroists in Miami have more or less sworn vengeance on Castro for 'despoiling' them of their rights and throwing them out of Cuba in 1959. These are the people who lobby the US authorities in favour of maintaining the embargo.

Dissident movements within Cuba consist of about a hundred disorganized, fragmented groups, many of them infiltrated by the police. They are made up of journalists, environmentalists and union members who have broken with the party line but whose first step is to disassociate themselves completely from the anti-Castroists. They do this by proclaiming loudly that they are neither in the pay of any foreign government (particularly not the US government), nor are they calling for an end to the regime.

During the Spanish-American summit in November 1999, when they met the international press and, more importantly, several foreign heads of state, these Cuban dissidents issued a declaration calling for national reconciliation and the release of political prisoners. In particular, they asked for a more relaxed regime – with or without Castro – and the granting of certain liberties: freedom of expression, freedom of access to the media, freedom of conscience and religion, freedom of association, political pluralism and the right to individual freedom of enterprise. While this last point is admittedly totally opposed to the basic idea of Communism, the remaining demands are widely shared and not at all incompatible with the principles of the Revolution. Castro, however, refuses to meet these internal dissidents halfway despite the opportunity this would give him to exit with a flourish.

THE APPEAL FOR TOURISTS

For foreigners, the idea of Revolution remains one of the main defining factors of Cuba (as was the case for the former Soviet Union and Vietnam). Many visitors are fascinated by the Cuban Revolution and its achievements in the fields of health, sport and education.

Che Guevara continues to enjoy a wide following and many tourists track down and buy anything bearing his name or image, some objects becoming collector's items. The pink three-peso notes bearing the legendary image of Che as captured by Korda proved so popular they have disappeared from circulation. They reappear from time to time in the hands of canny Cubans at a price of $1, $2 or even $3. Children will even try to sell you three-peso coins (at a premium), even though these are still in circulation. Other sought-after 'pieces' are the lovely but rare 1960 notes bearing Che's signature as 'Presidente del Banco'.

This fascination with Che memorabilia is not the same as the auctioning off of revolutionary imagery that accompanied the demise of the USSR. But there is a poignancy in this spread of commercial and marketing practices: this can't be how Ernesto intended it to be.

THE BARBUDOS

In December 1956, 82 of Fidel Castro's guerrillas disembarked from the *Granma* in eastern Cuba and sought refuge in the Sierra Maestra. Although legend has it that there were only 12 of them, their ranks were swelled daily by peasants prepared to face – and defeat – the troops of Fulgencio Batista. Known as the *barbudos* (the 'bearded'), they were prototypes of the South American guerrilla, armed to the teeth and dressed in olive-green combat uniforms. More than 3,000 of them marched victoriously into Havana at the beginning of January 1959, led by Fidel Castro, Che Guevara and Camilo Cienfuegos. It was the stuff of legend. Documents from the time immortalize these men, whose beards became a rallying sign.

Today there is only one *barbudo* – Fidel Castro, whose greying beard was of interest not only to American journalists, curious to know why he still wore it, but also to the CIA. Implicated in at least eight attempts on Fidel Castro's life between 1960 and 1965, the US agency also conspired to remove the Cuban leader's beard using a powerful depilatory made from thallium salts! By removing his beard, they hoped to destroy Castro's very image.

BACKGROUND

POLITICS

Political institutions and political life in Cuba are governed by the Constitution, which, however, only came into being in 1976. It defines the Communist Party as 'the governing force of society and the state'. It is stated that Cuba is a 'Socialist state of workers and labourers guided by Marxism-Leninism'. The Cuban Communist Party (founded in 1925, clandestine until 1937) only assumed its present name in October 1965. Fidel Castro is First Secretary of the Central Committee. The Cuban Communist Party (PCC) is an avant-garde party comprised of selected members, such as the *Juventud Comunista* (Communist Youth Union).

Between 1959 and 1976, the institutions in force were officially only provisional. It wasn't until the autumn of 1976 that the first elections for the various bodies as defined by the Constitution took place:

– **The National Assembly**: members are elected by universal suffrage.

– **The Council of State**: accountable to the Assembly and comprised of around 30 members. Its president (Fidel Castro) is both head of state and head of the government, contrary to the traditions of other (older) Communist countries.

– **The Council of Ministers**: elected by the Assembly.

– **Unions**: omnipresent since 1959, these have a fundamental role, from the CDR (Committees for the Defence of the Revolution), FMC (Federation of Cuban Women), CTC (Cuban Workers' Organization) and MTT (Territorial Militia Troops), to the UPC (Union of Cuban Pioneers) and mini-brigades (representing construction workers, for example) and so on. The CDR in particular has always united more than half of the population – 'a committee for every worker' was its original slogan – but no longer has the same powers.

For some the CDR is essential to the state machine; for others, it is a control mechanism. When times get really tough and people do what they can just to survive, the CDR serves as a network of local control and observation centres, poisoning the atmosphere and creating a climate of mistrust in some neighbourhoods. Things are no easier for the people in charge of the CDR, who are driven to the same extremes as local people. As a result, the CDR's role as a force for order is becoming a thing of the past. It does have one major advantage, however: when it comes to implementing vaccination or evacuation campaigns after a hurricane, nothing is as efficient as the CDR thanks to its knowledge of the area and huge network of contacts.

ECONOMY

The Cuban economy has huge problems. It relies on sugar and, to a lesser extent, cigars, but it is increasingly tourism that now brings in much-needed foreign currency. Although Cuba owes many of its difficulties to the US embargo, its inefficient economic system also contributes.

THE EMBARGO

The 'embargo' (*bloqueo* in Spanish) is still very much at the forefront of Cuban life. On 3 February 1962, a year after diplomatic relations with Cuba were broken off by Washington, the White House ordered a total trade embargo and, on 14 May 1964, food and pharmaceuticals, even medicines for children, were added to the blacklist. Today, the embargo is not only still in force, but it has also been systematically reinforced by both the Republicans and Democrats, particularly during US presidential election campaigns.

The key lies in pinpointing the exact role that the embargo has played, both in economic and political terms. Politically, it is undeniable that it has promoted an anti-American or anti-imperialist mobilization of the Cuban people. But expert opinions on the economic consequences of the embargo differ, ranging from 'that's right, blame the embargo' to 'without the embargo, Cuba would be Eldorado', and 'in any case, it has been constantly violated, not least by the Americans'.

Most Americans, especially if they are politicians, Cuban exiles or voters in Florida, continue to be extreme in their opinions, while industrialists and business people would like the embargo lifted.

In the late 1990s the US embargo was still the subject of intense protest, particularly in Latin American countries and the European Union. There is no doubt that, of all state-level persecutions, the Cuban embargo is one of the longest and most severe. However, it seems that light has appeared at the end of the tunnel. During his visit to Cuba in February 1998, Pope John Paul II described the embargo as 'morally unacceptable' but also asked Fidel Castro to make an effort in the field of human rights. As a result of his intervention more than 300 Cuban political prisoners were freed by the Havana government.

The US administration has also not been insensible to this gesture, and in March 1998 it announced an easing of the embargo, 'on humanitarian grounds'. Direct flights between the USA and Cuba have been reinstated. Shipments of money and medicine are now authorized, and Cubans in Florida can now help their relatives who are still on the island.

Following this favourable outcome for Cuba, the Pentagon reported to the US Congress that the Castro regime no longer represented a significant threat to the security of the United States. All that needs to happen now is a complete lifting of the embargo – despite efforts to the contrary by committed anti-Castroists in Miami – and the normalization of relations between Washington and Havana.

SUGAR

Sugar is Cuba's answer to the oil industry, and is one of the pillars of the economy and a primary source of currency. The sugar industry is the legacy of the *macheteros*, Cuba's slave workforce until the abolition of slavery at the end of the 19th century. The freedom fighter José Martí said, 'A people which depends on a single product will never be a free people'.

For a long time Cuba was by far the world's leading producer of sugar. The green cane fields that stretch from one end of the island to the other, the honey-coloured stalks and the unrivalled taste of *cafecito* are the legacy of the sugar industry.

Cuba has been freed from the slavery of the sugar industry, less by choice than by circumstance and due to the current state of the global economy. In 1959, when the *barbudos* seized power, sugar represented 83.6 per cent of Cuba's agricultural production and 81 per cent of its exports. Almost 50 per cent of agricultural labourers worked in this sector.

Sugar is especially important to Cuba since it doesn't really have any heavy industry, and there are few natural resources on the island. Since 1964, when agreements between Cuba and Moscow were drawn up, sugar has been a mainstay of Cuban Socialism, with production the number one objective. The failure of the 'zafra of the 10 million' resulted in the mobilization of Cuban forces, and artists such as the Los Van Van group were commissioned to boost the morale of the troops with their songs. This may have been where the Castro regime went wrong – this virtual monoculture, inherited from the Spanish colonization, was never really questioned – and when the Russians stopped subsidizing the price of sugar (in 1989) the Cuban economy collapsed.

Today, tourism is coming to the rescue of the sugar industry. The government's decision to open up the country to visitors was taken rather late, but hundreds of thousands of tourists now arrive each year. The Cuban people are bending over backwards to make them feel welcome, and the government has come full circle.

BACKGROUND

THE PURSUIT OF DOLLARS

Cuba is now the 'dollar cow' of the Caribbean. Aside from a few small businesses, notably in rural areas where it's necessary to pay in Cuban currency, almost everything – from accommodation to souvenirs – has to be paid for in dollars. Most shops accept dollars, not only from tourists, but also from Cubans (except in certain stores selling basic produce, and on public transport). Officially, this is known as 'currency capture'. In reality, it represents the 'dollarization of society'. In 1993, the Cuban government launched itself into the pursuit of greenbacks, to the point that today the volume of US currency in circulation outstrips the national money stock.

From the 1960s until the mid-1980s Cuba lived in a politically privileged although economically artificial sphere. Havana was spared payment for products bought from the USSR and from Eastern Bloc countries in Cuban currency because trade obeyed the laws of exchange (*intercambio*) or barter between brother countries. It was a fine and generous, if dangerous, arrangement whereby sugar cane could be exchanged for oil, tobacco for manufactured goods, or coconuts for Lada cars.

Cocooned from the machinations of the capitalist world, everything was going well until disaster struck. Castro, refusing to follow Soviet President Mikhail Gorbachov's *perestroïka* (reconstruction), lost his influential political ally, his strategic protector and his greatest economic and financial backer. In 1989 an angry Gorbachov decided to 'let go of Cuba', and terminated the laws of exchange between the two countries, which were not in Russia's best interests anyway. For example, under the trade agreements, Moscow would buy Cuban sugar cane at three times the global market price.

In 1990, virtually overnight, Cuba was forced to pay hard currency for its acquisitions. With dollars all but prohibited since the Revolution, the island awoke to a reality without any real means of payment. It was difficult to invent a currency in a country that prohibited the possession of dollars – until 1993, a Cuban found with dollars could be sent to prison.

Everything changed suddenly following the decriminalization of possession of the dollar that year. The pursuit of dollars has now become so common – indeed, so oppressive – that it has generated all kinds of new and worrying behaviour. Tourists are constantly solicited and hassled by *jineteros* and *jineteras* (the activity is known as *jineterismo*), goods are sold on the black market, an illegal parallel economy has developed, and pickpocketing and prostitution in certain towns have increased.

Following the US government's easing of the trade embargo and its authorization of the transfer of funds to Cuba, the amount of money sent by Cubans in exile (particularly in Miami, Florida) to help their families back home totalled $800 million in 1996, and dollars continue to pour in. Régis Debray, former political ally and friend of Castro, remarked 'The guerrillas wanted to kill the dollar, and in return the dollar killed them, body and soul'.

This obsession with currency is the economic reality in Cuba, and it has led to a disconcerting new form of human segregation. Cubans are often refused entry to hotels in the cities and seaside resorts (such as Varadero) on the understanding that their pockets aren't lined with dollar bills.

To have or have not is the new and terrible dilemma faced by Cuba, called an 'economic war' by the authorities. Will this 'dollarization' of Cuban life have a happy ending? Will Cubans ever be able to pay for their purchases in pesos? Is the pursuit of dollars the island's last hope? 'Dollarization' hasn't so far managed to hide the weaknesses of a paralyzed, inefficient and unjust economic system.

THE PEOPLE

According to the poet Nicolás Guillén, there will one day be a 'Cuban colour'. According to the writer Pablo Armando Fernandez, 'The sugar is white, brown or black. Like the island's population'. But it's a bit more complex than that. The permutations in Cuba of skin and hair colour, combined with facial features, hair type and traces of Indian or Asiatic ancestry, are endless. A native Indian may be dark- or red-skinned, with dull-looking hair but quite fine features; a *mulata* is a dark-skinned woman with straight hair, fine features and '*un buen cuerpo*' (a good body). Cubans, rather like Brazilians, may be *mulato claro*, *fino*, *jabao* and so on. But while *negrona* may be a pejorative term for a woman of clearly 'black' descent, Cubans have no time for overt racism.

Today, the 'whites' – of Spanish origin – are the dominant race in Cuba. Like Fidel Castro's parents, they are descended from Spaniards mainly from Galicia, but also from Asturia and Extremadura. For Cubans today, to be Spanish is to be *Gallego* (Galician).

Hundreds of thousands of indigenous peoples (Tainos, Siboneyes and Guanajuatabeyes) had been massacred or killed by disease by the end of the 16th century. The largest immigration at this time was of white people in search of fortune, adventure and exoticism. Meanwhile the importation of 550,000 black people, mainly from the African coast between Senegal and Angola, chained together in the cramped holds of galleons or caravels, took place between 1530 and 1873.

Cuba's first census (in 1774) showed 171,620 habitants, 25 per cent of which were African. At the beginning of the 19th century 'Africans' made up almost 46 per cent of the population. They belonged, as they do today, to four main groups: Yorubas or Lucimi, Congos, Carabalis and Araras.

In 1953 the geographer Antonio Nunez Jimenez reckoned that Cuba's population was 72.8 per cent white, 14.5 per cent mixed race, 12.4 per cent black and 0.3 per cent Asian. The first two figures are disputable, however. The population doubled to around 7 million between 1925 and 1962, standing at more than 11 million today.

With the Revolution, Cubans were faced with putting aside their inherited racism. Although Batista's Constitution did not actually include the term 'apartheid', many of its practices resembled this system, even if discrimination was based mainly on money and social conditions. As with other countries, since slavery was only abolished in 1886, black people often found themselves at the bottom of the social ladder.

BACKGROUND

FRENCH IMMIGRATION

At the end of the 18th century many French people emigrated to Cuba, fleeing the Haitian independence movement of 1791. From rich French settlers to employees and administrators working on the plantations in Haiti, they landed on Cuban shores near Santiago, where they settled as coffee and cotton planters. The women taught sewing, lace and the language of Molière.

The eastern province of Cuba still shows traces of French influence, mainly in the Creole language, words borrowed from French, music and dance styles, and in French surnames such as Fontaine, Armagnac and Dupont.

JINETERAS

Jineterismo, or prostitution, is a delicate subject and yet a vast problem in Cuba. A real social phenomenon attributed to the explosion in tourism, *jineteras* seem to be everywhere, particularly in Havana and Varadero. You will see them in hotel lobbies, nightclubs, at the entrance to cabarets, on pavements, beaches or even in restaurants.

Jinetera is a polite term for prostitute, literally meaning 'escort'. Most of the time, the *jineteras* are young girls in search of a few extra dollars to help them get by. The male equivalent is the *pinguero*. Many are students, while others are unemployed. The older ones are often teachers or hairdressers supplementing a meagre income.

Jineteras come from the poorer provinces such as Camagüey or Holguín and tend to live at home. They bribe local police officers to turn a blind eye, slip backhanders to hotel attendants, and get round taxi drivers. Everyone benefits from this parallel economy. Only the government and a few old revolutionaries object to the *jineteras*, on the grounds that they do little for the country's image.

In February 1999, the army methodically searched the houses and streets of Havana. More than 7,000 *jineteras* were rounded up; the lucky ones were expelled to their home towns, while others were sent to the 'detention and classification centre' in Havana. Later that year, Havana cleaned up its act again ahead of the Spanish-American summit.

For many women, however, a European boyfriend is the ticket out of Cuba. In 1998, the French newspaper *L'Evénement du jeudi* estimated that more than 3,000 European men had married Cubans and, according to official sources, the figure is rising.

HUMAN RIGHTS

Events surrounding the visit of Pope John Paul II to Cuba in 1998 suggested that there might be some improvement in the country's very poor record on human rights issues. This hope has not in the end been realized, and in some respects, the situation has become worse in recent years. Even monitoring the human rights situation is difficult due to the harassment of human rights observers and activists by the government.

The Communist Party is the only legal political group in Cuba, and the most pressing human rights issue is the repression of any groups or individuals that criticize or oppose the government. Amnesty International has identified numerous political prisoners in Cuban prisons. The constitution prohibits freedom of dissent and as a result the basic freedoms of speech, assembly and association are drastically curtailed in order to maintain the 'unity of the state'. Some of the offences of which dissidents have been convicted have been chillingly nebulous, including the crimes of 'dangerousness', 'insulting Castro' and the rather Orwellian 'resisting authority'. These offences have been criticized by the United Nations Committee on Torture. The vagueness of the laws used to convict dissidents is exacerbated by the serious question marks that exist over the fairness of trials in the Cuban legal system.

In addition to those actually convicted of these offences and imprisoned as a result, there have been very frequent instances of opponents and critics of the regime being subjected to various forms of harassment. These have typically included detention without trial (normally for relatively brief periods), interrogation (including ill treatment), threats to individuals and their families, restrictions on travel as well as random searches of both individuals and their homes. Members of both the domestic and foreign press have been particularly subject to these types of harassment. Religion, while still closely regulated by the government, is not so tightly controlled as it once was.

Cuba is one of the relatively small number of states that retains the death penalty for a variety of offences, and uses it on a regular basis. Government harassment of human rights monitors makes it difficult to make a reliable estimate of the number of executions and of the number of prisoners on death row, but at the end of 2000 there were thought to be around 20 prisoners awaiting execution. Cuba has recently extended the number of offences for which the death penalty is available. Prison conditions in Cuba are generally very poor, with reports of ill treatment of inmates by both guards and other prisoners. The UN Committee on Torture somewhat contentiously suggested that the poor and overcrowded conditions were in part due to the disruption of the Cuban economy caused by the US-led embargo that affects so much of Cuban life.

On a more positive note, the UN has found that women in Cuba have a strong position in the civic and state structures, amounting to 44 per cent of state employees, and 60 per cent of the judiciary, figures that few other states in the world can match. However, socially and in private employment, the situation is not so good. Gender stereotypes are still prevalent, and domestic violence against women is relatively common. The UN noted that traditional non-state women's jobs were particularly affected by the consequences of the US embargo. Racial discrimination is unusual in Cuba, due in part to the complex racial mix of many Cubans and the positive efforts of the government to eliminate it.

– **Amnesty International UK**: 99–119 Rosebery Avenue, London EC1R 4RE. ☎ 020 7814 6200. Fax: 020 7833 1510. Email: information@amnesty.org.uk. Website: www.amnesty.org.uk

EXILE AND EMIGRATION

Any exile is traumatic, though it is not certain whether an exiled Cuban in Miami is really to be pitied. He or she has left 'hell' for a much longed-for 'paradise'. There are no refugee camps (not even temporary ones), and, until recently, any Cuban who managed to set foot on American soil was considered a hero and rewarded with political asylum within the hour. He or she became a US citizen, and usually settled in Miami.

The background to Cuban exile can be divided into three chapters. Firstly, there were three major exoduses (1965, 1980 and 1994), which all made headlines around the world. Then came the odd news article when one or two Cubans managed to reach the US coast, an airline pilot landed on a US runway, a musician decided not to go back to Cuba, an athlete defected or a famous prisoner chose America as his country of exile. The final chapter began to unfold after the 'decriminalization' of possession of the dollar in 1993.

An exiled Cuban will probably try to get to Miami, where one of the largest districts is known as 'Little Havana'. Until recently, the flow of traffic between Florida and Cuba was one-way, but today people come and go. Armed with an exit permit, Cubans – now passport holders – can now apply for a US visa from Havana. Cubans can visit their (exiled) families and friends, go shopping, stock up on all kinds of goods and then go home to Cuba, paying for their excess baggage at the airport. From being a land of asylum, Miami has become a shoppers' paradise.

In the space of some 35 years, Cuba has lost a great many of its sons and daughters. It is reckoned that more than one million people (representing one tenth of the population) are direct exiles. These days a Cuban in exile is no longer called a *gusano* ('vermin' or 'earthworm'), but a 'member of the Cuban international community'. Some exiles are even casting off their anti-Castro feelings and are openly travelling back to Havana to negotiate with Fidel.

It was mainly Castro's Communism that first caused so many to flee (1959–65). Most of these Cubans belonged to the old Cuban bourgeoisie and tended to be professionals such as doctors, lawyers and architects. Like the second wave of exiles (*marielitos*) in 1980, this exodus was 'free', indeed 'authorized' or encouraged. The *marielitos'* ragbag assortment of vessels beaching on the Florida coast was organized by the American and Cuban authorities. As for the *balseros* (*see below*), their position was disputed for two years before they found their place of refuge.

A new story is now unfolding. Cubans who are US citizens are starting to come back to their homeland, either on extended visits or – more significantly – to settle here for good, to retire or to start up a business.

THE *BALSEROS*

July and August 1994 were the months of the *balseros*, people who left Cuba on a *balsa* (raft), usually made from inner tubes. Some, having set off for 'Eldorado' (the coast of Florida), were lost at sea in hurricanes, died of thirst or exhaustion or suffered shark attacks. Thousands fled Cuba, though very few bodies were ever recovered by the US coastguards.

This was the third such exodus since 1959. In 1980 the movement was known as 'Mariel' (after the port of Havana) and was political. But it is generally recognized that the *balseros* of 1994 were fleeing the terrible poverty caused by the collapse of the Soviet Union, upon which the Cuban economy depended. Since 1990, the country has been in what is described by the authorities as a 'special period in a time of peace', with the enforcement of draconian austerity measures.

On the beaches of Cojimar and at other points around the coast, the *balseros* – some having spent a long time preparing for their journey, others deciding to depart only the day before – set off before a pack of foreign journalists and under the scrutiny of indifferent police. Some even took to the seas from the Malecón, the promenade right in the centre of Havana. More than 30,000 *balseros* managed to leave the country in the space of a few weeks. Cuba accused Washington of having engineered the exodus, citing the fact that most of the exiles had applied for American visas, although their applications had been in vain.

The *balseros* affair ended abruptly on 18 August after Bill Clinton adopted a unique measure in the history of American-Cuban relations. Cuban immigrants would no longer automatically be entitled to a residence permit and would be held in detention centres like any other immigrants. Following this, an agreement was drawn up, according to which any Cubans entering the country illegally would no longer be automatically welcomed on to US soil. The *balseros* affair suggested for the first time that the United States would consider its relations with Cuba in a new light.

The Elian Affair

The last *balseros* episode to make world news concerned a six-year-old boy called Elian González who fled Cuba with his mother and stepfather in November 1999. US coastguards found him clinging to the side of the vessel, the sole survivor of the 13 passengers who set out. What followed was a political tug of war, as the authorities argued over whether to let him stay in the US (as his dead mother had wanted) or send him back to Cuba to live with his estranged father. The whole sorry business became a political tool, used on the one hand by anti-Castroists in Miami, who campaigned for the right of the boy to remain in a free country, and on the other by the Cuban authorities, who argued that Elian was better off with his father – and succeeded in having the would-be exile repatriated. The 'Elian affair' became both a national and a revolutionary cause, complete with the usual demonstrations, T-shirts, concerts and parades.

RELIGION

Relations between the Catholic Church and the Castro regime became strained soon after 1959. The religious hierarchy, which refused to acknowledge Communism, was accused of being in with the imperialists and reactionaries, a view encouraged by the Church's almost complete absence from the fight against Batista. Religious schools were nationalized and nuns invited to leave hospitals. Any religious instruction outside places of worship was prohibited. In these conditions, it is not surprising that Cuban Catholicism lost a lot of its strength and began to stagnate.

In the mid-1980s, Castro attempted a reconciliation with the Catholic Church. The state began to tolerate the free circulation of bibles and the presence of foreign priests. Today, the revival of religious worship is unmissable, as churches open and the number of priests rises into the hundreds. And in the more touristy areas, the state has taken over the renovation of colonial or republican sanctuaries that are of architectural interest.

Fidel Castro has since taken the process one stage further by meeting the Pope in the Vatican in November 1996; the Pope paid a much-awaited return visit to Cuba in January 1998.

However, Cuba has only around 100,000 churchgoers, and they do little to threaten the dominance of santería, the most popular religion in Cuba.

SANTERÍA

Santería is to Cuba what voodoo is to Haiti – a surprising syncretism of beliefs, animist practices, African rituals and Catholicism. Originally, slaves were forced to adopt the religion of their masters. African slaves came to Cuba from countries such as Nigeria, Dahomey (now Benin), Cameroon and the Congo, where animism was deeply rooted. In Cuba and in other nearby countries, such as Haiti, the Dominican Republic and Brazil, they suffered the savage destruction of their cultural identity. They were forbidden from speaking African languages, or from preserving their customs and beliefs, and fellow countrymen, ethnic groups, tribes and families were systematically dispersed. It was the Yorubas – the predominant African ethnic group in Cuba, from the Niger delta – who most successfully overcame this persecution and re-established their own culture, one of the richest on the African continent.

No longer allowed to practise their own religion, the slaves assimilated their own gods into Christian mythology, finding details, colours and objects that would remind them of their own beliefs. The gods represented particular natural forces such as forests, rivers, wind, storms, the sea, lightning, the African bush and so on. In Cuba and Brazil, these gods or spirits were given the name *orishas*. Around 400 of them have been identified in Nigeria. Around 40 are known in Cuba and 20 are devoutly worshipped. Each has its own colour. Over time, and because of the diminution of oral tradition, many have lost their aggressive nature and have incorporated Christian values.

Santería Practices

Santería is found particularly in the Oriente (Santiago, Guantánamo), but also in Havana and Matanzas. What with the economic recession, personal and family crises and the uncertainty of what tomorrow will bring, its influence has grown considerably, and it even has support now among white communities. The faith is particularly strong among artists, musicians, writers and even party representatives. It is believed that half of Cuba's population is involved in santería, which has become, in many cases, a solution for most of life's problems. There is an *orisha* for practically every aspect of daily life, from emotional, financial, health or employment worries, to overcoming hostility or even destroying an enemy.

The santería priests are known as *babalaos*, and are consulted regularly (sometimes up to 20 or 30 times a day). Young people increasingly visit the priests to interrogate the *orishas*, and use them as teachers. There are at least 10,000 *babalaos* in the country, compared with fewer than 300 Catholic priests. In their houses, several rooms are devoted to rituals, with statues of saints, dolls, small dishes filled with strange objects (money, amulets, pictures), shells, cowries, bottles of rum and various offerings. The atmosphere is mysterious, to say the least.

The *babalao* also officiates over ceremonies in honour of the saints, some of which are open to the public (including tourists). The ceremonies are spiritual, colourful and emotional. Music plays an important role, with percussion instruments, ritual chants and other accompaniments. Beginning slowly, the music increases in tempo and intensity, heightening the tension. The atmosphere is enhanced by the smell of incense and cigars, shouting, chanting and dancing. The *orishas* are invoked and given offerings such as flowers, food and fruit. At this point, some of the faithful go into a trance – allegedly a sign that the spirit is entering the body. The person will embrace the personality of the *orisha* and reproduce some of its characteristics and traits. The trance may also descend during initiation rites, which determine which *orisha* will be the believer's patron.

The beauty of santería rituals is a huge part of the celebration. Each *orisha* is characterized by an object, a day of the week, a colour, an ornament, a jewel, a special food preparation, a chant – anything that can be used to symbolize the god's presence.

Apart from these ceremonies and feasts, a whole series of practices maintains a permanent communication between believers and their gods. Believers may call upon *orishas* by making offerings or performing special rituals, or by consulting the tables of *Ifa*. The act of making offerings and sacrifices, or doing odd jobs and specific tasks demanded by an *orisha* who is asked to solve a problem or ease a situation, is known as *trabajos*, or 'works'. Few Cubans, even the most rational, can claim that they have never invoked the *orishas*, and Cuban life is full of strange and impressive stories about problems that have been solved in this way.

Santería and the State

After spearheading a vigorous campaign in the 1970s against religious obscurantism, aimed at eradicating 'retrograde beliefs through the propaganda of scientific materialism', Castro officially received His Majesty Alaiyeluwa Okunade Sijuwade Olubuse, king of the African Yoruba people in 1986 in Havana. It is also claimed that during a trip to Nigeria, Fidel was initiated under Obatalá, the *orisha* of peace.

The Cuban authorities eventually realized that santería was a means of maintaining social harmony. This was helped by the fact that being a Catholic is not an impediment to being a follower of santería – indeed, a man cannot become a *babalao* without being baptized. The Catholic hierarchy has adapted to the situation.

BACKGROUND

For many Cubans, santería is a good way to preserve their cultural identity, and recognize the country's African roots. A spiritual void was undermining Cuban society, and if so many people seek refuge in the arms of the *orishas* and saints, it must be because the Revolution, despite its undoubted achievements in areas such as health and education, cannot fulfil all the spiritual needs of the Cuban people. Castroism, while attempting to guarantee the earthly happiness of the people, has to understand and respect the fundaments of Cuban identity, as well as its deep-seated cultural roots.

TRADITIONS AND CUSTOMS

Despite their apparent nonchalance, politeness is important to Cubans. They are very tolerant of foreigners, but expect them to behave properly and to respect local people. Below is a list of customs to respect and blunders to avoid, which should help you make friends easily.

– Never openly criticize the situation of the country or political regime in the presence of Cubans. They won't say anything, but will be hurt.

– Don't go topless on the beach. Nudity is prohibited.

– Observe the dress code in upmarket restaurants and venues. Instead of a shirt and tie, wear a *guayabera* (traditional shirt).

– When you join a queue, ask who is the last person (*El ultimo?*), and stand behind him or her. Do not try to push in.

– If someone does you a favour, give him or her a small gift (*see below*).

- If you smoke, offer cigarettes to the people around you. American brands are particularly welcome.

– Punctuate your sentences with 'comradely' words such as *compañero* ('friend') for a man or *compañera* for a woman. However, refrain from using the expression *mi amor*, much beloved by Cubans, or you'll sound absurd.

– Don't be offended by the endless 'psst-psst!' from people in the street trying to attract your attention. This is common in Cuba and does not have the same rather dubious associations as in Europe.

– Don't be offended by compliments paid to you by strangers. Cubans love compliments and are quick to make them, so take them at face value.

– Finally, whatever happens, keep smiling . . .

EL AMOR

El amor – 'love' in Spanish – is one of the most frequently heard words in Cuba. Love is the essence of Cuban life, and Cuba is possibly the most sensual place in the world. In the early 1960s, 'Sex and Revolution' went together in Havana for the many who flocked here in search of excitement. Few were disappointed, apart from those who came to plant sugar or coffee in Pinar del Río, as in 1968 Cuban comrades were prohibited from entering into sexual relations with foreign comrades. Love is such a part of life here that even the government has issued recommendations on the subject in the past, sometimes encouraging, sometimes condemning.

Amor has become an all-purpose word to suit every occasion. It doesn't necessarily refer to love, and can sometimes mean quite the opposite. It's quite acceptable to use it to address a complete stranger, much as an older person might call someone 'dear' or 'love' in Britain. Common alternatives to *mi amor* are *amorcito* ('little love'), *mi cielo* or *mi vida* ('my life').

MAÑANA

Mañana (pronounced 'manyana') means 'tomorrow', and is frequently used in Cuba. *Mañana* is the buzzword of Cuban revolutionary hope – the promise of doing better, doing more. But tomorrow, not today. At one time, everything was put off until the next day in Cuba, and there are still signs of this today. Sometimes '*mañana*' could be a way of saying 'no', a discreet way of shirking responsibility, of dodging an issue or even a way of suggesting that you were unable to do what was being asked of you.

GIFTS

Cubans will often expect little gifts. However hard it may be to refuse, do not hand these out indiscriminately, but do give presents to thank people. A good rule is to offer gifts to Cubans with whom you have had rewarding contact and who seem the most needy, bearing in mind their average monthly wage of $10–15.

The most appreciated presents are soap (this is rationed to only one bar a month, sometimes less in the provinces), perfume (samples will suffice), shampoo, T-shirts, shoes, and repair patches and glue for the inner tubes of bike and car tyres. Cigarettes (preferably American brands) always go down well. Good ideas for children are clothes, school books and stationery, tennis balls and chewing gum (*chicle*). It's best to offer the school supplies direct to the teacher or head teacher. However, you'll need supplies for a whole class; the odd exercise book is not enough.

MUSIC AND DANCE

Cuba's extraordinary palette of music and dance has had a major influence on the 20th century. Since the arrival of the Spanish colonists in the 16th century and the subsequent importation of large numbers of African slaves, Cuba has served as a melting pot for all manner of musical styles. While the historical and political events of the country have helped shape its musical direction, the advent of radio in the 1920s and later television, has been fundamental in disseminating Cuban music to audiences around the globe.

With the demise of Cuba's indigenous Taíno Indian population (many were killed fleeing for their lives or succumbed to European diseases brought over with the Spanish settlers), vast numbers of African slaves were imported to work on Cuba's sugar plantations. By the mid-19th century almost half of Cuba's population was made up of slaves, it was inevitable, therefore, that

Africa's rich musical heritage and ancient tribal rituals would have a significant influence on the local musical culture. Living together in their respective tribal communities, the African slaves soon adapted their own songs and dances to the instruments and working tools that were available. The gradual integration of European and African musical styles gave birth to the distinctive sound of Cuban music that we are familiar with today.

SON AND RUMBA

Son, meaning sound in Spanish, is undoubtedly the most influential style of Cuban music and is believed to have originated in the eastern province of Oriente towards the end of the 19th century. The music is a combination of African call and response choruses, traditional Spanish song styles and musical influences from Oriente's immigrant population of Haitian refugees. The genre was brought to Havana at the beginning of the 20th century through the musical efforts of the Trio Oriental. They reformed in the 1920s as the Sexteto Habanero, popularizing *son* and defining the classic sextet line-up for future generations of *son* musicians. Instruments included *tres* (a cuban guitar with three sets of double strings), Spanish guitar, two vocalists (providing rhythmic accompaniment on claves, maracas and *guiro*, a scraper), bongos and double bass.

By the 1930s the sextet had evolved into a septet. The great band leader and innovative composer Ignacio Piñeiro integrated the trumpet into the *son* orchestra to form his spectacular Septeto Nacional which played a vital role in popularizing the genre abroad. The innovative style of Septeto Nacional and Septeto Habanero inspired many other artists in the field to experiment. Don Aspiazu's Havana Orchestra, trumpeter Felix Chappotín, *tres* player Arsenio Rodriguez and legendary *sonero* (singer) Beny Moré have all contributed to *son*'s success in America and the Caribbean, developing the genre with elements from the popular American swing style of the period. These include the addition of a horn section, extra drums and the use of a piano instead of a guitar. The various permutations of *son* continued to grow throughout the 20th century (including regional variations such as *changüí*, which was performed with additional African instruments such as the thumb piano), influencing subsequent musical styles and genres.

Outside the country *son* became known as rumba – a term that was later used in America to refer to any style of music encompassing Latin influences including *guaracha*, *danzón* and *bolero*. In Cuba, however, rumba had its own identity distinct from that of *son*: a dance accompanied by a combination of percussive, pulsating rhythms, chants from the Afro-Christian santería cult and repetitive Spanish song lyrics. Rumba's musical structure is based around the *sonero*, the singer. After a long vocal introduction with drumming accompaniment, the rhythm tightens, the chorus enters in response to the solo singer and the dancers swing into action. Nowadays the rumba consists of three principal styles: the *columbia*, the *guaguancó* and the *yambú*. The first is a physically demanding dance requiring acrobatic skill and precision, performed at great speed by a solo male dancer. The *guaguancó* is a fiery, flirtatious and sexually provocative dance performed by couples, whilst the *yambú* is a slower, more stately and less suggestive dance for couples.

If you want to see and hear live rumba while you're visiting Cuba, then keep an eye out for the Rumba Saturdays (*Sabados de Rumba*) staged by the Conjunto Folklorico Nacional in Havana. Alternatively, each town usually has at least one Casa de la Trova, where musicians congregate to sing, play music and dance. These are the best places to go if you want to sample some of Cuba's diverse musical styles.

DANZÓN, MAMBO AND CHA-CHA-CHA

Danzón was one of the major European influences in the development of Cuban *son*. A slow and stately country dance based on the classical French *contredanse*, it was brought to what is now Haiti and the Dominican Republic by French colonists. In the 19th century its popularity spread to Cuba's colonial households where the African servants adopted it, transforming it into a new instrumental genre which became known as the *habanera*. At the turn of the 20th century, innovative band leaders experimented with the traditional line-up of the *danzón* orchestra replacing the brass section with groups of violins and flutes, a double bass, percussion and piano. These became known as *charanga* ensembles, reaching the height of their popularity in the 1940s. Meanwhile, in Mexico City, singer Beny Moré and pianist Pérez Prado were working on developing the big band swing sound, adding more percussion, and an imposing brass section to the line-up. Prado's adaptation of a piece called '*Mambo*' by the López brothers eventually bore fruit and by the late 1940s, Prado had kickstarted the next Cuban craze to arrive in America – mambo – a flashy dance rooted in the old *danzón* style. Although the music of mambo kings Pérez Prado and Tito Puente proved popular, the fast, complex footwork required to perform the mambo stalled its success abroad. To counteract this problem one of the leading *charanga* ensembles, Orquesta America, developed a simpler version which became known as the cha-cha-cha. Adopted by other *charangas*, including Orquesta Aragón, cha-cha-cha became a popular alternative for English and American audiences in the 1950s.

SALSA

Cuban music lost its international footing in the 1960s during the Cuban Missile Crisis when the flow of musicians, recordings and sheet music to the US came to an end. In Cuba there was a return to traditional music where the Casa de la Trova once again became the centre of music-making for those left behind. Elsewhere, however, the cycle of musical creation continued. The 1970s witnessed an explosion in musical creativity and experimentation right across the globe with jazz musicians leading the way. In New York, the sizeable Latin community, many of them Cuban expatriates, began fusing their own indigenous musical styles with those that they heard around them. The creation of salsa, a term first coined in the 1970s, came out of the Cuban and Puerto Rican communities living in New York. Related to *Son montuno*, a fusion of *son* and rumba played by the big-band orchestras and *charangas* of the 1940s and 1950s, salsa (meaning sauce) comprises a myriad of musical styles. As well as fusing *son*, rumba, cha-cha-cha and mambo with big-band American jazz and Latin influences from Central and Southern America, salsa reinterprets these genres. Modern salsa bands, for example, include rock, pop and funk elements to produce a more up-to-date, hard-hitting style that appeals to younger audiences. These developments, coupled with the emergence of new musical styles after the Cuban revolution (including *Nueva trova* songs and experimental jazz fusions), clearly show that the success of Cuban music lies in its richly diverse heritage that allows any number of musical permutations.

CONTEMPORARY TRENDS IN CUBAN MUSIC

After the collapse of the Soviet Union in the 1990s and the subsequent social and economic changes in Cuba (including a boom in the tourist industry), musicians were once again able to travel and record abroad. In recent years they have proved what a valuable asset they are to the Cuban economy. Currently more than 500 top bands are paid by the government to play each week at a range of venues across the country. The major reason for this rebirth in popularity of Cuban music stems from the 1997 collaboration of American guitarist Ry Cooder, with several legendary Cuban musicians, including Compay Segundo (*see* 'Notable Figures'), Rubén González, Ibrahim Ferrer and Juan de Marcos González. The fruit of their collaboration, the Buena Vista Social Club album, has sold over two million copies worldwide and a film documenting the event has been a hit in cinemas across the world. In recent years, the music market has become saturated with new recordings and reissues of Cuban music. The virtuosic jazz improvisations of groups such as Los Van Van and Irakere have had an enormous impact on younger bands such as NG La Banda and Charanga Habanera. Founded in 1988, NG La Banda play a contemporary *son* style known as *timba*, including elements of jazz, rap, hip-hop and salsa mixed with slang lyrics. Charanga Habanera, meanwhile, are renowned for their controversial, heavily rhythmic creations mixing together salsa and *timba*. Other popular performers include Issac Delgado and Paulito FG, the talented songwriter Manolín, el Médico de la Salsa and Cuban rap group Orishas.

As octogenarian Cuban musicians steal the limelight along with young artists keen to push musical experimentation to the limit, it seems once more that Cuban music has a colourful future ahead of it.

DISCOGRAPHY

There are too many great Cuban recordings to list here. All the musicians mentioned in this article and many more besides have made significant contributions to the development of Cuban music. However, we have listed some suggestions below to get you started. Besides the major record companies, a handful of small publishers also distribute Cuban music.

– **Tumi Cuba as Classics**: all six volumes of this series are indispensable for getting to know Cuban music. So are the slightly more adventurous numbers on the **Lusafrica** label (distributed by BMG). The best of mambo and cha-cha-cha can be found on the **Caney** label, the excellent **Afro-Cuban Grooves** compilations of Radio Nova and the compilations of **Milán Latino Music** (BMG).

– The Salsa Masters' compilations by **Radio Latina Fania, Globe Music** and the Cuban compilations on the **Earthworks** label are all worth checking out. The **RMM** label that produces Cheo Feliciano, Celia Cruz and Oscar D'León is also good for salsa. The '**El inspector de la Salsa**' label distributed by Caribe Productions, although not widely available in Europe, is easy to find in Cuba and has all the great numbers by Los Van Van, NG la Banda and Adalberto Alvarez y su Son. Globe Music also deserves a mention for reissuing many of La Fania's most successful numbers in the Fania Legends compilation.

– **Afro-Cuban Jazz Project** (Lusafrica/Media 7, 1999): a chance to hear Tata Güines, Cascarita, Osdalgia and other musical heavyweights getting together for a memorable jam session with Orlando 'Maraca' Valle. Covers a range of musical styles including traditional *son* and *danzón*.

– **Aquí Está Portabales** (**Guillermo Portabales**; Evasion Records, 1998): 12 tracks from this master of dance-hall *guajira*, who sings of the joy and pain of rural life.

– **A Toda Cuba le Gusta** (**Afro-Cuban All Stars**; World Circuit, 1997): a mix of *sones*, *guaguancós* and *guarachas* that show the Afro-Cuban All Stars at their best.

– **Buena Vista Social Club** (World Circuit, 1997): a remarkable album that brought together some of Cuba's greatest musicians to play some of their favourite tunes.

– **La Charanga Eterna** (**La Orquesta Aragón**; Lusafrica/BMG, 1999): this band, originally from Cienfuegos, is famous for such songs as '*El bodeguero*' (covered by Nat King Cole) and '*Pare Cochero*'. A 60th anniversary album with a great selection of tunes.

– **La Charanga Soy Yo** (**La Charanga Forever**): innovative orchestration including solid backing from the brass instruments and piano. Excellent live band.

– **Concierto Eurotropical en La Habana** (The New Generation of Cuban Music; Éd. Manzana 1998): these two CDs of live recordings at the Karl Marx Theatre in Havana feature new arrivals such as Klimax, Manolito y su Trabuco, Sabrosura Viva, Los Soneros de Carnacho, Llubia Maria Hevia and Mayelin y el Sabor Oriental.

– **Euforia Cubana** (**La Ritmo Oriental**; Globe 1999): Ritmo Oriental come into their own on this recording conducted by Enrique Lazaga.

– **Introducing . . . Rubén González** (World Circuit, 1997): a debut album from this outstanding pianist who has been making music for over 50 years.

– **Lo Mejor de la Vida** (**Compay Segundo**; Dro East West Spain 1998): one of his finest albums comprising a compilation of long-forgotten tunes and personal compositions. Essential listening.

– **Sublime Ilusión** (**Eliades Ochoa y el Cuarteto Patria**; Virgin, Spain, 1999): a great collection of *son* and bolero tracks showing Ochoa at his best. Guest appearances from Ry Cooder and harmonica player Charlie Musselwhite amongst others.

BACKGROUND

– **Salsa Caliente** (Universal, 1998): an excellent compilation featuring the greatest names in salsa: Fania All Stars, Celia Cruz, David Calzado and other Caribbean artists such as Oscar D'León, Robert Torres and Johnny Pacheco.

BOOKS AND LITERATURE

Storybook island *par excellence*, Cuba has influenced a number of major Western writers, including Graham Greene and Ernest Hemingway (*see below*). In proportion to its size, Cuba probably has more internationally renowned writers than any other Latin American country.

The first literary giants are José Martí and Nicolás Guillén, both poets and national heroes. Aside from their important poetic works, Martí has published *Our America: Writings on Latin America* and the *Struggle for Cuban Independence*, and Guillén a magnificent posthumous tribute to Che Guevara.

The pillars of Cuban literature are Alejo Carpentier, Severo Sarduy, Jesús Diaz, José Lezama Lima, Guillermo Cabrera Infante (even if he did take British nationality) and the great contemporary novelist, Jesus Diaz. Influenced as much by their island as by European writers such as Proust and Joyce, they share several points in common – a love of art and history, nostalgia and a yearning for the liberalization of Cuban society. Despite their blend of styles, each has a very individual personality. Cuban style, invariably described by critics as 'baroque', tends to be a knowing mix of erudition, verve, musical rhythms, passion and truculence. Above all, these writers are great poets and it's a shame that so many works are still banned in Havana.

Other notables include novelist Reinaldo Arenas, who was exiled in 1980 and died in 1991 in New York; Virgilio Pinera, one of the greatest Cuban playwrights (as well as a notorious homosexual who was banished by the regime and then restored to favour); Severo Sarduy, literary adviser to two French publishing houses; Miguel Barnet, sworn enemy of slavery; and César Lopez, heir to the Surrealists and winner of the National Prize for Literature in 1999.

Increasingly, the public is recognizing exiled Cuban writers. In Spain, important literary prizes have been awarded since 1996 to writers such as Andrés Jorge (exiled in Mexico), Matias Montes Huidobro (who lives in Hawaii) and the poet Daina Chaviano (in Miami). Spain's pre-eminent literary prize, the Cervantes prize, was awarded in 1997 to Cabrera Infante.

Among the dozens of writers who are less well known in Europe, mainly because they still live in Cuba, are Abilio Esteves, Onelio Jorge Cardoso, Leonardo Padura, Pablo Armando Fernandez and the amazing Daniel Chavarria (of Uruguayan origin). This former gold prospector in the Amazon rainforest, former guerrilla and a defender of the Castro regime now writes spy novels in Havana.

FURTHER READING

– **Alejo Carpentier**: *El Siglo de las Lucas*, *The Chase*, *The Lost Steps* and *The Harp and the Shadow*. The only novels of the great Cuban writer set partly in Cuba. *El Siglo* evokes the French Revolution as perceived in the Caribbean, with lovely passages on colonial Havana. *The Chase* is a stunning political whodunnit, and *The Lost Steps* is a love story.

– **José Lezama Lima**: *Paradiso*, a largely autobiographical baroque novel, is 660 pages long and written in a convoluted but brilliant style. It tells the story of a young Cuban terrorized by his father, a colonel and aspiring English aristocrat. *Paradiso* caused a scandal when it was published, but enchanted many critics and was hailed as signalling the renaissance of the Latin American novel.

– **Graham Greene**: *Our Man in Havana*. This classic spy novel is recognized as the great British writer's best work, and a splendid example of British humour. Everything is a source of derision in this implausible story of a vacuum cleaner salesman who inadvertently becomes a spy. It also contains a wonderful insight into the atmosphere in the Cuban capital before the Revolution.

– **Ernest Hemingway**: *To Have and Have Not*, *The Old Man and the Sea* and *Islands in the Stream*. These three classics were written in Cuba, even if the Gulf of Mexico provides the local colour. (*See also* 'Ernest Hemingway' *below*.)

– **Guillermo Cabrera Infante**: *Three Trapped Tigers*. This first masterpiece pioneered a new genre. Packed with passion, Cuban slang and word play, it tells of the nocturnal wanderings of young artists in Havana in the 1950s. Funny and satirical, he describes a wild town that has changed little in the intervening years. Don't miss the superb sequel *Havana for a Dead Prince*, published 15 years later. The author lives in exile in London, and his books are banned in Cuba.

– **Zoé Valdés**: *La Nada Cotidiana* (*Everyday Nothingness*). Daughter of the Revolution, the heroine of this book has a poorly paid job, but can't do anything else. Yet still she survives, living from day to day, coping with the daily grind of life in Cuba. In true Cuban style, she collects lovers and adventures. A sensual tale set in a difficult period and the work of an author who is now exiled in France. Another work, *La Douleur du Dollar* (The Pain of the Dollar, 1997), tells the story of the uncertain existence of a young Cuban woman 'passionately in love, unbelievably patient and incredibly wretched'. Set in Havana, 'a sweet and honeyed town with hot and mellow nights' and the most romantic setting in Latin America, this is a superb portrayal of Cuban hardship.

– **Benigno**: *Life and Death of the Cuban Revolution*. This hero of the Cuban Revolution, scandalized by the country's situation, decided to make a point of telling 'his' truth. Reminding the reader of his contribution to Socialism, he embarks on a vivid account of the actions of certain governments, and even Fidel himself does not escape judgement. It's a captivating work, even if certain claims are unsubstantiated.

– **Patrick Glaize**: *Cuba, tierra caliente* is a book of magnificent and unforgettable black-and-white photographs, accompanied by a CD. The

BACKGROUND

author has a real passion for Cuba, its people and culture, vividly captured here. The CD includes some rare recordings made during the 1940s and 1950s, and tracks by some of the great musicians.

ERNEST HEMINGWAY

One of the best-known American writers, Ernest Hemingway (1899–1961) left a considerable legacy to Cuba, creating his own myth that is now part of the island's history.

In 1932, Hemingway checked into the Ambos Mundos hotel in the heart of Old Havana. His friend Joe Russell, a barkeeper and keen fisherman, introduced him to fishing on the island, where the waters teemed with sawfish. Hemingway's wife, Pauline, had just given birth; the writer had no desire to play the proud father, despite his nickname of 'Papa', so fishing was the perfect excuse to stay away from home. Marlin wasn't the only creature he chased. He also met the lovely Jane Mason here, who was as much of a barfly as he was. In between fishing, drinking and other activities, he even found time to write one of his masterpieces, *To Have and Have Not*, in his hotel room. Whenever he needed inspiration, he would end up in one of his favourite bars, either the Bodeguita del Medio or the Floridita, and invent new cocktails.

In 1940, fed up with the States, he bought the Finca Vigia, about 20 kilometres (12 miles) from Havana. He had just divorced Pauline and almost immediately afterwards married the journalist called Martha Gellhoven. Over the years, Hemingway filled his house with almost 6,000 books, and surrounded himself with 60 cats, plus dogs and fighting cocks. He also wrote some of his most famous works here, including *The Old Man and the Sea*.

But it was on the ocean that he was in his element, on board his yacht *Pilar*, whose captain, Gregorio Fuentes, from the fishing village of Cojimar, provided the inspiration for the swordfish catcher in the novel. During World War II the *Pilar* was fitted out with bazookas. Hemingway, having become a US 'intelligence' agent, was tracking German submarines. According to a recently unveiled secret report, he also worked for the US secret service to provide information on the Castro Revolution.

In 1960, Hemingway organized a fishing contest and invited Fidel Castro to present the trophy to the winner. As it turned out Fidel won the competition, and Hemingway had to present him with the award. It was the first and last time the two men met.

Shortly afterwards, Hemingway was forced to leave Cuba: as a US citizen the Cuban Revolution was putting him in a delicate position. A year later, he took his own life. Some believe that he did it in a fit of paranoia, convinced that he was being watched by both the Cubans and the CIA.

FILMS

For years, Cuban cinema was so low-key that it seemed to have disappeared altogether, a casualty of the dwindling inspiration of the country's film industry, or of the absence of the materials and equipment needed to make a film, or of a combination of both. Yet Cuban cinema was both a cultural and political tool, and a mouthpiece for those opposed to the US embargo. Since 1960, Cuba has earned more film awards than any other developing country, mainly thanks to the wonderful ICAIC (Cuban Institute of Art and the Film Industry), which has always been a forum for creation and a real breeding ground for talent.

In 1994, the cult film *Fresa y Chocolate* (Strawberry and Chocolate), by Cuban directors **Tomas Gutierrez Alea** (died 1996) and **Juan Carlos Taibo**, was released. Oscar-nominated, it enjoyed international success and launched the career of the Cuban actor **Jorge Perrugoria**. The film mirrored modern-day Cuban society, depicting the conflict between homosexuality and Cuban machismo, and an entire generation empathized with it. At the beginning of the Revolution, Cuban homosexuals were considered criminals and were exiled to what was the Isle of Pines, now the 'Isle of Youth', just off the coast. Today, there is more tolerance, and there is a gay village in Havana – and yet a certain ambiguity persists, and Castroists still view homosexuality as a crime. The film illustrated questions that divide the nation: respect for differences, non-alignment of art with propaganda, the monolithic ideology of some and the despair of others. The movie owed its release in Cuban cinemas to Alfredo Guevara, one of Fidel Castro's entourage.

Fresa y Chocolate, followed in 1996 by *Guantanamera* and recently by *Madagascar*, the work of another director, are proof of the return to health of the Cuban film industry.

Alfredo Guevara (no relation to Che), the master of Cuban cinema, remains one of the most outspoken figures in Havana. It is thanks to Guevara, (famous for wearing his jackets over his shoulders) that up-and-coming film-makers such as **Gutierrez Alea** (*Death of a Bureaucrat*, *The Last Supper*), **Pastor Vega** (*Portrait of Teresa*) and, above all, **Julio García Espinosa** (*Reina y su Rey*) have been able to gain a foothold. All the films are influenced heavily by Italian neo-realism and the New York school.

It would be a mistake to ignore the importance of the Cuban documentary. Its post-1959 leading light, **Santiago Alvarez**, was the author of a number of geopolitical programmes touching on the subject of internationalist solidarity. Another great documentary is Wim Wenders' *Buena Vista Social Club*, named after a famous Havana cabaret from the early 1950s, and glorifying some of the living legends of Cuban music, including Compay Segundo, Rubén González and Ibrahim Ferrer.

NOTABLE FIGURES

– **Néstor Almendros**: reputed to be the best director of cinematography in modern cinema, Oscar-winning Almendros has worked with all the great directors. An active Cuban dissident, in 1989 he made two shorts denouncing the human rights situation in Cuba.

– **Fulgencio Batista**: in September 1933 this lowly sergeant was suddenly promoted to colonel thanks to the intervention of an American diplomat. Batista, in charge of the army by the end of the same year, virtually deposed

BACKGROUND

the government of Ramón Grau San Martín in January 1934, backed by the Americans. Even though he coveted no government post, Batista became the henchman of the new regime, effectively running the country for the next 10 years and getting himself 'elected' as president of the Republic in 1940. Defeated in the 1944 elections again by Grau San Martín, exiled in the States, Batista seized power again in March 1952 during another coup. Overthrown by Castro, on 1 January 1959 Batista fled Cuba in a plane with his family, close friends, generals and police officers, and suitcases full of dollars. He died in Spain at the age of 72 on 6 August 1973. He had promised to deliver Cuba from 'gangsterism', but became a crook, dictator and corrupt ruler *par excellence*.

– **Benigno** (Daniel Alarcón): at the age of 17, Benigno's fiancée was killed in front of him by Batista's soldiers. Picked up by the *barbudos* (*see* 'The Barbudos'), he became the protégé of Cienfuegos and Fidel in the Sierra Maestra, then went to work for Che Guevara in Bolivia. He was one of the few survivors of the Bolivian escapade, witnessing Che's assassination, which he later recounted in his first book, *Surviving Che*. He then became an instructor for the special commandos, a spy appointed to infiltrate the counter-revolutionaries, head of the military police in Havana and head of Fidel's security. However, after years of working for the government, he decided to settle in France, and to give vent to his creative urges. The revelations in his book *The Life and Death of the Cuban Revolution* launched a huge debate. The Cubans thought he was in the pay of the CIA and the French treated him like a double agent, while others believed that he was illiterate, and had been manipulated by his publishers. In fact, it seems that it was Che Guevara himself who taught him to write. Benigno remains a mystery, in true Cuban style.

– **Cachao** (Israel Lopez): this musician was born with music in his veins, with no fewer than 35 double-bass players in his family. Born in Havana in 1918 (in the same house as José Martí), this blue-eyed mulatto learned to play a variety of instruments and soon proved himself an outstanding composer and arranger. In 1939, with the song entitled *Mambo*, Cachao became one of the pioneers of the mambo genre, together with Perez Prado. He went on to invent *descarga*, a frenzied improvisation inspired by the *danzón* and new cha-cha-cha. After the 1950s, the fashion passed; Cachao went to Miami and ended up playing at weddings and bar mitzvahs. Admired by a new generation and a hero to his compatriots Gloria Estefán and Andy García, Cachao is back in the limelight once again with a re-release of his wonderful *Master Sessions*.

– **Alejo Carpentier**: born in 1904 in Havana of a Breton father and Russian mother, Carpentier is still the most famous Cuban novelist. A musicologist first and foremost, he studied Cuban music, and became the first to devote a book to the island's musical history. In 1928, the visiting Surrealist poet Robert Desnos invited him to Paris. Carpentier ended up staying there for 11 years, working as a journalist. After supporting the Castro Revolution, Carpentier was appointed cultural adviser to the Cuban Embassy in Paris (with the official title of Minister). At the same time, he pursued his career as a novelist in France, winning that country's award for best foreign novel (1956), then the prestigious Cervantès prize. He died in Paris in 1980.

– **Fidel Castro** (*see* 'History').

– **Raúl Modesto Castro Ruz**: Fidel's younger brother by five years was also his right-hand man from the start of the guerrilla warfare in 1956, although at the beginning of the Revolution he was eclipsed by Guevara and Cienfuegos. Although constantly overshadowed, above all by his brother, Raúl Castro has had real power for almost 40 years, and is completely loyal to Fidel. His organizational qualities, particularly in the Cuban Communist Party and FAR (armed revolutionary forces), of which he is minister, and the way he performs his public duties are in marked contrast to his private persona. He is reputed to be a keen dancer, to have a talent for making people laugh and to partake occasionally of the national drink. Considered to be the natural successor to his brother, Raúl is much liked by the Cuban people, despite the fact that he lacks Fidel's charisma.

– **Carlos Manuel de Céspedes**: he played a key role in the first War of Independence (against the Spanish) which started in 1868. A lawyer and owner of much land in southeast Cuba, Céspedes famously freed the slaves on his Demajagua estate, with the rallying cry 'Independence or death'. The rebels proclaimed a Republic in 1869, with Carlos Manuel de Céspedes as its president. He was killed in action in 1874.

– **Camilo Cienfuegos**: after Castro and Che Guevara, Cienfuegos is the most famous of the *barbudos* who arrived on board the *Granma*, yet his life as a heroic and popular revolutionary was all too short. On 28 October 1959, he took off in a plane from Camagüey heading north. He was never seen again, and no trace of his plane, which crashed somewhere off the coast of Havana, was ever found. Ever since, this handsome young man, one of Che Guevara's best friends, has been venerated in Cuba. His brother Osmany, still closely linked with Fidel, has always been appointed to key posts.

– **Máximo Gómez**: this general of Dominican origin joined forces with Maceo (*see below*) in the struggle for independence; he died on 17 June 1905. Together with Martí, Gómez is synonymous with the legend of the Cuban Revolution, and constantly remembered by Cubans today. Gómez and Maceo fought in the provinces of Oriente, Santiago de Cuba and the Sierra Maestra, which is also where Fidel Castro and his men launched their guerrilla attacks in 1956.

– **Che Guevara**: (*see* 'History').

– **Hatuey**: symbol of the fight for independence, Hatuey was the first native Cuban to lead other indigenous peoples against the Spanish *conquistadores*. The uprising took place in Yara, in southeastern Cuba. He was captured and burned alive on 2 February 1512. Today, a Cuban beer still bears his name, even though it has been taken over by a firm based in Florida.

– **Korda**: the great Cuban photographer who took *that* photo of Che, hair streaming in the wind, beret on his head, wearing a semi-determined, semi-dreamy expression. The image is now recognized everywhere and has been reproduced ad infinitum since 1967 – in books and magazines, on posters, T-shirts, flags, transfers, huge murals, postcards, record sleeves and even banknotes. Yet, in true revolutionary style, Korda has never received a single centavos in royalties.

– **José Lezama Lima**: born in 1910, this writer virtually never left his family home in Old Havana. The founder of a famous review, an essayist and poet, he only wrote one book, *Paradiso*. It was a runaway success all over Latin America and earned him the nickname of 'the Caribbean Proust'.

– **Antonio Maceo**: this mulatto general took up the cause of Céspedes (*see above*) until 1880. He died in 1896.

– **Celia Sanchez Manduley**: this daughter of a Manzanillo doctor was often by Castro's side. She was one of the few women who fought in the Sierra Maestra episode. A strong, unconventional woman, she went on to become one of Castro's principal collaborators, and they remained loyal to each other, even when the chips were down. She served as Minister of State responsible for the general secretariat, and her small apartment in the Vedado district of Havana was the party's unofficial headquarters. She died of cancer in 1980.

– **José Martí** (1853–95): considered a national hero by all Cubans, Martí's memory lives on throughout the country. This charismatic figure was a rebel, writer, poet, journalist, orator and thinker. He distinguished himself at the age of 15 by writing his first poems. Arrested on charges of treason in 1867, he was convicted and then banished to Spain. He met Victor Hugo in France. After founding the Cuban Revolutionary Party, he went on to organize the War of Independence. He was shot and killed by the Spanish during the Battle of Dos Ríos, and his remains lie in Santiago.

– **Jorge Perrugoria**: born on 13 August 1965, this actor has been the darling of Cuban society ever since he starred as a gay man in the cult film *Fresa y Chocolate* (he also appeared in *Guantanamera*; *see* 'Films'). Although he has achieved international fame, rubbing shoulders with actors Antonio Banderas and García Marquez, and working with Almodovar, Julio Cortázar and Imanol Arias, he still lives in Cuba. For the time being he is respected by the regime, despite minor criticisms that he voices from time to time. In Havana, he's known as 'Pitchi' ('playboy').

– **Pedro Sarria**: Fidel owes his life to this second-lieutenant in Batista's army. Sarria led the patrol that found and then arrested Fidel Castro after his attack on the Moncada de Santiago barracks in 1953. Castro managed to escape with eight of his friends. Acting against orders, Sarria prevented his soldiers from shooting Fidel; as they raised their guns, he cried 'Don't shoot, don't shoot! We mustn't kill ideas!' Pedro Sarria Tartabull saw out his days peacefully in Havana, where he died in September 1972.

– **Compay Segundo** (Francisco Repilado): born in Siboney in 1907, music and cigars were very important to Compay's family. Initially a farm worker in the Santiago region, he went to Havana in 1934 to play the guitar. He made an auspicious start, featuring on the first record to be cut in Cuba. But it was in Mexico that he became famous, as a singer for the Cuarteto Hatuey. He then became a clarinet player during the triumphant tours of Miguel Matamoros, and in 1948 formed the duo Los Compadres, popular with an entire generation of Cubans. Seven years later, having fallen out with his colleague, Compay packed it all in and became a cigar roller at the Upmann factory. In the 1970s, when he was a grandfather with three marriages behind him, and seemingly forgotten by the world, he was invited by Eliades Ochoa to join his Cuarteto Patria. Compay dug out his old *armonico*, the seven-string guitar that he had invented, and since then he has been on the road again, even though he is now over 90 years old. Invited to play on Ry

Cooder's Buena Vista Social Club album (*see* 'Music and Dance'), Compay has become one of the most famous musicians in Cuba, and a valuable national export. He claims to have three passions in his life: cigars, women and flowers.

FOOD AND DRINK

Frankly, the Cubans do not eat well. Food in Cuba hardly varies at all, and is never enhanced with spices (bring your own tabasco!). Rice, chicken and pork are the staples of Cuban *criollo* (creole) cooking. You will also find *res* (beef), which is usually of poor quality and often overcooked (possibly to disguise its age). By law, rock lobster and beef are reserved for export and restaurants only – personal supplies are forbidden, and the penalties are severe for locals caught with any.

You will find virtually no green vegetables in Cuban cuisine, although, with a bit of luck, you'll come across the odd yam or malanga (a sort of Jerusalem artichoke). The only alternatives to rice are potatoes or fried bananas. For a balanced meal, try ordering a salad, invariably lettuce, tomato and *pepino* (cucumber), or sometimes avocado.

As well as the ever-present classic dishes, you'll find assorted *tortillas* (omelettes) and *perro caliente* (hotdogs) on most menus. Dessert is usually cheese with jam, a curious combination that Cubans love.

The situation is different in the major towns, however, where you'll find a number of foreign restaurants, especially Chinese and Italian.

CUBAN SPECIALITIES

– **Rice and black beans**: the lifeblood of creole gastronomy, these are eaten together and referred to as *moros y cristianos* ('Moors and Christians'), in reference to their colours.

– **Cochinito**: pork is the dish of choice for Cubans, roasted, grilled or fried.

– **Rock lobster**: this is mainly reserved for export, although you can still find it in most tourist restaurants. Prices are no longer as attractive as they used to be since the authorities decided to cash in on the Westerner's love of lobster and doubled the price. This went down rather badly with the tourists who decided not to play ball, and so most of the lobster found now is tucked out of sight in *paladares*. The other problem with lobster is that it is seldom properly prepared, particularly since the rule that the lobster should be carved up alive before being grilled is rarely observed. You will find better lobster in private houses, provided it was caught the same day. Touts will try to sell you lobster, particularly in Varadero.

– **Cangrejo** (crab): the alternative to lobster is abundant, although few restaurants serve it.

– **Crocodile**: you'll only find this in Guama and in a few restaurants in Playa Girón in the Zapata peninsula. Occasionally, you may also come across tortoise on a menu.

BACKGROUND

Fruit: although this tropical island produces many different fruits, you'll only find one in local cuisine – the humble *plátano* (plantain). This type of banana is prepared as a vegetable, usually sliced and cooked like French fries. Thin slices are known as *mariquitas* and thick ones as *tostones*. This is not a Cuban speciality, since the plantain is eaten in most tropical countries. When they can get it, some of the best places serve *fruta bomba* (guava), often with jam and cheese. You may also find pineapple and delicious mango, mainly available as juice.

DRINKS

– **Water**: the tap water is not for drinking, so it's best to buy the bottled version, which is found virtually everywhere at a reasonable price – except in cafés and some restaurants where bottled water costs the same as beer. It's a great deal cheaper if you buy it from somewhere like CUPET service stations. The most widely available bottled water is Ciego Montero. Ask for *agua con gaz* if you want sparkling, or *natural* if you want still.

– **Fizzy drinks**: Cubans call these *refrescos*, even if they aren't actually that refreshing due to a lack of ice. Real Coca-Cola, sold under Mexican licence, can be found almost everywhere, as can substitutes such as Tropicola or Fiesta Cola.

– Cuba makes several good **beers**, which are not that expensive. Cristal is light and refreshing, but the best are probably La Bucanero (light or strong) and Mayabe (*blanca*, light and *negra*, strong) – look out for the black label). All the beers are brewed in Holguín. Hatuey, a famous Cuban beer before the Revolution, is now made under licence in Florida and Santiago by Bacardi, so it's considered American rather than Cuban. The *claras* tend to be more popular with locals than tourists, even though these beers are cheaper and more traditionally made.

– **Wine** is rarely available in Cuba, but some upmarket restaurants serve Cuban and French wine, although many wine lists tend to favour wines from Italy and Spain. Prices are at a premium. Opt instead for rum, which goes well with the local cuisine.

– Cuban **coffee** is well known, even though it doesn't hold a candle to the Colombian version. Here it's served good and strong, Italian-style. About 250g (half a pound) of coffee costs $6.

– **Guarapo**: This pressed sugar-cane juice is called *Guararón* when drunk with rum.

– You will also find Maltas, a refreshing, sweet non-alcoholic drink.

Rum

Together with the cigar, *ron* (rum) is the pride and joy of Cuba, and there are numerous great brands, all with their aficionados. Alongside beer, it's the national drink – a tradition that dates back to the 16th century. The first rum was sold under the Havana Club label, but Caney and Paticruzado are also popular. There is even a six-year-old Reserve available now. Watch out for the so-called 15-year old rum marketed by the brand leaders – the ageing process is entirely artificial. Pinilla, or 'poor man's rum' is very strong and is popular in rural areas.

Cuban rum is made from ground sugar-cane molasses. You can try it *carta blanca* (white), *carta oro* (golden), amber, *anejo* (matured), *a la roca* (on the rocks) or in cocktails. Cuban rum is so flavoursome, light and treacherous that it's quite likely to leave you feeling rather wobbly, so find yourself a rocking chair – that other ubiquitous tropical item – sit back and savour the taste. Ask for a *sillón* in Havana, a *balance* in Santiago or a *comadrita* anywhere else. Look out also for the *aguardiente*, a traditional, dry and fiery version (45 per cent proof) found in rural areas. Otherwise, the little-known but no less fabulous Havana Club is now available in supermarkets in Europe following its acquisition by Pernod Ricard.

For Cubans in Miami the best rum in the world is not Havana Club, but Bacardi, the old Cuban rum that has enjoyed international success. During the Revolution, the Bacardi family fled from Cuba, taking the patent and trade secrets with them. In the USA, the Arechabala family did not register the trademark which remained in the public domain until 1974 when it was registered by the Cubans. In 1994, the Cubans relaunched the Bacardi brand on world markets. Bacardi meanwhile marketed Havana Club. Predictably, Pernot Ricard filed a claim with US courts, who immediately threw it out. The battle continues . . .

Cocktails

In Cuba, any self-respecting bartender should know how to make no fewer than 100 cocktails, rum-based or otherwise. Some are made with sugar, fruit or fruit juice, others with angostura bitters, mint leaves, dairy products and spices.

Whatever you do, don't just pick up the cocktail menu and work your way methodically down the list. You'll end up in hospital! Restrict yourself to sampling the island's best. These range from the classics and winter warmers to long drinks and shorts, which are the most common.

It was Ernest Hemingway who made two classic cocktails popular in 1934 in two of Havana's biggest bars, the Daiquiri in the Floridita and the Mojito in the Bodeguita. The Floridita barman, Constante, also invented the Hemingway Special for the writer – a double Daiquiri served over ice in a cone-shaped glass, and made using light dry rum, half a teaspoon of sugar, the juice of half a lemon, a few drops of maraschino and crushed ice. In the Bodeguita del Medio, the Mojito is made by putting two ice cubes in a conical glass and adding the juice of half a lemon, half a teaspoon of sugar, sparkling mineral water, *yerbabuena* (mint leaves), two drops of Angostura bitters and some Havana Club light dry rum. Of the others, the classic Tom Collins, the Mary Pickford and the Mulata are also wonderful.

Finally, ask the barman (especially if he's old) to tell you a story or two about Cuban cocktails. All Cuban barmen think their island is the cocktail capital of the world, so you'll probably be there for hours.

SPORTS

Cuba ranks high among the world's leading sporting nations. At the 1992 Olympic Games in Barcelona, Cuba was ranked fifth in the medals table after the former Soviet Union, the USA, Germany and China. However, the 1996 games in Atlanta weren't such a success, as some of Cuba's top athletes defected at the last minute.

Cuba's great sporting heroes include **Alberto Juantorena**, twice Olympic 400m and 800m champion (Montreal, 1976), the sprinter **Leonard**, the hurdler **Casanas**, the high-jump world champion and record-holder **Javier Sotomayor** and the boxers **Teofilo Stevenson**, **Félix Savon** and **Pedroso**. At the Olympic Games in Barcelona Cuba came away with three-quarters of the boxing medals.

One sporting heroine, **Ana Fidelia Quirot**, is particularly admired by the Cuban people. The 800m athlete, silver medal winner in Barcelona, came back to win silver again in Atlanta after being badly burned in an explosion in her kitchen.

The leading sporting nation in Latin America and the developing world, Cuba owes its success to the sports policy of the Revolution. Before January 1959, Cuba finished only 11th in the 1959 Pan-American Games, and its only Olympic gold medal before the Revolution was in 1904 (St Louis, USA).

Surprisingly perhaps, few people in Cuba play **football**, and the country's team is not highly regarded. Instead, *beisbol* (**baseball**) is the island's national sport, and the Cubans are top dogs – even beating the USA at their own game at the Atlanta Olympics. Baseball is played everywhere and has created sporting legends. Cubans even reckon that they invented the game, since the Spanish invaders saw the indigenous Indians hitting a ball made from rolled leaves with a stick. On Sunday 28 March 1999, the legendary Estadio Latinoamericano sports ground in Havana saw the Baltimore Orioles play against an elite, hand-picked Cuban team. This was the first time in 40 years that the Americans had played a match in Cuba, paving the way for a thaw in relations between the two countries. The Americans won but the Cubans won the return match in Baltimore.

After 1959, other sports developed, such as volleyball, (the women's team were world champions in 1978 and 1992), fencing, basketball and judo.

DIVING

Cuba is a real diver's paradise. With a coastline thousands of kilometres long and lots of little islands surrounded by coral reefs, Cuban waters are rich in sea life. You can glide over schools of fish and shipwrecks on the seabed, entertain curious and attentive grouper, brush past fan-shaped gorgonia, admire the coral and make friends with inquisitive exotic fish. As long as you steer clear of anything that doesn't scuttle out of your path, plus scorpion fish, sea anemones and fire coral (and don't touch anything) you should be fine; the danger from sharks is exaggerated.

Two of the most stunning places to dive are María La Gorda (on the western tip of the island) and Isla de la Juventud. The spectacular setting of María la Gorda offers the better value for money as the equally impressive Isla de la Juventud is much too expensive. More details are available from the sites.

Take the Plunge

Cuba's quiet, warm and inviting waters are ideal for beginners, and the clubs and dive centres can provide equipment and full instruction – from safety procedures to depth control using stabilizer jackets (these stop you leaning on the seabed, rocks or coral for support). You don't have to be the athletic type, or even a good swimmer (but you do need to be able to breathe out while holding your nose). You just need to be over the age of six and in good health. It's a good idea to have a dental check-up before you leave home. Unless it's a try-dive, you'll need to produce a medical certificate. In addition to a qualified instructor and suitable equipment, for children over six the environment must also be suitable (warm water with no currents).

First-timers will start with a short try-dive lasting around 30 minutes (perhaps in a swimming pool). It should be one-to-one with an instructor, who should hold your hand. Try to relax and enjoy yourself. On land, you may feel weighed down by the equipment, but you will forget it once in the water. You shouldn't descend below 5 metres (16 feet). The suit should fit properly so that pockets of water don't chill you. You will then go on to a progressive training course lasting from three to five days until you reach level 1, after which you can dive down to 20 metres (65 feet).

BACKGROUND

Diving Centres

Diving is still in its infancy here and only a handful of spots are visited by tourists. Facilities remain very limited but the clubs that do exist are usually well set up and offer decent equipment, enthusiastic instructors and good security.

All centres should be affiliated to an international organization such as the PADI (Professional Association of Diving Instructors) or NAUI (National Association of Underwater Instructors). Each organization has its own training courses and internationally recognized diplomas. If you're an experienced diver but the club does not recognize your qualification, it will ask you to do a test dive to assess your level. All the clubs issue a 'dive logbook', which is both an essential record of your diving activity and a souvenir. Keep it safe and remember to take it with you whenever you go on holiday.

A good diving centre should respect all safety regulations, and make sure you have a good time. Be wary of any club that offers to take you diving without asking about your level of experience. Look around the centre to see if it is well maintained (look for signs of rust, check cleanliness and so on). Make sure there is safety equipment (oxygen, first-aid kit, radio) on board the boat, that the boat provides some shade from the sun, that you don't have to lug heavy equipment around and that there aren't too many divers (ideally a maximum of six). It's up to you whether you prefer a large, professional centre or small, flexible outfit offering a more personal service.

Note: You must allow between 12 and 24 hours after diving before taking a plane or climbing to any altitude.

– **Centre UCPA de Guajimico**: Based on the south coast around 40 kilometres (25 miles) west of Trinidad, on the way to Cienfuegos, this centre arranges 'discovery' holidays combining sport and sightseeing. Experience fine coral gardens, and some sharp drops, a few metres under. There are 10 instructed or accompanied dives, two per day morning and afternoon. Basic equipment is supplied, and accommodation is in fully equipped chalets.

ARTS AND CRAFTS

Crafts are not a forte of the Cubans, who have never really gone in for the kind of objects that tourists seem to like so much. However, the recent influx of foreign visitors has resulted in the emergence of a small-scale crafts industry, especially in busy tourist centres such as Varadero. Products include 1930s-style model cars, which are not too badly made but quite pricey and not at all typical. Cigar boxes and cases are also popular. Elsewhere, you'll find straw *machetero*-style hats, *guayaberas* (traditional cotton shirts) or santería objects of worship. You will also find plenty of jewellery and trinkets made of black coral, which is an endangered species, so don't make matters worse by buying it. Alternatively, opt for musical instruments such as congas, maracas and *tumbadoras*.

On the arts side, the island's best-known painters include Amelia Pelaez, René Portocarrero, Manuel Mendive and Wifredo Lam. Graphic art is also important in Cuba – particularly in film posters and political propaganda.

Cubans apply to all practical matters a skill for invention, for dextrous repairs, for making something out of nothing. It is thanks to local mechanics that you can still see American Chevrolets, Pontiacs and Fords from the 1940s and 1950s cruising slowly around Cuba's towns.

CIGARS

A cigar bearing the name 'Habana' is something special. Even in Cuba itself, Havana cigars are referred to simply as *tabaco* or *puro*, rather than *Habana*. The Mecca for cigars is situated in the valleys of Vuelta Abajo, near Pinar del Río, west of Havana.

In early December 1492 (or perhaps 1495) a certain Jerez, a member of Christopher Columbus's expedition, landed on the north coast of Cuba. There he discovered a Taino Indian with a lit stick of rolled leaves in his mouth, and imitated him on the spot. Unfortunately, on his return to Madrid, he was condemned by the Inquisition to two years' imprisonment, apparently for breathing smoke and having sparks in his eyes.

Five centuries later, more than 60 million Havana cigars go up in smoke around the world each year. There are more than 40 different brands. Cubans, who are inveterate smokers, consume more than 200 million cigars each year, albeit everyday cigars made from second-rate tobacco not destined for export.

The Havana cigar has played a major role in the country's history. The tobacco growers were the first to rebel against the Spanish; national hero José Martí's written order to start the war was concealed in a cigar. The Havana has always belonged to revolutionary imagery: Che Guevara (an asthmatic) smoked huge quantities of them. When he was in the Congo, Castro sent him a favourite gun accompanied by Havana cigars 40 centimetres (16 inches) long. According to one cigar-lover's journal, 'Che did manage to reduce his consumption to a single cigar, but this was one metre long!'. Fidel Castro gave up Havanas as long ago as 1985 – yet he still has his own brand, Cohiba, and regularly presents boxes to foreign heads of state.

John F. Kennedy was also a lover of Havanas. According to Pierre Salinger, a former adviser to the president, shortly after the Bay of Pigs, Kennedy asked for a huge quantity of Havana cigars as a matter of some urgency. The very next day, the cigars were acquired. Satisfied that he now had enough to be getting on with, the President felt able immediately to sign the order establishing the Cuban trade embargo.

Making cigars is an art form, requiring, according to an old saying, 'the instinct of a chef and the dexterity of a conjurer'. Castro once said that it was 'easier to imitate the finest Cognac than a Havana cigar'. No fewer than 170 meticulous operations are necessary before one of these fat cigars is ready to be smoked. Each brand has different characteristics, varying in length, flavour, bitterness and strength.

Most cigarette smokers enjoy Havana cigars and, while cigarette smoking is now viewed as antisocial, cigar smokers – men and women alike – can increasingly be found behind a cloud of blue smoke in the most prestigious clubs.

Jean-Paul Sartre once wrote that 'jazz is like bananas; you have to consume it in the place where it comes from', and it is true that cigars taste very different in Cuba from in London or Paris. This is because the humidity in Cuba is perfect for cigars. In Europe, you really need a humidifier to recreate the atmosphere. There's also something about Cuba that gives the cigar smoker anonymity and the knowledge that no one is being bothered, so you can enjoy it just the way it was intended.

Obviously, there are a few pitfalls to avoid, such as the 'real bargain' that turns out to be a fake. There is a thriving black market in Havana cigars, and the authorities are cracking down on small illegal factories and those who fence stolen cigars. Large numbers of boxes have 'disappeared' from factories and have been smuggled into Europe, giving customs officers new cause for concern.

Note that Cuban customs officers can ask you for a *comprobante* (receipt) if you have bought more than 50 cigars. Beware of fake cigars being sold on the street with a forged receipt. A good tip, before you leave Cuba, is to wrap your boxes in a damp cloth (a T-shirt will do) and try to keep them warm.

SMOKING A CIGAR PROPERLY

There are a few rules to follow. First, the humidity and taste of the cigars must be protected, so they must be stored in a wooden box with a humidifier; the box must be kept cool (not in the fridge) and well ventilated.

BACKGROUND

Before lighting up, cut the end of the cigar with a cigar cutter, or with a sharp knife. Don't push the match too far into the head of the cigar (an error of taste). There is no point in taking off the band when the cigar is cold. The beauty of the band is no indication of quality. Finally, don't use a petrol lighter to light the cigar, since this can affect the odour. Keep the flame upright and turn it regularly, drawing on the cigar gently. Relight it if it goes out, and make sure you don't overheat it. The last third of the cigar is rather bitter (from the concentrated tar). The cigar will go out on its own, so don't bother stubbing it out. Once it is cold, dispose of it in the proper place.

VINTAGE CARS

Cuba has more 1950s American cars per square kilometre than any other country, including the United States. This was a decade when money flowed like water in Cuba, and American ostentation pervaded the island's way of life. This extended to the ownership of fine cars, and tens of thousands were imported from the States during the island's rich years.

However, this came to an end with the Revolution at the beginning of the 1960s, when Cuba rebelled against the USA and its strict trade embargo. The only cars to reach the island at this time of amicable Soviet-Cuban relations, were a few thousand Ladas and Moskviches. Cubans started to hold on to their old cars rather than take them to the breaker's yard where they probably belonged.

Many drivers became renowned as star mechanics, especially in Old Havana, Camagüey, Trinidad and Santiago. Many of the cars that you will see on Cuban streets are authentic collectors' items, vintage vehicles that have been renovated and lovingly cared for by their owners. Their leather upholstery is remarkably well looked after, and the engines are endlessly tinkered with to make them last as long as possible.

The average cost of these fabulous machines is a few thousand dollars, and they are in great demand from European enthusiasts. However, Castro has banned their export, declaring them part of the national heritage. These old Studebaker 48s, candy-pink Buicks, gleaming Bel-Airs, chromed Oldsmobiles, apple-green Mercurys and other legendary Chevrolets and Cadillacs of the rock-and-roll years will cruise Cuba's streets for some time to come.

Don't be surprised if you see a Cuban hot-wiring his engine, or starting it up using a screwdriver or a penknife. The car's original owner probably fled during the Revolution, taking his keys with him!

SOUVENIRS

The most popular souvenirs for visitors to Cuba are rum, cigars and coffee. Be careful, though, as many brand-name 'Havana' cigars and coffee products are fakes (*see* 'Cigars').

Salsa and other records in tourist shops are overpriced, so visit a local market instead. The sound quality of tapes sold in the markets isn't too bad but, just in case, ask if you can listen to them before buying.

A *guayabera*, or traditional white cotton shirt, makes a lovely souvenir. For Revolution enthusiasts, street children sell three-peso coins and banknotes showing the image of Che Guevara. Note, however, that if they're in good condition, they're probably forgeries. Banknotes that have been signed by Guevara are much rarer. You will also find lots of Che merchandise such as T-shirts, photos, posters, stickers, badges, postcards and even plates, on sale in Havana.

Many books have been written about Che Guevara and the Revolution, and Spanish-speakers will be spoilt for choice. Bookshops and hawkers sell copies of Che's writings, as well as a plethora of biographies, some illustrated with rare photos. For aficionados, there is ample opportunity to find out all there is to know about the life and work of the Comandante.

BACKGROUND

Havana and surroundings

For maps of Havana, see the colour plate section.

HAVANA (LA HABANA)   DIALLING CODE: 7

Havana, the capital of Cuba, was founded on its present site in 1519. Little has changed architecturally in this impressive colonial city since the Revolution and the old town, La Habana Vieja, was declared a UNESCO World Heritage Site in 1982. Here you will discover sumptuous colonial churches, graceful arcades, elaborate balconies and Spanish-style courtyards – a far cry from the other capital cities in South America, which swarm with cars, neon lights and advertising hoardings. The lack of rampant commercialization and modernization in Havana is immediately apparent and the nostalgic feel adds to the laid-back mood which prevails. This is enhanced by the distinct lack of cars, and those that you do see will doubtless be classic 1950s American models. Restoration work to reveal the former glory of the shabbiest buildings has been started, but those on the sea front which are continually exposed to the erosive sea air are slowly cracking and crumbling.

The heat during the day is not really conducive to much action, and patience is a virtue since the relaxed attitude means that even if something is urgent it is still dealt with in the same slow way as everything else. At night however, Havana shakes off its languor, and once the partying starts it usually goes on into the wee small hours. Salsa dancing is a national passion and the rhythm of the Cuban people is contagious – you will be welcomed on to the dance floor if you dare!

A Brief History

Havana is one of the oldest towns in the Americas. In 1492, Christopher Columbus set foot here before discovering the continent. It may seem comical now, but at the time he thought he was in Southern China. He was even expecting to be met by the Aga Khan and had taken an Arabic and Hebrew interpreter with him. He must have been disappointed by the strange, naked men who greeted him. They were in fact Taíno Indians. The island didn't disappoint him though because he is supposed to have declared that: 'No one had ever laid eyes on a more beautiful place'. He returned two years later and named it the island of Juana, in homage to Prince Juan of Spain. But it was Diego Velázquez, sent by Columbus's son, who conquered the territory with a force of 300 men.

The Key to the New World

The town of San Cristóbal de la Habana was founded not long after, in 1514, and was named after an Indian chief called Habaguanex. It expanded rapidly, due to the influx of masses of slaves from Africa, and tobacco and sugar plantations spread all around. In 1553, the governor took up residence in the town. With its natural anchorage, Havana was a perfect safe haven on the route from Veracruz to Seville, and so it became the springboard of Spanish colonialism. Every year, between March and August, the galleons of the *conquistadores* nestled in its well-protected roads. One chronicler of the time wrote: 'We could pave the streets of Seville with gold and silver thanks to the riches we receive from the New World'. The ships' holds were stuffed with goods from Latin America: emeralds, pearls, silk, perfume, indigo and cochineal, as well as coconuts and even multicoloured birds. The colonists in Cuba filled the ships with tobacco, leather and wood. Ships arrived from Africa full of slaves, while other boats came from Europe loaded with fine wine, lace and mirrors.

But this immense wealth meant that the town was constantly pillaged by all the pirates of the Caribbean. In the 18th century, the waters around Havana were such a hotbed for pirates that it spawned the Jolly Roger, the black flag with the death's head. In 1582, the slaves built the ramparts and the first fortress: the Castillo de la Fuerza. On 29 May 1586, Francis Drake fired his guns on Havana, but by 4 June he had abandoned his attempt to take the town.

Then the Spanish built the fortresses of El Morro and La Punta, to fortify the entrance to the roads. This proved a deterrent to even the best pirates of the Caribbean, l'Olonnais, Henry Morgan, John Rackam, Ann Bony and Mary Read, but they continued to attack the ships at sea. The prosperity and a sense of security enabled the colonists to indulge themselves in grandeur and the first grand, Spanish-style colonial mansions date from this era. The island quietly prospered and, by the 17th century, the capital had 10,000 inhabitants.

In 1762, the English captured the town, but they only kept it for a year and traded it back to the Spanish in exchange for Florida. It became a free port and continued to increase in prosperity throughout the 19th century, in spite of riots by the slaves and attempts by Cuban nationalists to gain independence.

In 1863, the ramparts were pulled down and two new distinctly different areas were built: the old town (Habana Vieja) and the new town (Vedado and then Miramar). But the fight for independence was renewed with a vengeance. In 1898 an incident occurred which was to have far-reaching consequences for the whole country: a battleship, the *Maine,* sent to protect American citizens, exploded mysteriously. As a result, the United States declared war on Spain . . . and won. Thus Cuba became a kind of American 'protectorate'.

The Caribbean Babylon

With Batista's return to power in 1952, American gangs strengthened their hold on Havana. Connections with the North American underworld were so strong, that Batista made Meyer Lansky his advisor on tourism (a kind of semi-official post). Lansky, like the other great American Mafia gang leaders, Lucky Luciano and Bugsy Siegel, took over the Sevilla-Biltmore hotel and controlled the gambling at the Montmartre, the Nacional, and the Monseigneur. He cleaned up the sordid gambling dens and the corruption became highly organized. Only a few hours flight from New York and with nearly 270 brothels, Havana became a major centre for prostitution, a paradise for gringo tourists. All forms of vice thrived in the Americanized part of Vedado, which was dominated by big hotels and high-rises.

Liberated first of all from the tyrant Batista by the guerrilla Camilo Cienfuegos, then by Che Guevara and then Fidel Castro, the capital became totally Cuban for the first time on 2 January 1959, but that's another story . . .

The Wind of Restoration

For some years now, the government has given carte blanche to the expert architect-historian, Eusebio Leal, to restore and save from impending disaster the entire sector of Havana Old Town that has been placed on the World Heritage list by UNESCO. As a result, a few ancient palaces, carefully selected for their history and architectural detail, have been transformed into luxury hotels and restaurants. The revenue they produce is immediately reinvested to restore other sites, many of them transformed into museums, schools and other administrative buildings. The aim is to restore as many of the ancient buildings as possible to their original condition before they became dilapidated. This is a high-minded venture, not motivated by any element of property speculation. The Herculean works are going ahead with financial support from UNESCO and Spain, but in 10 years' time it is unlikely that more than 10 per cent of the Old Town will have been pulled from the wreckage. The truth is that while the area is undeniably charming as it crumbles Venice-style into oblivion, it is quite definitely moribund. In many places, the cramped housing facilities are positively dangerous, and thousands of families live in conditions of grinding poverty that most tourists rarely get to see. The greatest danger is from heavy rains, when rainwater collects in the walls that threaten to crack and collapse on top of the inhabitants.

Naturally, the palaces selected for restoration are home to dozens of families who are evicted and rehoused in relative comfort in the suburbs. Paradoxically, what they gain in comfort they lose in terms of quality of lifestyle, closeness to town and journey times into the centre.

The result is that Old Havana looks different from one year to the next and may well have to forfeit a decadence that seems quite charming to tourists who don't have to live there. Such is the price of survival. In any case, the style of restoration is nicely judged: no architectural adventures, no loud colours, respect for historical detail and remarkable quality of conservation.

GETTING THERE

✛ **José Martí International airport** (map 1, off B4). About 17 km kilometres (10.5 miles) south of Havana.

– At customs: customs officers sometimes ask visitors to show that they have a reservation coupon (voucher) for two nights in a hotel in Havana. (*see* 'Entry Formalities'). If you cannot prove that you have a reservation for two nights, you may have to pay the authorities at the airport the equivalent of two nights (about $60), and sleep in whatever hotel you can find, on penalty of deportation.

> **TIP** If you don't have a hotel coupon or voucher, just give the name of the hotel where you intend staying, or give the first name that comes into your head and you should not have too much trouble.

Transfers to the Centre of Havana

– There is no bus to the town centre: you have to take a taxi, payable in dollars. There are two kinds of taxis: the official ones with a meter ($16–18 and the private ones (*taxis particulares*), where the price is negotiable (about $10). That said, private taxis were recently banned from the airport.

> **TIP** Ask an official taxi driver what the price should be so that you have a guideline when negotiating with the others. You can also hire a car locally if you have not already reserved one. Ask at the office of Havanautos, in the airport car park.

ORIENTATION

It is very easy to find your bearings because all Havana's roads are laid out in a regular grid pattern, as in American towns. To make things even easier, in the modern part all the roads are numbered. However, there are some subtle differences: the even numbers run at right angles to the roads with odd numbers. So don't expect number 23 to follow number 22, because the next road will be number 24! Another exception: to the east of Paseo (which more of less divides Vedado from north to south), the roads have letters instead of numbers and they run from A to P. But at least in this case they follow alphabetically.

Addresses are written in such a particular way that it helps to know how to decipher them. Firstly, the name of the road, then the number in the road, then the location in relation to adjoining roads and finally the name of the area. For example: 'calle 15, 21, e/ 18 y 20, Vedado' means: at No. 21 in road No. 15, between roads 18 and 20, in the Vedado area. The word *entre*, meaning 'between' can be abbreviated as e/ or with the symbol %. The word *esquina* (abbreviation *esq.*) means 'at the corner of' but it is often replaced by a simple 'y', meaning 'and'. It's easy when you know how.

THE MAIN AREAS

Havana is made up of several distinct areas, three of which are really important. It is easy to wander about the old town by foot but advisable to take a taxi to the other areas.

– **Habana Vieja** (map III): Old Havana to the east, around the port. It is the historical centre, or Spanish colonial area and incredibly charming. The most important sights, the old palaces and the famous bars are all concentrated here. The most ancient part is bordered to the west by a famous promenade: the Paseo de Martí, also known as Prado, which leads to the no less famous Capitolio (a loose copy of the one in Washington). The dome serves as a useful landmark. The most interesting roads for tourists are around the Plaza de la Catedral and the Plaza de Armas, an area that has been undergoing major restoration for some years.

– **Centro Habana** (map IV): sandwiched between Old Havana and Vedado, this dilapidated area finishes at avenida Galiano (to the east) and avenida Infanta (to the west) but is not of great interest to tourists, except for the beautiful colonial mansions. It looks a bit like Beirut, with lots of cafés and restaurants where you can sit outside and read a good book. The faded seafront is where director Wim Wenders shot his famous film *Buena Vista Social Club*.

– Vedado (map V): is the real town centre and full of activity, bordered to the north by the **Malecón** and to the south by the gigantic **Plaza de la Revolución** (on the other side of which is Nuevo Vedado). A rather chic residential area, Vedado is also a great place for nightlife. Most of the hotels, discos and restaurants are here, as well as the Coppelia ice-cream parlour, which is always immensely popular. Havana's most important street, the **Rampa** (officially calle 23) runs from here to the sea. But the biggest attraction of the Vedado is still the Malecón, a breakwater protecting the town from the sea for 7 kilometres (4 miles) and stretching from the old town to Miramar. It forms a huge, romantic promenade making it a popular meeting place for lovers.

– Miramar (map VI): through the tunnel to the west, past the river Almendares is the most up-market residential area of Havana. All the foreign embassies are located here, as well as the best restaurants. Miramar stretches along the coast for quite a distance, but the beaches are not sandy. However, the palaces, old casinos and luxurious residences are not to be missed. But you'll need some form of transport to get around.

– Siboney, la Coronela and around the 'laguito' (off map I): this is where most of the political elite live and, to party hardliners no doubt, it looks for all the world like a little Miami, with grand colonial houses and not a blade of grass out of place. Even the birds seem to cheep in an orderly fashion! The whole place is guarded by armed police, but it's definitely worth a look. Be discreet, however, because prying eyes (foreign or Cuban) are not welcome in some of the streets in case they disturb the peaceful enjoyment of a good cigar.

– Regla and **Guanabacoa**: on the other side of the bay, to the east of the Old Town, there is a famous church and museum of santería.

GETTING AROUND

Rickshaws

These bicycle-taxis provide a fairly rapid, environmentally friendly means of transport for short distances and, since the town is flat, they are not very strenuous. You'll find them in the centre and around the main squares and streets. Expect to pay $1 for short trips and $3–4 to go from Vieja Habana to Vedado (but it will take nearly half an hour). Miramar is further out, so take a taxi. The driver pedals in front, the passenger sits behind and some even have music!

Taxis

These are found in front of all the hotels and short trips are not too expensive. Cars belonging to the three official companies (Panataxi, Turistaxi and Transtour) are in excellent condition and all metered. They are often air-conditioned and no more expensive than *taxis particulares*. The drivers are usually nice too. You can even hire one for the day: if you agree the price in advance, the driver will turn the meter off.

– **Taxi rates**: the official rates are $3 between Vieja Habana and Centro Habana, $5 from Vedado to Vieja Habana. These fares are metered, so there's no room for argument.

– **Collective taxis**: these are old American cars that ply the same streets. Usually, these taxis are for Cubans only (hardly surprising, given that the fare may be 10 times cheaper than a normal cab). They're usually packed and display a taxi sign behind the windscreen. You can pay the 50-cent fare in pesos or dollars (but your change will be in pesos). Just tell the driver the road and the *esquina* (intersection, for example 27 *y* 4). However, if you're not a fluent Spanish speaker, the driver is very unlikely to take you.

– *Taxis particulares*: private taxis are more expensive than official taxis and, since they're not metered, expect to be charged more than the 'normal' price. But be prepared to bargain *after* you get into the car, not before. There are two reasons for this: Cubans are not officially supposed to accept payment in dollars, so if you start to haggle on the street, it can get a bit awkward. Second, offer the driver a reasonable price and if he doesn't accept, ask him to let you out – that will probably make him change his mind. It doesn't usually come to this, but some drivers have been known to take advantage of tourists by charging extortionate prices.

To hail a *taxi particular*, just raise your hand. Few drivers will refuse to take you, especially if you have dollars. You are also highly likely to be approached by private drivers offering their services.

You can hire a *taxi particular* for a whole day in Havana. Again, agree the price in advance and expect to pay around $20.

– **Note**: taxis in Havana are not officially allowed to leave the capital. The only taxis able to take you to the beaches in the east are those who pay for their licence in dollars. Most of the drivers are aware of this and will refuse to take you in any case – unless, of course, you are on your own and could be mistaken for a Cuban.

The *Guagua* (urban bus)

An alternative for those on a tight budget is the *guagua* (pronounced 'wawa') or urban bus. However, because of the petrol shortage, there are very few, and consequently they are packed. The advantage is that they cost peanuts and you pay in pesos (or, more precisely, in centavos).

Make sure you have some 10-centavo coins because you must have the exact fare. It costs 20 centavos to take a *camelo* (the camel-shaped bus with two humps) and 40 centavos for all other buses. Above all, allow plenty of time because the queues are very long. The average wait is 30 minutes, although waits of up to an hour are not uncommon. In main stations you take a ticket assigning you a place in the queue, but this does not necessarily guarantee you a place on the bus. Invariably there is someone around prepared to sell their ticket to a tourist in return for a few dollars. The network does serve the town centre well. Just ask the driver where the bus is going.

The Vaiven Shuttle Minibus

This is a new means of transport especially for tourists. Comfortable buses provide a regular shuttle service between 8.45am and 9pm, from the port of Old Havana (the square next to Castillo de la Fuerza) to the Convention Palace (Miramar), via Révolution Square (the central stop) and the Vedado (the stop next to the Coppelia).

It makes a total of 23 stops on its route. There is a commentary and you can get off and on as many times as you like. Tickets, valid for the whole day, cost $4 and are sold on the buses, in tourist offices and in hotels.

USEFUL ADDRESSES

Tourist Offices

⌈ Infotur (map III, B2): this is a tiny kiosk at the corner of calle Obispo and calle Ignacio, Old Havana. ☎ 33-33-33. Open Monday to Friday 8.30am–7pm. However, there is no information available and the service is almost non-existent, so this new office is even more useless than the old one that used to be on calle Obispo.

⌈ El Palacio del Turismo (La Habana tourist office: map VI, A2): calle 28, 303, between avenida 3 and 5, Miramar. ☎ 24-06-24 or 24-81-64. Open Monday–Friday 9.30am–5.30pm. This large, new centre is slightly more useful than the office in the old town, but not worth a detour.

⌈ Infotur (map VI, off A2): calle 5, 112th floor, Miramar. ☎ 24-70-36. Open 8.30am–8.30pm. Yellow prefabricated building in the second rotunda, just behind the Cecilia (see 'Where to Eat'). Don't expect too much because this office is only there to give advice of a state-run nature, so it will not provide you with a list of rooms to let in private lodgings. Next door is a small car-rental agency called Transtur.

■ **Roots Travel** (map V, D2, **1**): Hotel Colina (room 201, 1st floor), calle L, between 27 and Jovellar, Vedado. ☎ 55-40-05. Open Monday–Saturday 9am–7pm. This Paris-based travel agency offers various services including: hotel bookings, bungalows, transport (buses, cars, airline tickets). They charge $5 a night to reserve rooms in private lodgings, which is reasonable for the guarantee of a good-value room. French and English spoken.

■ **Roots Travel** (map V, B3, **1**): calle 4, 512 between 23 and 21, Vedado. Email: cuba@rootstravel.com. Open 10am–6pm. There is someone on duty to meet night flights. This is a prime address for backpackers, with young, friendly people who speak English and French and can provide lots of useful information about accommodation. Their rooms range from (budget) double rooms in private lodgings to rooms in colonial houses. Most of the private lodgings suggested in 'Where to Stay' come from their catalogue. Try to contact them before leaving home to ensure that you not only have a reservation, but also a room for the night when you arrive in Cuba. The people at Roots can also tell you about all sorts of cultural activities and give you the kind of tips you would never get from a conventional tourist office.

■ **Havanatur** (map VI, B1, **1**): calle 2, 17, between 1 and 3, Miramar. ☎ 24-21-61 or 24-22-73. Fax: 24-28-77. These are agents for Havanatour Paris, specialists in Cuban travel. They provide a full travel agency service: hotel reservations, car hire, excursions, air tickets, etc. They also have an office on the ground floor of the Hotel Habana Libre Tryp in Vedado (*see* 'Where to Stay').

■ **Cubatur** (map V, B1, **2**): calle F, 157, between Novena and Calzada, Vedado. ☎ 33-41-55. Fax: 33-35-29. This is the main tourist agency on the island and the staff are very professional. They can book shows (including the *Tropicana*), and they also exchange currency. There is another office at the Hotel Nacional (*see* 'Where to Stay').

■ **Cuba Autrement** (map III, B2, **1**): Lonja del Comercio (first floor on the right), plaza San Francisco de Asis, Habana Vieja. ☎ (537) 66-98-74. Fax: (537) 66-98-73. Website: www.CubaAutrement.com. Email: info@Cuba Autrement.com. This is another French-run agency staffed by a friendly, efficient team who can put together every kind of trip imaginable. They cater for people who want to go off the beaten track and get to know the country and its people, and specialize in last-minute arrangements (hotel reservations, private lodgings, car rental). For Cuba enthusiasts who plan ahead, this is one of the only agencies to offer a *Habano Passion* tour. This is your chance to meet some of the country's greatest *torcedors* (professional cigar rollers) and visit the tobacco plantations of such legendary names as Partagas, Cohiba, Romeo y Julieta and other celebrated cigars. Their website has useful ideas on budgeting your trip.

Currency Exchange

You can obtain dollars in all the major hotels, but the exchange rates are higher than at the bank. The international Visa card is increasingly accepted in hotels, particularly at the Habana Libre Tryp, the Riviera, the Presidente and the Nacional (*see* 'Where to Stay'). Don't forget your passport. Service is fast but there have been cases of overcharging.

You can get pesos at *casas de cambio* in the banks at better rates than those offered by the hotels.

– Steer clear of the black-market traders who operate all over town.

In Habana Vieja
■ **Assistur** (map III, A2, **2**): paseo del Prado 212. ☎ 33-83-39 or 33-89-20. Open daily 8am–10pm. This is probably the only insurance company in the whole of Cuba where you can exchange American Express traveller's cheques. There is a 5 per cent commission charge. You can also take out an insurance policy and, if you fall ill, the agency can make arrangements with your insurance company at home.

■ **Banco Financiero Internacional** (map III, B2, **3**): corner of Brasil and d'Oficios, near plaza San Francisco de Asis. Open Monday–Friday 8am–3pm. Cash withdrawal facilities (dollars) for Visa and MasterCard.

In Vedado
■ **Banco Financiero Internacional** (map V, D1, **3**): Linea and O. Open daily 9am–7pm. You can exchange any kind of traveller's cheques (except American ones).

■ **Banco Nacional de Cuba** (BNC; map V, D1, **4**): 74 avenida 23 (Rampa), Vedado, at the end of la Rampa, coming from the Malecón. Facilities for withdrawing cash (dollars) with Visa and MasterCard.

■ **Banco Popular de Ahorro** (map V, C2, **5**): avenida 23 (Rampa) and J. Cash withdrawal facilities with Visa and MasterCard.

■ **Cadeca** (map V, C–D1, **6**): calle M, between 17 and 19, opposite La Torre bar. Peso exchange and Visa cash withdrawal facilities.

■ **Cadeca** (map V, B2, **6**): calle 19, between A and B. Site in the farmers' market where you can change dollars into pesos.

Post and Telephone

✉ **Main post office** (map V, C3): avenida de la Independencia. Stamps can only be bought here with Cuban pesos, but tourists never need come here because all the hotels have posting facilities. Most shops that sell postcards also sell stamps, which you can buy with dollars. There are also stalls on all the main avenues.

✉ **Post office** (map III, B2): plaza San Francisco de Asis, Habana Vieja. Open Monday–Friday 8am–6pm. This is a big, modern post office mainly for tourists and offers a full range of services.

■ **International telephone**: You can make international calls from a hut next to the Riviéra hotel in Vedado, and from a place next to the Banco Popular de Ahorro at calle 23 (Rampa) and J. It's actually much cheaper to send a message abroad by fax than to phone (calls to Europe cost $4 a minute). Prepaid phonecards cost $10 and $20. Note that you can also pay at the time of making the call but it works out much cheaper with a card.

Embassies and Consulates

For details of embassies and consulates in Havana, *see* the 'General Information' section at the beginning of the guide.

Transport

Buses

🚌 **National bus station** (map V, D3): avenida Rancho Boyeros (Independencia), corner of calle Arroyo. ☎ 70-94-01 to 09. Terminal for buses from the provinces. Tickets may be bought at the back of the station. They are cheaper here than in the travel agencies because you can pay in pesos, but it's easier to get a seat if you pay in dollars.

■ **Viazul Agency** (map II, A3): avenida 26,1152, corner of Zoológico Nuevo, Vedado. ☎ 81-14-13, 81-11-08 or 81-56-52. Fax: 66-60-92. Has air-conditioned and very well-equipped Mercedes buses. For more details *see* 'Leaving Havana' at the end of this chapter.

Trains

🚆 **Railway stations**: there are three, one for the eastern part of the country, one for the west and a third for local train journeys. Note that it is essential to book in advance. Foreigners can buy tickets at the station, and they can also buy them with dollars in travel agencies and in the tourist offices of large hotels such as the Habana Libre Tryp or the Inglaterra. You can also buy tickets at Assistur (*see* 'Currency Exchange').

– **Ferrotur** (train reservation centre): calle Egido y Arsenal, next to the central station. ☎ 62-17-70. Service here is much more efficient than at the station and you pay in dollars.

● **Estación Est-Central** (central station; map III, A3): calle Egido y Factoria, south of Habana Vieja. Information: ☎ 62-80-21 to 25. Information: ☎ 62-19-20 (for Santiago) or 70-99-00 (for Pinar del Río and Cienfuegos). There is a small information office (Ladis) for those paying in foreign currency: ☎ 62-19-20.

● **Estación Cristina** (map IV, off B3): avenida de Mexico (Cristina) 7, opposite Cuatro Caminos market (Mercado Unico). This is much smaller than the central station and most trains go to the airport (but there is quite a walk when you get there). Three departures a day, and tickets cost 90 centavos. In July and August trains from this station also go to Playa del Este.

● **Estación de Casablanca** (map II, off D1): avenida de Gamis 7, Casblanca. ☎ 624.888. An electric train fitted out by the Spanish (mysteriously called the 'Jersey train') goes to Mantanzas.

Taxis

There are three official companies, which are dependable and not much more expensive than *taxis particuliares*.

● **Panataxi**: ☎ 81-01-53 or 81-41-42. One of the cheaper companies.

● **Turistaxi**: ☎ 33-55-39 to 42. 24-hour service that's reliable but slightly more expensive than Panataxi.

● **Taxis OK**: ☎ 33-14-46.

● *Collectivo* **taxis**: Collective or shared taxis are the cheapest option and are often old American cars that you can take on long tours around Havana for around $1 (*see* 'Getting Around').

Car Hire

● **Micar** (map V, B2, **8**): Riviera Hotel, avenida 1 and Paseo, Vedado. ☎ 55-35-35. Also at the airport (☎ 55-88-80). This agency, part of the Cubalse consortium that imports cars, is probably your best guarantee of a car in good condition. Prices are very much the same as in other agencies. Micar only has Fiats for hire and only for periods of three days upwards.

● **Transtur** (map V, B2, **8**): Riviera Hotel, avenida 1 and Paseo, Vedado. Central bookings: ☎ 24-55-32 or 24-39-39. Website: www.transtur.cuba-web.cu. Email: comerc@rentcar.transtur.com.cu. Choice of various Suzuki and Daihatsu four-wheel-drive vehicles, but beware of vehicles in poor condition and overcharging.

● **Havanautos**: has branches in all the large hotels such as Inglaterra, Nacional, Habana Libre, Sevilla, etc. (*see* 'Where to Stay').

● **Transgaviota**: has several offices, including at José Martí international airport and in the restaurants of the Parque Histórico Morro-Cabaña. ☎ 23-70-00 or 33-17-30. Fax: 33-27-80. Car hire with driver, by the hour or by the day. More expensive than normal car hire of course, but useful if you don't have a driving licence.

Bicycle hire

There is no longer anywhere in Havana where you can *officially* hire a bicycle. Your only possibility, if you have rented a room, is to ask the landlord of the *casa particular* where you are staying. Every family owns one or more bikes and will be delighted to lend you one for about $3 a day. Be sure to check the condition of the bicycle very carefully.

There are many cycle tracks in the capital but it is not wise to ride at night because there is not enough light. Don't forget your waterproofs in the rainy season.

Take the usual safety precautions and beware of the numerous thieves. Bring your own anti-theft devices because they are not readily available here. More and more private hotels offer secure parking places for bicycles (*parqueo*), payable by the hour.

CUPET service stations

There are several stations in town, all open 24 hours and you can only pay in dollars.

● Linea y Malecón, in Vedado. Between the Hotel Nacional and the former US embassy.

● Calle M y 17, in Vedado.

● Paseo y Malecón, in Vedado; in front of the Hotel Riviera. Note that this station has a tendency to put up the price of petrol by $2.

● Calle 31 y 20, in Miramar.

● Calle 41 y 72, next to the Tropicana.

● Avenida 5 y 110, in Miramar.

Airports and Airlines

✪ **José Martí international airport**: 17 kilometres (10.5 miles) south of Havana. ☎ 33-57-77. By car, take plaza de la Revolución, then avenida Rancho Boyeros, then continue straight ahead. It is well signposted. There are two terminals: the T1 (Cubana) and the T2 (AOM, Iberia and Air France), so check which one your plane departs from.

✪ **Domestic airport**: about 1 kilometre from the international airport. If you are taking one of the rickety little planes to the islands, they leave from T5, the Aero Caribbean charter terminal.

All the airline companies below can be found on the ground floor of the Cubana de Aviación building, calle 23 (Rampa) 64, between P and Infanta, Vedado; map V, D1, **9**.

■ **Air France**: ☎ 66-26-42 or 66-26-44.

■ **AOM**: ☎ 33-40-98 or 33-39-97 (flight confirmation). Fax: 33-37-83.

■ **Iberia**: ☎ 33-50-41 or 42.

■ **KLM**: represented by the ALM Antillean Airlines office. ☎ 33-37-30.

■ **Cubana de Aviación**: ☎ 33-44-46 to 49. The other office (domestic flights) is at calle Infanta y Humbolt, Centro Habana. Same telephone number.

■ **Aero Caribbean**: ☎ 79-75-24 or 78-68-13.

Emergencies

■ **Emergency**: ☎ 113.

■ **Cira García Central Clinic** (map VI, B2, **3**): calle 20, 4101, esquina avenida 41, Playa. ☎ 24-28-11 to 14. Fax: 24-16-33. Just across the river coming from Vedado is the best clinic in town, catering for embassy personnel. Fees for services are payable in cash (dollars) only, and a basic consultation costs $20 plus any medication. The clinic offers a full range of services, including a well-stocked pharmacy, so you can be sure of good treatment. It also caters for a range of specialized requirements.

Bookshops (road maps, maps, guide books)

🔒 **El Navegante** bookshop (colour map III, B2, **4**): 115, calle Mercaderes (Old Havana) between Obispo and Obrapía. ☎ 57-10-38. Open Monday to Friday, from 8am to 5.30pm and Saturday from 8am to 1pm. This is one of the best places to buy maps and road maps. It sells guides and maps of Havana and the various regions of Cuba, and sailing charts. If you are travelling by car you should buy the excellent *Guía de Carreteras de Cuba*. It is a road atlas in pocket form, edited in Mexico. It's very well done, in colour, highly detailed and shows all the existing road networks, even little country roads. It is indispensable.

– **Geotech**, (colour map V, C2, **10**): 409 calle 13, corner of calle F, in Vedado. Open every day of the week from 9am to 5pm. Sells maps, guides, and atlases, which are particularly good for hikers.

🔒 **Librería La Internacional** (colour map III, A2, **5**): calle Obispo y Bernaza, Habana Vieja. Open from Monday to Saturday from 10am to 5.30pm. Post cards, magazines and books in (almost) any language. It is very near the Floridita so you can write your postcards while sipping a daiquiri!

Newspapers

You will find international newspapers at the hotel Nacional (at the reception) and at the hotel Habana Libre (on the ground floor, between the gents and ladies' toilets) and at the hotel Sevilla. Don't expect a huge amount of choice, but they do have the *Herald Tribune*, the *New York Times,* the *Wall Street Journal* and *El País*.

Cultural Events

Cultural events are published in the daily newspaper the *Granma* (on sale everywhere). The Spanish edition is cheaper because you pay in pesos, unlike the international editions, which are priced in dollars. See also *Cartelera* published in Spanish and English, and *Bienvenidos, la guía del ocío de Cuba,* available in the big hotels and from the tourist office. Both publications are rather too commercial to be really useful but they include one or two articles on current cultural events that might be helpful to non-Spanish speakers. The best sources of advice are the Cubans themselves.

WHERE TO STAY

See the colour maps of Havana in the centre of the guide.

The Old Town may have very few hotels, but those it does have are definitely the city's most beautiful. However, most tourists stay in the Vedado area, where you'll find all the large hotels and the private lodgings, with accommodation costing around $15–25 a night.

Havana is noisy because of the late-night cabarets and discos, and also the cockerels that wake you at dawn. Another inconvenience is the shortage of water in the bathrooms because the supply is often cut off (especially at night). But this is rare in the good hotels.

Habana Vieja

Casas Particulares (private lodgings)

♙ Gustavo L. Enamorada Zamora 'Chez Nous' (map III, B2, **10**): calle Brasil 115, at the corner of calle Cuba. ☎ 62-62-87. Double rooms cost about $25 in this early 20th-century colonial house with bags of character right in the heart of old Havana. One of the only reliable addresses in the area, it's run by a friendly family who let out two pleasant, high-ceilinged rooms (one large, one small) with fan, mini bar, TV and shower (hot water). Popular, clean and quite charming, with a homely atmosphere. Good value. There's also a pleasant terrace reached via a narrow iron staircase.

♙ Chez Amalia (map III, A1, **11**): Prado 20, apartment 7A (seventh floor). ☎ 61-78-24. Here you'll find one ridiculously small room at $25 and another at $35, excluding breakfast. The shared bathroom is clean and has hot water. The building dates from the 1950s and is undeniably charming, but its main attraction is the sensational view of the Prado, the Capitole and especially the bay from the huge terrace. Nice welcome.

♙ Sra. Elvira Parra (map III, A1, **12**): calle Cuba 60, apartment 5B (fifth floor). ☎ 63-26-97. Also facing the bay is this modern but dilapidated building with two double rooms at $30 each. The rooms are clean and quite pleasant (no view) and share a bathroom with hot water. There's also a small balcony with a view. Pleasant welcome.

Hotels

☆ Budget

♙ Hotel Lido (off map III, A2, **13**): calle Consulado, between Animas and Trocadero. ☎ 57-11-02, 03 or 04. Fax: 33-88-14. This is one of the cheapest places in the area – simple, old fashioned and rather dreary. Rooms with bath (no hot water) range from $25 to $35 depending on the season. The rooms without windows are really depres-

sing, so try for one with a balcony overlooking the street and the Capitole. Watch your belongings when out at night in this rather dodgy area.

♙ Casa del Científico (map III, A2, **14**): 212, Paseo Martí (Prado Street). ☎ 62-45-11 or 63-81-03. Fax: 60-01-67. The building is a real baroque palace complete with stucco and colonnades in the foyer and a lovely balcony on the first floor overlooking the Prado. Expect to pay from $31 for a room with shared bathroom to $55 for one with private bath, excluding breakfast. Try to get a room on the terrace (with bath). Simple, with loads of charm and full of character, this friendly place offers excellent accommodation.

≜ **Convento Santa Clara** (Residencia Académica; map III, B3, **15**): 610 calle Cuba, corner of Santa Clara, between Sol and Luz, south of Plaza Vieja. ☎ 61-33-35, 66-93-27. Fax: 33-56-96. Email: reaca@cencrem. cult.cu. Away from the hustle and bustle, this beautiful 17th-century convent has nine spacious, clean and peaceful rooms, and a delightful gallery. There are also two dormitories with six beds and a charming suite (bedroom, sitting area and terrace) in the internal courtyard. There are about 30 beds in a superb setting with just a touch of decadence. Expect to pay from $25 per person for a double room or dormitory accommodation with hot water and shower. The staff are extremely attentive. The convent is run by the Ministry of Education and closes at midnight, but there is a back entrance for use after hours. Highly recommended; booking essential.

≜ **Hotel Caribbean** (map III, A2, **16**): 164 Prado, between Colón and Refugio. ☎ 62-45-11 or 63-81-03. Fax: 60-82-10 or 66-04-79. On the border between Centro and Habana Vieja is this modern building with a narrow, pastel blue facade. Expect to pay $50–55 for a double room with bath. Nice welcome but the corridor rooms are small and drab (but clean), and not cheap.

[☆☆–☆☆☆] Moderate to Expensive

≜ **Hostal Valencia** (map III, B2, **17**): 53 calle Oficios, corner of Obrapía. ☎ 51-10-37. Fax: 33-56-28. In the heart of the Old Town, two blocks from Plaza de Armas, is this adorable and very chic little palace that will appeal to lovers of the Andalucían style, with its colours, courtyard and galleried corridors. Apparently King Juan Carlos himself has stayed here. Prices range from $60 for a twin room to $75 for one of three suites (plus breakfast). The tastefully renovated rooms with high ceilings have loads of charm, and some are spacious. There are only 12 rooms so early booking is recommended. There's also a bar and restaurant (see 'Where to Eat').

≜ **Hotel Florida** (map III, A2, **18**): calle Obispo, corner of calle Cuba. ☎ 62-41-27. Fax: 62-41-17. Expect to pay about $105 a night excluding breakfast. This charming little hotel, minutes away from all the best places, is a real little palace that has been tastefully and beautifully refurbished. With no more than 30 rooms, it has quite an intimate feel. Features include a magnificent two-storey patio with stone columns, marble floor and huge, very comfortable rooms with high ceilings, bath, telephone, safe, etc. The restaurant, on the other hand, tends to be rather amateur.

≜ **Hostal Conde de la Villanueva** (map III, B2, **19**): calle Mercaderes 202, on the corner of Lamparilla. ☎ 62-92-93. Fax: 62-96-82. Email: hconde@villanueva.ohch.cu. This former palace is now a charming, discreet, luxury hotel with a cigar theme. It features a large patio with photos of famous cigar lovers and is furnished with the inevitable rocking chairs without which it is impossible to do justice to a good Partagas D4 cigar. Its nine rooms are named after the leading brands and are spacious and classy, with one or two tasteful architectural flourishes, especially in the bathrooms. Expect to pay from $95 for a patio room (with shower) to $105 for one overlooking the street (with bath). Service is a bit slow. The excellent cigar shop on the first floor offers a wide choice of individual cigars; there's also a small tasting room and regular meetings are held for cigar lovers. The restaurant on the ground floor is recommended.

🛏 **Ambos Mundos** (map III, B2, **20**): corner of Obispo and Mercaderes. ☎ 60-95-30 or 31. Fax: 60-95-32. Double rooms cost $90–$105 at this legendary hotel where Ernest Hemingway wrote the first chapters of *For Whom the Bell Tolls* in his top-floor room (No. 511 in the corner) before moving to Finca Vigia (*see* 'What to See'). The hotel may be steeped in history, but the rooms are nothing special for the price. Those off the corridor-patio are small and dark and best avoided, even if they are cheaper. The bar in the light, airy foyer (that opens onto the street) has good background music, and the sunny Roof Garden bar on the large terrace (open 7am–10pm) has magnificent views on three sides.

☆☆☆ – ☆☆☆☆ Expensive to Splash Out

Despite their reputation, the hotels listed below are not as charming as those in the former two categories and are more places to visit than places to stay. They also attract lots of groups.

🛏 **Hotel Inglaterra** (map III, A2, **21**): 416 Prado, between San Rafael and San Miguel. ☎ 60-85-93 to 97. Fax: 60-82-54. This splendid palace, dating from 1875, is both neo-classical and Moorish and has long been a favoured haunt of celebrities and artists, including the Spanish poet Federico García Lorca (1898–1936). Sarah Bernhardt met her lover, the *torero* Mazzantini, here. Enjoy the courtyard and the elegant dining room, the decorative mouldings and coffers on the ceilings, the wrought ironwork, the mosaics and the stained-glass windows. However, the rooms are not so luxurious, even a little disappointing, but they are spacious and their balconies overlook a nice park. This is by no means the most expensive hotel in town, and you could always treat yourself to a drink in the foyer or on the terrace and just savour the atmosphere.

🛏 **Plaza Hotel** (map III, A2, **22**): 267 calle Zulueta. ☎ 60-85-83. Fax: 60-85-91. Directly opposite the Hotel Inglaterra, this is another hotel for lovers of palatial architecture. Recently restored, it is admittedly quite attractive with its yellow facade, Belle Époque foyer, colonial-style galleries, marble fountain, fifth-floor terrace and various embellishments dating from 1900. Many artists have stayed here, including dancers Isadora Duncan and Anna Pavlova and the great Cuban musicians Paulina Alvarez and Pacho Alonso. Expect to pay about $120 for a double room with breakfast. It is rather noisy, however, and the rooms are very disappointing.

🛏 **Sevilla** (map III, A2, **23**): 55 Trocadero, between Prado and Zulueta. ☎ 60-85-60. Fax: 60-85-82. Besides a fascinating history, this splendid palace has little to recommend it: second-rate rooms (vast, sparsely furnished), dingy paintwork and very poor facilities for the price. Expect to pay $130–150 for a double room, excluding breakfast. Built in 1880, the Sevilla is a perfect replica of the Mudejar style of the capital of Andalucía – Moorish columns, panelled ceilings, mosaics and a delightful courtyard where you can enjoy a glass of wine. Numerous celebrities have stayed here, including former Yugoslav President Tito, American dancer Josephine Baker, Enrico Caruso, actress Gloria Swanson and the ubiquitous Ernest Hemingway. Some guest portraits in the main corridor include

Errol Flynn, Al Capone and Merle Oberon. As the Seville-Biltmore, the hotel proved an inspiration to Graham Greene, who set the meeting between the hero of *Our Man in Havana* and his boss in room 510.

Even if you don't actually stay here, don't miss the fantastic view over the town from the top floor. The hotel also has a lovely pool but, once again, the facilities are pretty poor.

Centro Havana

Casas Particulares

♠ **Tommy Reyes** (map IV, A1, **20**): 218 Gervasio, between Virtudes and Concordia. ☎ 62-71-09. After seeing this unbelievably crazy, kitsch place you'll never want to leave Havana. Tommy is a former dancer with the Havana National Ballet and his blue-and-white painted house is easy to spot. Tommy is not difficult to spot either – just look for the man with rings and piercings from top to toe who delights in tall stories (and much quoting of Oscar Wilde). There are four rooms, all with a certain charm, in powder-pink and sky-blue. The downside – and it's not enough to detract from the exceptional quality of the place overall – is the shared bathroom. The price ($20 for a double) includes 'mini' breakfast.

♠ **Amada Pérez Guelmes – 'chez Tony'** (map IV, B1, **21**): 262 calle Lealtad (altos), between Neptuno and Concordia. ☎ 62-39-24. Four quite decent rooms ($25 for a double) adjoin each other around an inner courtyard hung with long lines of washing that attach to pulleys, just like in *West Side Story*. The refurbished bathrooms have hot showers. There is also a lovely little colonial terrace where you can watch the world go by from your rocking chair. Lunch or dinner can be requested in advance.

♠ **Gladys Cutiño** (map IV, A1, **22**): 272 calle Soledad, between Concordia and Virtudes. ☎ 79-43-73. All the available space in this little house has been optimized (Cuban style) to make it as functional as possible. As a result, more rooms have been added on the first floor although there's hardly room to swing a cat in the rooms downstairs. They all have air-conditioning and shared bathroom and cost $25 for a double. There's also a little kitchen for guests, which is particularly handy as the farmer's market is right next door. This place is very popular so advance booking is recommended. Meals are also available by arrangement.

Vedado

This is your next best bet if places are full or too expensive in Old Havana. You might even be better off here because, along with Centro Habana, this is where most Cubans live.

Casas Particulares

♠ **Mélida Jordán** (map V, B3, **19**): 1102 calle 24, between 6 and 4. ☎ 35-219. This delightful place, probably the nicest in the area, is run by an adorable grandmother whose energy and good humour put even her daughters to shame. She rents three rooms (two on the first floor, one on the ground floor) in a magnificent house surrounded by dense vegetation and protected from prying eyes by tall black gates. Double rooms cost from $20 (excluding breakfast). Probably the best room is the one with its own entrance and small colonial windows. The bed is comfortable and there's a (hot) shower in the room. Breakfast is a bit on the small side, but the people are so friendly that you are unlikely to notice.

â **Manuel Arena Musa** (map V, C3, **20**): 710 calle B, between 29 and Zapata. ☎ 31-25-52. All three guest rooms in this beautiful colonial house, owned by a financial and accounting expert, are quiet and clean with fan. It's $20 for a double room with breakfast. There's no view but you can be sure of a warm welcome.

â **Dr Manuel Alvarez Alonso** (map V, C1, **21**): 260 calle 1, between 13 and 15. ☎ 32-47-13. Expect to pay about $30 for a double room without breakfast. Before the Revolution this was the house of a Cuban aristocrat and is painted in the traditional faded pink. Time seems to have stood still since then and the decor is exactly as it was in the 1940s. The accommodation has an old-fashioned charm that appeals to filmmakers, so early booking is recommended. Ask for the room with its own entrance on the terrace. Nice welcome but the service is a bit slow.

â **Margarita o Jorge Villazón** (map V, C2, **22**): 203 calle 21, between J and K. ☎ 32-10-66. Double rooms cost from $25 in another beautiful colonial house that could easily be taken for a museum, particularly with its guest lounge in the foyer and towering ceilings painted old-fashioned green. There are rooms on the ground floor and terrace accommodation consisting of a clumsy ar-rangement of rather drab little huts. Both cost the same but the ground-floor rooms are nicer. This place is particularly suitable for families. Car-parking available.

â **Milagros Cordero** (map V, D1, **23**): 6 calle Linea, between N and O (ninth floor). ☎ 32-67-29. A big building like this is not the kind of place to hang about the ground floor at night. However, a quick trip in the ancient lift and a warm welcome from Milagros will soon put you at ease. The budget furnishings are post-modern and quite basic. All the rooms ($30 for a double) have bathrooms and there's a lovely view over the Malecón and the straits of Florida. Nice place, nothing fancy, but very serviceable.

â **Alicia Hernández Padrón** (map V, D1, **23**): 6 calle Linea, between N and O (15th floor). ☎ 32-91-66. This is more attractive than Milagros Cordero because of the large bay window and the popular cocktail lounge. The pleasant rooms cost $30 for a double and have original furnishings and a TV. Warm welcome.

â **Chez Josefa** (map V, B3, **24**): calle 25, between 4 and 2. ☎ 30-10-65. There are three double rooms from $25 in this tidy house hung with cheap reproductions of Che Guevara that testify to the hosts' unshakeable faith in the Revolution. The toilet seat cover in cherry-red fabric is revolutionary kitsch, as are the CCCP stickers recalling the Soviet origins of the earthenware tiles. One look at the old American fridge (a real collectors' item) says that this place is full of memories, and a certain humility is expected of guests. The humble water heater can be temperamental. Make sure you check the price.

â **La Kakatua** (map V, A3, **25**): 1211 calle 15, between 18 and 20. ☎ 31-10-82. This offers small but well-equipped rooms that are almost comfortable. Each has its own bathroom but the hot water is unpredictable. Double rooms cost from $30. Warm welcome. There's also a restaurant of the same name (*see* 'Where to Eat').

♠ **Casa de Craciela** (map V, A3, **26**): 208 calle 18, between 15 and 187. ☎ 31-36-41. This small, single-storey apartment (owned by a doctor whose practice is next door) costs about $25 a night. Recently renovated, it has its own entrance and there is free parking in the courtyard. The bathroom is nothing

special, but it's clean and has hot water. There's also a kitchenette so you can save money on eating out.

♠ **Chez Josefina Gomez Villar** (map V, B3, **34**): 507 calle 4, between 21 and 23 (first floor). ☎ 30-68-43. The owner is a former seamstress who (before the Revolution) used to work for Cuban high-society ladies. Now she welcomes tourists to her spacious, peaceful home that opens onto a terrace. The two guest rooms are clean (with fan) and there's a communal bathroom.

Hotels

☆☆–☆☆☆ Moderate to Expensive

♠ **Hotel Bruzón** (map V, D3, **27**): calle Bruzón, between Pozos Dulces and Independencia. ☎ 57-56-84. This small, garrison-style hotel right next to Plaza de la Revolución has clean but fairly basic air-conditioned rooms with cold showers only, at $50 for a double with breakfast. Rooms overlooking the rooftops are quieter than those overlooking the bus terminal. It's fine if you arrive too late to find anywhere else. The Maison du Tango is in the basement.

♠ **Hotel Colina** (map V, D2, **28**): corner of calle L and 27. ☎ 32-40-71. This small building opposite the university is nothing much to look at but well located between Vedado and Old Town. It's slightly more appealing since the corridors were done up, but that's all that was renovated and the rooms could be a lot more comfortable. Prices are $54 for a double room with breakfast. There's a bar and restaurant and currency exchange facilities. Fairly indifferent welcome.

♠ **Hotel Vedado** (map V, D2, **29**): calle O, on the corner of 25th street. ☎ 33-40-72. Occasionally known as the Hotel Flamingo, this consists of

two vaguely art-deco buildings either side of a tiny, rather uninviting swimming pool that gets the sun for a few minutes a day. Think twice before taking the plunge. Refurbished to quite a good standard, there are small but comfortable rooms all with private bath (hot water). Expect to pay $54 for a double. Ask for one on the upper floors away from the street. Good welcome, efficient service and the reception staff speak some English. There is a good restaurant with tables on the street next door on the right.

♠ **Hotel St John's** (map V, D1-2, **30**): calle O between Humboldt and 23. ☎ 33-37-40 or 33-35-61. This mid-priced hotel has been completely refurbished to a high standard: new bathrooms and beautifully furnished rooms with Mediterranean-style printed fabrics. Expect to pay $80 for a double room with breakfast. The hotel is famous for its concerts and there's even a rooftop cabaret (so make sure you ask for a quiet room).

☆☆☆☆ Splash Out

♠ **Hotel Habana Libre Tryp** (map V, D2, **31**): calle L, between 25 and 23 (la Rampa). ☎ 30-40-11. Fax:

HAVANA

33-31-41. Email:hotel@rllibre.com. cu. Right in the heart of Vedado, this former Hilton hotel is now owned by a Spanish chain. However, it remains as much a (package) tourist factory as ever. The accommodation and facilities include 500 rooms, five bars, three restaurants, cabaret, disco, various boutiques, a post office and information bureau. The hotel also carries most foreign newspapers. The rooms are decorated in shades of pale blue and come with serious air-conditioning and a view over the whole of Vedado, central and old Havana. It's very expensive, at $130–160 for a double room.

â **Hotel Nacional** (map V, D1, **32**): calle O, corner of 21. ☎ 33-35-64. Fax: 33-50-54. Ideally located 200 metres from the Malecón, Vedado's other legendary hotel is probably the most widely photographed; with its line of palm trees and its twin towers, it looks like a public building or a presidential palace. In front, two enormous Krupp cannon face the sea. They date from the beginning of the 20th century and used to defend the bay. It is hardly surprising that many celebrities have stayed here – from Winston Churchill to Josephine Baker, Errol Flynn and Ava Gardner. There are still some old photos of these illustrious guests on the walls of the bar Visto al Golfo, including one of the Mafia leader Meyer Lansky (with his gigantic bodyguard), who ran the casinos in Batista's era (see 'History'). In the 1950s, there was even a casino where Frank Sinatra used to sing. With nearly 450 rooms, the Nacional is immense and caters to every need, with restaurants, bars, cabaret, bureau de change, car hire, tennis and a superb swimming pool. It's great, if you can afford the $140–165 for a double room with breakfast. The pool is open to the public for a hefty entrance charge of $15; but, after all, there's no beach in Havana.

â **Hotel Riviera** (map V, B1–2, **33**): Paseo and Malecón. ☎ 33-40-51. Fax: 33-37-39. With double rooms at about $110 a night, this huge American-style, typically 1950s hotel is included here mainly out of interest. It's now run by the Gran Caribe chain and retains an old-fashioned charm and air of glitzy razzmatazz characteristic of a mythical era – such as rooms painted lurid green. There's a magnificent swimming pool with diving board, where Ginger Rogers, Esther Williams and other celebrities have enjoyed a dip.

Nuevo Vedado

This is a mainly residential area to the south of Vedado and therefore quite some distance from the main centres of interest.

â **Sra Maria Elena Hernandez** (map II, A3, **21**): 130 calle 35, between 41 and 43. ☎ 81-05-03. Four rooms are available to let at $25 for two people, which is dirt cheap for a place of this standard. This exceptional address, admittedly fairly ordinary from the outside, is originally laid out inside to create numerous open spaces. The colour scheme is equally original, with pastel blue, pink, pale violet and peachy tones. The rooms are magnificent – light, spacious and each with air-conditioning and private bathroom with hot water. The welcome is discreet, the service efficient and the pool in the garden is surrounded by inviting deckchairs. However, it is far from town, so private transport is essential (otherwise, allow for cab fares).

♠ **Chez Micheline Marie** (map II, A3, **20**): avenida del Bosque 58, between calle Nueva and avenida Zoológico. ☎ 81-08-81. Take bus No. 27 from Old Havana, or it's 30 minutes' walk from the centre of Vedado and 5 minutes from the Viazul Terminal. As you leave the terminal, take the road uphill on the right. Go past Pablo Milanes's house (ask) and this place is the second on the right going downhill. The charm-ing, French-born Micheline has lived in Cuba since 1956. Totally bilingual, she works as a translator, and often used to accompany Castro on tour. She has followed the history of the country very closely, and can talk about it fascinatingly at length. The light and pleasant studio apartment for less than $30 has a bedroom, lounge area, bathroom (cold water only) and kitchenette. Advance booking is essential.

Miramar

This is not an ideal area for backpackers, but there are a couple of surprising places to suit most pockets. It's great if you want to escape the hustle and bustle of town, but a car is absolutely essential.

Casas Particulares

♠ **Arelis Sera** (map VI, A2, **20**): 118 (bajos), calle 30, between 1 and 3. ☎ 22-94-02 or 23-31-24. There's not a great deal to say about this except that it's a bit pricey – $35 for a large double room with a separate entrance – so be prepared to bargain. And you definitely need private transport.

♠ **Frank de Armas** (map VI, off A2, **21**): 37 Calle 3, between A and B, Playa. ☎ 29-52-97. This former civil servant lets out several whole houses, all ideally located in the green and pleasant areas of Mira-mar and Siboney. Prices vary, so be prepared to bargain, although prices are not as high as they might appear at first. Some houses have a pool, and most of the guests are Amer-ican executives.

Hotels

♠ **Hotel Mirazul** (map VI, A2, **23**): 3603 avenida 5, between 36 and 40, Playa. ☎ 24-00-45 or 24-00-88. This house with a tiled roof used to belong to the proprietor of Partagas, the cigar manufacturers, and is now a rather unusual hotel. All the rooms are individual and well decorated, with air-conditioning, cable TV and other mod cons. Prices are $60 for a double and $70 for the Partagas suite. There's a sauna and solarium on the top-floor terrace, an international restaurant in the former reception rooms and a self-service restaurant in a central courtyard with a fountain. Service is absolutely charming.

♠ **Hotel El Bosque** (map VI, B2, **24**): calle 28A, between 49A and 49C, Kholy, Playa. ☎ 24-92-32 to 35. Fax: 24-56-37. Surrounded by greenery and away from the traffic, this is popular with rich Cubans attracted by its spacious rooms in warm colours (each with small bal-cony) and good facilities, including swimming pool. It's $74 for a double room. There's also a decent disco.

♠ **Château Miramar** (map VI, off A2, **25**): calle 1, between 60 and 70. ☎ 24-19-51 to 57. Fax: 24-02-24. Email: reservas@chateau.cha.cyt.cu. Despite every effort to make it look like a real château, this is really just a modern building. Nevertheless, it has all the advantages of a luxury hotel facing the sea. (Less attractive is the feverish construction work on all sides.) It has a superb lobby with a terrapin pool. Service is cheerful and the very comfortable rooms have all amenities, including balcony. However, the price is $130 for a double room. It's very popular with businessmen drawn by the famous *torcedor* (cigar roller) in the cigar shop.

In the Area

♨ **Villa Cocomar**: kilometre 23, Carretera Panamericana, Caimito. ☎ 53-680 Fax: 33-01-84. Located 15 kilometres (9 miles) west of Mirama on Salado beach going towards Mariel, these bungalows are quite a long way out but worth it for the price (around $30 for two) if you have a car. This is perfect for peace and quiet and the chance of a swim, but the beach does get quite busy. The bungalows, arranged around a large swimming pool, have good facilities: private bath, air-conditioning, cable TV, minibar and telephone. 'Standard' rooms are the cheapest. Activities on offer here include canoeing, cycling, table tennis, sailing and pedaloes. Excellent welcome.

WHERE TO EAT

See the colour maps of Havana in the centre of the guide.

There are more than 400 *paladares* (private restaurants) in Havana, especially in Vedado. By law they're not allowed to serve more than 12 guests, which means that very few make a profit, particularly since they have to provide the authorities with bills for supplies in dollars only. The result is that many businesses are short-lived (*see* 'Practicalities: Restaurants and Paladares').

– At lunchtime, more or less everywhere on the island, Cuban workers with no canteen buy pizzas and sandwiches from armies of little stalls where a handful of Cuban pesos will buy quite enough to eat.

Habana Vieja

☆ Budget

– **Calle Obispo**: stalls selling pizzas with ham and cheese abound. They are very good value and you can pay in Cuban pesos.

✕ **El Rincón de Elegguá** (map III, A2, **30**): 257 Aguacate, between Obispo and Obrapía. Open daily until 11pm. The food is pretty good, the setting simple and unpretentious (small first-floor dining room), but soaring prices have made this *paladare* less attractive than it was. However, it's worth a mention because of the friendly family owners.

✕ **Isaman** (map III, B2, **31**): avenida del Puerto, opposite the castillo de la Fuerza. Open daily 24 hours. Just a few seats outside, under a straw canopy, this serves the cheapest fried chicken in the area and a selection of sandwiches. Eat in or takeaway.

✕ **Hanoï** (map III, A2–3, **32**): Brasil and Bernaza (further on from the Capitolio). Open daily noon–11pm. Dine at wooden tables and benches in a small courtyard in a pretty and unusual 18th-century residence. Its small, minimalist rooms are well ventilated and have a nice atmosphere and lots of charm. Undoubtedly the cheapest restaurant in the area, serving a limited selection of good quality, simple, traditional Creole cooking. Not to be missed.

✕ **Café Taberna** (map III, B2, **33**): calle Teniente Rey, on the corner of Mercaderes. ☎ 61-16-37. In this huge, airy, neo-colonial style dining room you can sit and listen to music all day, particularly *son*. You can enjoy a *mojito* and, at around $4–6, the good chicken and *bistec* (steak) dishes won't break the bank.

☆☆ Moderate

✕ **La Paella** (map III, B2, **17**): 53 calle Oficios, corner of Obrapia. ☎ 57-10-37. Open daily noon–11.30pm. Located on the ground floor of the Hostal Valencia (*see* 'Where to Stay'), this Hispanic-style restaurant serves a wide range of delicious paellas (as good as any you might find in Spain) at $6–12. The *sopa de cebolla* and the *gazpacho* is also worth a try. Crisp white tablecloths and napkins, fresh flowers on every table, and professional, courteous service.

✕ **Velta Abajo** (map III, B2, **19**): Hostal Conde de Villanueva, 202 calle Mercaderes, corner of Lamparilla. Open daily lunch and dinner. This restaurant in the hotel vaults may be a bit too formal and neat for some, but actually it's pretty classy with a good track record. It serves a wide choice of dishes from $5 to $15, but the more expensive dishes are better value – nothing revolutionary but good, traditional cooking with a touch of imagination, such as expertly prepared *filete de pescado grille en salsa de almendera*. The *paella de la casa* is also pretty good.

✕ **La Bodeguita del Medio** (map III, B2, **34**): 207 Empedrado. ☎ 57-13-74. Open daily noon–midnight. This legendary place has been in business since 1942 and is not to be missed. Along with the Floridita, it's the best-known restaurant in Cuba and is often packed. Until

recently it was an old, crowded tavern – noisy, cheerful and lively – with a bar at the front and lots of little rooms at the back. Today it's not so much crowded as overrun with tourists. The interior is covered with graffiti, posters, photos, banners, drawings and trophies all muddled together with poems, the Corsican flag, Cuban artists' portraits, newspaper cuttings and old advertisements. Its celebrity patrons have included Errol Flynn, Nat King Cole, Brigitte Bardot and Chilean president Salvador Allende, García Márquez, Perez Prado and Beny Moré, Alejo Carpentier and Pablo Neruda. But it was Hemingway who adopted the Bodeguita as his local. The musicians try to drown out the cacophony with their eternal Cuban refrains. The food is good too, with the best Cuban *criollo* (Creole) specialities on the island. Dishes cost $7–11 and lots of nibbles for about $3. Service is fast and Visa cards are accepted (with a passport).

✕ **La Torre de Marfil** (map III, B2, **35**): calle Mercaderes, between Obispo and Obrapía. ☎ 62-34-66. Open daily noon–11pm. One of the few Chinese restaurants in Havana, this reliable, friendly place serves a wide range of Cantonese style chicken and pork dishes from $5 (double for seafood dishes). There's a Buddha in the window, a revolving table beneath a red pavilion, tables on the street and a small indoor garden.

✕ **XII Apostoles** (map III, A1, **36**): Parque Histórico Morro-Cabaña. ☎ 63-82-95. This is at the foot of Castillo del Morro, opposite the Old Town. Drive through the tunnel towards Playa del Este, then turn left after the motorway toll booth. More intimate and cheaper than its neighbour La Divina Pastora (*see below*), the Apostoles serves good Creole cooking in a spectacular setting, with dishes at $6–11. The terrace

HAVANA

just above the restaurant is particularly striking and perfect after a visit to the fortresses.

✕ **La Mina** (map III, B2, **37**): calle Obispo, between Mercaderes and Oficios. ☎ 62-02-16. Open daily noon–midnight. Overlooking Plaza de Armas, the restaurant's attractive terrace is surpassed by the shady, intimate patio complete with strutting peacock, well and climbing vine. Its traditional Cuban dishes aren't too bad at all and the service is courteous even if the touristy side of things is a bit irritating. But you can be sure of some soothing music to aid the digestion.

✕ **El Patio** (map III, B2, **38**): 54 Plaza de la Catedral. ☎ 57-10-35. Open daily noon–11pm. Ideally located, this large, colonial house is always packed and is a great place at any time. There's a beautiful courtyard, fountain, galleries on several levels, parrot cages, a wonderful bar under the arcades and a terrace facing the magnificent cathedral. It has starters at $9–14 and a complete *cena cubana* set meal at $16, or you could just have a coffee on the terrace while listening to one excellent band after another. There's such a great atmosphere that the waiters even dance with the customers sometimes. (*See also* 'Where to Have a Drink'.)

✕ **Don Giovanni** (map III, B2, **39**): 4 Tacón, corner of Empedrado. ☎ 33-59-79. Open daily until 11pm. Another beautiful Spanish-style residence with terrace and courtyard, the Don Giovanni in question was a military strategist who masterminded Havana's defences in the 16th century. The large and quite classy, but old-fashioned, dining room on the first floor is lit by a heavy bronze chandelier. The service is friendly if a bit stiff and catering-college-style, rather like the food: dependable Italian cooking but nothing more – decent pasta,

fairly meagre lasagne, good pizzas for $7–12 and a set meal for about $15.

✕ **Al Medina** (map III, B2, **40**): Casa de Los Arabes, calle Oficios, between Obispo and Obrapía. ☎ 57-10-41. Open daily noon–11pm. The restaurant of the Cuban Arabic Cultural Centre serves dishes of plainly Arab inspiration and others of more humble Cuban origin. The *combinación mezze* meal is not bad at about $8 and the traditional dishes at $6–12 are quite reasonable. Meals are served in the shady, peaceful courtyard with occasional musical performances – a rarity in Cuba. This is a nice place to relax, even if the food is a bit disorientating.

☆☆☆ Expensive

✕ **Divina Pastora** (map III, A1, **41**): Parque Histórico Morro-Cabaña. ☎ 60-83-41. Open daily 12.30–11pm. This classy restaurant probably has the most enviable location in the whole of Havana, on the bay watched over by numerous cannon from the fortress. It's housed in a long building with a pleasant covered terrace and specializes in well-prepared fish and lobster. Few dishes cost less than $15 and most cost more than $20, with the lobster – fished straight out of the tank – really extortionate. If you can't afford to eat here, have a drink in the El Mirador bar next door.

✕ **El Floridita** (map III, A2, **50**): This very high-class place is the best restaurant in town and famous for its seafood. The superb menu is very enticing but the prices are really over the top and the service, although extremely gracious, is so stiff and formal that it makes you feel quite uncomfortable. You could always just have a drink (a daiquiri, naturally), *see* 'Where to Have a Drink'.

Centro Habana

☆ Budget

✕ **Seeman** (map IV, A–B2, **30**): 306 Zanja, between Lealtad and Escobar. ☎ 78-64-84. Open daily noon–midnight. You'll find this at the end of a little alley, above a huge picture commemorating the People's Republic of China, the only sign that you're in the Chinese quarter. There's one air-conditioned room and one with a bar. Don't be put off by the decor (fancy blue mirrors and marble everywhere). This restaurant serves generous portions for next to nothing, and is the only place open to both Cubans and tourists with lobster that everyone can afford – $5 for grilled lobster in a sauce or '*al ajillo*'. Recommended, even if the service is a bit stiff.

✕ **Restaurant Bellomar** (map IV, B1, **31**): 169A Virtudes, between Industria and Amistad. Open daily noon to about 10.30pm. Three blocks from Paseo Martí is this small *paladar* with a bright pink facade, a few tables, flowers, red curtains and a wall covered in graffiti like La Bodeguita del Medio (*see above*). Expect to pay $10 for a complete meal.

✕ **Lung Kong** (map IV, B2, **33**): 364 calle Dragones, between Manrique and San Nicolas. ☎ 62-53-88. Open daily noon–midnight. The restaurant is up the narrow stairs on the first floor. Despite the rather gloomy dining room and an atmosphere more Chinese than Cuban (that is, not very lively) the food offers excellent value for money and includes probably the cheapest (and most delicious) lobster in Havana. The prices are unbelievable, with *Pollo Lung Kong* for less than $2 and grilled lobster tail for just $3.

☆☆☆ Expensive

✕ **La Guarida** (map IV, A1, **32**): 418 calle Concordia, between Gervasio and Escobar. ☎ 62-49-40. Open Monday to Friday noon–midnight. Saturday and Sunday 7pm–midnight. The first floor of this sumptuous, mysterious but shabby old bourgeois building, typical of the style of the town, has been turned into a *paladar*. Some of the most moving scenes from the film *Fresa y Chocolate* (Strawberry and Chocolate) were shot here, and some items from the shoot remain, such as the blue fridge, the Chinese robe and the little corner altar. During the Spanish–American summit in Havana, the owner received a call telling him to expect an important guest. A few minutes later he opened the door and found himself face to face with the Queen of Spain. Presumably it was this momentous occasion that entitled La Guarida to serve more than 12 people and charge rather more for its food. Expect to pay at least $20 for a complete meal. However, despite the rise in prices the food is delicious and well prepared according to traditional recipes. The *cherna compuesta a lo caimanero* (braised back of red snapper) is excellent, served with the traditional *buñuelos, malanga* and *yuca con mojo*. The jazzy atmosphere seems a bit incongruous, however. Booking is strongly recommended.

Vedado

☆ Budget

It's wise to steer clear of the cafeterias in the area except for those listed below.

✕ **Le Kakatua** (map V, A3, **25**): 1211 calle 15, between 18 and 20. ☎ 31-10-82. Open Monday–Saturday 11am–11pm. This competitively priced place has dishes at $5–7 and facilities you wouldn't expect of a *paladar*. Very professional service, young, friendly atmosphere, attractive setting with bamboo walls and green plants everywhere. It serves good local food, especially the *pierna de cerdo asado*.

✕ **Juana la Cubana** (map V, B3, **40**): apartment 7, 961 calle 17, between 8 and 10. ☎ 31-11-65. Expect to pay about $3 per person. This *paladar* is unsigned, but just ask anyone. You order your meal in advance (fried chicken, *bistec de cerdo*) and wait patiently, chatting with fellow guests or passers-by.

✕ **El Racauto** (map V, B3, **41**): calle 17, between 8 and 10. ☎ 70-50-47. Closed Wednesday. This is on the first floor, up the stairway on the right at the end of the hallway, behind a barred door. The motto here is '*la boca se sobra, el bolsillo no se queja*' ('good food at prices you can't grumble about'). Generous Cuban, Chinese and Italian meals (at around $2–3) are served on the terrace overlooking the rooftops. The chicken and pork are particularly good and prepared in a variety of ways. Very friendly family welcome.

✕ **El Hueco de 23** (map V, A3, **42**): 1414 calle 23, between 20 and 22. ☎ 30-07-52. Open noon–10.30pm. You'll find a small, covered terrace at the end of a long passageway. All dishes here are served with rice and salad ($2–6); and the service is rather sullen.

✕ **El Farallón** (map V, A3, **43**): 361 calle 22, between 21 and 23. Next door to El Hueco de 23, at the end of a cul-de-sac and alongside the Cristóbal Colón cemetery, this small, quiet pizzeria with covered terrace serves good pizzas for less than $3.

✕ **Pizzeria Decamerón** (map V, B2, **44**): 753 Linea, between Paseo and calle 2. ☎ 32-24-44. Open Wednesday to Sunday noon–10pm. Expect to pay less than $5 per person at this small *paladar* that has such a reputation that it could easily be mistaken for a real restaurant. The meat dishes are a bit expensive but the pizzas are very good value.

✕ **Casa de la Amistad** (map V, B2, **48**): 406 Paseo, between 17 and 19. ☎ 30-31-14. With prices at less than $5 per person, this state-run cafeteria is a good place for a beer and a pizza or a sandwich – but nothing more. Be prepared for slow service.

✕ **Villa Babi** (map V, B3, **50**): 965 calle 27, between 6 and 8 (up the stairs on the left). Individual dishes $6–10. Despite the graffiti on the walls in the manner of La Bodegita del Medio (*see above*), this little place is not bad at all and takes a lot of trouble with its food. For Cuban cinema buffs, the owner is an actress and an ex-wife of one of the directors of *Fresa y Chocolate* (*see* 'Background: Films').

♦ **Coppelia** (map V, D2, **60**): corner of L and 23. Open Tuesday to Sunday 11am–11pm. This gigantic 'flying saucer in the park' was restored in 1998 and is the favourite meeting place of young *Habaneros* who think nothing of queuing for a *copa* for several hours. On Sunday, queuing is practically an end in itself. With nearly 40 different flavours, this is one of the best ice-cream parlours on the island, particularly since you can still pay in Cuban pesos, but don't expect to pay the same as the Cubans. The tourist price ranges from $2 to $6.

✕ **Pain de Paris** (map V, D2, **130**): 160 calle 25, between O and Humbolt. Open until 8pm. As the name suggests, this is a French-style *boulangerie* specializing in baguettes and eclair-type pâtisseries – not something you see every day in Cuba. There's another branch at calle 41 esquina 26, next to the Viazul bus station in Nuevo Vedado (map II, A3, **130**).

☆☆ Moderate

✕ **Huron Azul** (map V, D1, **45**): 53 Humboldt, esquina P. ☎ 79-16-91. Despite its prices – at $5–10 per person – this place is not bad at all.

✕ **El Gringo Viejo** (map V, C2, **46**): 454 calle 21, between E and F. ☎ 32-61-50. Expect to pay $5–10. Open Monday to Saturday 1–11pm. This little restaurant is tucked out of sight down a garage approach ramp. Ring the doorbell for entrance to a small, wood-panelled dining room covered in photographs, reminiscent of a sea captain's cabin. It's run by an affable, bearded owner and his family, who offer a warm welcome and efficient service. The

food is traditional (chicken, pork) and also includes certain red-shelled crustaceans. You can pay in pesos or dollars, but the price is the same in either currency. Booking is recommended.

✕ **Paladar Amor** (map V, C2, **47**): 759 calle 23, between B and C ☎ 38-150. Unlike so many *paladares* that have turned their houses into anonymous-looking restaurant dining rooms, this magnificent apartment looks as gorgeous as ever, with its silver displayed in cabinets and on tables, grandiose statues, cosy lounge and small, Arab-style fountain. The food is equally stylish and includes an elegant fish selection (which makes a change in Havana). Meals cost about $10–13. With very friendly service as well, this is the perfect place for a romantic dinner.

✕ **Restaurant-Bar 1830** (map V, A2, **49**): 1252 Malecón, on the corner of 22. ☎ 55-30-90. Open daily noon–midnight. Located just after the fortress of la Chorrera, heading towards Miramar, this luxurious, palatial seaside residence has seven particularly elegant dining rooms serving international cuisine at very reasonable prices (less than $15). The service is charming, but this is best known for its huge ornamental garden with little Japanese island – a delightful place to enjoy a walk in the fresh air after a drink or a good meal.

Miramar

✕ **Paladar 'La Cocina de Lilliam'** (map VI, A2, **40**): 1311 calle 48, between 13 and 15. No telephone. Open noon–4pm, 7–11pm. This magnificent house in a remote, quiet area is the ideal place to enjoy the cool of the evening on the terrace sipping a glass of Cuban

rum or Spanish wine. The food is well prepared and served in generous portions; expect to pay $10–15. This is a favourite haunt of embassy personnel who live around here, so it's best to book (in person).

✕ **El Aljibe** (map VI, A2, **41**): avenida 7, between 24 and 26. ☎ 24-

15-84. Open daily noon–midnight. Set in an enormous room under a canopy of palm trees, this is a real gem that belies everything you hear about official restaurants. Here you'll find probably the best Creole cooking in Havana, together with very fast and efficient service. The house speciality, *pollo criollo*, is the best anywhere in Cuba. It's served any way you like – with rice, black beans, salad or even fried bananas – offering a full meal at a reasonable price (around $15 per person). For a really good evening, come and eat here after seeing the show at La Maison (*see* 'Nightlife').

✕ **La Cecilia** (map VI, off A2, **42**): 11010 avenida 5, between 110 and 112. ☎ 224-15-61 or 22-67-00. This is another well-known spot in Miramar that even features in songs by Charangua Habanera (*see* 'Background: Music and Dance'). There is an enormous tropical garden full of parrots, and a patio where you can sit and have a drink at night as you listen to music. The buffet from $15 offers an astonishing range of local dishes: chicken, beef, maize, rice, banana fritters, etc. More original, but also more expensive, is the à la carte menu (chicken and fish from $16). Visa accepted.

WHERE TO HAVE A DRINK

Habana Vieja

Old Havana is full of music bars where, depending on who's playing, people either get up and dance or just groove to the music as they sip their *mojito*. If you're only in town for one or two nights then it's probably better to check out the places listed below rather than go to some famous cabaret that costs a fortune or to one of the more 'traditional' nightclubs. Legendary places such as La Bodeguita del Medio or the Floridita simply ooze music from every pore. The atmosphere is intoxicating and the people irresistible, including young Cubans who take you by the arm and delight in showing you other places.

– One relatively inexpensive way of enjoying the city's former palaces is just to have a drink. Try the courtyard of the Sevilla or the lobby of the Hotel Inglaterra, which serves better *mojitos* than the Bodeguita del Medio, at almost a third of the price (*see* 'Where to Stay').

♟ **La Bodeguita del Medio** (map III, B2, **34**): 207 Empedrado. ☎ 57-13-74. Open daily noon–midnight. This legendary bar is where you'll find the best *mojito* in town ($4) – the most refreshing cocktail there is. Take a tip from Hemingway, who wrote on the wall: 'My *mojito* in the Bodeguita, my daiquiri in the Floridita.'

♟ **El Patio** (map III, B2, **38**): 54 Plaza de la Catedral. ☎ 57-10-35. Open daily noon–11pm. Have a drink under the arcades or on the pleasant terrace from where you can admire the cathedral, especially in the evening when the square is empty and the music echoes through the arcades. *See* 'Where to Eat'.

♟ **El Floridita** (map III, A2, **50**): 557 Obispo, corner of Monserrate (avenida Belgica). ☎ 57-13-00. Open daily 11.30am–midnight. This other Cuban institution is where, in 1817, Havana's high society ladies came to sample the ice-cream, and it gained its name at the end of the 19th century. In 1914, a Catalan called Constante became a cocktail waiter here and invented the now-famous, refreshing daiquiri – lime juice, rum, sugar, a hint of maraschino and lots of crushed ice. In the 1930s, Hemingway became Constante's best customer, his friend and his biggest publicist, drawing many Hollywood stars in his wake, including Marlene Dietrich, Ava Gardner, Gary Cooper, Spencer Tracy, Errol Flynn and Robert Taylor. He also invented his own, somewhat stronger, cocktail – the Hemingway Special (or simply 'Papa') – a daiquiri without sugar but enhanced with double the rum and a dash of grapefuit juice to sharpen it up. In 1943, the magazine *Esquire* listed the Floridita as one of the seven best bars in the world, and it has lost none of its cachet; the decor hasn't changed either (except that Hemingway's stool is now chained to the floor). However, the atmosphere has become rather stiff, the guests loaded and not always very pleasant and the waiters (still with bow tie and red waistcoat) perfectly unpalatable. The daiquiri, however, continues to steal the show and is available in six different varieties, at $6 a shot. You can also eat here but prices are rising all the time (*see* 'Where to Eat').

Café París (map III, B2, **51**): Obispo and San Ignacio. Open daily 24 hours. Despite its name, there's nothing remotely Parisian about this rather ordinary looking place with fans and ancient bar. But it's popular with all sorts of people and gets busy even in mid-afternoon. But it's best at night when all the customers, tourists and Cubans alike, go wild to the music. Beers and Coke are quite good value, the *mojitos* are nearly half the price of the Bodeguita del Medio's and you can also get a slice of pizza if you're feeling peckish.

Café O'Reilly (map III, B2, **52**): 203 O'Reilly. Open daily, 9am–1am. This is an old café with an ancient facade and a spiral staircase leading to a room on the first floor. There, on the little balcony overlooking the street, you can sit and have a drink as you listen to a small group of musicians who play requests.

Lluvia de Oro (map III, A2, **53**): calle Obispo, corner of Habana. No tour of Havana nightlife would be complete without a visit to this huge bar whose very walls seem to rock to salsa. There are tables outside and lots of tourists and Cubans.

Castillo de Farnés (map III, A2, **54**): calle Monserrate, on the corner of Obrapía. ☎ 57-10-30. Open daily 24 hours. Not as grand as its name suggests, this consists of a rather old-fashioned, working-class bar with tables outside and a little restaurant at the back. Nothing very special, but this was once a favourite haunt of a certain student called Castro. On 9 January 1959, the day he liberated Havana, he came back here with Che Guevara. After four years of guerrilla warfare, the first place he honoured with his presence in the capital was where he used to eat as a student. At 4am, he woke up the cook and together they enjoyed a peaceful meal and savoured the taste of victory. You'd expect the Spanish-style food here to be something special but it isn't, unlike the prices which are very high. Give the food a miss and settle for a *mojito* at the bar.

Mirador (map III, B1, **55**): behind the restaurant Divina Pastora (*see* 'Where to Eat'). Open until midnight. This is definitely the best located bar in Havana thanks to the wonderful view from the terrace that slightly overhangs the Bay of Havana, with its cannon and the Old Town directly opposite. Drinks are a bit pricey but the setting is more than worth it. The best time is at sunset when the sea and the fortress stand out against the light. It does get a bit quiet in the evening however.

HAVANA

Vedado

❦ **Casa de la Amistad** (map V, B2, **48**): 406 Paseo, between 17 and 19. ☎ 30-31-14. Admission $5 when groups are playing. This fine old colonial house, with charming colonnaded terrace at the back on the garden side, has become very fashionable and functions both as a bar and twice-weekly music club. Tuesday is usually an evening of traditional *son* music inspired by Compay Segundo who occasionally pops in for a drink with his wife (*see* 'Background: Music and Dance'). Saturday is *fiesta cubana* night from 10pm to 2am.

❦ **Café La Fuente** (map V, C2, **62**): calle 13, between F and G. Open daily until 11pm. At the foot of a beautiful colonial palace (Institute of Tropical Geography), a large shady enclosure shelters this pleasant café around a pond that's home to a solitary turtle. It's a good place to

enjoy a late-afternoon drink, with few tourists and lots of Cubans.

❦ **La Torre** (map V, C–D1, **61**): Focsa building, calle 17 and M. ☎ 32-56-50. Open daily 10.30am–2am. Take the lift, press button 3 and get out on the 34th floor, where you'll find a nondescript, dusty panoramic bar/restaurant with nothing to recommend it except the spectacular view of the Hotel Nacional, the Capitolio and the Old Town, often featured in magazines. On the right of the bar an army observation post keeps a watchful eye on the horizon and the area round the Florida coast.

❦ **Colonial Bar** (map V, A2, **49**): 1252 Malecón, corner of calle 20. Open daily noon–4am. ☎ 345-04. Restaurant 1830's elegant bar has stained-glass windows and creates its own cocktails, which can also be enjoyed in the beautiful gardens (*see* 'Where to Eat').

NIGHTLIFE

Night-time in Havana is not for sleeping. With its Spanish and African roots, when the sun goes down the city starts to party. This is when you can really get a feel for the place and understand what it means to be Cuban. So have a siesta in the afternoon, then dose yourself up with vitamins, coffee, rum – anything to keep you awake – but don't miss the wealth of festivals and concerts, great shows and the seemingly endless stream of fantastic music of every description.

Nightlife in Havana is too spontaneous to categorize easily. Venues can change atmosphere according to the time of day – from a *peña* in the afternoon, to a salsa place in the evening and later a disco. A bar can suddenly turn into a dance hall just because the customers get the urge. People always dance at concerts too. Some places are too expensive for the locals, so music bars are the best bet for meeting young Cubans because they're free and, with any luck, someone will buy them a drink. Just make sure you pick a place that does what you want when you want, and you can have a great time anywhere.

In addition to **concerts** and **cabarets** there are *peñas* – improvised parties typical of Havana – which can happen anywhere, anytime, in apartments or simply on the street. However, some *peñas* have regular venues, so try to catch one while in town because these are no ordinary parties. They are moments of great charm and sharing, conviviality and sensuality but, above all, *peñas* are what you make of them. Bring a bottle of rum and the locals take care of the music.

❢ **Peña of the National Union of Cuban Writers and Artists** (UNEAC; map V, C2, **15**): corner of calle 17 and H, Vedado. The UNEAC holds some great *peñas* every Wednesday 5–8pm (*see* 'Cultural Activities').

❢ **Peña de la Rumba** (map V, D2): callejón de Hamel, between Aramburu and the hospital. This Sunday morning *peña* in the heart of Havana, with its festive, villagey atmosphere, is not to be missed.

❢ **Discos**: You'll find most of the nightclubs either in Miramar or Ve-dado, especially around la Rampa. Young women who can't afford the entry fee often hang around the door waiting to be invited in by any man on his own. There are also discos in all the major hotels, often with live bands. If you have a car, there are lots more discos, including the famous Finca on playas del Este. In addition to the places listed below, there are many other semi-improvised, semi-official discos all over Havana. Just ask any young Cuban for a recommendation.

Vedado

❢ **Pico Blanco** (Rincón del Feeling; map V, D1–2, **30**): Hotel St John's, calle O, between Humboldt y 23 (*see* 'Where to Stay'). This rather small and exclusive rooftop piano bar-type place is popular with actors, TV people, Cuban artists and the occasional tourist. There are often some very good bands, but most of the performers are singing comedians who specialize in a kind of comedy that goes down well in Havana but is completely lost on anyone who doesn't speak Spanish. But it's a lovely dance venue, with the town lights gleaming through the huge bay windows.

❢ **El Turquino** (map V, D2, **31**): Habana Libre Tryp Hotel, calle L, between 25 and 23 (*see* 'Where to Stay'). Open nightly. Admission by passport. On the top floor with a lovely view over Havana, this is one of the most select tourist discos in town.

❢ **El Parisien** (map V, D1, **32**): Hotel Nacional, calle O, corner of 21 (*see* 'Where to Stay'). ☎ 33-35-64 Closed Thursday. Admission $30. Shows from 10 to about 11.30pm; closing time 3am. This offers a big, fantastic Caribbean show in a luxurious setting, formerly a casino that rivalled the Tropicana in the 1950s where Frank Sinatra (among others) used to sing (*see below*). After the performance there's usually a comedy or music act and then a disco.

❢ **Café de la Amistad** (map V, B2, **48**): 406 Paseo, between 17 and 19. Saturday night is concert time here (*see* 'Where to Eat').

❢ **Jardines de 1830** (map V, A2, **49**): Open daily 10pm–4am. The nightclub of the Restaurant-Bar 1830 (*see* 'Where to Eat') features little shows on the open-air dance floor every evening, and also dance demonstrations sometimes. There's Cuban and European music and live groups as well as a disco.

❢ **Tropicana** (map II, off A3, **80**): 4504 calle 72, corner of 45, Marianao. ☎ 27-17-17 or 27-01-10. Nightly cabaret from 10pm, followed at midnight by traditional music and a disco at 1am. Admission is expensive to say the least, at $60 ($45 on Monday). The price includes a bottle of rum (for four people) and a Coke each. Booking is highly recommended, particularly if you want a good seat. Although it's quite a way south of Vedado, there's a shuttle bus and the hotel will have details. This is quite simply the biggest cabaret in the world, partly because it's in the open air – a tropical version of the Paris Lido. Built in 1939, a little old-fashioned and certainly very expensive, it's a monument of its kind. Many big names have played here, from Perez Prado to Nat King Cole. The shows are sumptuous, the dancers superb and the tropical vegetation spectacular. When the weather's fine the whole show takes place in the open air. Hundreds of dancers mill around the bedazzled tourists and the atmosphere quickly becomes incandescent. After a few glasses of rum, take a stroll along to the 'paradise under the stars', as it's known.

❢ **Café Cantante** (map V, C3, **81**): Paseo and 39. ☎ 33-57-13. Open daily 11pm–4am. Also a *peña* Monday to Saturday 4–6pm. Admission $15. Underneath the national theatre, opposite Plaza de la Revolución, this huge dance and concert hall dedicated to salsa has long been the alternative venue for fashionable *Habaneros*. There's a young ambience, with more Cubans and fewer tourists than elsewhere. It attracts some fantastic bands both known and unknown (Los Van Van, Charanga Habanera, etc.) and there's usually a disco after the concert, although everybody dances all the time anyway. Sometimes there's a long queue for entry to this hugely successful place that's often full right until closing time. Despite rather too many *jineteras*, this is still one of the best places in Havana.

❢ **Salón Rojo** (map V, D1, **82**): calle 21, between N and O, next to the Hotel Capri. ☎ 33-47-47. Open 11pm to about 1am. Admission $10 (including unlimited drinks – known as an 'open bar'). The atmosphere here is quite conventional and well behaved (rather too much perhaps), somewhere between light comedy and dance hall, with naff singers and bands. It reminds you of a tea dance – funny and sad at the same time; fine for anyone over 60.

❢ **Mi Conuco** (map V, B1, **84**): Malecón, on the corner of calle E. Open daily from 11pm. Admission $3–5. This consists of a few straw huts along Malecón, where *pepes* (tourists) and Cubans come to dance. Performances depend on the night (groups, comedians, fashion shows) but since it's so central and everything happens outside, you can find out what's on just by looking.

❢ **Habana Café** (map V, B2, **85**): Paseo, between Primera and Tercera. ☎ 33-36-36. Admission $10 (or you pay for a compulsory locker – the price is the same in either case). This place is rather like the Hard Rock Café, with its American cars, Cubana airways plane hanging from the ceiling and walls lined with photos. Most of the guests are youngsters out to make an impression, lots of locals but some tourists too. The main attraction is the Afro-Cuban dance show and salsa concert, which usually starts at around 11pm. The shows are pretty good on the whole even if the atmosphere does feel a bit contrived and touristy.

❢ **La Zorra y el Cuervo** (map V, D1, **90**): 155 calle 23, between N and O. ☎ 66-24-02. Open daily 11pm–3am. Admission $5. This highly respected Latin American jazz club, whose name means 'The Fox and the Crow', is in the middle of Vedado and entered, Dr Who style, via an English telephone box. Go early because it's always crowded and the place is tiny, making it that much easier to appreciate the music of the mainly young bands, which is truly excellent.

❦ **Casa de la Cultura de Plaza** (map V, B2, **91**): 909 calle Calzado, on the corner of Ocho. Setting aside one or two other cultural events, this place is principally interesting to tourists during the International Jazz Festival in January.

❦ **Jazz Café** (map V, B1–2, **92**): esquina 1 and Paseo; on the top floor of a new shopping centre opposite the Melia Cohiba Hotel. ☎ 55-35-54. Performances nightly 11pm–2am. Admission moderate. Apart from the view, with its wall-to-wall marble and ferocious air-conditioning, this place is nothing to write home about. It appeals mainly to Cubans with a few dollars to spend and is not really worth going out of your way for, but go and see for yourself.

❦ **Las Vegas** (map V, D2, **93**): 104 Infanta, between 25 and 27. Admission $5. This disco is one of the last places in the centre of Havana where you still get good salsa bands (although not the best known). It's quite authentic despite its shady reputation.

Miramar

❦ **Casa de la Música** (map VI, B2, **80**): calle 20, between 33 and 35. Open daily 10pm–3am; gigs start at 11.30; also a *peña* at 4–7pm Monday to Saturday. ☎ 24-04-47. Admission $10 or $15 (evening concerts), $10 (*peña*). Despite dreadful acoustics because of the coffered ceiling that deaden the sound, this is where all the best salsa bands play (but often at a price). Drinks are also a bit pricey.

❦ **La Maison** (map VI, B2, **81**): 701 calle 16, corner of avenida 7. ☎ 24-01-26 (bookings). Shows daily at 10pm (except when it rains). Admission $25 or $30. (It may be possible to slip in through the back, via the Piel Canela jazz 'club', as nobody seems to check.) This isn't really a concert hall or even a disco, but a fashionable clothes shop. Regular fashion shows, lasting about 45 minutes and featuring superb models, are held in the garden of this very stylish building. After the show, there's a concert of Cuban music. Actually it's all a bit over the top and reeks of a place for bored ex-pats, but check it out.

❦ **La Tropical** (map VI, B3, **83**): avenida 41 and calle 46, Playa. Admission varies, but around $10. This huge open-air dance hall is some way from town, so take a taxi or make sure you leave your car in the car-park. Officially known as the Salon Dorado Benny Moré, La Tropical is the most popular club in Havana and where most Cubans come to dance, particularly since they can pay in pesos (tourists pay in dollars). Inside there's a big pit for Cubans and a sort of giant mezzanine floor for tourists, where it's best to stay as there are pickpockets in the pit and fights break out all the time. In any case, a huge police presence enforces an apartheid system, with black and mixed-race clubbers on one side and whites on the other. Anyone who steps out of line risks getting whacked with a truncheon. Such niceties apart, this is *the* place to hear all the best groups.

❦ **Havana Club** (map VI, off A2, **100**): calle 86 and 3, next to the hotel Comodoro. ☎ 24-29-02. Open daily 10.30pm–5am. Admission $10. This is one of the most fashionable nightclubs in Havana and has quite a lot going for it, including several bars and an excellent sound system that churns out a kind of dance music that's somewhere between techno and salsa. When it's really busy, the dance floor is quite a sight.

❦ **Casa del Bolero** (map VI, A2, **101**): calle 7 and 26. With its traditional

HAVANA

music and somewhat stiff, old-fashioned manner, this place is highly amusing despite being off the scale in style terms. It feels like a talent contest – make of it what you can.

☛ Papa's (map VI, off A2, **102**): Hemingway Marina. This open-air disco with a tropical atmosphere is not as popular as it used to be.

– One of the coolest places at the moment is the **Rio Club**, which is not listed here because its bouncers are insufferable even by European standards.

WHAT TO SEE

Havana is sadly lacking in signposts, so it's best to take your guide with you if you want to track down the many sites and museums, which have something to suit all tastes. Many of the sights are also subject to long-term restoration programmes, so check details before setting out.

The Old Town (Habana Vieja)

Allow at least two days to see Havana's Old Town, which was placed on the UNESCO World Heritage list in 1982. It is a rare sight, and one of the richest examples of Spanish colonial architecture in the Americas. Its appeal lies in its originality and in its crumbling authenticity, far removed from the neatly renovated, quaint old quarters of most European cities.

There is vibrant and intense activity behind the dilapidated facades and along the bumpy roads of Old Havana. A little exploration will reveal hundreds of unusual and picturesque architectural details, such as original roofs, friezes and window frames, as well as a variety of Spanish colonial architecture, with balconies, wrought-iron grills and awnings reminiscent of Andalucía. It's a feast of faded pastels and aristocratic mansions, adorned with elaborate ironwork on either side of the front door; even if many of the doors are now rotting, the metalwork remains.

The best way to explore the town is to stroll along the cobbled streets, linger in the squares and grandiose courtyards, and savour the languorous charm, the noble decadence of this extraordinary testament to four centuries of colonial architecture. Take the opportunity to visit Old Havana as soon as possible; in the next few years, immaculate restoration is likely to have 'saved' these beautiful buildings from their present decrepit state, and they will have lost much of their appeal. For more details of the restoration, *see* the introduction to 'Havana'.

There are hundreds of palaces still standing in Old Havana but they are not easy to spot beneath the layers of dust. The term *solar* refers to former palatial homes where today dozens of families live in cramped conditions of appalling squalor. You are highly likely to be invited to see round one of these places and, if so, don't hesitate to accept. There is absolutely nothing to fear. The invitation is a sincere one, honest and direct, even if your guide does hope to get a dollar for his pains. In exchange you get a real insight into what it's like for a Cuban living in Havana, how unsanitary these houses are and, in particular, how promiscuous it all is.

This tour begins in Plaza de Armas, the oldest part of town. For details of the fortresses, houses and museums, *see below*.

Around Plaza de Armas

★ **Plaza de Armas** (map III, B2): built in the 16th century, the square is surrounded by prestigious buildings, mostly housing military operations such as the Castillo de la Fuerza. Others house administrative or residential property. They were all rebuilt in 1776 to their original dimensions. In the middle is a large garden with a statue of Carlos Manuel de Céspedes. Every day except Sunday, there are many second-hand book stalls on the square selling a wide range of books on Che Guevara, history, geography and politics.

★ **Palacio de Los Capitanes Generales** (map III, B2, **71**): this palace occupies the whole of the west side of the square, between O'Reilly and Obispo streets. Built in superb late-baroque style in 1776, while the square was being refurbished, it served as both the island's seat of government and as a public prison. It was the presidential palace after the founding of the Republic in 1902 until 1920, then it became the town hall and now houses the Museo de la Ciudad (Museum of the City) (*see* 'Museums'). There is a statue of Christopher Columbus in the beautiful internal courtyard. Note the wooden cobbles in front of the museum were put down to muffle the sound of horses' hooves.

★ **Palacio del Segundo Cabo** (or de l'Intendancia): calle O'Reilly, on the north side of the Plaza. Open Monday–Saturday 10am–5pm. It costs $1 to go up to the first floor, but the view of the elegant courtyard below is free. Built in 1770, this palace later became the headquarters of the post office, home of the royal taxation office, of the treasury and the army and, in 1854, the residence of the governor's deputy. In the 20th century it became the home of the senate. Today it houses a cultural centre, art gallery and two bookshops.

★ **Palacio de Los Condes de Santovenia**: Baratillo and Narciso López on Plaza de Armas. Also dating from the end of the 18th century, this building, which is now a hotel, has a beautiful wrought-iron balcony incorporating the initials of the Count of Santovenia.

Next door, immediately on the left, rises **El Templete**, built in 1828 and the town's first building in the neo-classical style. Open daily 9.30am–6.30pm. Admission $1. It contains three paintings by the French artist Jean-Baptiste Vermay. A column marks the spot where the city was founded with a Mass in the 16th century.

★ **Castillo de la Real Fuerza** (map III, B2): Calle O'Reilly, next to the Plaza de Armas. Open daily 9am–5.30pm. Admission $1. Built in 1588 by King Philip II, this is the oldest fortress in the country, with diamond shaped eaves, a deep moat on all sides and mighty stonework. Until 1762, it was the residence of senior military officers. The tower was added in 1632, topped by the famous *Giraldilla*, the weathercock that symbolizes the town (and appears on the label of Havana Club rum). Today, in the cool of the arcades, the Castillo houses a small, first-class gallery showing the best contemporary ceramics in Cuba. There is a magnificent view from the first-floor terrace, where there is also a shop and (very expensive) bar.

★ Many of Havana's oldest dwellings are found on **calle Obispo**, especially along from the Palacio de los Capitanes Generales (*see above*). Nos. 117 to 119 are the oldest, completely blue and white with tiled roofs and circular windows. No. 113, the **Casa de Obispo** houses a tiny museum. At this level, holes in the road reveal the ancient excavations beneath. As the tourist lifeline of Old Havana, Calle Obispo was the first to be restored, and works are well under way.

★ A little further along, on the corner of Mercaderes, the **Hotel Ambos Mundos** (*see* 'Where to Stay'), is an all-pink, 'modern' construction that integrates surprisingly well with the area. Ernest Hemingway sometimes used to stay here; his room, No. 511, now houses a small museum (open Monday–Saturday 10am–5pm. Admission $2). It is an elegant corner room lit by three windows (with a lovely view of the old town) and contains many souvenirs. There is Hemingway's bed, the Underwood typewriter he used (one of them), a reproduction of the manuscript of *For Whom the Bell Tolls*, display cabinets full of giant fishhooks, a swordfish spear and a few photographs.

★ South of Plaza de Armas, leading from **calle Oficios**, are several points of interest, and the whole area is undergoing a considerable restoration programme.

At No. 8, the former Monte de Piedad contains the **Numismatic Museum** (map III, B2, **78**). It was the residence of the bishops of the town from the 17th century to the first half of the 19th century. Next door is the Casa de los Arabes (*see below*).

Opposite, at No. 13 (corner of Justiz), is a small **Automobile Museum**, and the **Casa de la Comedia** is on the corner of Justiz and Baratillo.

★ On the corner of Mercaderes and Obrapía, the **Casa de la Cultura de Mexico** (centre of Mexican culture) is a beautiful colonial building with a pink courtyard and a small fountain. Almost opposite is the **Casa Guayasamin**, a lovely little colonial palace and the residence of the Ecuadorian painter (*see* 'Casas'). Still on Obrapía, between Mercaderes and San Ignacio, you will find **Casa de África** (map III, B2, **75**), both a cultural centre and a museum.

★ Opposite, at No. 158, is **Casa Obrapía** (open Tuesday–Saturday 10.30am–5.30pm. Sunday 9am–1pm), which has a splendid monumental portal (quite rare in Havana). When it was built, in the first half of the 17th century, this was one of the town's most prestigious residences. It has a charming galleried courtyard.

★ **Plaza de la Catedral**: (map III, B2). Here you'll find the most harmonious and homogenous collection of colonial architecture, including the cathedral, a masterpiece of Jesuit baroque, the museum of colonial art and several other palaces. At night it is enchanting.

★ **The cathedral**: built by the Jesuits in the 18th century, with an elegant, Italianate baroque facade, twin lateral bell-towers and elegant columns, the cathedral is dedicated to San Cristóbal. It is very rarely open; try visiting during Sunday Mass, from 10–11am. Inside, there are three naves and eight chapels. The style is Franco-Italian, with paintings by Jean-Baptiste Vermay and frescoes by Giuseppe Perovani. Christopher Columbus's ashes are supposed to have rested here in the central nave until 1898 when they were repatriated to the cathedral in the Spanish city of Seville.

★ Other monuments in the plaza:

– The **Casa de Lombillo** on the right (facing the cathedral, on the corner of Empedrado), next to the Casa del Marqués de Arcos, was built in 1730 and now houses the museum of education (under restoration).

– The **Casa del Marqués de Arco** is a beautiful arcaded mansion built in 1746 for the king's treasurer, Diego de Peñalver Angulo y Calvo de la Puerta. It is full of beautiful baroque detail. The semicircular (*medio puntos*) windows allow light in while keeping out the heat. Today, it houses the municipal centre for graphic arts and an art gallery on the ground floor.

– The building at the end, the **Palacio de Los Condes de Casa Bayona**, opposite the cathedral, was built in 1720 for the governor. The facade is fairly restrained. At one time rum was made here but now it is a museum of colonial art.

– Finally, to the left of the cathedral (on the corner of San Ignacio and Empedrado), is the **Casa de Los Marqueses de Aguas Claras** (map III, B2, **38**). Built in 1751, it is one of the most elegant *casas* in the area and is now a restaurant with a pretty internal courtyard.

★ On **Empedrado**, just behind the cathedral, is the **Wifredo Lam Centre** (*see* 'Museums'). A little further along you can relax with a few *mojitos* at the famous **Bodeguita del Medio** (*see* 'Where to Eat' or 'Where to Have a Drink').

Near by, you will find the **Casa del Conde de la Réunion**, which has a very beautiful internal staircase and houses the little Alejo Carpentier Museum (*see* 'Museums').

South of the Old Town

★ **Plaza Vieja** (formerly Plaza Nueva; map III, B2–3): this 'old square' is one of the best spots in Old Havana. Less touristy than the other two main squares, and with quite a few beautiful palaces, the plaza is undergoing almost complete restoration. The only disaster so far is to have covered over the central fountain with some very ugly wrought-iron bars. The square was built in the middle of the 16th century as part of the first urbanization programme extending the town, to replace Plaza de Armas, which was purloined by the military. In the 17th and 18th centuries it was a very important square, where the nobles, affluent bourgeoisie and wealthy merchants built their homes. Nowadays, there is something quite moving about its noble decadence, reflected in a feast of porticoes, loggias and ornamental facades. Some of the buildings deserve attention for their fascinatingly picturesque details.

★ Look first at the **Casa de los Condes de Jaruco**, built in 1733, on the corner of Muralla and San Ignacio. Also known as the *Casona*, it is currently used as an art gallery maintained by the Cuban Cultural Foundation. (Open Monday–Friday 10am–5pm. Saturday 10am–2pm. Admission free). Inside is a very beautiful staircase and a splendid galleried courtyard on the first floor. The overall impression is of simple elegance and serenity. Exhibitions and occasional musical soirées are held here.

★ On San Ignacio, between Muralla and Brasil (Teniente Rey), take a look at **Casa del Conde Lombillo** as well (under restoration).

★ To one side, on the corner of Ignacio and Brasil, lies the **Casa de las Hermanas Cardenas**, which dates from the end of the 18th century and has an impressive galleried courtyard. In 1824, it was the home of the Philharmonic Society, the most prestigious musical circle in Havana. Today, it is the Centro de Desarrollo de las Artes. Opposite, on the corner, is the **Antiguo Colegio El Salvador** (old college).

★ On the other side of the square, on Mercaderes 307, between Brasil and Muralla, is the **Casa de Estebán José Portier** (1752), a beautiful, entirely blue, arcaded building. Inside you will find the Photographic Library of Cuba, containing 25,000 photos from before 1920.

★ On the corner of Mercaderes and Muralla is the **Casa de Franchi Alfaro**, which dates from the end of the 18th century. Although these buildings have little historic value, they are still quite interesting. On the corner of Brasil and Mercaderes is an eclectic 19th-century building.

★ On the corner of Muralla and Inquisidor, the former **Hotel Cueto** (Palacio Viena) was built in 1906. It has a distinctly art nouveau feel to it with its wavy balconies, but it's urgently in need of restoration.

★ To the northwest of Plaza Vieja, the late-Renaissance style church of **San Agustín** (calle Cuba and Amargura) dates from 1608, but has been restored, mostly during the first half of the 19th century. The adjoining former convent contains the **Museo Histórico de Ciencias Carlos J. Finlay** (historical science museum).

★ The **church and convent of San Francisco de Asís** (map III, B2) houses the **Museo de Arte Religioso**. Open daily 9am–7pm. Admission $2. It was built at the end of the 16th century on a dried-out creek and rebuilt in 1730 in baroque style. There is a magnificent nave with many religious paintings displayed along the aisle. Despite the heavy square columns, the overall impression is quite elegant. The crypt used to be a burial chamber for the most aristocratic families.

The cloister chapels now house a museum of religious art containing a display of colourful wooden statues, furniture and archaeological finds (ceramics). The rooms upstairs are empty except for a hugely enlarged photograph of Fidel Castro with the Pope (proving that anything is possible)! As you walk through the various rooms, one of them opens onto the church tribune (view of the nave) and the terrace, where there is a magnificent view of the square below. At the far end is another cloister with arcades on three levels (which is quite rare) and a charming central fountain in a green and serene setting.

For a long time, the church's magnificent three-pillared tower was the highest point in Havana. It is open to visitors (admission charge) and affords a truly splendid view of the Old Town. There are also some lovely houses facing the church.

In the square in front of the church the **Fountain of Lions** dates from 1836. To the north of the square (on the corner of Amargura), the **Lonja del Comercio** (Stock Exchange) is an imposing construction built in 1909. Dominated by a dome and the bronze statue of the god Mercury (patron of merchants and flight), it now contains many different high-tech offices. Its restoration was inaugurated by Castro and paid for by Spain.

– There are several fine churches to the south of town, back down San Ignacio, past two interesting houses at Nos. 411 and 414.

★ The imposing yellow mass of the **Santa Clara convent** (map III, B3) dominates the Sol, Habana, Luz and Cuba quadrangle. Built in 1638, this was the first convent to be created in Cuba. Today it contains the National Centre for Restoration, Conservation and Museology, as well as a hotel, and is a UNESCO World Heritage Site. In principle, there is a guided tour during the week (check details).

★ On Cuba and Agosta, the church of **Espíritu Santo** dates from 1674 and is the oldest in the state of Havana. Built in beautiful white stone, it has a very simple triangular pediment and a bell-tower.

★ On Merced and Cuba, the church of **La Merced** dates from 1755. It has a classical facade with columns. The interior gives an impression of vastness, with gilded columns, three naves and a barrel vault, mostly covered in frescoes.

★ The old promenade of Alameda de Palma was much used by the Habaneros in the 18th century. In the middle is a charming baroque church, the **Antigua Iglesia de San Francisco de Paula** of 1730 (undergoing restoration).

★ Near the central station, by the seafront on avenida Pesquera, is the monument to those who died on the steamship *La Coubre* in 1960, which locals claim was sabotaged by the CIA for carrying arms for the budding Cuban Revolution. On avenida de Belgica there are late 17th-century remains of the old town wall (cortina de la Muralla, Puerta de la Terraza).

★ **José Martí's birthplace** (map III, A3, **72**): Leonor Perez and Egido 314. Open Tuesday–Saturday 9am–5pm. Sunday 9am–1pm. It's appropriate that such a hugely important figure in the Cuban liberation movement should have been born in this modest house in a working-class area of Old Havana. The house dates from the beginning of the 19th century. The Martí family rented two small rooms and a minuscule corridor on the first floor; the owner lived on the ground floor. José was born here on 28 January 1853. There is a great deal of memorabilia on display in changing exhibitions, including letters, prison irons, photos taken in exile, cartridge pouches, spurs and flags. There's also José Martí's desk from time spent in New York, his books and various publications, numerous photos, poems (*Versos Sencillos*), the fork he used while travelling through Mexico and a very rare photo of Martí with General Máximo Gómez, taken in New York in 1893. Various personal items add a sentimental touch, such as the lock of hair from the four-year-old José.

★ **La Estación Central de Ferrocarriles** (map III, A3): Egido and Arsenal. This huge, rather graceless edifice, with its two massive square towers, is a monumental railway station typical of those built in the early 19th century throughout the world. It is also very Spanish with its scalloped decorations. Inside is a venerable machine dating from 1843 called 'La Junta' that was the first steam engine ever bought by the Compagnie de Matanzas. The trains leaving this station are the slowest and the longest in this part of the world!

Opposite are remnants of the **cuerpo de guardia de la Puerta Nueva** (guardhouse of the old wall, 1674–1740).

★ The church and convent of **Nuestra Señora de Belén** (map III, A3): Luz and Compostella. Dating from 1712, this baroque-style convent was ceded to the Jesuits in 1848. Today it belongs to the Science Academy. It has a single nave, a beautiful ornate facade and bell-tower, and a porch over a window shaped like a scallop shell, decorated in red and blue. On the left is an entrance to the massive and beautiful cloister (being restored). The arcades will house offices, a theatre and hotel. In front there is a popular and picturesque little market (*mercado campesino*).

– There are many interesting buildings in the area, especially on Luz, where noble facades remain among the squalor and decay. On the first floor, arched windows are decorated with grotesque masks and wonderful carved friezes; one good example is the building on the corner of Agosta and Compostella. The upper floor has an arcade and a long wrought-iron balcony, with carved window frames. Continue along Compostella towards the north. On the corner of Brasil is a picturesque old pharmacy (*farmacia de Sarrá*) and, on the other corner, the church of Santa Teresa and an early 18th-century baroque convent.

★ The church of **Santo Cristo del Buen Viaje** (map III, A2) is located on a pretty little square between Brasil (Teniente Rey), Bernaza and Villegas. Initially, in 1640, there was a hermitage here, then in 1755 the charming little church was built with two hexagonal bell-towers surrounding a large arched portal. Inside it has three naves with Doric arches and an open cupola. There is a small primary school next door on the right.

– On the corner of Teniente Rey are some very old houses, including the 17th-century **Casa de la Parra**, now the Hanoï restaurant.

★ Calle Obispo takes you back to the lively avenida Belgica. Obispo is one of the most picturesque streets in the area, but it is over-commercialized, with bookshops, art galleries and so on. 'Facadism' is much in evidence here – the facades are kept, and new buildings are put up behind them. Naturally, many of the shops are three-quarters empty. Restoration work is under way on many of the buildings in this street.

– On the corner of Obispo and Havana is a large, traditional department store, where the shelves are almost empty. A long, pleasant bar offers *refrescos* (refreshments) at Cuban prices. With its old counter in polished wood, the **Lluvia de Oro** opposite is the venue for some good bands at night (*see* 'Where to Have a Drink').

– Further along, you come to an area that used to be a kind of mini Wall Street in the 1920s and 1930s, with the headquarters of major banks and important financial organizations. As in Paris, London, New York or San Francisco, the overly ornate facades reflected the wealth and prosperity of the time, resulting in a grandiloquent, even pompous style of architecture. On the corner of Obispo and Cuba is the **Commit Estatal de Finanzas**, with its huge Corinthian columns and Greek frontage.

– On the corner of San Ignacio, the **Café de Paris** is the place to rub shoulders with the local wheelers and dealers (*see* 'Where to Have a Drink'). At No. 155 Obispo, the **Farmacia Taquechel** (pharmacy) has an aged mahogany bench and 19th-century bottles. It dates from 1898 and still functions as a herbalist. Open daily 9am–6.30pm. Worth a look.

– On O'Reilly and Cuba, note the opulent, highly sculpted facade of the **Bank of Nova Scotia**, with its glut of pilasters and columns, Corinthian capitals and so on.

★ At No. 311 O'Reilly (between Habana and Aguiar) is the Casa O'Reilly. Follow Habana, across the Cervantes park. On the corner of Chacón and Habana, the **Palacio del Arzobispado** (archbishop's palace) was built in the first half of the 19th century for the O'Farrell family and taken over by the archbishop in 1870. It's an interesting example of neo-classical architecture, with a huge porch opening onto a central courtyard surrounded by arcades.

★ On the corner of Cuarteles and Compostella rises the church of **San Ángel Custodio**, dating from 1690 and rebuilt in neo-Gothic style in 1866. José Martí was baptized here.

★ **Former presidential palace** (map III, A2): Refugio, between Belgica and the Prado. Building on this began in 1913 and it became the residence of the presidents of the *República* in 1920. True to the eclectic and pretentious neo-baroque style of the masters of the neo-colonial Republic, it has enormous staircases and huge rooms, decorated by the famous New York firm of Tiffany. On 13 March 1957, the revolutionaries attacked the dictator Batista and the palace. Today it houses the Museum of the Revolution (*see* 'Museums'). In front is the **Granma Memorial**.

– In the north of the Old Town there are fragments, here and there, of the old city wall; the **Palacio Pedroso** and the **Museum of Music** (map III, A1, **83**); and the monumental **statue of General Máximo Gómez** on horseback. At the top of Prado lie the remains of the old prison (1834), where José Martí was incarcerated in 1869.

★ At the furthest point of this part of town stands the **Castillo de San Salvador de la Punta**, built at the end of the 16th century in the form of a fortified trapezium. In the 17th century, a chain linked to the Castillo de Los Tres Reyes del Morro controlled entry to the harbour.

★ **Edificio Bacardi** (Bacardi building): avenida de Belgica, between San Juan de Dios and Empedrado. This former property of Emilio Bacardi, the exiled king of rum, is a superb example of 1930s architecture, juxtaposed with multicoloured art-deco tiles. At the top of the tower is a huge bat (said to have inspired the author of *Batman*, who used to work at Bacardi).

★ **The Prado** (or Paseo de Martí, map III, A1–2): between Malecón and the Capitol, this is the most beautiful avenue in town (the Rampa in Vedado has comparatively little charm). The best way to see round the Prado is on foot or to take a leisurely trip in a bicycle-taxi. Lined with prestigious residences, this airy, noble promenade recalls the area's glorious past. With its shaded stone benches and art-deco street lamps, you can well imagine members of the Belle Époque's elegant society strolling along here with the rich Creole merchants waving to them from their barouches. The facades of the houses, the beautiful pastel colours and the elaborate old balconies are truly delightful. Some of the houses are being restored.

The paseo is also a perpetually busy meeting place. Here you will find *jineteros* trading in cigars, Revolutionary currency and even girls, in return for dollars, as well as workers and swarms of children in school uniform queuing for buses.

★ The Parque Central (map III, A2) borders the Prado, just before the Capitol. Despite its name, it's a pretty, tree-lined plaza that doesn't really look like a park. In fact, there's so much traffic round this square that the *parque* itself tends to get a bit choked up. The most interesting buildings on either side are the **Inglaterra** and the **Plaza** (see 'Where to Stay'), two splendid palaces that have been facing each other for many years. Inside the square itself is the statue of José Martí, now famous as '*la esquina caliente*' because it's where people go to engage in heated discussions, not about a new Revolution, but about pelota, or *cesca punta*, the national sport and main topic of conversation. A lot of betting goes on and there is much talk about the chances of the Industriales, Havana's team.

★ Towards the **Capitolio** (Capitol) there are a few interesting buildings. On the corner of Paseo de Martí and San Rafael, the **Teatro Nacional García Lorca** (Gran Teatro, map III, A2), built in 1915 in marble, is a prime example of neo-baroque style. It's a feast of over-elaborate turrets, balconies, columns, balustrades, long bays, arches and carving, and amazingly ornate, undulating dormer windows. The actress Sarah Bernhardt and the operatic tenor Enrico Caruso both performed here.

★ Next door is the equally exotic neo-classical architecture of the **Hotel Inglaterra**. Its café, the Louvre, was a popular meeting place for pro-independence conspirators in the first war of 1868. Appropriately, the white marble statue, dedicated to José Martí at the height of his influence, lightens the shady plaza. The ever-busy calle San Rafael runs between the Hotel Inglaterra and the theatre leading to the rather ugly concrete gateway into the tiny **Chinese quarter** (see 'Centro Habana' *below*) that's worth exploring and is just as popular (though less impressive) than Old Havana.

★ The **Capitolio Nacional**, (map III, A2–3), built between 1920 and 1929 with a 61-metre (195-foot) high cupola, is an exact replica of the Capitol in Washington DC. Thousands of labourers were employed to build what was the most imposing construction in Cuba at the time. It was the seat of the chamber of representatives of the senate until the Castro revolution. Visitors can stand at the entrance (free of charge) and admire the vast hall that seems to go on forever. In the middle, a diamond set in the floor marks the theoretical centre of Havana, from where all distances are measured. A colossal statue, 14 metres (49 feet) high and weighing 30 tonnes, symbolizes the Republic and is purported to be the largest in the world to be found inside a building. The Capitolio houses the **Science Academy**, a small museum dedicated to the history of the Capitolio itself (not essential viewing, particularly as there is an admission charge) and a large café under the arcades at the front (with a view).

– Behind the Capitol stands the **Fábrica de Partagas** (see 'Cigar Manufacture' *below*).

★ **Palacio de Aldama** (map IV, B2): avenida de Bolívar and Máximo Gómez. This palace was built in 1840 in neo-classical style for a rich Spaniard, Domingo de Aldama y Arréchaga. His son-in-law hosted a famous literary salon here. His son Miguel was a pro-independence partisan during the first war, and was forced to emigrate to the USA. The palace was plundered by the Spanish during the war in 1869. The facade is interesting despite a third, inappropriate floor that was added at the beginning of the

19th century when the building was transformed into a cigar factory. It now contains the Institute of the History of the Communist Movement and the Socialist Revolution in Cuba (not open to visitors).

The Fortresses

The admission charge for the fortresses varies according to the number of visits and the time of day. They are a few hundred metres apart so, if you go by taxi, ask the driver to wait.

★ **Fortaleza San Carlos de la Cabaña** (map III, B1): opposite the old town, on the other side of the bay. ☎ 62-40-92. Open daily 10am–10pm. Admission $3 before 6pm, $5 after 6pm. Guided visits in Spanish.

This imposing fortress dominates the port. Built by the Spanish in 1763 following the English capture of Havana the previous year, this enormous military complex, constructed in triangles and protected by thick walls, accommodated over a thousand soldiers. It became one of the most important garrisons in Latin America. Although it served as a prison during the wars of independence and again during the Revolution, the complex is now a barracks once more. Take a look at the small vaulted chapel, with its interesting, 18th-century, baroque wooden altar, and note the excavations at the entrance where bones have been discovered. There are also a few original exhibitions funded with foreign subsidies in the fortifications at the foot of the walls. But the highlight is the **Che Museum** (see below).

If you come in the evening you can watch the famous ceremonia de cañonazo followed by a little show. This ceremony of cannon shots, which used to signal the closing of the town gates, is still carried out in historic costume using an authentic Spanish cannon. The ceremony takes place every evening at 8.30pm and the cannon is fired at 9pm sharp. Cover your ears – the noise is deafening.

★ **Castillo de Los Tres Reyes del Morro** (map III, A1) to the west of La Cabaña, still on the other side of the bay. Open daily 9am–8pm. Admission $1 to enter the site and $1 to tour the entirely unmemorable museum (not worth it). This fortress is less imposing than Fortaleza San Carlos de la Cabaña, but important all the same. It was built at the end of the 16th century to defend the access to the port and the town. The English seized it in 1762, and subsequently declared themselves masters of the whole country. With its old lighthouse (admission $2) that juts out to sea, it is perhaps more photogenic than its huge neighbour. Before you enter the fortress, there is a magnificent view of the port from the terrace that also attracts Sunday afternoon painters, and one or two people selling indifferent items of craftwork. Inside, at the far end of a passage punctuated with regularly spaced loopholes, is another area of terrace at the foot of the lighthouse. There is nothing in particular to see inside except for courtyards and passageways that lead to various viewpoints, but there is a restaurant.

Houses

★ **Casa de Simón Bolívar** (map III, B2, **73**): Mercaderes, between Obrapía and Lamparilla. Open Tuesday–Saturday 10.30am–5.30pm. Sunday 9am–12.30 pm. Admission $1. This beautiful colonial mansion was donated to the Cuban people by Venezuela. It is typical of the style of the old *casas* of the area – verdant courtyards with an upper floor of arcades – but the traditional parrots in cages have been replaced by magnificent Amazonian macaws (watch out – they bite!).

On the ground floor is a minuscule chapel with a stained-glass window that portrays an extremely potted history of South America. The room here is dedicated to the life of Simón Bolívar, whose story is told in a highly original manner, through painted terracotta figurines. It's particularly amusing because the artist has left little to the imagination; the great South American liberator is even shown naked beside a young woman.

A beautiful marble staircase leads to the first floor, where there is a contemporary art exhibition and various souvenirs of Bolívar. Particularly worth seeing is the reproduction of the golden sword covered in diamonds which was a gift from Peru. There are also many paintings and sculptures by Venezuelan and Cuban artists, some of them very good.

★ **Casa de Los Arabes** (map III, B2, 74): calle Oficios, between Obispo and Obrapía. Open 9.30am–6.30pm. Admission $1. This is another noble 17th-century mansion, simply decorated and typical of Old Havana. But the decor is more reminiscent of North Africa than of Spain, probably because the Spanish settlers were from Andalucía and deeply influenced by Arabic culture. Besides some *mudejar* (Spanish Muslim) furniture and carpets, there's not a great deal to see. Access to the small square tower with three green shuttered windows is from the second floor. To get up there you pass in front of a small classroom and a minuscule prayer room, which is still in use. Every Friday all the Muslim diplomats from Nigeria, Algeria and the Congo congregate here. The carpet hanging on the wall indicates the direction of Mecca.

★ **Casa de África** (map III, B2, **75**): Obrapía 157, between Mercaderes and San Ignacio. Undergoing lengthy restoration works, but in principle open daily 9.30am–6pm (to be confirmed). This former palace is not so much a museum as a showcase for contemporary African culture. Allowing for whatever changes may take place once restoration is complete, the items on display include carved wood, fabric, clothes, bronzes, drums and basketry. There is also a small section dedicated to santería. Other exhibits feature African-Cuban ritualistic objects; paintings depicting the uprisings and sufferings of the slaves; an 18th-century collar shackle; santería dolls; musical instruments and painted ceramics; ceremonial robes, drums, embroidered fabrics; ancient furniture and antiques; and masks, costumes and musical instruments of the secret Abakuá society.

★ **Casa de Guayasamín** (map III, B2, **76**): Obrapía 111, between Oficios and Mercaderes. ☎ 61-38-43. Open Tuesday to Saturday 10.30am–5.30pm. Sunday 9.30am–12.30pm. Admission $1 to see round the painter's apartments upstairs, but access to the patio is free. A small charge is made for taking photographs. This is the residence of Oswaldo Guayasamín,

Ecuador's most important contemporary painter, who died in March 1999. It is both a centre for the promotion of his work and an opportunity for visitors to admire one of the Old Town's most beautiful and elegant palaces, with its imposing colonnaded courtyard, marble floor and incredibly light and fresh interior. Visit the first floor to see the remains of 18th-century frescoes and the beautiful furniture in the painter's bedroom. These apart, the other exhibits are not of any great interest and smack rather too much of a personality cult. They include: the artist's shirts and flip-flops neatly tidied away in the wardrobe; his razor and toothbrush in the bathroom; and the dining room – not exactly earth-shaking and all a bit obsessive. Actually, setting aside Guayasamín's talent, it is easier to understand why the authorities are so keen on him when, among the other works on display here, you see the strange portrait of Fidel with the hands of Christ. There's also a shop selling books, postcards and reproductions.

Museums

★ **Museo de la Ciudad** (Museum of the City; map III, B2, **71**): Plaza de Armas. ☎ 61-28-76. Open daily 9.30am–6.30pm. Admission $3. Havana's city museum is tucked away in the superb Palacio de Los Capitanes Generales (*see above*). This building is remarkable for its size and its architecture, and is certainly one of the three most beautiful museums in Havana. It contains detailed exhibitions about the history of the city until the Revolutionary era as well as art collections.

– **Ground floor**: on the right are the former stables, where the oldest statue in Cuba (1630), the *Giraldilla*, or weathercock, is kept. Symbol of the city of Havana, it was originally intended to decorate the tower of the Real Fuerza fort. Highlights here include a collection of military standards, costumes, wrought-iron work and more. There are also old hackney carriages and other beautiful items dating from the colonial era, strange caricatures of Africans, a large-scale model of a locomotive, an old fireman's pump and a coal-seller's barrow.

There are several rooms full of portraits of 18th-century bishops, tomb-stones, frontages of brass altars, porcelain discovered during the restoration work in 1967, gold and silver plate, sacerdotal robes and religious and Slavonic evangelical statuary adorned with superb lustre and miniatures. Also worth seeing are the large wreathed wooden pillars and a fine 18th-century Christ.

– **First floor**: there are lots of huge rooms, some still in their original splendour, others transformed into museum exhibition halls housing thematic collections. The main ones, which do not have to be visited in any particular order, are as follows:

– **Salas de la Capitanía General** and **salon verde** richly furnished with pieces from the 18th and 19th centuries, including Regency uniforms and collections of arms (swords, rifles, etc.). A number of edicts include the amazing call of 1850 to the inhabitants of Matanzas, intended to discredit the rebels.

– **Salas del Cabildo**: the town council used to meet here from 1791 to 1967, and it now houses portraits of the great patriots – Aguilera, Céspedes and Mármol – and insignias of soldiers killed in the fighting of 1868 and 1898.

– **Sala de las Banderas**: this contains new portraits of all the great independence leaders, Antonio Maceo's machete, the flag of Máximo Gómez HQ (1868), his saddle and sword, and the first Cuban flag.

– **Sala de Maceo**: this room contains various souvenirs, personal effects, letters (from the war of 1895), a first edition of *Versos Sencillos* by José Martí, the boat from which Maceo landed when he arrived in Cuba, and a large painting depicting his death. There is also the Cuban flag, letters written by José Martí, personal effects (comb, glasses, boots) and papers relating to the War of Independence.

– **The Republic Room**: displays many items relating to the years before the Revolution, vestiges of the 'Eagle of Imperialism', as well as other symbols of the *compradore* republic, and of the great events of 1960–61.

– Other rooms and exhibitions include the white room, the throne room, the mirror room, the huge dining room full of trophies, and others. These house displays of colonial furniture, Italian, French and German porcelain, portraits of the kings of Spain, beautiful artefacts, paintings and so on, under the stucco and gold of the Republic.

★ The **Che Museum** (map III, B1): in the fortress of La Cabaña (*see above*). One of the buildings in this old fortress has several rooms dedicated to the *guerillero heroíco*, who took the place by storm in 1959. Che Guevara fans will not be disappointed. On display are a number of his personal effects from the war – rucksack, gun, radio, binoculars and so on – which have become cult items. A large map of the world traces his many journeys, from the era of *Easy Rider* across the American sub-continent, to his official trips to Asia, via the attempts at uprising in Africa. Che was certainly an intrepid traveller. To the right of the main room is a photo gallery offering a rare glimpse of this era, including several photographs of Che as a lad; to the left there's a reconstruction of his ministerial office. Take whatever the museum guards tell you (the official story) with a pinch of salt. It's a pity the museum authorities never put together a collection of items inspired by Che – as if it all ended with his death on 9 October 1967.

★ **Museum of Colonial Art** (map III, B2, **77**): Plaza de la Catedral. ☎ 62-64-40. Open 8.30am–6.30 pm. This museum is located in a former 18th-century palace with a pretty courtyard.

– The **ground floor** contains paintings and tableware from the 19th and 20th centuries. The **Salas de elementos arquitectónicos** houses decorative ironwork, windows in carved wood, old doors, locks, knockers and so on. The **Sala cochera** has barouches, old lamps and spurs.

– **First floor**: There are several rooms with beautiful colonial furniture, one with an English piano, rocking chairs, low tables, chairs on castors, sacristy sideboard and desks – all extremely beautiful. But there are also some super-kitsch items, like the vase on feet decorated with cherubs, Sèvres porcelain, cabinets, a carved game of draughts, an enamelled aristocratic toilet, splendid collections of chairs and armchairs. The large dining room has chandeliers, elaborate ceilings, colonial sideboards and chests of drawers. Note also the wood and leather armchairs, with their curious ear flaps, and the inlaid desk.

There is also a superb collection of *mamparas* (internal doors typical of bourgeois residences) and the bedroom contains some fantastic crystal.

★ **Numismatic Museum** (map III, B2, **78**): Oficios 8. Open Tuesday to Saturday 8.30am–5pm (4pm on Thursday). Sunday 8.30am–1pm. Next to the Plaza de Armas, this contains collections of old coins and money. The notes from 1960 are signed by Che, as 'President of the Bank of Cuba'.

★ **Vintage Car Museum** (map III, B2, **79**): Oficios 13, opposite the Numismatic Museum. Admission $1. This old hangar contains a dusty display of Yankee charabancs from the 1940s and 50s: Chevrolets, Fords, Chryslers, even an old Mack lorry and, stranger still, a Citroën Mahari. There are some fine old models to be sure, but it's not really worth a visit. Anyone short of cash can simply take a look from the street.

★ **Museum of the Revolution** (map III, A2): Refugio 1. ☎ 62-40-91. Open Tuesday to Sunday 10am–5pm (until 6pm on Tuesday). Ironically located in a magnificent former presidential palace. Allow at least 90 minutes to do justice to more than 30 rooms relating the entire history of Cuba in meticulous detail, with commentaries (in Spanish and sometimes English) on every piece and photographic exhibit. Even if you don't understand everything, the richness of the collections allows you to follow what's going on. The museum is organized chronologically and the collections are quite exhaustive. As you might expect, the sections on recent events are not quite as extensive, and any political analysis tends to be a bit partial. The tour starts on Level 3 (second floor) and descends through history as you make your way downstairs: colonial era, neo-colonial Republic, the War of Independence, the foundations of Socialism and the room commemorating Che. It is impossible to cover everything, but the following are some of the more important sections:

Level 3
– **Colonial era, neo-colonial Republic (1899–1952) and the War of Independence**: exhibits here include the conquest, the aborigines, slavery, cane and a model sugar refinery; the Ten Years War (1868–78); the formation of the Cuban Revolutionary Party by José Martí; the international context; the Russian Revolution; history of the workers and the revolutionary movement of the 1920s and 30s.

– Next comes the history of the Republic and the social and cultural situation of the country until the Revolution. There's an interesting list of 'presidents' picked by the USA. Look out for the first cards of the Cuban Communist Party in 1925 and a reproduction of the Cuban declaration of war on Japan. There are photographs of Castro, particularly during the 1948 demonstration when he was wounded by police, and a letter in his handwriting dating from 1951 congratulating his friends in the orthodox party, and the broom symbolizing his will to 'sweep' the Republic free of demons. It's a poignant illustration of how poor the country was under American rule.

Dictatorship: displays include preparation for the insurrections of 1953; a model of the *Granjita Siboney*; storming the Moncada; photos and blood-stained uniforms, a model of Santiago and of the barracks. There's also a detailed map of the roads involved in the attack of 26 July 1953, with a precise account of events. There is even Batista's shirt from when he was wounded in the student demonstration of 1952.

The amnesty: The departure for Mexico and preparation for the *Granma*'s landing – everything you could ever want to know about revolutionary guerrilla warfare and the liberation, including portraits of the protagonists involved in the fight against imperialism. There are reconstructions of the main battles; 'bounty' taken by the *guerilleros* for funding and various weapons. Look out too for the small 'Liberty or death' banner, photographs and instruments of torture used under Batista's rule.

Level 2

The foundations of Socialism: everything to do with the victory march of Castro, Che and Cienfuegos. Agricultural reform, the new power, the assault on Playa Girón, the 'first defeat for imperialism in Latin America', the founding of the Cuban Communist Party, the regime's achievements.

1975–90: photographs of the congresses presided over by Fidel, evidence of social progress, the notion of voluntary work, photos of this new and 'perfect' world, the Soviet-Cuban 'friendship', with the accent on education and health. Also cosmonauts' equipment of Cuban origin as proof of scientific exchange. Finally, there are press articles on the breakdown in Soviet-Cuban relations.

– In passing, take a look at the different state rooms dating from the time when this palace was still the seat of executive power, including the golden room, the mirror room, the presidential office and the chapel.

Level 1 (ground floor)

There's a curiously small room dedicated to the 'special period', with a disappointing lack of detail when it comes to explanation. There are photographs of Che, personal effects, a copy of the fake passport he used to get into Bolivia and a great portrait. The exhibition reaches overkill with hairs from Che's beard, his socks, instruments used during the autopsy and much, much more, including a sort of shroud.

★ *Granma* **Memorial** (map III, A2): access to this outdoor memorial is via the Museum of the Revolution, but you can also see it from the street. This is an exhibition of the famous yacht that brought Castro and his 82 companions from Mexico to the Sierra Maestra. You can only see around the exterior and there are military vehicles on all sides.

★ **Palacio de Bellas Artes** (Fine Arts Museum ; map III, A2): Trocadero, between Agramonte (Zulueta) and Belgica (or Monserrate). Closed for refurbishment until around 2003. The new museum will be divided into three adjoining buildings. The main building is modern, dating from the 1950s and slightly incongruous in this part of town. It will house 20th-century Cuban paintings, while the other two will display important collections of Egyptian, Greek and Roman art as well as paintings from the 18th and 19th centuries.

★ **Alejo Carpentier Museum and Cultural Centre** (map III, A2, **80**): Empedrado 215, between Cuba and San Ignacio. Open Monday to Saturday 8.30am–4.30pm. Admission free. This palace, with its pretty 18th-century patio, is not really a museum at all but the house where Carpentier set the scenes in Havana in his novel *El Siglo de las Lucas*. It is also a research centre devoted to this great Cuban writer, journalist and composer.

As you enter, two rooms on the right contain his first writings, the novel *Ekoué Yamba* and numerous translations (in 24 languages, to be precise), plus the 1977 Cervantes prize for literature and more. The palace also houses a small theatre and, if you ask nicely, the guard will show you round. Failing that, come back on Thursday after 2pm when there are lectures in the theatre.

★ **Wifredo Lam Centre** (map III, B2): San Ignacio and Empedrado. ☎ 61-20-96. Open Monday to Saturday 10am–5pm. Admission $2. In a beautiful colonial mansion behind the cathedral, near the Bodeguita del Medio and the Alejo Carpentier Centre, this elegant building is named in tribute to the great Cuban Surrealist painter, but does not actually present any of his works. All the more reason therefore, to give a brief account of his life here.

Born in 1902 in Sagua La Grande, Lam left Cuba to study in Spain, where he came up against the dictator Franco. Lam's friend Pablo Picasso helped him escape to France, where he mixed with the cream of the art world – Éluard, Matisse, Léger, Braque, Leiris, Tzara, Breton. Lam returned to his own country to support the Revolution, but died in Paris in 1982. His works had a considerable influence on Cuban painting.

If it doesn't show any works by Lam, what does this museum show? The answer is temporary exhibitions of usually quite interesting works by artists from all over the world, including Asia, Africa and South America.

★ **Museo de Armas** (Arms Museum; map III, B2, **82**): Mercaderes 157, between Obrapía and Lamparilla. Under restoration but in principal open Tuesday to Sunday 10.30am–5.30pm. A kind of annexe of the Museum of the Revolution, this former armoury inherited a very impressive collection of Castro's own weapons. Like any self-respecting revolutionary, the *Comandante* was always interested in weaponry of all kinds, and there is an extraordinary range of pieces on display here, from knives and machetes to highly specialized guns and grenades. Castro was also a great lover of hunting (another thing he had in common with Hemingway), which he did mainly in Africa, and his trophies hang on the walls. Small display cases contain various souvenirs; some are rather unusual, such as the underwear belonging to Marcelo Salado, a hero of the Revolution.

Other Sights

★ **Casa del Tabaco** (Tobacco Museum): calle Mercaderes 120, between Obispo and Obrapía, Habana Vieja. On the first floor of la Casa de Porto Rico. Open daily 9am–5.30pm. Admission free. This little museum contains the longest cigars in the world – one is 6m (nearly 20 feet) long and supported on trestles, while another measures a mere 2.2m (7 feet). These cigars were never intended for smoking but were produced specifically to establish records of size. The biggest one was made in four days by just one worker. The museum also has a large papier-mâché model of Fidel Castro with a cigar in his mouth. Cuba's leader no longer smokes, but he apparently still enjoys the smell of tobacco. The display cabinets contain an assortment of gifts given to the leader of the Revolution during official visits: a tobacco pouch here, an ash-tray there, elsewhere a cigar lighter or cutter. In addition, there are various 19th-century black-and-white lithographs of the first designs used for cigar rings, and a selection of stones delicately engraved with *sellos* designs (official stamps).

★ **Museo Nacional de la Música** (National Museum of Music; map III, A1, **83**): calle Capdevila 1, between Habana and Aguiar, Habana Vieja. ☎ 61-98-46. Open Tuesday to Saturday 9am–6.30pm. Sunday 9am–noon. Admission $2. This museum is often overlooked by tourists, but it's actually a treat for any music fan. On the ground floor is a rather dusty little room and a small shop where CDs are roughly the same price as anywhere else. It's a shame they don't actually play any music here but, that apart, it's a great museum and well worth a visit.

It all starts rather oddly at the top of the stairs where you come across a room full of very fine antique pianos, including an elegant Sassenhoff built in Bremen. But everything becomes clearer once you reach the second room, where the tour proper starts. This room is dedicated to Fernando Ortiz, one of the greatest historians of Cuban music. All the instruments are clearly labelled in display cabinets with a commentary about each one (in Spanish only, unfortunately) including such intriguing remarks as: 'The white man [has] sugar and the guitar, the black man tobacco and the drum, the mulatto milk, coffee and the bongo.' The African tradition is well represented by drums brought over by slaves from Dahomey, others of purely Yoruba tradition, some Haitian and 20th-century Cuban. There is a fine collection of *abwes* or *chekere*, enormous colocynth-type objects (on sale everywhere to tourists) with a net full of glass marbles. There are some great handmade *bembés* with dead-straight barrels and others made from truncated casks. Note also the odd-looking drums with grass skirts and a sort of feather duster, known as *abakuas* or *ekueñon* by *ñañigo* blacks. There are also magnificently sculpted *guiros'* (dried gourds with notches that the musician scrapes with a drumstick) and a wonderful lute encrusted with ivory.

The third room focuses on the drums used by *comparsas* (groups of musicians) at carnival time throughout the country. Because popular music is forever changing, Cuban music reflects a variety of influences. The range of 'native' instruments is enriched by various new instruments that have evolved from different styles (*minuet*, *rigodones*, *lanceros*, *contradanzas*, *danzas*, *danzónes*).

This is a good time to mention the national dance, the *danzón* that developed in the 19th century as a transitional style between *contradanza* and the *danza cubana*. For more about *son* (and the many other forms of Cuban music) *see* 'General Information: Music and Dance'.

– In the fourth room is a fine collection of *tres* guitars (used in *son*), *demi-cinco* and *seis* guitars with splendid 'horns', proving that Rock 'n' Roll didn't invent everything! Next comes a collection of instruments from rather colder climes such as Finland with its strange flat *kantele*. Before you go downstairs, take a look at the elegant Cuban-Andalucían patio which is a great place to sit and read.

★ **Museo de la Ceramica** (map III, B2): in the Castillo de la Real Fuerza (*see* the entry on the Castillo).

★ **Palacio de las Artesanías** (map III, A1): Cuba 64, corner of Tacón, Old Havana. All the shops open daily 10am–7pm. Cuban handicrafts are presented in an 18th-century palace (worth visiting for its architecture alone), with artisans producing jewellery, clothes, fabric, paintings, traditional musical instruments, cigars and rum. You don't actually see the craftspeople at work here, but the fruit of their labours is sold in shops arranged round the patio. Many of the items are aimed at tourists and quite expensive, but the courtyard itself is remarkable and you're bound to find something to take back to friends.

– Other museums include the **Máximo Gómez Museum** (avenida Salvador Allende, Quinta de Los Molinos), the **Museum of the History of Sport**, the **Finance Museum**, the **Museum of Humour** and the **Museum of the Capitolio** (in the Capitolio).

Cigar Manufacturers

Most of the factories are in Havana but only two of the most famous (with Upman and Laguito) are open to visitors. Admission $10. Tours start at 10am and last about an hour. Individual tours are not really on the agenda so it's best just to tag along with a group. For anyone going to Pinar del Río, it's a lot cheaper to visit the small local factory there.

In each factory there are hundreds of people working on several floors and you can see the entire production process, always by hand, of a real Havana cigar. Contrary to popular belief, the workers do not roll the leaves between their thighs or under their armpits, but spirally in huge rollers. In each room, a 'reader' entertains the workers by reading newspapers and entire novels. The work was deemed to be so boring that this provision was the first cause championed by the unions at the beginning of the 20th century.

It's not necessarily a good idea to get carried away and buy cigars from the factory, since the price charged by the different factories and by their shops is virtually the same given that it's all state-owned anyway. If you do decide to buy your cigars at one of the factories, take a little time to chat with the sellers.

★ **Corona** (map III, A2, **70**): calle Zulueta (Agramonte) 106, between El Refugio and Colón; next to the Museum of the Revolution and the monument to *Granma*. Guided tours of the factory Monday to Saturday 10am–2pm. Admission $10. The shop on the ground floor, El Palacio del Tabaco has the widest range of cigars in town.

★ **Partagas** (map IV, D2, **40**): calle Industria 524, behind the Capitolio. ☎ 33-80-60. Guided tours Monday to Friday at 10am and from 2pm, in English or Spanish with a demonstration of cigar hand rolling. Admission $10. The shop is open Monday to Saturday 9am–7pm and Sunday until 3pm. There are two *torcedores* (tobacco rollers) working there regularly. This is a good-quality cigar house patronized by many celebrities, including the French actor Gérard Depardieu, with photos on the walls to prove it. It sells a wide choice of cigars but few *vitoles* are available singly.

Centro Habana

★ **'The 'Wonderful World of Salvador Escalona'** (map V, D2, **100**): callejón de Hamel 1054, between Aramburu and Hospital. ☎ 78-16-61. Salvador Escalona – 'I am the one who paints messages to the human soul on walls' – is a self-taught mural painter and sculptor, inspired by Dalí, Miró and Picasso. He is also a *santo* from Camagüey, belonging to the most primitive branch of santería, the religion that combines African gods with Christian saints.

Inspired by the spirit of this Afro-Cuban culture, he has transposed his artistic vision onto the grey walls and dilapidated facades of a number of buildings in the centre of town. After eight years of work, his tropical colours and universal messages have brought new life to the area. Even the guttering has been transformed by the magic of his paintbrush.

No cars are allowed in Callejón de Hamel, only pedestrians and residents. A wooden hut contains a pile of jumble and a couple dressed in painted rags; it's an altar where passers-by pray and make offerings (for luck, health and money). Numerous sculptures and baroque and Dadaist works of art (suspended baths, cash registers – discover the rest for yourselves) add more colour still.

Next door there is a gallery where Escalona's five companions, dressed in black, display and sell his paintings. Free shows for the people take place in the street. The best day to come is Sunday (noon–3.30pm) for the 'El Callejón rumba', or every third Saturday of the month (10am) for children's entertainment. On the last Friday of the month, at 8.30pm, El Tecón is a cultural *peña* (festival), at which tea is served with milk and honey. '*Tecón*' literally means 'tea with' whatever you want.

Salvador Escalona, considered to be one of the great muralists of Latin America, travels extensively and is in demand all over the world, yet he remains humble, and when he is in residence it's quite easy to meet him. During one visit there was a partial eclipse of the sun and he was seen giving homage to the heavenly king in the middle of the road.

When he has covered all the facades in the area, Salvador plans to build a tunnel under the road so that he can continue to paint his messages on walls. He says, '*Vengo de una realidad oculta a una realidad abierta para que me conozcas*' ('I come from a hidden reality to an open reality so that you may know me'). The project should see the light of day in the years to come, but at the moment Salvador's greatest problem is obtaining paint.

– **Colonial houses**: at calle Concordia 418 is a very beautiful private house with a superb sculpted facade and a spectacular staircase. It achieved cult status in Havana as the setting for Cuba's most famous film, *Fresa y Chocolate*. Today the apartment houses a well-known *paladar* called La Guarida (*see* 'Where to Eat in Centro Habana').

– **The Chinese quarter**: at the heart of this popular yet neglected district, very near Zanja and Dragones, is a tiny rectangle rather inappropriately known as the *barrio chino* (the Chinese quarter). It dates from 1920 when Cantonese Chinese were sent to work for major companies in Cuba. They came expecting El Dorado, but what they found was a life of semi-slavery. Unlike migration from other countries, Chinese immigration never caught on in Cuba and ended abruptly in 1959. Today there are few remaining survivors from those days, as most Chinese have integrated with the local population, and a mere 400 Chinese people remain in this area.

The heart of the quarter is in fact concentrated along a little lane called the cuchillo de Zanja that has been artificially transformed (with Chinese backgrounds and decorations among other things) to create a sense of 'local colour' that is false and even close to being ridiculous. There is however a small, unfussy authentic Chinese restaurant called Lung Kong along here that's well worth a visit.

Vedado

★ **El Malecón** (map II, A–B–C1): this site is unmissable, in more ways than one. This thick, 7-kilometre (4-mile) barrier has protected Havana from the violence of the waves for decades. El Malecón is one of the finest symbols of the town and is hugely popular with the local *Habaneros*, who spend a great deal of time on and around it. It's claimed that many declarations of love have been made here, possibly helped by the influence of the Gulf Stream, which is only a few hundred metres away.

A gigantic promenade stretches along the barrier, from the Castillo de la Punta in the old town to the Castillo de la Chorrera, just in front of Miramar. All human life comes here for romance and parties, or just to hang out during the day, but it is not the safest place to be at night, so be cautious.

The largest part of the Malecón is in the Vedado area, but it is not the most beautiful. The old part, in Centro Habana in the area around the (Mafia-built) Hotel Deauville, is much more attractive. The famous row of houses, all freshly repainted, is really worth seeing. In his *Esquisses havanaises* (*Sketches of Havana*), Jean-Louis Vaudoyer wrote of 'Spanish forts portside, sky-scrapers starboard,' and, in between, 'a stunning row of houses which are not particularly beautiful but are all covered in rough-cast paint in the colours of meringue, butter and milk'.

★ **La Rampa**: officially 'Street No. 23', the Habaneros' favourite street begins at the Malecón and rises to the centre of the Vedado. Lined with shops, cafés and small nightclubs, it's lively day and night. The two largest hotels in the town are found here – the Nacional and the Habana Libre (formerly the Hilton) – as well as the famous Coppelia ice-cream parlour, where there is always a seemingly never-ending queue.

★ **The Focsa**: calle 17, between M and N. One of the last buildings constructed in Havana under Batista, this is also the most ugly and spoils the view for miles around. It is the tallest building in Cuba and the first building in the Americas to have been constructed according to a new technique of cabling and concrete. The only point of interest is the La Torre bar on the top floor, which gives a fantastic panoramic view of the town.

★ **The University** (map V, D2): calle San Lazaro. Situated on a hill, Havana's university was established in 1728, but black or mixed-race students were not admitted until 1842. The present building dates from the beginning of the 19th century, and was built in a pompous neo-classical style with a huge staircase and Corinthian columns topped by a triangular pediment. Demonstrations are often held in front of the building. In the square is a monument to Julio Antonio Mella, founder of the Federation of Communist Students, who was assassinated in 1929.

★ **Plaza de la Revolución** (map V, C3): south of the Vedado. This vast square can hold up to a million people. Since 1959, it has witnessed all the important events in Cuban history, from the launch of the literacy campaign to the farewell ceremony for Che Guevara. It is also here that Fidel Castro delivered his most important speeches, which could last for anything from three to six hours! Today, every time there is a speech, the Communist Youth Movement draws in the crowds with food and alcohol at unbeatable prices. So to a visitor it often seems as if the revolutionary fervour has not changed since the early days.

The **monument to José Martí** in the centre of the square is a strange concrete pyramid of vaguely Soviet inspiration, even though it was built under the dictator Batista. All around it are the most important administrative buildings – the Central Committee of the Cuban Communist Party, the Government Palace, the Ministries of Justice and Communications, the National Library and the National Theatre. On the facades of the Ministry of the Interior there is a giant portrait of Che Guevara, his eyes fixed on the eternal Revolution.

★ **Colón Cemetery** (map V, B3): calzada de Zapata and calle 12. Admission $3. This large necropolis of the bourgeoisie and Cuban aristocracy is as fine as the famous Père Lachaise cemetery in Paris or the Recoleta in Buenos Aires. The main surrounding wall was built in 1871. Through the monumental Roman gateway, a wide avenue, lined with elaborate, often grandiloquent and kitsch tombstones and mausoleums, leads to a church. A huge variety of styles, evoking many different civilizations and mythologies, is on display here. Note the monument to the firemen – a masterpiece of funereal art. Among the personalities buried here are Alejo Carpentier and Cecilia Valdés. While here, look for the tomb of the 'Hero of the Fatherland', Arnaldo Ochoa Sanchez, the general who was condemned by Castro as an example to others. For a long time his tomb was guarded by video cameras, and his family was even pressured into not revealing its whereabouts to journalists. Today the tomb remains anonymous, but every Cuban knows where it is.

★ Although newer than the houses in the old town, the **houses** scattered about this area are still interesting. Of rococo inspiration but built in 'modernist' style, they serve as a reminder that the area was inhabited by the upper-class bourgeoisie. It was also a place of pleasure; brothels and casinos were a major source of income in Havana before the Revolution. At every turn there are other, even more beautiful houses, some of which have been converted into *paladares* (private restaurants) for visitors. The following are some of the most interesting, but there are many more.

– On calle 19, between N and O (opposite the Nacional), there is a surprising medieval facade, among the most original of the area.

– The sumptuous dwelling at calle 17 and H is now the headquarters of the Writers' Union.

– There is no point looking for Fidel Castro's house; there are so many claims that no one really knows which is the right one.

Museums in Vedado

★ **Napoleon Museum** (map V, D2, **101**): San Miguel 1159, between Ronda and Mazón, next to the University. ☎ 79-14-12. Open Monday to Friday 10.30am–5pm. The museum is housed in a kind of Florentine palace, built by Julio Lobo, a millionaire who idolized Napoleon and wanted a place worthy of his fabulous collection. Stretching over four floors, it is probably the richest Napoleonic exhibit in the world. Here are some of the highlights:

– First floor: a few items such as the last letter from Louis XVI, a note from Marie-Antoinette, original badges from the national police force, etchings by Barras, Madame de Staël, busts, stamps, *Bonaparte* by J.B. Régnault, *Caroline Bonaparte* by François Gérard, arms and so on. In the large room is *Wellington* by John Boaden.

– Second floor: *Napoleon Prepares for the Coronation Ceremony* by Jean-Georges Vibert; note the great attention to detail. Rooms furnished in the style of the Empire. Fine pieces of ormolu by the French master, Thomire.

– Third floor: a touching bronze of *Napoleon at Saint-Helena*. Admire the vibrant colours on the drapes and the beautiful falling light in François Flamens' *Versailles*. Several pieces of Sèvres porcelain, superb polished wooden desks and an unusual 'gondola-bed' with a sphinx. Various relics include a piece of Napoleon's coffin and a lock of his hair.

– On the top floor, the dark wood of the library creates a solemn atmosphere. It contains an incredible number of works on the life and times of the emperor. There is access to the terrace, which is decorated with ceramic tiles.

★ **Museo Nacional de Artes Decorativas** (Museum of Decorative Arts; map V, C2, 102): calle 17, 502, between D and E, Vedado. Open Tuesday to Saturday 11am–6.30pm. Admission $2. In a townhouse dating from the beginning of the 19th century, this museum houses a collection of beautiful works of art from all over the world that were used to decorate opulent Cuban interiors. There is furniture by the grand masters of the 18th century, creations from the famous workshops in Sèvres and Chantilly, and a collection of rare porcelain. That said, there must be better things to do in Havana than to go into raptures over French 18th-century tapestry.

★ **Museo Postal Cubano** (Postal Museum): corner of avenida Rancho Boyeros and Plaza de la Revolución, Vedado; next to the main post office. Open Monday to Friday 10am–4pm. This contains stamps from all over the world and, entertainingly, a Cuban rocket that was supposed to send mail into space. The label does not say whether or not the mission was successful.

★ **Museo Antropológico Montané** (Anthropological Museum): Plaza Ignacio Agramonte, in Havana University, Vedado. Open Monday to Saturday 9am–12pm and 2.30–4.30pm. Rooms here are dedicated to archaeological digs of early Cuban and pre-Colombian civilizations.

Miramar

★ **Avenida 5**: the continuation of the Malecón, this sumptuous avenue lined with alleys and small squares crosses the whole of the fashionable part of Havana. The name may have been chosen by some of the American millionaires who came to live here.

★ **The 'mansions'**: the American-style name is given to the small palaces of the area. They are everywhere, scattered between the embassies and the chic little bungalows, often hidden behind wrought-iron gates and garden vegetation. There are many different styles, from neo-classical to neo-baroque, and they are in better condition than the houses of the Vedado.

★ **Hemingway Marina**: at the end of Miramar. A town within a town, this huge tourist complex (covering more than 5 kilometres/3 miles) provides moorings for hundreds of yachts along its internal canals. It looks a little out of place in a socialist country, with its luxury hotels, nightclubs, restaurants, bungalows, swimming pool, watersports and so on. It provides every facility, and all for the pleasure of rich foreign visitors. Hemingway never even set foot here. However, the deep-sea fishing competition he established in 1960 still exists, and attracts many enthusiasts every June.

★ **Museum of the Ministry of the Interior** (map VI, B1): 5 and 14 Miramar. Open Tuesday to Friday 8.30am–5pm. Housed in a villa in the chic part of Miramar, directly opposite the French Embassy (and in the course of refurbishment), this museum is dedicated to the acts of sabotage attributed to Uncle Sam, including the graphically illustrated biological warfare of dengue fever and sugar-cane blight. It covers all the failed assassination attempts on Castro, as well as the bomb in 1976 on the plane transporting the national fencing team. Cuban 'international operations' in Guinea, Bolivia, Vietnam, Venezuela and Angola are also documented. This should appeal to espionage enthusiasts and anti-imperialists.

CULTURAL ACTIVITIES

– Cultural events are published in the daily newspaper the *Granma* (on sale everywhere). The Spanish edition is cheaper because you pay in pesos, unlike the international editions, which are priced in dollars. See also *Cartelera*, published in Spanish and English, and *Bienvenidos, la guía del ocío de Cuba,* available in the big hotels and from the tourist office. Both publications are rather too commercial to be really useful, but they include one or two articles on current cultural events that might be helpful to non-Spanish speakers. The best sources of advice are Cubans themselves (but *see also* 'Useful Addresses' at the start of the section on Havana).

Cinema and Theatre

– **Cinema** (map V, D2, **14**): Yara, on la Rampa (calle 23), Vedado. Next to the hotel Habana Libre and opposite the Coppelia ice-cream parlour is one of the most popular cinemas in town; but there are many others as the Habaneros are great cinema-lovers.

– **Teatro Nacional García Lorca** (Gran Teatro; map III, A2): corner of paseo de Martí (Prado) and calle San Rafael. ☎ 61-30-78. This is Havana's main theatre with a superb auditorium, where you should try to see one of the truly splendid national ballets. Performances are every evening at 8.30pm (Saturday and Sunday only out of season). Tickets are not very expensive and you can book through the large hotels.

Literature and Music

– **Poetry readings** take place at the home of the poet Dulce María Loynaz, at the corner of 19 and J (Vedado).

– **National Union of Artists and Writers (UNEAC)**: map V, C2, **15**): calle 17 and H, Vedado. ☎ 32-45-51. This is a great place for the more erudite, offering rare books, video-club and frequent visits from the most important Cuban artists. But the big music night, not to be missed, is Wednesday between 5 and 8pm. One week it is the *peña del ambia*, and another it is the *peña de la trova*: musical performances for an audience of Cuban students and tourists. Thanks to separate entry charges of $5 for tourists and 10 pesos for Cubans, there is a good mix of people. It all happens in the garden where even the trees seem to drip with sweat in the steaming atmosphere. On Sunday there is rumba from 3–7pm.

Events

– **The Festival of Latin Jazz** takes place in Havana from 3–13 December.

– **The Latin American Film Festival** also takes place from 3–13 December.

– **The Havana Carnival** takes place during the last two weekends of February and August.

SHOPPING

Bookshops

For road maps, maps and guidebooks try **El Navegante** (map III, B2, **4**) and **Geotech** (map V, C2, **10**) bookshops. There is also the **Librería La Internacional** (map III, A2, **5**) for postcards, magazines and books in (almost) any language. *See* 'Useful Addresses' in Havana.

Music

🔒 **Casa de la Música** (map VI, B2 **80**): calle 20, between 31 y 35, Miramar. Open Tuesday to Sunday 10am–12.30am. ☎ 24-04-47. This is a great place for salsa fans, with cassettes, CDs (and even vinyl for real aficionados) and also a few instruments for sale. But it's a bit of a shambles and so mainly for connoisseurs. There are shows and live salsa bands later in the evening (*see* 'What to Do').

Rum

🔒 **La Casa del Ron** (map III, B2, **6**): 53 calle Baratillo, Habana Vieja, next to Plaza de Armas. Open 9am–5pm. It's hard to decide between all the different types of rum since there are more than 80 . . . but tasting is free! It also sells cigars. If you need to clear your head later the Maison du Café is right next door at No. 51.

Cigars

Generally speaking, it is best not to buy cigars on the street no matter how many times you may be offered them. They are usually counterfeit and even if they are a lot cheaper than the real thing, you can never be sure of getting a good deal. In any case, you have to be a real expert to tell a fake from the genuine product. Remember too that Cuban customs are unlikely to be a problem, but that you might have trouble with customs on your return if you exceed the allowance. (*See* 'General Information: Cigars'.)

El Palacio del Tabaco (map III, A2, **70**): 106 calle Zulueta (Agramonte), between el Refugio y Colón. ☎ 33-83-89. Open Monday to Saturday 9am–5pm. Sunday 9am–3pm. This is the retail outlet of the Corona cigar factory on the ground floor and, as you might expect, one of the best-stocked places in town.

Partagas cigar factory retail outlet (map IV, B2, **40**): 520 calle Industría, behind the Capitolio. ☎ 33-80-60. Open Monday to Saturday 9am–7pm. This is where the celebrities buy their cigars (*see* 'What to See'). It sells a wide range of cigars, but few are available singly. There are usually two *torcedores* at work.

Hostal Conde boutique of the Villanueva factory (map III, B2, **19**): 202 calle Mercaderes at the corner of Lamparilla, Old Havana. Relatively unknown, this place is rapidly becoming popular with cigar lovers. It stocks a wide range, including many available singly. *See also* 'Where to Stay'.

La Casa del Habano (map V, B2, **48**): 406 Paseo, between 17 y 19, Vedado. ☎ 30-31-14. Open 9am–6pm. You'll find this on the right as you enter Casa de la Amistad (*see* 'Where to Have a Drink'), and there is a *torcedor* at the entrance. It's one of many boutiques in the Casa del Habano chain.

La Casa del Habano (map V, B3, **120**): calle 12, between 23 and 25, Vedado. Open 9am–6pm. At the far end of a bar and next door to an off-licence, this offers less choice than the previous shop (there is no *torcedor* either), but the humid conditions are the same.

La Casa del Tabaco (map VI, B1, **120**): 5 y 16, Miramar. Open Monday to Saturday 10.30am–6.30pm. This is a good shop not well known by tourists (above a restaurant) selling quality cigars.

Château Miramar Hotel Shop (map VI, off A2, **25**): 1st calle, between 60 y 70, Miramar. On the right of reception as you enter the hotel, this is where you can see the famous *torcedor* Crisanto Cardenas at work. Now retired, Cardenas owes his success (and much travelling) to his years of experience as head *torcedor* at the Partagas factory in charge of all the other *torcedores*.

La Casa del Tabaco (map VI, off A3, **121**): avenida 244, Miramar, in the Giraldilla shopping complex. Open 11am–midnight. This is the newest shop in the Cubanacan chain, and has a *torcedor* to advise customers.

Fashion

🔒 **La Maison** (map VI, B2, **81**): in Miramar. Well-known fashion boutique. *See also* 'What to Do', 'Nightlife').

Crafts

🔒 **Palacio de las Artesanías**, calle Cuba 64, at the corner of calle Tacón, Habana Vieja. There are lots of boutiques arranged around an elegant patio, selling a wide range of Cuban craft products. It's very touristy and not especially cheap, but a good source of CDs, cigars, rum, dolls and more. *See also* 'What to See'.

Markets

Thanks to numerous people's markets, Cubans without access to dollars can buy cheaper goods in pesos at prices subsidized by the state.

🔒 **Farmers' markets** (map V, B2, **6**): calle 19, between A and B. Prices are in pesos. There is another market in old Havana on calle Egido opposite the convent of Nuestra Senora de Belen (map III, A3). Some markets are more touristy and sell a range of more-or-less original products.

🔒 **La Feria** (map V, B1, **12**): Malecón, between F and E, behind the Ministry of Tourism. This is a large daily market where you can buy or exchange just about anything: old books, things you find in the attic, santería relics, 1950s furniture, family jewellery, etc. It used to be a people's market but it's now mainly for tourists.

🔒 You should also take a look at the **craft market** on La Rampa (calle 23, between O and P; map V, D1, **13**) next to the Ministry of Health and opposite the International Press Centre.

IN THE AREA

★ **Finca Vigia** (Hemingway's house): at San Francisco de Paula, about 15 kilometres (9 miles) southeast of Havana. Open Wednesday 9am–4pm. Sunday 9am–noon. Closed public holidays. Admission $3. There's no bus, so take a taxi and keep it for the return journey. Visitors are not allowed into the house beyond the threshold, but you can see inside through the many open bay windows. Ask for a guidebook (in Spanish or English and included in the price) as the guards on duty inside the house are not very communicative.

You approach the house via a long and beautiful tree-lined drive, in the style of a Caribbean manor house. Built at the end of the 19th century, in a luscious tropical park on a hillock overlooking the valley, Finca Vigia, where 'Papa' Hemingway installed himself in 1939, is a pretty Creole house of neo-colonial inspiration. The internal decoration, just as he left it, is reminiscent of Key West on the other side of the Gulf of Mexico. The house is light and airy, and its northern side has views of hills, Havana and a little bit of sea in the distance.

The house reflects the life of the writer/adventurer, with its dilapidated elegance, Spanish furniture, impressive hunting trophies from his many

African safaris, bullfight posters and books everywhere, even in the toilets. Among the most interesting items are the typewriter at which he used to stand to type his novels, some pretty African statuettes, a plate by Picasso with a bull's head on it, Hemingway's Nobel Prize certificate, and the little Winchester cannon with which he used to greet his guests! In the office is the sofa with which actor Gary Cooper had to make do when he stayed, because he was too tall for the guest bed. There is also the stuffed head of a large, twisted-horned kudu, the African antelope that was one of Hemingway's obsessions. Another amusing detail is the stamp that he used to put on his envelopes, saying 'I never write letters'.

Behind the house stands a 12-metre (39-foot) tower with a small study containing a little desk decorated with the skin of a bright-eyed cat and a telescope. This is where Hemingway used to shut himself away to put the final touches to his manuscripts. His cats had the floor below. The garden is full of magnificent palm trees and the relics of the worldwide fame that his best-sellers brought him: the swimming pool where he entertained Hollywood stars and, in its boathouse, the famous, well-preserved wooden yacht *Pilar*, which could take up to six people on deep-sea fishing trips. On the roof, in place of a boring old wheelhouse, Hemingway found it more useful to install a bar. You can also see the graves of his four dogs (but not those of his 60 cats), the only creatures who were allowed to disturb him when he was writing.

★ **Parque Lenin**: 20 kilometres (12 miles) southwest of town. Open Wednesday to Sunday 10am–6pm. One of the few parks in Havana, this is where Cubans like to go for family picnics at the weekend. There are one or two old-fashioned attractions and a dilapidated sports ground, there is a lake for swimming, fishing or boating. The rest of the week, this huge place is quite deserted and the rusty merry-go-rounds are not a cheerful sight. But there are some little cafés and a very classy restaurant called Las Ruinas.

★ **Jardín Botánico** (National Botanic Garden): Carretera Rocio, after the Parque Lenin. Open Wednesday to Sunday 9am–5pm (6pm in summer). Admission 60 cents just to visit, $1 for a guided tour and $3 to tour the park in a little train. This magnificent and extensive park contains tropical species from all over the world (some of them extremely rare) as well as a very impressive collection of orchids that blossom from mid-December to mid-January. Don't miss the Japanese garden and the prehistoric palm tree known as the 'living fossil'.

Guanabacoa

About 4 kilometres (2.5 miles) southeast of the centre, this straggling old independent colonial village has been engulfed by sprawling Havana. It was founded in 1743 by decree of King Philip V as a sugar and tobacco centre. The many Afro-Cubans and Creoles in the town are descendants of the slaves who were transported here to work in the cane fields. Religious fervour is very strong in Guanabacoa, and one of the rare museums dedicated to santería is located here. This Afro-Cuban religion is firmly rooted in popular culture (*see* 'General Information'). Guanabacoa has retained much of its character, and it's worth spending a good half-day here.

★ Try to find a Cuban to take you to the following sights because they are not easy to find: **Potosí Hermitage**, the oldest church in the country (dating from 1644); the **Santo Domingo Monastery** (1748), built in honour of Saint Domingo Guzmán (one of the instigators of the Inquisition), and the **San Francisco Monastery**.

Regla

This area on the other side of the bay of Havana is reached by *lancha* (a small motorboat) from the old town (from Desamparados San Pedro), at the top of Lonja del Comercio. The area is now in its fourth century of existence. Its population is mostly black or of mixed race, and santería rituals are very strong here.

★ **Church of the Santísima Virgen de Regla**: the patron saint of sailors and of Havana, the famous black Most Holy Virgin of Regla holds a white baby Jesus in her arms. She is much venerated by the local people and a huge festival takes place in her honour on 8 September, with lots of music and santería rituals.

LEAVING HAVANA

By Car

– **Eastwards** (Playa del Este, Varadero, Matanzas): take the Malecón all the way to the end (in old town), then the tunnel to Habana del Este then continue straight ahead. There's a toll booth before Cojimar.

– **Westwards** (Viñales, Pinar del Río): take the Malecón to Miramar (after the tunnel, then 5th Avenue), then follow the signs to the *autopista* (motorway).

By Bus

If you are patient and determined it is possible to travel from Havana by bus, but book at least one day ahead.

🚌 **Bus station** (map IV, D3): avenida de Independencia and calle 19 de Mayo. Open 7.30am–9pm. There is an information desk next to the waiting room opposite the bookshop. Reservations and tickets (in US dollars only) are available from an air-conditioned office just past the pharmacy, in a passage on the right off the grand hall (open 24 hours).

– Fares: **Pinar del Río** $7, **Varadero** $6, **Trinidad** $17, **Holguín** $25, **Santiago** $35, **Cienfuegos** $14.

– For **Pinar del Río**: nine buses a day, from 7am–9pm. Journey takes about 3 hours.

– For **Viñales**: one bus, after 9am, taking just under 3 hours.

– For **Matanzas**: two buses a day, at 5am and 6.30pm.

– For **Varadero**: two buses a day, at 4am and 2pm. Journey time 2 hours 45 minutes.

– For **Playa Girón**: one bus late morning. Journey time 6 hours.

– For **Cienfuegos**: five buses from 6.15am to 9.15pm. Journey time 5 hours.

– For **Trinidad**: one bus at 5.45am. Journey time 5 hours 30 minutes.

– For **Sancti Spiritus**: two buses very early in the morning.

– For **Camagüey**: two buses, at 8am and 5.30pm. Journey time over 8 hours 30 minutes.

– For **Holguín**: one bus in the morning and one at the end of the day. Journey time around 12 hours.

– For **Santiago**: two buses, after 12am and 7pm ('express'). Journey time about 14 hours.

By Coach

– **Agence Viazul**: avenida 26 and Zoológico, Nuevo Vedado. ☎ 81-14-13, 81-56- 72 and 81-11-08. Fax: 66-60-92. Tickets on sale from 7am–7pm. This new, state-run bus terminal feels like a small airport. The company (also new) has modern, almost luxurious 40-seat Mercedes buses, with air-conditioning and toilets. It runs a service to and from the biggest towns in the country. Timetables may change, so phone to check. It's best to reserve seats in advance (at least 1–2 hours ahead) but it is not possible to reserve seats for the return journey. Fares are payable in dollars. The advantages of Viazul buses are punctuality, speed, comfort and safety, and the fact that they operate when the others don't. Best of all, Viazul buses are regularly filled with petrol. The disadvantage is that the Cubans never use them, so they are usually half empty and not particularly interesting.

– Fares: **Pinar del Río** $11, **Varadero** $10, **Trinidad** $25, **Sancti Spiritus** $28, **Santiago** $51, **Viñales** $12.

– For **Varadero**: departures at 8am, 8.30am and 6pm arriving at 10.45am, 11.15am and 8.45pm. Return coaches from Varadero to Havana depart at 8am, 4pm and 6pm, arriving at 10.45am, 6.45pm and 8.45pm.

– For **Trinidad**: departs at 8.15am, arrives at 1.50pm. Trinidad to Havana departs at 3pm, arriving at 8.35pm.

– For **Santiago de Cuba**: departures daily at 3pm, arriving in Santiago the next day in the cool of the morning (6.50am). Santiago to Havana departures are Monday and Thursday 4pm and 8pm, arriving at 8am and 10am. This coach also goes to **Santa Clara**, **Sancti Spiritus**, **Ciego de Avila**, **Camagüey**, **Las Tunas**, **Holguín** and **Bayamo**.

– For **Viñales**: departures every two days at 9am, arriving at 12.15pm, stopping at **Pinar del Rio**.

By Train

Trains are slightly more comfortable than buses, and are booked up a long time in advance by Cubans. However, some seats are set aside for foreign tourists paying in dollars, who must book in advance at the central station or, even better, at the Ferrotur agency (see 'Useful Addresses'). A passport is needed when booking. There is only one class, with no couchettes, but there are reclining seats. Drinks are served on the train, but no food, so take some provisions, including plenty of water. Journey times vary, and departure times on the boards are not very reliable.

– **Central station**: ☎ 61-42-59. Open daily 8am–4pm. Bookings in person only. There is always a crowd, but foreigners with dollars are often allowed to jump the queue. Tickets are on sale in the small former Ladis office at the side of the station. Some of the staff speak English.

– **Fares**: **Bayamo** $26, **Cienfuegos** $9.50, **Holguín** $27, **Las Tunas** $27, Mantanzas $2.80 (bought well before departure), **Pinar del Río** $6.50, **Sancti Spiritus** $13.50, **Santiago** $30.50 for an ordinary train ($43 for an air-conditioned train).

– For **Santiago**: a night train departs late afternoon, and arrives the following morning (more than 14 hours).

– For **Las Tunas** and **Camagüey**: an early-morning train.

– For **Sancti Spiritus**: a night train arrives early next morning, taking just under 8 hours.

– For **Cienfuegos**: one train at about 1pm arriving 11.35pm. Duration over 10 hours.

– For **Bayamo**: one train every two days leaves shortly after 8pm arriving the following day at 10.20am (about 14 hours). There is a connection for **Manzanillo**.

– For **Holguín**: one train a day departs in the afternoon and arrives the following morning at about 4am.

– For **Pinar del Río**: there's an evening train every two days arriving during the night. Journey time 5 hours 15 minutes.

– For **Matanzas**: three trains a day at 4am, 8.30am and 9pm from Casablanca station (avenida de Gamis; map II, off D1). ☎ 62-48-88. Try to catch the 8.30am train that only makes five stops (taking 3 hours), compared to 49 stops by the other two services.

By Plane

There are three airports in the same area, so be sure to go to the right one. Check with the ticket agency. In high season, reservations are strongly recommended. For the islands, reservations at special rates are often included in the hotel booking. For details of **airports** and **airlines** *see* 'Getting There' at the start of the section on Havana.

Airport bus: green-and-white French buses, given to Cuba by the Paris Transport Association in 1997, depart for the airport from la Rampa (in Vedado). The fare (payable in pesos) is about $1.

Note: an airport tax of $20 is payable on departure, in cash only. Make sure you put the money aside on arrival in Cuba, since the minimum amount of cash you can withdraw at the airport is $100.

– **Fares**: **Baracoa** $180, **Bayamo** or **Camagüey** $72, **Cayo Coco** $50, **Cayo Largo** $60, **Ciego de Avila** $50, **Guantánamo** $100, **Holguín** $82, **Las Tunas** $80, **Manzanillo** $82, **Santiago** $90, **Trinidad** $50, **Varadero** $30.

– For **Santiago**: 24 flights a week on Cubana. Duration (non-stop): between 1 hour and 20 to 30 minutes.

– For **Varadero**: three flights a day with Lacsa. Duration: 30 minutes.

– For **Trinidad**: one flight a week with Lacsa. Duration: 50 minutes.

– For **Camagüey**: nine flights a week (Cubana). Duration: 1 hour 35 minutes.

– For **Holguín**: nine flights a week with Cubana. Duration (non-stop): about 1 hour 30 minutes.

– For **Guantánamo**: seven flights a week with Cubana. Duration: 2 hours 40 minutes.

– For **Bayamo**: four flights a week (Cubana). Duration: around 2 hours.

– For **Ciego de Avila**: two flights a week with Cubana. Duration: 1 hour 25 minutes.

– For **Isla de la Juventud** (Gerona): 19 flights a week with Cubana.

– For **Cayo Coco**: four flights a week with Cubana and one a week with Lacsa. Duration: 1 hour 40 minutes.

– For **Cayo Largo**: two flights a day with Aero Caribbean and two a week with Lacsa. Duration: 50 minutes.

– For **Las Tunas**: three flights a week with Cubana. Duration: 2 hours.

– For **Manzanillo**: four flights a week with Cubana. Duration: 2 hours.

– For **Baracoa**: three flights a week (with stopover). Duration: 3 hours 30 minutes.

The West of Cuba

The west, commonly known as the province of Pinar del Río, will show you just one of the many faces of this island, and a pretty one at that! For many people, it is quite simply the most beautiful area in Cuba. However, it has not attracted vast numbers of tourists, for its beaches are not particularly special (with a few exceptions that we shall cover later). So much the better then, for this means that you will find peace and tranquillity here and the people will give you a warmer welcome.

The A4 *autopista* leaves Havana and runs through this typically Cuban region as far as Pinar del Río. After the first 20 kilometres (12 miles) you will find yourself in the countryside. Along the roadside locals will flag you down to try to interest you in their strings of garlic, jars of guava jam and even homemade cheese. Such items, exorbitantly priced in the cities, are much cheaper here.

The wild landscape of the west is initially made up of the gently rolling mountainous countryside of the Guaniguanico mountain range. This low-altitude chain (we're not talking about the Andes here), which is divided into two distinct sierras, Rosario and Los Oganos, is full of gigantic caves. It is clear why Che Guevara sought refuge here during the Cuban Missile Crisis in 1962. That said, the caves will not be the first thing to come to your attention, rather the thick pine forests interrupted by deep ochre or brick-coloured layers of earth, hence the name given to the province and to its capital, Pinar del Río.

In the heart of this region is the Viñales Valley, a wonderful place that alone is well worth the detour. Together with the Vuelta Abajo triangle, this fertile oasis is tobacco country, where the aromatic leaves are gathered before being sent around the world to be smoked as Havanas (because they are manufactured in Havana). However, the main attraction at Viñales are the *mogotes*, strange geological formations covered in vegetation that give the enchanting landscape of the valley its magic feel.

An Unspoiled Region

Geologically speaking, this is the oldest part of the island. In the course of the various glacial periods, the water level in this region rose extensively, but the tips of the *mogotes* remained above the surface. So when the waters finally abated, part of the primary forest had consequently survived. One species surviving from this period is the cork palm (*palma corcho*). There are also lots of pine trees, generally at moderate altitudes (500–900 metres/1,640–1,970 feet). Other species include tree ferns; introduced eucalyptus trees and numerous *altea* (from the hibiscus family), which enjoy a special place in Cubans' hearts as the wood is used to make baseball bats. There's also the *almacigo*, a very attractive tree nicknamed the *árbol del turista* (tourist tree), as its red bark and two main branches resemble the sunburned foreign legs seen on the island's beaches.

Beyond Viñales, towards the end of the mountain range, is the Guanahaca-bibes peninsula. It is virtually deserted and its shape is strangely reminiscent of a crocodile's head (this is how Cuba got its nickname of the 'green

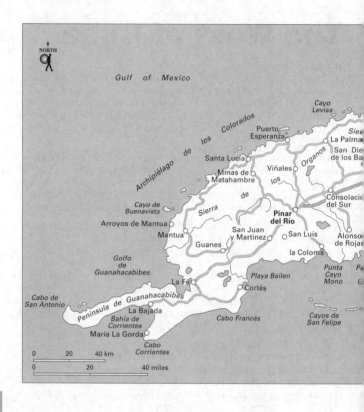

crocodile'). There is a small dream of a beach called María La Gorda, just on the croc's tail.

GETTING THERE

The region is very poorly served in terms of trains, and buses are virtually non-existent, so you are strongly advised to hire a car for travelling through this region. You won't regret it, as there are numerous drives and some routes are absolutely superb. With a car you can also get away from the main roads and explore the province in more depth. Having said that there are numerous excursions from Viñales organized by locals – including horse-riding, hiking and cross-country trips in four-wheel-drives – so if you just want to do one of these excursions a car isn't necessary.

There are several itineraries: via the main motorway (the A4), for those in a hurry; along the main road for those with a little more time; and via the northern coastal road for those who have plenty of time. The itinerary below starts on the motorway, continues on the main road and ends with a tour

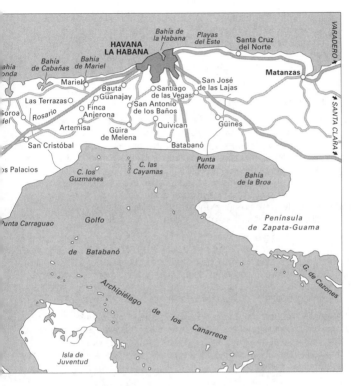

HAVANA TO PINAR DEL RÍO

around the coast. You can of course make up your own circuit, starting from these three routes.

> **TIP** Make sure you have a good map, as road signs are almost non-existent, and fill up with fuel wherever you can, as petrol stations are also quite rare. It is worth noting that, although the busier roads are generally in reasonable condition, you should be particularly careful on minor mountain roads where there are potholes and ruts everywhere. Even on the good roads the smooth surface can suddenly give way to a stretch of potholes.

LAS TERRAZAS   DIALLING CODE: 085

The resort of Las Terrazas is set in the Sierra del Rosario, a sumptuous landscape (replanted to a great extent) 51 kilometres (30 miles) from Havana. It is here that Che Guevara carried out his training before his Bolivian expedition. From the motorway travelling towards Pinar, take the turning to the right around 700 metres after the 'advertising' hoarding announcing it, then continue straight on. Follow the arrows for 7 kilometres (4 miles). The road isn't very exciting at the start, but it's the right one! There's a small admission charge to the estate ($2 per person).

An Ambitious Project

As in many other parts of the island, the forests that cover this area were gradually cut back over the centuries. Whether the land was needed for sugar-cane plantations, or the wood required for ship repairs or the production of *charcola* for cooking, the landscape suffered radically. Stripped of trees, the once-superb hillsides became a pitiful sight. But in 1968 a political decision was made to carry out reforestation and thousands upon thousands of trees were planted. Hundreds of country people worked on the project – and a real little community grew up around what was initially intended as temporary accommodation (the long buildings that can be seen on arrival).

Once the trees had grown, the authorities decided to turn the area into a sort of eco-tourist resort. In 1985, 50,000 hectares (123,550 acres) were declared biosphere reserves, and in 1994 the Moka, a luxury hotel beside a large artificial lake stocked with trout, opened its doors. The next (and more difficult) stage of the project was to attract tourists to the nature-based activities – nature trails, birdwatching, boat trips, horse-riding, fishing, cycling and the like.

The lake in the heart of this region is surrounded by *cabañas* on stilts – typical homes in this rural area. There's also a hospital, a disco and even a rodeo arena (that doubles as a football ground when no shows are scheduled). They are all connected by dozens of steps, hence the name, which literally means 'terraces'.

Despite all this, few people seem aware of the site's existence and it certainly seems very quiet. The original eco-tourism concept hasn't really caught on as much as expected, and it all seems rather low key, which is excellent if you're looking for a bit of peace and quiet.

If you have the time, there are around 50 abandoned plantations to visit in the area. As the hotel is very expensive, a cheaper alternative is to arrive early and simply spend the day here. A swim in the San Juan river makes a trip well worthwhile and the area is home to the *zunzuncito*, one of the world's smallest birds, although you will be lucky to catch a glimpse of it.

USEFUL ADDRESS

■ **CUPET service station**: on the outskirts of the village towards Soroa.

GETTING AROUND

If you turn right just after the toll booth at the entrance, you come to an attractive terrace, where the ruins of an old coffee-planter's house have been turned into the Buenavista restaurant (the fairly pricey set menu is $13). This is the island's narrowest point, from where (before the trees had grown so much) it was possible to see both sides of the island. Otherwise, continue straight on and you'll come out at the lake and, a little higher up, the hotel.

WHERE TO STAY AND EAT

⌂ El Taburete campsite: On the edge of Río San Juan, reached by a path, on the left before the Hotel Moka. Allow $5 per person. Open all year. There are around 50 very basic *cabañas* in the middle of the forest for two to four people. No facilities and somewhat unhygienic, but very cheap and so really for hard-up nature lovers. It's possible to bathe in the river.

⌂ ✕ Hotel Moka: turn left before you get to the lake. ☎ 24-37-39 and 24-37-40. For bookings ☎ and fax: 24-53-05. Double rooms cost around $105, which is expensive even given the level of comfort and facilities, but still worth it if you can afford it. Surrounded by tropical vegetation, this is a very beautiful hotel with neo-colonial charm, built in 1994 around an algarrobo tree and tastefully designed by none other than the Minister for Tourism himself. Splendid rooms all have balcony, air-conditioning, TV, international telephone and bathroom with a picture window so that you can enjoy the garden from the tub. Fantastic! Overhanging the garden is a splendid swimming pool with bar. There are several restaurants: the one near the swimming pool does *parillada*, while the other is more sophisticated (grilled chicken, lobster, shrimps, veal, etc.). Lots of activities are available: tennis, horse-riding, bicycle hire and tours of the reserve. Reservations prior to arrival are essential. Visa accepted.

WHAT TO SEE AND DO

★ **Angerona**: 46 kilometres (28 miles) west of Havana. Leave the motorway (A4) at Artemisa, then take the road to the left and continue for around 7 kilometres (4 miles). There is no sign. Turn down the track to the left, marked by some square stone pillars, and continue through the sugar-cane fields. Follow the dirt track for around 700 metres and Angerona is at the end.

Angerona is not a village, but rather an old coffee plantation, founded in 1820 by a Franco-German married to a Haitian, that has fallen completely into ruin. This plantation was once the second largest in the country, employing 500 slaves. Several films have been shot here, including *El Siglo de Las Luces* (The Age of Enlightenment) from the historical novel by Alejo Carpentier. Nevertheless, the place seems to be little known either to tourists or to many Cubans (this can sometimes lead to problems if you are asking for directions), which means you will receive full benefit from the tranquillity.

The Greek statue of Angerona, goddess of fertility, greets you against a backdrop of romantic ruins. The site warden will act as a guide if you can find him. The mansion house, which must once have been the height of luxury, has burned down – nothing remains but a few ruins supported by thick columns. At the back, the house with a tower was the slaves' dormitory. Those who died while working were buried behind it in a cemetery that has disappeared beneath the vegetation.

★ Pleasant **walk** and fantastic **swim**: leave the village of Las Terrazas and near the rodeo, on the way to the Hotel Moka, take the road on the left and continue for about 3 kilometres (1.5 miles) through the gently rolling hills of El Salón and El Taburete. You can't go wrong as the road follows a massive metal pipe. At the end is a small car-park. From there the path follows the San Juan river and you will soon come across some superb natural swimming pools formed by the rapids – where you should dive in without further ado. There are a few little huts where you can shelter, and this is a favourite picnic spot among weekending Cubans.

SOROA

Also off the Havana–Pinar del Río motorway, level with Candelaria, is this charming holiday village at the foot of the mountains. Nature's fertility and exuberance abound in this little haven of calm, renowned for its waterfall and botanical gardens. There are also some nice walks in the area.

The village owes its name to a French landowner who, like many others, settled here after fleeing Haiti at the time of the Revolution. He planted coffee and made his fortune. As in Las Terrazas, there are numerous ruined plantation buildings in the area.

GETTING THERE

If you are travelling from Las Terrazas to Soroa, the easiest route is along the road inside the park to come out at the other side. If you come across anyone en route, check that you are going the right way as there are no signs. There are striking landscapes, but the road is fairly poor.

WHERE TO STAY AND EAT

🛏 ✗ **Villa Soroa**: in the centre of the resort. ☎ 85-21-22 or 85-20-41. A double or twin room costs $38–43 and in the restaurant main dishes are around $5–8.The only hotel in Soroa, with architecture akin to a 1960s motel. It is part of the Horizontes chain. The concrete chalets surround an attractive swimming pool in a lovely, well-kept garden and have very clean, simple, colourful rooms with air-conditioning, shower and fridge. The portions in the restaurant are small, but the food's decent enough: spaghetti bolognese, chicken and pork.

✗ **El Salto**: Open daily 11.30am–4pm. At the starting point for the walk to the waterfall is this nice and lively thatched restaurant, fre-

quented by artists and local craftsmen. While some perform massages, others draw portraits of Che or even sing '*Guantanamera*' to the amusement of the tourists setting off on their walk. Chicken or *bistec de cerdo* for $3–5. Tickets for the waterfall are sold here.

✗ **El Castillo de Las Nubes**: 2 kilometres (1 mile) above the botanical gardens. Open 11.30am–4pm. You can't miss it, for this strange stone castle dominates the village. It is just a restaurant, not a hotel. A meal costs around $10, with chicken and pork reasonably priced. There is a terrace with a beautiful panoramic view over the valley. Continue a few hundred metres along the road to the end for more superb views.

WHAT TO SEE AND DO

★ **Botanical Gardens** (Orquideario): on the way into the village, on the left. Generally open daily 9am–4pm, with restricted hours on Sunday. Admission $3; guided visits only. This garden was created on land belonging to a lawyer of Spanish origin who wanted to pay homage to his deceased daughter and who adored orchids. It was his Japanese gardener who devised the majority of hybrids that you can see here. There are some beautiful varieties of orchid (more than 700), which are at their best in November or December when they flower, and less interesting between May and November.

★ **The 'Rainbow' waterfall**: entrance by the El Salto restaurant, down the steps from the roadside on the other side of the botanical gardens. Admission $2. Allow 30 minutes to get there, and a little longer to get back as it is uphill. At around 9am, if it is sunny, a rainbow appears above this beautiful 22-metre (72-foot) high waterfall. After the exertion, you can bathe under the cascades.

★ **The 'Baños Romanos'** (sulphurous swimming pool): This 2- by 3-metre (6- by 9-foot) pool, built in 1945, is on the left before the road to the *mirador*. The admission charge is negotiable. The water has therapeutic benefits for rheumatism and arthritis. A curious man called Pedro, a specialist in Chinese medicine, will show you his massage technique, which may not necessarily conform to the usual hygiene standards, but nevertheless has undeniable psychological benefits!

– **Walks**: Ask your hotel staff to recommend the best places. You can take a pleasant walk to the *mirador* in around 30 minutes, starting from the car-park of the El Salto restaurant. There are beautiful panoramic views, as expected. You could also go on horseback.

SAN DIEGO DE LOS BAÑOS DIALLING CODE: 7

THE WEST OF CUBA

Also off the motorway, to the right when coming from Havana, is this little spa town of no great charm on the banks of a river. Virtually devoid of tourists, this place is, however, very well known among Cubans, who come here for treatment at least once in their lives. It caters mainly for skin disorders and is a very tranquil spot. The spa is 100 metres away, opposite the Hotel Mirador. You can take a shared or individual bath in the warm, sulphurous water (renowned for its benefits to the skin and joints), and then have a massage.

USEFUL ADDRESS

■ **CUPET service station**: on the left-hand side as you enter the village from the Soroa direction.

WHERE TO STAY AND EAT

There are not many hotels and restaurants in the resort, and the one at the Municipal Spa Centre is the only one open to tourists.

🛏 ✕ **Hotel Mirador**: At the end of calle 23. ☎ 783-38. Rooms are pricey – up to $40, but it's the only place to stay in town. The building has a vague colonial charm, freshwater swimming pool and pretty flower garden. The rooms are decent enough, but nothing amazing, with all mod cons and in some cases a view over the park. The restaurant (chicken or pork for around $6) and bar are next to the swimming pool. It all sounds nice, but it lacks atmosphere and the service is mediocre.

IN THE AREA

★ **Cueva de los Portales** (Los Portales cavern): not at all easy to find, around 15 kilometres (10 miles) along the San Andres road northwest of San Diego de los Baños. Make sure you have a good map and check with passers-by that you are going the right way at every opportunity. Needless to say, there are no signs and many people won't even have heard of this cave, even though it is classed as a national monument. Open generally 8am–5pm. The caretaker also acts as a guide.

It is a huge cave hidden in the undergrowth, and a stream passes under the arched entrance. The site itself is rather impressive, with jungle noises providing the background music. Inside, the high roof of the cave is adorned with enormous stalactites. Although there isn't a great deal to see, its wild setting and the play of light on the rocks and plants is a delightful sight.

This cave has been a tourist sight since the end of the 1950s. It was after Che Guevara's visit as a tourist that he thought of hiding here during the 1962 Missile Crisis – he couldn't have found a better hidey-hole, especially as the missiles themselves were hidden not far away. Guevara used the cave as a strategic base and refuge for his platoon, and he and around 30 men spent 45 days inside, communicating with Castro by radio. In the centre is a water reservoir. Narrow steps lead to smaller caves and some natural balconies. On one of them is the stone table where Guevara used to sit and write. In a recess is a tiny, roughly built, breeze-block and cement hut – his headquarters. There is also the iron bed of his second-in-command, an old mattress and his desk. In an inner chamber right at the back of the cave is Guevara's camp-bed. There is alleged to be a secret tunnel out of the cave – which would seem sensible given that otherwise Guevara would have been trapped in his bed in the event of enemy attack.

★ **La Guira National Park**: around 20 kilometres (12 miles) west of San Diego, on a little road. You can't see very much of the park, for even though it's huge, it is poorly organized. Tourists can visit the garden belonging to the former owner of the estate, Cortina, who was the richest man in the area. His mansion was destroyed by fire, and all that remains are the French-style gardens, the lake covered with water lilies, and a little waterfall. It makes a pleasant walk, but nothing spectacular.

★ **Parque Huéspedes**: about 12 kilometres (7 miles) from Guira Park, on the forest road to Viñales. This is also difficult to find – you will need to ask the way although, once again, not many people will have heard of it. This is the heart of the sierra del Rosario, and far from civilization. Lizards and iguanas seem to be the only inhabitants. There are a few log *cabañas* on stilts to welcome campers (but only in summer). It's fine for travellers with a sense of adventure, with lots of walks. At the foot of the camp, steps lead to the San Salvador cave.

VIÑALES   DIALLING CODE: 8

Viñales is situated 30 kilometres (18 miles) north of Pinar del Río. No matter where you are coming from (the motorway, the coastal road or from the interior), you will reach this charming village by crossing the lush valley of the same name, where life continues, it seems, just as it always has.

Some enduring images in this bucolic landscape are the *bohíos,* small, traditional peasant dwellings, often made of wood and painted in bright colours, with palm-covered or metal roofs and a tiny veranda, often complete with rocking-chair. The inhabitants of these houses are most likely to be *bugueros* (tobacco planters) who are also often in their *casas de tabaco –* tall, strange-looking buildings with high roofs in the shape of an inverted V, used for drying the tobacco leaves from which thousands of families in the region make their living. There are ox-carts and *macheteros* at work in the sugar-cane fields.

Impressive rocky outcrops, known as *mogotes,* rise up from this untouched, peaceful landscape, lost in time. A colourful local legend says that these limestone formations, dating back to the Jurassic period, are the supporting columns of a gigantic cave that collapsed when a dinosaur sneezed! This is a sight not to be missed. Fortunately, you will have plenty of time to admire it from the balconies of the two best hotels in the village, which are in a fantastic location.

As for Viñales itself, the streets are very colourful and well shaded and the pleasant central square is overlooked by a delightful colonial church. The main road is characterized by great architectural unity: the houses are modest, one-storey buildings, often painted pink or blue, each with entrance steps leading to columned porches.

Viñales is the ideal place to take a breather for a few days, or even longer, especially since there are lots of walks in the area. And to top it all, the people are very hospitable, the climate is milder than on the coast and you can eat better here than anywhere else.

USEFUL ADDRESSES

✉ **Post office** (map II, A–B1): calle Fernandez.

🚌 **Bus station** (map II, B1): 63A calle Salvador Cisneros, opposite the main square and church. There are two buses a day from Havana, one operated by Viazul and the other public transport (Astro). There are also buses from Pinar del Río that stop at Viñales en route to La Palma, Bahía Honda and Puerto Esperanza.

■ **Currency exchange**: there are two banks side-by-side, both with currency exchange facilities – **Banco Popular de Ahorro** (map II, B1, **1**): 56 Salvador Cisneros. Open Monday–Friday 8am–noon and 1.30–4.30pm. You can withdraw money with a VISA card. **Banco de Credito y Comercio** (map II, B1, **1**): 58 Salvador Cisneros. Open 8am–noon and 1.30–

3pm. Changes cash and travellers' cheques but no credit card transactions.

■ **Bicycle hire**: there are plenty of hire outlets and all the proprietors of rented rooms will be happy to help you find one. Although such trade is not really authorized, it is not formally banned either, and the authorities seem to turn a blind eye. Hire costs around $3 per day.

■ **CUPET service station** (map II, B1, **2**): at the edge of the village, towards Puerto Esperanza and San Cayetano. It's the only one in the village, and has a phone booth.

■ **Policlinico de Viñales** (medical centre): calle Salvador Cisneros interno. ☎ 93-245 and 93-246.

WHERE TO STAY

Casas Particulares

Rooms in private homes are ideal if you haven't got the cash for a hotel. There are around 50 homeowners offering one or two rooms in their houses for rent. The rooms often sleep three or four people and the price is the same however many of you there are – generally around $15 a night. You will often be approached with the words: *Psst, una habitación!* There are all sorts of places, and taking a chance with someone you meet could lead to anything from a hovel to somewhere really special. The most important thing, apart from the size of the room, is that you get on well with the owners. Generally, even though there's not much traffic in the evening, it's best to choose a house in a street set back from the main road. If the one you opt for is full, the owners will always find you another room with their aunt, cousin or brother-in-law. Here are a few suggestions:

■ **Useful Addresses**

✉ Post office (map II)
🚌 Bus station (map II)
 1 Currency exchange (map II)
 2 CUPET service station (map II)

🛏 **Where to Stay**

 10 Nery Hernandez Rodriguez (map II)
 11 Villa Lioska (map II)
 12 Teresa Martinez Hernandez (map II)
 13 Regla Paula (map II)
 14 Villa Dulce Maria (map II)
 15 Sra Maria Elena Urra (map II)
 16 Hotel Las Magnolias (map I)
 17 Hotel Ranchón San Vincente (map I)

 18 La Ermita (map I)
 19 Los Jazmines (map I)
 20 Camping Dos Hermanas (map I)

✗ **Where to Eat**

 30 Casa de Don Tomás (map II)
 31 Mural de la Prehistoria (map I)
 32 El Palenque de Cimarrónes (map I)
 33 El Ranchón de San Vincente (map I)
 34 Cueva del Indio (map I)

🍷 **Nightlife**

 19 Hotel Los Jazmines disco (map I)
 32 El Palenque de Cimarrónes (map I)
 40 Patio de Decimista (map II)

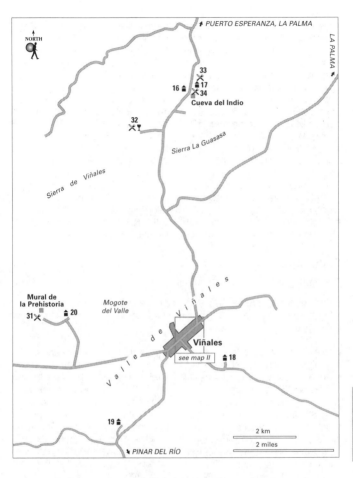

VIÑALES (MAP I)

♨ **Nery Hernandez Rodriguez** (map II, A2, **10**): 6 Carretera Pinar del Río. On the way into the village, on the left when arriving from Pinar. ☎ 93-331. Rooms (decorated in pink and sleeping up to five) cost around $15, and dinner costs $6 per person. The bathroom has hot water. The owners and their son, Noël, are kind and hospitable. Noël has made it his duty, as well as his pleasure, to act as your guide on various excursions. He has many strings to his bow: potholing, walking, horse-riding, etc.

♨ **Villa Lioska** (map II, A2, **11**): 129A calle Rafael Trejo. Two rooms for $15 with fan and $20 with air-conditioning, each sleeping up to four people. Meals available for $6. The spotless rooms are at the back of this pretty little blue-painted house and so are very quiet. The owner speaks English and the whole family is charming. If it is full **Villa Mercia** next door (No. 129) offers a room for four people. Next door again, **Villa Campana** (No. 127) offers something similar. The latter are not as nice as Villa Lioska.

Teresa Martinez Hernandez (map II, B2, **12**): 10 calle Camilo Cienfuegos. ☎ 93-267. Just one, ultra-clean room sleeping three or four people, for $15. There is a tiny lounge in front and a small balcony behind. The owners are delightful. Highly recommended.

♠ **Regla Paula** (map II, A2, **13**): 56 calle Camillo Cienfuegos. Two rooms costing $15 each. Regla (usually known as Nena) speaks English and is very kind and hospitable, as well as a very good cook. The rooms are small but respectable.

♠ **Villa Dulce Maria** (map II, A2, **14**): 11 calle Adela Azcuy. ☎ 93-340. One room sleeping up to four people for $15 in a little pink house in a tree-lined street.

♠ **Sra Maria Elena Urra** (map II, A2, **15**): 5 calle Adela Azcuy. ☎ 93-138. One nicely decorated, air-conditioned room sleeping up to four people for $20 in a small blue house with a little balcony above the street. Delightful owner.

In the Area

☆☆ Moderate

Listed below are a few moderately priced hotels, but bear in mind that for just a few dollars more, you could stay in one of the delightful hotels in the next category up.

♠ **Hotel Las Magnolias** (map I, **16**): on the Puerto Esperanza road. ☎ 93-60-62. Around 6 kilometres (4 miles) from Viñales, to the left of the Cueva del Indio car-park. Doubles cost $35 (breakfast not included), which is far too expensive for what it is. A small, plain, completely white and extremely clean house with three rooms, each with bathroom (hot water), TV and air-conditioning. It feels like a private home, but is actually state-run. The setting is marred by the neighbouring car-park. Lunch and dinner available. Only in case of dire necessity.

♠ **Hotel Ranchón San Vicente** (map 1, **17**): on the Puerto Esperanza road, 6 kilometres (4 miles) from Viñales, next to the Cueva del Indio. ☎ 93-62-00. Fax: 93-62-65. Bungalows for two people cost $40–45, including breakfast. The main building, on the edge of the road, is a spa undergoing construction work that may take some time as there isn't enough money to finish it. However, there are around 30 chalets (with showers, hot water and air-conditioning) on the other side of the road, set in a very nice park full of tropical trees. There is a small swimming pool, more for paddling than swimming lengths. It is possible to bathe in the garden's sulphurous spring water, but you have to pay for the pleasure (and it's expensive).

☆☆☆ Expensive

♠ **La Ermita** map I, **18**): carretera La Ermita, 2 kilometres (1 mile) above the village. ☎ 93-60-71. Fax: 93-60-69. Double rooms cost $55, including buffet breakfast. Modern, 1960s neo-colonial style hotel with pillared balconies and long galleries. It consists of several long buildings set in a big garden, all of which blend well with the landscape. Spotless rooms, each with bathroom. Although breakfast is OK, the restaurant itself is rather disappointing. Organized excursions, horse-riding. The main attraction, apart from the swimming pool (open to the public; admission $1) and the tennis courts, is its strategic position – you overlook the whole valley from its gardens and some rooms have panoramic views too. Sitting on the edge of the pool sipping a *mojito* from the bar and admiring the sunset over the *mogotes* is a very pleasurable way to start the evening.

▲ **Los Jazmines** (map I, **19**): carretera Viñales, on a hill 4 kilometres (2 miles) from the village, well signposted. ☎ 93-62-05. Fax: 93-62-15. A double room with breakfast costs $60. Very beautiful, pastel pink colonial house with a flower garden and swimming pool. La Ermita's main competitor and equally well maintained. There are three choices: you can stay in the main building (spacious but slightly more old-fashioned rooms), the annex building (quieter and very well kept)

or the chalets with terraces, nicely arranged in tiers on the hillside. The view of the valley is perhaps even more beautiful here, and the terrace round the splendid swimming pool is a very good spot from which to admire it. The only problem is that you are a bit far from the restaurants in the village. At least there's a disco. Also hiking and horse-riding.

Campsites

▲ **Dos Hermanas campsite** (map I, **20**): at the entrance to the Mural de la Prehistoria site (*see below*). ☎ 93-223. Pitches cost around $5 per person. Fidel Castro formally opened the site in 1996, and there are around 50 permanent chalets for two to four people, with rudimentary facilities. The standard of upkeep and cleaning leaves a lot to be desired, there is however a sweet little swimming pool, and the location at the foot of the twin *mogotes* from which the campsite takes it name (the 'two sisters') is very pleasant.

WHERE TO EAT

✕ **Private homes**: Eating in the place where you are staying is without doubt the simplest way to enjoy an inexpensive meal that will be better than in a restaurant. A really good meal could set you back only $6–8. You may even be able to choose what your hosts cook, and it's a good way of getting to know the Cubans.

✕ **Casa de Don Tomás** (map II, A2, **30**): calle Salvador Cisneros.

In the Area

✕ **Mural de la Prehistoria** (map I, **31**): 4 kilometres (2 miles) from Viñales, well signposted. ☎ 93-62-60. Open daily 11am–7pm. Note the

Dishes cost $6–8 or $10 for *las delicias* (the speciality). The oldest house in Viñales, built in 1889 from wood, with a terrace at the back and a balcony on the first floor, is the classiest restaurant in town. The speciality, a sort of homemade paella with chicken, pork, Spanish sausage and a touch of lobster, is unfortunately not particularly well-prepared or good value, so you may be better off choosing something else.

admission charge for the site and the car-park at the entrance ($1). A full meal costs $15, and don't worry if you are advised to order one between two – the portions are so large this is often the best idea. This is the most renowned restaurant in the area, serving the best pork in Cuba. Extensive set menu, including smoked and roast pork, rice, cassava (or yam), salad, bananas, fruit salad and coffee. Come early or late to avoid large groups of tourists. Outdoor dining beneath a large thatched canopy, next to the famous rock paintings (see 'What to Do'). The young, dynamic 'Director of Public Relations' will proudly show you behind the scenes, taking visitors on a tour of the kitchens. It's very touristy, as all the coaches visiting the valley stop here. But don't let that put you off, for the atmosphere is still good, thanks to the trio of Cuban musicians who drown out the noise of the tourists.

✕ **El Palenque de Cimarrónes** (map 1, **32**): on the Puerto Esperanza road, just before the Cueva del Indio, on the left. To get here, you can either go by the tunnel through one of the *mogotes* ($1), or circumnavigate it by car. Open noon–4pm. Large portions for around $5. A lovely restaurant under

a thatched canopy surrounded by superb *mogotes*. Pleasant background music. A few groups come, but it is rarely too crowded for comfort. Specialities are *pollo a la cimarrón, cerdo asado* and *arroz mixto*. The cave at the front of the tunnel is a bar and nightclub (see 'What to Do').

✕ **El Ranchón de San Vicente** (map 1, **33**): the restaurant at the Hotel San Vicente, behind the Cueva del Indio (see 'Where to Stay' *above*). Leaving the caves, turn right and cross a little bridge. Open from noon–5pm. There is a set menu for $11. Same type of food (specializes in pork), and same long tables under a thatched canopy as at the Mural de la Prehistoria restaurant. This is more intimate, but the Mural has better food.

✕ **Cueva del Indio** (map I, **34**): on the Puerto Esperanza road, opposite the eponymous cave. ☎ 93-62-80. Open 11am–5pm. The surroundings are somewhat austere, and dishes cost $5–8. Not particularly recommended, especially as other places enjoy a nicer setting.

Nightlife

❢ **El Palenque de Cimarrónes**: on the left-hand side of the Puerto Esperanza road, well signposted just before the Cueva del Indio. Open all day, but the nightclub only functions at night. There are shows every night except Sunday, then a disco. Admission $5, including a drink. In a superb setting in a real cave is this amazing bar and disco, where dancers shake their stuff under an enormous stalactite suspended above the dance floor! For romantics there are small, intimate caves around the edge. Not many people come during the week, but on Saturday it's definitely *the* place to be. During the day it's a tea-room and bar where you can

have a drink before or after visiting La Cueva del Indio (see *below*). As for the Mural de la Prehistoria site, you don't have to pay for access to the caves during the day if you've just come to eat or drink.

❢ **Hotel Jazmines disco**: see 'Where to Stay'. Another popular meeting place for young people. It's not particularly close to the village, but then Cubans can hitch lifts here from the hotel clients. It's fairly average as night-spots go, but very popular nonetheless.

❢ **Patio del Decimista** (map II, A2, **40**): 120 calle Salvador Cisneros. Tiny and singularly lacking in charm, this is the only place within the village itself with any nightlife. Small local groups play regularly from around 10–11pm.

❢ **Open-air disco**: every Saturday evening a disco for younger people is staged on a sort of patio area to the right of the Casa de la Cultura. Entrance costs next to nothing, and the atmosphere is that of a big, jolly house party.

WHAT TO SEE

★ **The Valley**: you will get the best panoramic views from the hotels Ermita and Los Jazmines. Otherwise, take advantage of the little country roads (*see* 'What to Do and See in the Area' *below*).

★ **The Botanical Garden** (Casa de la Caridad; map II, B1): on the way out of Viñales towards Puerto Esperanza, on the bend after the service station. There is no sign on the small gate, but look out for the fruit laid out to dry in the sun. No admission charge; donations suggested. Two nice old ladies open the gates to paradise – a garden in an extraordinary setting adorned, among others, with splendid orchids and planted with mango trees, cocoa and coffee trees, sapodillas, trees bearing oranges, grapefruit, avocados, jackfruit and breadfruit, royal palms and many other exotic species. The ladies' Chinese grandfather planted the first trees in this garden and, consequently, the scent of Cuba mingles with that of Indonesia, China and Malaysia. The garden passed to his son and then to the latter's daughters. Their generosity compels you to give something in return. But make sure that you go there on your own, as some hotels abuse their kindness by taking you to the place without giving anything in exchange. Anyway, you will be 10 times more welcome on your own. Come early to avoid groups.

★ **La Casa de Cultura** (map II, A1): an old colonial house on the village's main square is used as an exhibition room for local artists. Entry is free. There's not a great deal to see, but the old municipal theatre on the first floor is worth a quick look and has a pleasant balcony. Downstairs is the traditional small gallery of portraits of courageous and heroic revolutionaries – *malagenes* as they are called here, after the head of the first local militia and one of Castro's brothers-in-arms.

WHAT TO DO

– **Hiking**: There are numerous possibilities for walking and hiking in the area – anything from 2 hours to a full day out. All the hotels mentioned earlier are in contact with the guides. Just put in a request the night before (it doesn't matter whether or not you are staying in the hotel). In general, expect to pay $5 per person. If you are renting a room in a private home, the owners may well offer to take you on a walk themselves. Particularly worth seeing are the **Camino Hacia el Arte**, the **Mayor Caverna de Cuba**, **Viñales desde adentro**, and **San Vicente**.

Another walk is to the **Acuáticos**, a little, remote community at the top of a mountain around 3 kilometres (2 miles) from the village. Its members have a particular veneration for water. Part of this area has been taken over by the military and it can be more difficult to get there.

– **Horse-riding**: you can hire horses everywhere, particularly from the hotels. This is the easiest way of arranging an outing, although the villagers will often offer you better rates. Allow around $5 per hour. The trek is quite fun – the horses are small and generally of a nervous but determined disposition, tending to go where they want rather than respond to their riders' timid commands.

– **Potholing**: the region boasts hundreds of caves, many of which have never been explored, and only a few are operated specifically with visitors in mind. A few have up to 150 kilometres (90 miles) of galleries; others harbour a subterranean lake. A rather good characteristic of these caves is that they tend to remain on much the same level as the entrance and do not descend far below ground level. The busiest is **Cueva del Indio** as it's popular with tour groups. If you prefer something a little off the tourist trail ask in the hotels – they will be able to find a qualified speleologist to guide you round some of the lesser-known places. The proprietors of rented rooms may also be able to find you a guide. Tours cost about $8 for 90 minutes.

Make sure you are wearing appropriate footwear and warm clothing, and take a torch.

IN THE AREA

★ **The Viñales Valley**: having taken in the best views from the La Ermita and Los Jazmines hotels, enjoy a drive round the little country roads, each more charming than the last. One of the region's main points of interest are the hundreds of caves – some are well known and cater specifically for tourists, whereas others have practically never been visited.

★ **La Cueva del Indio** (map I): on the Puerto Esperanza road, 6 kilometres (4 miles) from Viñales. Open daily 9am–5.30pm. Admission $3. The Indian Cave gets its name from the people who lived here. The best thing about visiting these caves is that after walking 500 metres, you continue by boat. There are one or two things of interest (such as the rocks that look like Christopher Columbus's ships or the 'molar' and 'ballerina' stalactites), but the explanation stops there. A local man found a few pieces of bone in the 1920s. It's a very attractive spot, but the tour is rather too brief and you only actually get to see a small part of the cave.

★ **El Mural de la Prehistoria** (map I): 4 kilometres (2 miles) from Viñales. Take the road towards Moncada and after 3 kilometres (2 miles), turn right at the sign. Continue for almost 2 kilometres (1 mile) and you will see the wall painting on the left; it's well signposted. Car-parking $1. This is the big local draw – a giant fresco painted on a cliff – and a fine example of a tourist attraction that has been conjured out of thin air. Hardly surprising, it was Fidel Castro who commissioned this work of art. In the 1960s, with the aim of attracting tourists to the area, he chose a Cuban artist, Leovigildo Gonzáles, an ex-pupil of Diego Rivera (the Mexican mural painter), to execute the frescoes on a cliff face. It took Gonzáles 10 years to complete the work. The naive paintings narrate the region's prehistory, when snails shared the land with dinosaurs.

It almost seems a shame that the surroundings have been marred with such a thing, but it is a nice area nevertheless, with an attractive area of lush grass

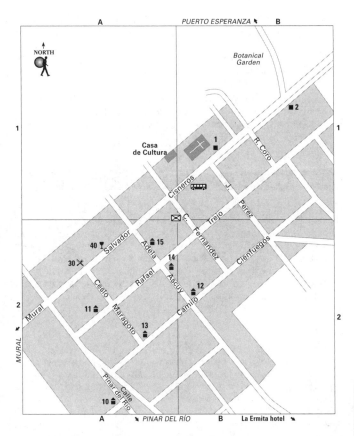

VIÑALES (MAP II) – TOWN CENTRE

in front of the cliff and a good-quality restaurant at its foot (*see* 'Where to Eat'). Take a walk in the countryside after eating a good meal in the restaurant. Locals will be delighted to show you around their homes and their small plots of land.

★ **The Santo Tomás Cave**: in El Moncada, a hamlet 18 kilometres (11 miles) southwest of Viñales, on the Miñas de Matahambre road. ☎ 38-44. After about 16 kilometres (10 miles), turn left towards Montada and it is on the right. At the roundabout, ask for the Centro de Espeología Santo Tomás. A Visitors' Centre (open daily 8.30am–6pm) has been built a stone's throw from the biggest cave in Cuba (47 kilometres/30 miles in all), which is also said to be the third largest in Latin America. There are always properly qualified guides (from the speleological school) on hand to show you round the cave with the help of a hard hat and torch. You can make advance reservations from the hotels in Viñales, although there isn't really any need.

The big plus point of this cave is that it remains unspoilt: it is a vast and majestic natural monument that has been variously inhabited by Indians and slaves. Nowadays its only residents are bats, freshwater shrimps and crabs. The basic visit, lasting one hour, costs $5; a two-hour visit costs $8, but you could easily spend more time here. Prices increase according to the amount of time spent in the cavern and the level of difficulty.

The more adventurous can spend the night here: comfort is not the primary concern and the facilities are minimal (bunks and neon lighting). Half board is around $17 per person, but it's only really for pros.

Other excursions can also be arranged for walkers and horse-riders.

PINAR DEL RÍO
DIALLING CODE: 082

If you come from Viñales then the hustle and bustle of Pinar del Río may at first seem a bit overwhelming, with people on bicycles whizzing all over the place and street traders offering countless different items and services, but the capital of the province has its own special charm. The pace of life is relaxed, and the streets are lined with attractive multicoloured houses complete with neo-classical columns, and there are other interesting architectural details. The town is famous for its thriving tobacco industry and it is possible to tour one of the factories (*see* 'What to See').

A Brief History

The town is actually fairly recent, dating only from the 19th century, when the descendants of a number of pirating families settled in the south of the province. Pinar expanded rapidly, with a wealth of elegant houses springing up in imitation of the neo-classical style of other towns and, of course, of Havana. A sumptuous theatre was also built. The town rapidly became known as the 'Cinderella of Cuba', as many people profited from its fertile soil to make their fortune, only to leave and invest their wealth elsewhere. Consequently, despite being right in the heart of the main tobacco-

■ **Useful Addresses**

   🚂 Railway station
   🚌 Bus station
   1 Banco Financiero Internacional
   2 Banco de Credito y Comercio
   3 CUPET service station

🛏 **Where to Stay**

   10 Casa Colonial
   11 Hotel Pinar del Río
   12 Hotel Globo

✕ **Where to Eat**

   20 Casa 1890
   21 Rumayor
   22 La Casona
   30 Coppelia

▼ **What to Do**

   21 Cabaret Rumayor
   31 Casa de la Música

🔒 **Shopping**

   41 Francisco Donatien cigars outlet
   42 La Casa de Garay

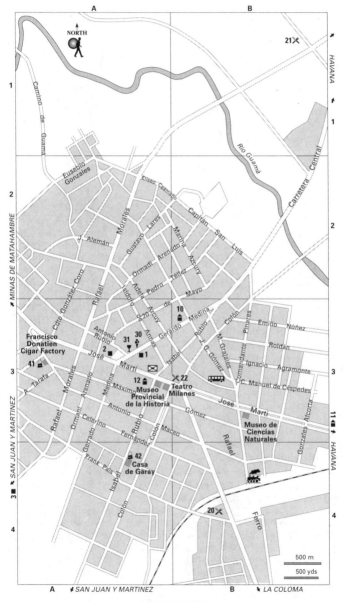

NORTH

PINAR DEL RÍO

growing region, the town did not have its own cigar-manufacturing facilities until 1965. This is doubly amazing since it is the third largest province in the country and practically all Cuban cigar *capas* (the outside layer or wrapper that represents 70 per cent of the cigar's price) are grown here. As a result, the region is obviously of great economic importance.

The singer Willy Chirino was originally from Pinar (he now lives in Miami). It is likewise the home town of Omar Linares, the great baseball champion, who refused the $40 million offered by the Americans to play in their league.

GETTING THERE

By bus: direct buses from Havana take about 3 hours. The train is not recommended as the journey is interminable.

USEFUL ADDRESSES

🚂 **Railway station** (map B4): calle Ferrocarril, in the Jamaica district.

🚌 **Bus station** (map B3): calle Adela Azcuy.

■ **Banco Financiero Internacional** (map A3, **1**): 46 calle Gerardo Medina. Open Monday to Friday 8am–3pm. You can change traveller's cheques and withdraw cash using Visa or MasterCard.

■ **Banco de Credito y Comercio** (map A3, **2**): 32 calle Martí. Open Monday to Friday 8am–noon and 1.30–3pm. Saturday 8–11am. You can change travellers' cheques and withdraw cash using Visa or Master-Card.

■ **Car hire**: There are three outlets attached to the Pinar del Río hotel (*see* 'Where to Stay'): **Havanautos** (in the car-park, ☎ 78-015): **Transautos** (in the hall, ☎ 78-278), **Micar** (in the car-park, ☎ 50-70–74).

■ **Car-parks**: at the Pinar del Río hotel (charge $1), 5-minutes' walk from the centre. Practical and safe solution for a carefree stroll around the busy streets of Pinar.

■ **CUPET service station**: (map, off A4, **3**): on the right 1 kilometre outside the city in the San Juan y Martinez direction.

WHERE TO STAY

🏠 **Casa Colonial** (map B3, **10**): 67 Gerardo Medina, between Adela Azcuy and Isidoro de Armas. ☎ 31-73. Private home with a few rooms (some with private bathroom) sleeping one to four people for $15–20. This building has a noble look about it – its welcoming facade looks neat and colonial. It has carved columns and chapters, a large lounge and a restful garden overlooked by the bedrooms. Impeccably maintained. Very simple but quite charming, with

a delightful owner. Highly recommended.

🏠 **Hotel Pinar del Río** (map off B3, **11**): at the end of calle Martí, on the way into town from Havana. ☎ 50-70 to 74. The biggest hotel in town has almost 150 rooms and a few chalets. A double room costs around $40, and chalets slightly more. The modern building lacks charm, but does have a large, attractive swimming pool. Basic rooms, with small balcony, telephone, air-conditioning, TV and shower. Note that the rooms above the swimming pool also have the nightclub just below . . .

♠ **Hotel Globo** (map A3, **12**): corner of José Martí and Isabel Rubio. ☎ 42-68. A room sleeping two to four costs around $25. A large yellow colonial building with red shutters, built in 1917, the Globo has retained a certain cachet or, more precisely, some cachet. Large old foyer with red leatherette benches, and a beautiful staircase. The high-ceilinged rooms are unfortunately rather antiquated (some could even be called dilapidated) and very poorly decorated. Avoid those next to the noisy roads. Air-conditioning and fridges, but no hot water.

In the Area

♠ **Villa Aguas Claras**: 7.5 kilometres (4.5 miles) along the Viñales road. ☎ (082) 784-27. Double chalets cost $24 (with fan) and $28 (air-conditioning). Without doubt this is the best place to stay if you are not staying in Viñales. Accommodation is in brick chalets set in a magnificent flower garden, full of mango trees and palms overlooking a large, but not particularly clean, swimming pool with a solarium and bar. Simple rooms but very reasonable and clean, each with a shower but no hot water. Restaurant on site. Lots of activities available from the information office: excursions, horse-riding, salsa classes, etc. Disadvantages are the mosquitoes and the music around the pool, which is sometimes too loud.

WHERE TO EAT

Strangely enough, Pinar del Río doesn't have much to offer in the way of restaurants, but here are a few that may be worth a visit. Otherwise, the little *confiterías* sell doughnuts and other deep-fried cakes.

✗ **Casa 1890** (map B4, **20**): corner of Rafael Ferro and Sol, 200 metres from the railway station. Open daily 11am–10pm. Denoted by the word '*Rumbos*' on the outside is this excellent, good-value establishment in a large house furnished in the 1970s. Dishes are a bargain $2–4, though the pizzas (dough with sauce) are probably best avoided. Staff are very welcoming.

✗ **Rumayor** (map B1, **21**): 2 kilometres (1 mile) from the centre of Pinar, on the Viñales road opposite the military hospital. Open daily noon–10pm. The classic main dishes cost from $5. This typical, large wooden house with thatched roof has a superb entrance hall decorated with mysterious Afro-Cuban masks used in santería ceremonies. The well-maintained garden is pleasant for lunch. There is also a bar and cabaret. More popular in the evening than at lunchtime.

✗ **La Casona** (map B3, **22**): on corner of Martí and Colón, opposite the theatre. Open Tuesday to Sunday 11am to around 8pm. Dishes only cost around $2, but the food is fairly average and depends on what is delivered. It's one of the least bad eateries in town, and centrally located.

♥ **Coppelia** (map A3, **30**): calle Gerardo Medina. Open Tuesday to Sunday noon to midnight. This branch of the famous Havana ice-cream parlour is a rather strange, almost surreal, place. Sometimes there is very little ice-cream and there may be a queue outside while the dining room and terrace are half empty. Payment is in pesos.

NIGHTLIFE

♪ Cabaret Rumayor (Arcoiris; map B1, **21**): *see also* 'Where to Eat'. Open for drinks from 9pm; shows start at 11pm Tuesday to Sunday. Admission $5. This is an open-air Afro-Cuban spectacular of music and dance in a magnificent green setting, with clumps of bamboo. Pinar's best night spot has a good reputation. It serves reasonably priced *mojitos*, and there's a disco after the show.

♪ Casa de la Música (map A3, **31**): calle Gerardo Medina, near calle Martí. Open Tuesday to Sunday 9–11pm. Nice, yet inexpensive, outdoor arena where the *trova* and bolero are played.

WHAT TO SEE

★ Francisco Donatien Cigar Factory (map A3): 152 calle A. Maceo. Open Monday to Friday 9am–4.30pm. Saturday 9am–noon. Admission $5. Shop open Monday to Friday 9am–4.30pm. Saturday 9am–noon. There is a guided tour in Spanish or English and you will be put with a group if there is one.

This little factory, opened in 1965, is far more modest than those in Havana and is housed in an old prison. It is named after a revolutionary who fought against Batista. The cigars made here can be purchased, but they can be of variable quality as some are intended for the Cuban market and others for export (under the Vegueros brand name). All the same they're not bad.

★ La Casa de Garay (map A4): 189 Recreo, between Sol and Virtudes. Open weekdays 9am–4pm. Admission $1. This tiny factory, using wholly manual labour, makes *guayabita* – a very sweet, fruit liqueur that is only consumed in Pinar del Río, probably because the fruit required, a small species of guava, only grows in this region. The drink was invented by an Asturian who serendipitously mixed *guayabita* with rum. He then sold the formula to a Señor Garay, who marketed it and set up the factory in 1892. It is possible to look around the small workshop where there are two production lines: one for local consumption and the other for sale to tourists. Practically nothing has changed since the factory first opened, and only 1,300 bottles are made each day. There's nothing else of great interest, but you can taste the product (be careful, 30 per cent alcohol in the tropics will soon raise your temperature!). If the tasting session gives you a hankering for the stuff, make sure you buy some here as it can't be found anywhere else in the country.

★ Museo de Ciencias Naturales (Natural History Museum, Palacio Guasch; map B3): corner of Martí and Cabada. Open Tuesday to Saturday 9am–4.30pm. Sunday 9am–12.30pm. Admission $1. This amazing building has very tacky decor – a mixture of neo-baroque and oriental fantasies (Greek columns and gargoyles in the shape of sea horses). The wildest is in the inner garden, which is adorned with concrete dinosaurs. Built in 1909, this megalomaniac mansion was home to a rich doctor named Guasch, whose extensive travels inspired him to commission this mixture of styles.

Today it houses the Museum of Natural History, full of dusty, kitsch curiosities that somehow seem to fit the setting very well: collections of cacti, coral, shells, exotic insects, artificial fish and snakes. There's also a flying squirrel, a lion and one of the smallest birds in the world, the *zunzuncito*, which is Cuban. But the real star is a 4.3-metre long (14-foot) crocodile that terrorized the population of Los Palacios for 10 years; all the chickens and pigs in the village kept disappearing mysteriously. Captured in 1984, it put up a valiant struggle before being overcome.

★ **Teatro Milanes** (map AB–3): corner of Martí and Colón. This large, 19th-century theatre was completed in 1842 and is the town's main monument. Built of wood, it has been restored several times.

★ **Museo Provincial de la Historia** (map A3): 58 Martí. Open Tuesday to Saturday 8am–4pm. Sunday 8am–1pm. Admission $1. Housed in a large, colonial building, one room is devoted to the history of the area and there are temporary exhibitions in the other rooms. It's less interesting than the natural history museum.

★ **La Casa del Ron**: calle Maceo, on the corner with calle Galiano, just beyond the Francisco Donatien cigar factory. They offer tasting sessions and there are many different sorts of rum to buy. It also sells CDs.

WHAT TO DO

★ **The Alejandro Robaïna plantation**: it is possible to visit various plantations in the area. You could either take a drive and see where you end up, or visit this highly renowned plantation owned by the Robaïna family. Open Monday to Saturday from around 9am to 5pm. There are no official guided tours but, as they take the time to show visitors round the plantation, a contribution of $2 per person is suggested.

From Pinar del Río, follow the San Juan y Martinez road for about 13 kilometres (8 miles) – keep an eye on the mileometer. Then turn left (there is no sign but there's a cafeteria on the left-hand side of the road). From this point on you really need to ask because there are lots of little roads and it's not clear which one to take. There are always children around who will be happy to accompany you – they are quick to spot people who look lost (don't forget to give them something for their trouble). The plantation is called Finca El Pinar (Barbacoa district).

Alejandro Robaïna is an imposing looking man and a veritable patriarch. He is very well known and respected in the small, closed world of cigar enthusiasts. He has one of the most beautiful plantations in the region and since 1997 has been the only living planter after whom the state has named a brand of cigar. This is the height of achievement for this long line of planters. Only the *capas* (the outer layers or wrappers of the cigar) are grown here. These leaves must be absolutely faultless, without holes or imperfections, otherwise they are simply thrown away. This is why the plants are covered in vast white nets that not only protect the harvest from insects but also prevent the wind and sun drying out the leaves. The cigar's wrapper must be very solid but must also have a certain elasticity, as well as a uniform colour. This is effectively the *haute couture* stage of the cigar-making process.

The tour is often led by Hirochi, Alejandro's youngest son (who speaks a little English) and includes the nurseries where the tobacco is grown, the drying barns and the family house with its numerous mementoes and photographs. The cigars are sold under the family brand for export, but the family does not have the right to sell them, as all their produce is bought by the state. However, you could ask your guide to give you a rolling demonstration and show you some of the things that can be done with tobacco leaves.

LEAVING PINAR DEL RÍO

By Bus

🚌 **Bus station** (map B3): calle Adela Azcuy. Generally speaking there are very few buses serving the west of Pinar del Río. You will waste a lot of time if you do not have your own transport. There are no buses to **Maria La Gorda**.

For **Viñales**: two buses per day, one with Astro and one with Viazul.

For **Havana**: around eight buses a day with Astro and one with Viazul (journey time 3 hours).

By Train

🚆 **Railway station** (map B4): calle Ferrocarril.

For **Havana**: there is only one train a day, at around 9am, stopping at several towns in the province en route: **Consolación**, **San Cristóbal**, **Candelaria**, **Artemisa** and **Paso Real** (not far from **San Diego de Los Baños**). It should arrive in Havana at around 3.30pm, but is always late. Reservations are essential – book as early as possible. The bus is by far the better option as it is much faster.

SAN JUAN Y MARTINEZ

San Juan is located 20 kilometres (12 miles) south of Pinar del Río via the main road, in the heart of Vuelta Abajo. It's a colourful, completely untouristy village typical of the area, with rows of pillared houses. At the edge of the village a large sign tells you that you are in '*La tierra del mejor tabaco del mundo*' ('the land of the best tobacco in the world').

As you come into the village, you will usually find children making signs at the cars, indicating a puncture. This is just a harmless way of getting cars to stop, so that the children can offer their services to visitors.

This is where the *vagueros* (plantation workers) live. Although 80 per cent of the land is privately owned, the planters may only sell the tobacco to the state. Planting takes place from October, and harvesting is three months later. The leaves are hung out to dry in *secaderos*, the thatched tobacco barns dotted around the fields. They are then sent to Havana to be made into cigars, hence their name. If you want to help with the harvest there are no formal arrangements, just ask one of the workers. In any case, you will often find that on arrival in a village, the locals will quickly offer you a visit to a *casa de tabaco*. However, visits to premium plantations are not allowed. It is essentially the wrapper of the cigar that is cultivated here, and as in Pinar del Río you will see huge white nets protecting the tobacco fields. Maize and rice are also grown here.

PLAYA BAILEN

Located 80 kilometres (50 miles) south of Pinar on the Cortés bay, Playa Bailen is to the west of San Juan y Martinez. Continue for around 10 kilometres (6 miles) after San Juan. A big advertising hoarding on the left points you in the right direction. Continue for another 8 kilometres (5 miles) and it is at the end. It is a huge, wild beach, virtually unknown to tourists but very popular with local families, who spend the weekends here from July to September. Playa Bailen is best visited in summer just to experience the friendly atmosphere and to make contact with the locals who go about their daily business in the shade of the palm trees. From September to May the beach is almost deserted.

> **TIP** ✗ Bring a picnic with you to eat on the beach as the 'café' at the entrance to the Villa Turística Bailen site and the restaurant behind the beach are best avoided. The Cubans tend eat in their chalets and some may invite you to share their crab soup or beans.

IN THE AREA

★ **Cocodrilos Sabanalamar** (crocodile farm): roughly 2 kilometres (1 mile) from Playa Bailen on the left; not easy to find and there are no signposts. There's a brown gate and then a sandy road for 600 metres. Open daily all day. Small admission fee and an extra charge for photos. Agree on prices before you visit. Poorly signposted and not very well maintained, the farm is run on conservation grounds rather than for profit. It is still worth the trip, however, as you will find the largest crocodiles in the country here (4–5 metres/13–16 feet). There are several pools, some for breeding and the smaller ones for rearing. The best time to see the crocodiles is at mealtimes, but they're only fed twice a week. The area, which is very swampy, is also infested with the creatures roaming free.

MARÍA LA GORDA

María La Gorda is not a town or village but a superb site at the tip of the peninsula, on the Corrientes bay. Development consists of little more than a hotel and a few outlying houses. This whole area of Cuba was designated a biosphere reserve by UNESCO in 1987, and it covers 101,000 hectares (250,000 acres). This is the **Guanahacabibes nature reserve** where one of the richest collections of fauna and flora in the world is completely protected from exploitation. The site includes part of the sea bed area which is very rare. Before entering this isolated area, visitors must pass through a military checkpoint where identities are checked (you must carry your passport). If you want to explore the reserve (access is only possible by four-wheel-drive) you must hire a vehicle and guide (*see below*). Access to the María La Gorda site is free.

María La Gorda derives its name from a pretty young woman who was captured by pirates in a faraway country, and then abandoned here. She built a hut and stayed here on her own. With nothing else to do, she began to eat and became so big that, when the pirates returned, they called her Maria *la gorda* (fat Maria)!

GETTING THERE

The only way of getting to María La Gorda is by private car. Allow three hours from Pinar. The road is, on the whole, very good – there are a few dodgy stretches but nothing really bad.

The Site

The area crosses one of the wildest parts of western Cuba: the forest is inhabited by wild boar, deer, wildcats and also snakes, crocodiles and wild bulls. But don't panic, as you are unlikely to meet these wonderful creatures en route. Compensation is at the end of the road, where you will find several small, tranquil beaches lapped by wonderful waters. The setting is idyllic and the view of the sunset is one of the finest in Cuba.

The area does not boast any big, long beaches – there are a number of small, white-sand coves, but the coast is lined mainly with chalk rocks. The landscape is really very beautiful but the real sights are under water, which is why the area is above all renowned among scuba-divers. In fact, professionals consider María La Gorda to be one of the five best sites in the world. There are dozens of dives, each lovelier than the last. Even for non-divers, it's a great place to relax for two or three days as the hotel is pleasant, it's very peaceful and the place is simply gorgeous.

WHERE TO STAY AND EAT

🛏 ✕ **Hotel María La Gorda**: on the beach. ☎ 78-131. Fax: 78-077. The only accommodation around has about 30 rooms. It is completely isolated and gives the impression of being at the end of the world. Reservations are recommended through the big agencies in Havana or Pinar del Río. Otherwise, at least phone in advance to check availability. Double rooms are $30 or $40 (plus $5 for the buffet breakfast). Lunch and the buffet dinner cost $15 each but are rather disappointing. Some of the older beach chalets are rather dilapidated and do not have hot water (avoid those that do not face the sea). Accommodation in the long, modern two-storey building is very comfortable (with hot water, air-conditioning, etc.). Ask for a room on the ground floor facing the sea. Activities include fishing, diving and excursions with the obligatory official guide. In front of the hotel is a small beach but the coral shelf makes it difficult to swim. If you continue for a few hundred metres, you will find a beautiful, white, sandy beach.

WHAT TO DO

🤿 **Scuba-diving**: there is a very efficient diving club attached to the hotel. ☎ 78-131. There are two excursions per day at 9am and 3pm. You can book a place by phone, and dives cost $38 for divers without their own equipment. If you have never tried scuba-diving, you can still go out on the boat ($5), or if you want to swim you can hire snorkelling gear ($12 including equipment hire and the boat trip).

The water here is crystal clear, with an average temperature of 28°C (80°F). The site offers 45 different dives, from a simple beginners' dive (between 3 and 5 metres/10–16 feet) to amazingly colourful exploratory dives. The coral reefs are covered with sponges and gorgonians. A simple dive (with fins) close to the coast will reveal schools of grouper, barracuda and all sorts of tropical fish.

One of the highly recommended dives on offer is the 'Gorgonians' garden' (15 metres/50 feet), where you will find yourself surrounded by inquisitive little groupers. Beginners are taken on a dive known as the 'Aquarium' to see hordes of multicoloured fish and crayfish. 'El Almirante' takes in one of the largest fields of black coral in Latin America (between 12 and 40 metres/39 and 131 feet). The more daring will no doubt enjoy 'El Encanto' (30 metres/ 98 feet) which includes a number of caves.

– **Other activities**: on the way into the site, in **La Bajada** (14 kilometres/9 miles before María La Gorda), there is a small building which audaciously calls itself an Estación Ecológica, giving a rudimentary introduction to the reserve. Two footpaths – **Cuevas las Perlas** (Pearl Caves) and **Del Bosque al Mar** (From the Wood to the Sea) – start from here and offer some nice little walks. But not many people take advantage of them as you're expected to pay $6 and $8 respectively for barely 1-hour's walk in the forest.

It is also possible to take a trip in a four-wheel-drive through the reserve, but vehicles must be hired from Havanatur (at the hotel) and a guide must be hired from the reserve.

PUERTO ESPERANZA

You'll find this to the north of Viñales, on the Gulf of Mexico. There are some beautiful, gigantic *mogotes* along the road to the left. The route takes in some pretty little valleys lined with a wide variety of plants and trees. Puerto Esperanza is a modest fishing port, abandoned by tourists once the boat for **Cayo Levisa** stopped leaving from here several years ago. Arrival in the village is heralded by a large avenue lined with lawns that leads straight to the sea. There's no beach, but the village, which is very pleasant, appears to be ideal for meeting people as the inhabitants are so friendly. There is absolutely nothing to do but it's a really nice stopping-off place, off the beaten track, on the coastal road taking you either to Cayo Levisa or Havana.

USEFUL ADDRESS

■ **CUPET service station**: turn left at a fork in the road 3 kilometres (2 miles) before Puerto Esperanza – it is not very clear, but the pump is on the right-hand side. Note that when you set off you need to get back onto the right fork to continue on the road to Puerto Esperanza.

THE WEST OF CUBA

WHERE TO STAY AND EAT

🏠 **Teresa Hernandez Martinez**: calle 4 ter. On arrival in the village via the main road, turn left at the Policlínico then take the third on the left. The house is on the left-hand side. ☎ 93-803. Two very well-maintained private rooms (sleeping two and four) for $10 a night. Meals cost $5. The house is owned by a delightful Cuban family who will help you with any problems. The attractive terrace under the straw-covered canopy, decorated with warmth and taste, is the perfect spot to enjoy a drink. Highly recommended. Advance booking by phone advisable.

🏠 ✗ **Paladar**: Dora Gonzalez Fuentes, 5 Pelayo Cuervo. ☎ 93-805 and 93-813. Once in Puerto Esperanza, go right to the seafront. Facing the bust, turn right then take the second on the left. The house is on the right (it has a little backpacker painted on the facade). The two rooms cost $15 each and sleep up to three people. The rooms are simple and clean and the house modest. Guests are quickly made to feel at home. If this isn't enough, it's certainly the best restaurant in the village (the mother was a school cook), and run by a very welcoming family. A meal costs $8 and portions are very large – excellent grilled fish served with rice, bananas and salad. Guests eat on the small terrace behind the house.

IN THE AREA

★ **Santa Lucía**: located 31 kilometres (19 miles) west of Puerto Esperanza, the road crosses a beautiful agricultural region, with glimpses of the sea in the distance. Santa Lucía, a village off the beaten track, has a superb, long, white sandy beach bordered by palm trees. There are few tourists, and just one small bar near the beach.

★ **The Puerto Esperanza to Palma Rubia road**: this is a delightful road along the foot of red hills, with superb views of the sea on the left and some impressive *mogotes* to the right. Occasional rural villages are dotted among fields of pineapple, cassava, Jerusalem artichoke and rice, and some vast pine forests.

CAYO LEVISA

This is a little island, surrounded by breathtaking translucent waters, first green, then turquoise, and has a stunning landscape of mangroves. But, unlike others (such as Cayo Coco or Cayo Largo), this one has remained virtually wild and has only really undergone any sort of development since the 1990s. There is a single hotel, and a few steps away is a deserted beach. There is a wooden walkway across the island that leads to the superb, white-sand beach, fringed with palm trees. At last – Robinson Crusoe's paradise!

GETTING THERE

Access is **by boat** only from **Palma Rubia**, 62 kilometres (40 miles) north of Viñales, via La Palma. It is signposted from the coast road. Allow a 1-hour drive from Viñales then a 30-minute crossing. If you have your own car, you can leave it in the harbour car-park without any problem. You can either make it a day trip or spend the night there.

– **Departure times**: from Palma Rubia to Cayo Levisa 11am (sometimes around 10.45) and 6pm. From Cayo Levisa to Palma Rubia 10am and 5pm.

– **Day trips**: a return ticket (including a welcome cocktail) costs $15 (it's $10 extra for lunch). Tickets are available from the coastguard station in Palma Rubia harbour (note the *mirador*). It's a good idea to book, but not essential. Divers can head out to the island in the morning, do the 1pm dive (you must book in advance) and return on the 5pm boat.

– Note that Cubans are not allowed to board without special authorization (due to the proximity of the USA), or to accompany tourists.

– With a **stop-over** at the hotel: it is essential to reserve in advance if you want to stay the night as it is often full. The return boat journey, a cocktail and a chalet for two people costs $70.

WHERE TO STAY AND EAT

🛏 ✕ **Caya Levisa Hotel**: this is the only hotel on the island: 20 brick-built chalets with palm-covered roofs, set among vegetation. ☎ 66-60-75. Bookings can be made at any hotel in the Horizontes chain. Meals in the restaurant are just $5–8. The rooms are nice, but not sensational, and have well-appointed bathrooms and air-conditioning. They aren't cheap but the location makes up for that. The airy, tropical restaurant is adorned with the trunks of palm trees and a stuffed swordfish. Good cuisine – a rarity in this type of place; the à la carte menu features whole grilled fish, beef fricassée, etc.

WHAT TO DO

– **Swimming, sunbathing, lazing around**: . . . the usual stuff! The beach is really extraordinary and the lagoon looks like a swimming pool. The downside is that the coral-less sea bed means there is not much to see underwater – and there are no fish around the shore. To see anything of interest you will need to go out in a boat. On the beach note the flat sea urchins, blanched by the sun, and admire the unbelievably delicate shells.

The hotel hires out snorkelling equipment, pedalos, canoes and the like. It also offers **snorkelling** trips by boat as well as day trips to Cayo Paraíso.

🤿 **Scuba-diving**: the club attached to the hotel organizes two dives per day at 9am and 3pm (and sometimes 1pm on request). The coral reef is 3.5 kilometres (2 miles) offshore. It is very expensive – $45 for the first dive and $20 for the second if both are done on the same day.

BAHÍA HONDA

East of Cayo Levisa, further along the coast road towards Havana, is this small, lively town in one of the largest bays in the country. It's very noisy and has nothing of particular interest; the rather mundane beach is 2 kilometres (1 mile) from the centre (not signposted). Bahía Honda was destined to be an American naval base, but local protests defeated the plan.

By contrast, further along the coast are some magnificent beaches not yet discovered by tour groups and often difficult to find. One, known as **playa La Altura**, is 10 kilometres (6 miles) south of Bahía Honda. Another is **playa San Pedro**, off the road to Havana.

WHERE TO STAY AND EAT

🛏 ✕ **Motel Punta de Piedra**: in Punta de Piedra, just south of town; 2 kilometres (1 mile) on the left coming from Cayo Levisa via Bahía Honda. ☎ 086-341. Set in a garden on a cliff with fine views over the bay. The rooms have all mod cons but are very badly kept.

COLOUR MAPS

INDEX OF COLOUR MAPS

MAP OF CUBA

NORTH

UNITED STATES
(FLORIDA)

GULF OF MEXICO

Florida Straits

Tropic of Cancer

Arch. de los Colorados

Cayo Levisa

Arch. de Sabana

Mariel   HAVANA   Varadero

Soroa   Matanzas   Cardenas   Cayo Fragos

Viñales   Artemisa   Batabanó   Güines   Jovellanos   Sagua la Grande

G. de Guanahacabibes   B. de la Broa   Guama   Santa Clara

Pinar del Rio   Golfo de Batabanó   Península de Zapata   Playa Larga

San Juan y Martinez   G. de Cazones   B. de Cochinos   Playa Girón   Cienfuegos

la Bajada   Cabo   Arch. de los Canarreos   Sancti Spiritus

Maria La Gorda   Francés   Nueva Gerona   C. el Rosario   Cayo Largo   Trinidad

Cabo Corrientes   la Demajagua   Cayo Piedra   C. Cantiles   Arch. d

Península de Guanahacabibes   Isla de Juventud   Punta del Este

CARIBBEAN SEA

0	50	100 km

0	50	100 miles

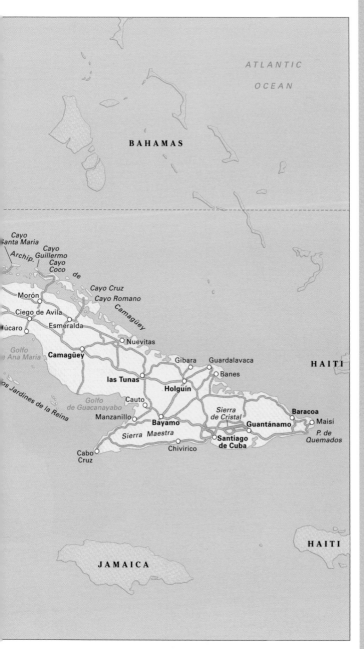

MAP OF CUBA

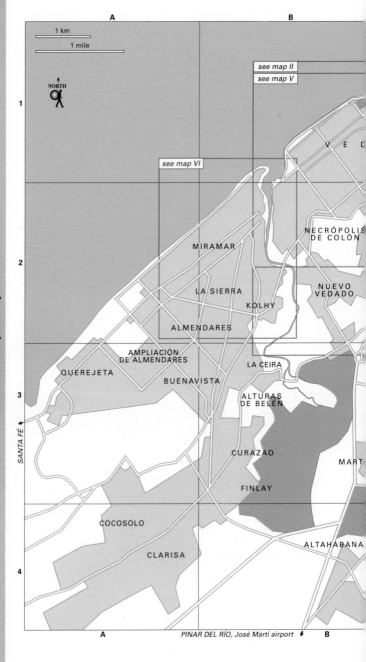

HAVANA (MAP I)

1 km
1 mile

NORTH

A

B

see map II
see map V

1

V E D

see map VI

NECRÓPOLIS
DE COLÓN

MIRAMAR

2

NUEVO
VEDADO

LA SIERRA

KOLHY

ALMENDARES

AMPLIACIÓN
DE ALMENDARES

LA CEIRA

QUEREJETA

BUENAVISTA

SANTA FÉ

3

ALTURAS
DE BELÉN

CURAZAO

MART

FINLAY

COCOSOLO

ALTAHABANA

CLARISA

4

A

PINAR DEL RÍO, José Martí airport

B

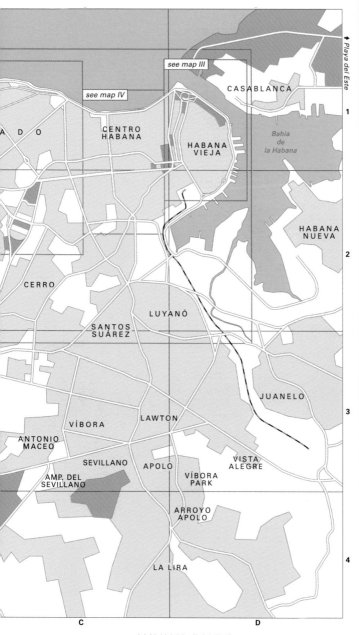

see map III

see map IV

CASABLANCA

CENTRO
HABANA

HABANA
VIEJA

Bahía
de
la Habana

A D O

HABANA
NUEVA

CERRO

LUYANÓ

SANTOS
SUÁREZ

JUANELO

VÍBORA

LAWTON

ANTONIO
MACEO

VISTA
ALEGRE

SEVILLANO

APOLO

AMP. DEL
SEVILLANO

VÍBORA
PARK

ARROYO
APOLO

LA LIRA

Playa del Este

C

D

1

2

3

4

HAVANA (MAP I)

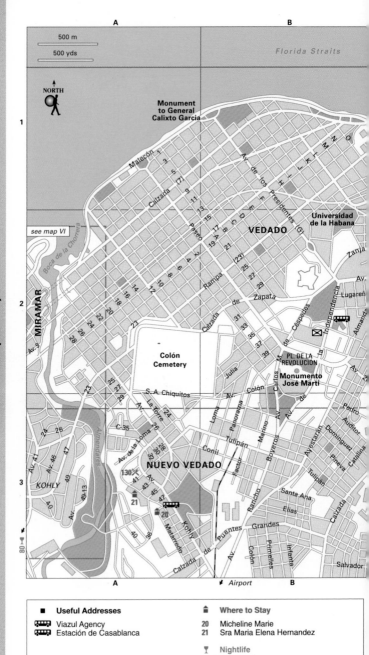

HAVANA (MAP II)

500 m
500 yds

NORTH

Florida Straits

Monument to General Calixto Garcia

Malecón

Calzada

Paseo

VEDADO

Universidad de la Habana

see map VI

Boca de la Chorrera

MIRAMAR

Rampa

de Zapata

Calzada

Colón Cemetery

S. A. Chiquitos

NUEVO VEDADO

KOHLY

Av. de la Loma

C-35

Tulipán

Conil

Colón

Loma

Panorama

Malino

Boyeros

PL DE LA REVOLUCIÓN

Monumento José Martí

Ayestarán

Zanja

Av. Lugareño

de Cespedes

de Independencia

Almanci

Pedro

Auditor

Dominguez

Nueva Catalina

Santa Ana

Elias

Rancho

Factor

Tulipán

Calzada

Grandes

Primelles

Infanta

Salvador

Kohly

Matadrecto

Calzada

de Puentes

Av.

Colón

Airport

■	Useful Addresses	🏠	Where to Stay
🚌	Viazul Agency	20	Micheline Marie
🚌	Estación de Casablanca	21	Sra Maria Elena Hernandez
		🍸	Nightlife
		80	Tropicana

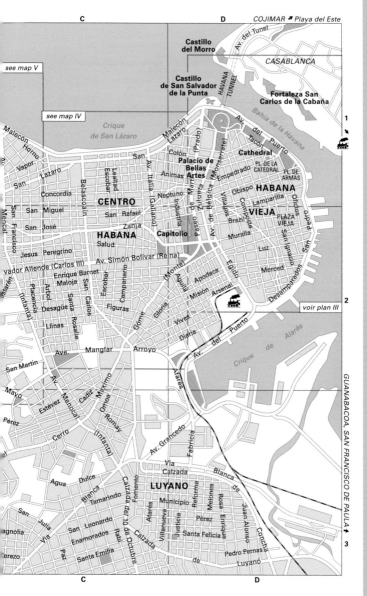

HAVANA (MAP II)

KEY TO HAVANA MAP III

■ **Useful Addresses**

🏨 Infotur
✉ Post office
🚆 Estación Est-Central (Central station)
1 Cuba Autrement
2 Assistur
3 Banco Financiero Internacional

🛏 **Where to Stay**

10 Gustavo L. Enamorada Zamora
   'Chez Nous'
11 Chez Amalia
12 Sra. Elvira Parra
13 Hotel Lido
14 Convento Santa Clara
16 Hotel Caribbean
17 Hostal Valencia
18 Hotel Florida
19 Hostal Conde de la Villanueva
20 Ambos Mundos
21 Hotel Inglaterra
22 Plaza Hotel
23 Sevilla

✕ **Where to Eat**

17 La Paella
19 Velta Abajo
30 El Rincón de Elegguá
31 Isaman
32 Hanoï
33 Café Taberna
34 La Bodeguita del Medio
35 La Torre de Marfil
36 XII Apostoles
37 La Mina
38 El Patio
39 Don Giovanni
40 Al Medina
41 Divina Pastora
50 El Floridita

🍷 **Where to Have a Drink**

34 La Bodeguita del Medio
38 El Patio
50 El Floridita
51 Café París
52 Café O'Reilly
53 Lluvia de Oro
54 Castillo de Farnés
55 Mirador

★ **What to See**

70 El Palacio el Tabaco
71 Palacio de los Capitanes
   Generales
72 José Martí's birthplace
73 Casa de Simón Bolívar
74 Casa de los Arabes
75 Casa de África
76 Casa de Guayasamín
77 Museum of Colonial Art
78 Numismatic Museum
79 Vintage Car Museum
80 Alejo Carpentier Museum and
   Cultural Centre
81 Wifredo Lam Centre
82 Museo de Armas
83 Museo Nacional de la Música

🔒 **Shopping**

4 El Navegante bookshop
5 Librería La Internacional
6 La Casa del Ron

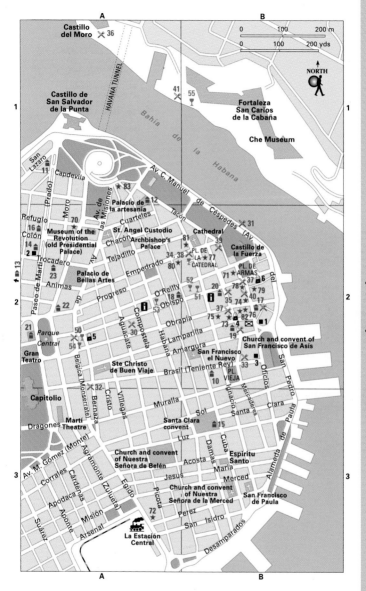

HAVANA (MAP III) – La Habana Vieja

■   **Useful Addresses**

🚌   Estación Cristina

🛏   **Where to Stay**

20   Tommy Reyes
21   Amada Pérez Guelmes –
     'chez Tony'
22   Gladys Cutiño

✕   **Where to Eat**

30   Seeman
31   Restaurant Bellomar
32   La Guarida
33   Lung Kong

★   **What to See**

40   Partagas cigar factory
     retail outlet

HAVANA (MAP IV) – Centro Habana

HAVANA (MAP V) – VEDADO

A   B

0   200   400 m
0   200   400 yds

NORTH

Florida Straits

1

Monument
to General
Calixto García

🔲 12

★ 🏛 84
72

🏛 16

2 ◼

Malecón   1

🍷 92
3

🏛 8 33   85 🍷

5

Calzada   (7)

(9)   11

Línea   13
44

15

Paseo   17 🏛
A   6

🍷 91   19

48
2 🍷   4

49 🍷   6
8

10   40, 41   1 🔲 34
12   Rampa

14   16   19 🏛   24

25   18   50 🍷
20   26   120 ⛳   Calzada

22

24   23

26   28

49
42
43   Colón
Cemetery

23   25   S. A. Chiquitos

27   La Torre   24

29

A   B

MIRAMAR

Av. 3

Almendares

Boca de la Chorrera

HAVANA (Map V) – Vedado

■ **Useful Addresses**

✉	Main post office
🚌	National bus station
1	Roots Travel
2	Cubatur
3	Banco Financiero Internacional
4	Banco Nacional de Cuba
5	Banco Popular de Ahorro
6	Cadeca
8	Micar and Transtur
9	Cubana de Aviación
14	Cinema
15	National Union of Cuban Writers and Artists

🛏 **Where to Stay**

19	Mélida Jordán
20	Manuel Arena Musa
21	Dr Manuel Alvarez Alonso
22	Margarita o Jorge Villazón
23	Milagros Cordero and Alicia Hernández Padrón
24	Chez Josefa
25	La Kakatua
26	Casa de Craciela
27	Hotel Bruzón
28	Hotel Colina
29	Hotel Vedado
30	Hotel St John's
31	Hotel Habana Libre Tryp
32	Hotel Nacional
33	Hotel Riviera
34	Chez Josefina Gomez Villar

✕ **Where to Eat**

25	La Kakatua
40	Juana la Cubana
41	El Racauto
42	El Hueco de 23
43	El Farallón
44	Pizzeria Decamerón
45	Huron Azul
46	El Gringo Viejo
47	Paladar Amor
48	Casa de la Amistad
49	Restaurant-Bar 1830
50	Villa Babi
60	Coppelia
130	Pain de Paris

🍸 **Where to Have a Drink**

48	Casa de la Amistad
49	Colonial Bar
61	La Torre
62	Café La Fuente

🍸 **Nightlife**

14	Cinema
15	Peña of the National Union of Cuban Writers and Artists
30	Pico Blanco
31	El Turquino
32	El Parisien
48	Café de la Amistad
49	Jardines de 1830
81	Café Cantante
82	Salón Rojo
84	Mi Conuco
85	Habana Café
90	La Zorra y el Cuervo
91	Casa de la Cultura de Plaza
92	Jazz Cafe
93	Las Vegas

★ **What to See**

102	Museo Nacional de Artes Decorativas
101	Napoleon Museum
100	The 'Wonderful World of Salvador Escalona'

🛍 **Shopping**

6	Farmer's market
10	Geotech
12	La Feria
13	Craft market
48,120	La Casa del Habano

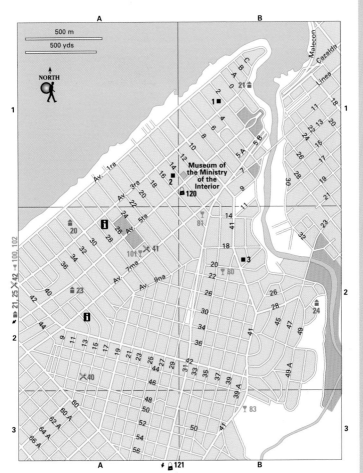

■	**Useful Addresses**		🍸	Where to Have a Drink
🅑	Infotur		80	Casa de la Música
1	Havanatur		81	La Maison
3	Cira Garcia Central Clinic		83	La Tropical
			100	Havana Club
🛏	**Where to Stay**		101	Casa del Bolero
			102	Papa's
20	Arelis Sera			
21	Frank de Armas		🛍	**Shopping**
23	Hotel Mirazul			
24	Hotel El Bosque		25	Château Miramar Hotel Shop
25	Château Miramar		80	Casa de la Música
			81	La Maison
✕	**Where to Eat**		120,121	La Casa del Tabaco
40	Paladar 'La Cocina de Lilliam'			
41	El Aljibe			
42	La Cecilia			

HAVANA (Map VI) – Miramar

The Beaches in the East and the North

Once you have passed through the tunnel linking Habana Vieja with Habana del Este, the road runs along the north coast to the famous playas del Este (eastern beaches) that extend for 30 kilometres (18 miles). In 1976 Havana was divided in two: the city and its suburbs, and the province of Havana, which extends east as far as the Bacunayagua bridge, just before Matanzas. The beaches to the east (Bacuranao, Santa Maria del Mar and Guanabo) are, therefore, officially part of the city of Havana. This is where the Habaneros come at weekends – especially during July and August when the heat is at its most stifling. If you are here in summer it is best to come during the week when it is not so crowded. There are major traffic jams in the morning and evening so you should set off early and return late.

Further on is the historic town of Matanzas, providing a short cultural interlude before you reach the beaches of Varadero, the undisputed jewel in Cuba's tourist crown.

GETTING THERE

– **By bus**: although there are public buses, they are not a good option as they take so long and are very unreliable. But if you are determined, bus No. 400 goes direct to Guanabo from the bus station near the railway station in Old Havana.

– **By truck**: numerous trucks run for a few pesos per person. The truck terminus is along central station in Havana, between calle Arsenal and Misión (Havana map III, A3). Many of Havana's inhabitants will rent a truck between several families to get to the beaches rather than use public transport.

– **By taxi**: it is possible hire a taxi to go to Cojimar for the day (at least $5), but arrange for it to come back to collect you as there are no taxis at the beaches.

COJIMAR   DIALLING CODE: 7

This is an attractive little fishing village, once you get past the unprepossessing buildings on its outskirts. This is the bay where the English disembarked on their way to Havana. They then attacked the town from the land. Cojimar is most famous thanks to Hemingway, whose friend, a fisherman named Gregorio – immortalized in *The Old Man and the Sea* – lived here. The place has become equally well known since the *balseros* made it one of their favourite places from which to set sail. You shouldn't come across many tourists here. Enjoy a pleasant walk around the harbour.

WHERE TO EAT

☒ Budget

✕ **El Barco**: Moré No. 2, on the corner with Malecón. In the centre of the village, at the end of the jetty, turn left at the small stone fortress and continue for 100 metres. There's no sign but it's the building with blue window frames. You can have a good, cheap meal in this tiny, unpretentious fishermen's restaurant. The menu doesn't bear much relation to what is actually on offer – it's up to you to ask. There's fried fish, octopus, squid or chicken, all for Cuban pesos. It's not as good as La Terraza (*see below*), but a lot cheaper and you will get a warm welcome.

✕ **Restaurante La Terracita**: via Nueva 9606, between Concha and Pezuela. An unpretentious yellow house with a welcoming terrace offering good, simple, traditional family cooking for just a few dollars. A warm homely atmosphere.

☒☒ Moderate

✕ **La Terraza**: corner of calle Real and Candelaria, on the right-hand side of the main road leading down to the port. ☎ 55-32-94. Open daily from around 11am to 11pm. Dishes range from $7 to $20. This legendary restaurant where Hemingway loved to relax is very attractive, with 1920s furniture. The superb dining room has large windows directly overlooking the water. In a corner, you can see the old fishing port. There are lots of photos of Hemingway on the walls, fishing for sharks and swordfish, or in the company of Castro during the famous fishing tournament at the marina. This was in fact the only time they met. Another photo to look out for is the one of Gregorio, the fisherman who was the inspiration for the character of the old man in Hemingway's famous novel (*see above*). The place is, however, quite smart. The seafood isn't particularly cheap but some of the specialities are more affordable. The lobster is certainly fresh – it is plucked from the big fish-tank when you order. You could also just have paella, which is more reasonably priced, or a *mojito*, if you want to do as Hemingway did!

WHAT TO SEE

There is no real beach in Cojimar, and the bay is not very good for swimming. The town's attraction lies more in its tranquillity and gentle charm. On the harbour there is a small square fortress flanked with lookout towers. Just in front, under a cupola, is a bust of Hemingway. As soon as the fishermen of Cojimar heard the news of their friend's death, they each contributed their bronze anchors, which were then smelted down to make this bust in homage to their fishing companion. There is a small error in his date of birth – he was in fact born in 1899 not 1898.

Gregorio, the captain of Hemingway's boat (the *Pilar*) still lives in Cojimar and is over 100 years old.

NORTHERN BEACHES

SANTA MARÍA DEL MAR — DIALLING CODE: 7

Just 21 kilometres (13 miles) from Havana, this is the largest of the playas del Este. The beach is nice, although not always very clean, but the surrounding area is not particularly interesting as there are no villages to explore. Santa María is little more than a beach and a few pseudo-posh hotels scattered along the coastline. There are lots of young Cubans here, and also hordes of Italian tourists. Although there are plenty of things to do, it's not the sort of resort where you would necessarily want to stay – just make a quick stop for a swim. If you are driving, park in one of the hotel car-parks.

On a more serious note, there is a treatment centre for the children of Chernobyl between Cojimar and Santa María del Marl.

WHERE TO STAY

The hotels here are typical examples of Soviet architecture – namely exceedingly unattractive.

Private homes: there are very few private rooms to rent, and those that do exist are illegal. If you want to stay in a private home, go to Guanabo.

Tropicoco: corner of avenida Sur and Las Terrazas. ☎ 97-13-71. Fax: 97-13-89. The first hotel when coming from Havana. A double room costs around $65, including breakfast. A huge, ugly, modern building with lukewarm hospitality, but one of the few hotels in the area not to insist on full board. The beach is 50 metres away and the rooms, which are comfortable, clean and fairly cheap, have sea views. It costs a bit more for a balcony. There is a swimming pool, bars, restaurants, disco, tennis, car and motorcycle hire, foreign exchange and an information office. The hotel management doesn't advertise this, but there are also lots of *jineteras* (prostitutes) on the beach.

⚑ **Hotel Atlántico**: avenida de La Terraza, next to the sea. ☎ 97-10-

85/86/87. Full board for two people costs around $142. This is a lot more intimate than the Tropicoco, with tennis, swimming pool, disco etc. The rooms are very well kept and have full facilities, but the obligatory full board means it is not particularly recommended.

GUANABO

DIALLING CODE: 7

Around 10 kilometres (6 miles) from Santa María, Guanabo is the first proper village that you get to after Havana. This is the new meeting place for the '*chicas*', driven out of Varadero. If you are driving from Santa María del Mar, follow the main road (via Blanca), looking out for a single flashing orange traffic light mounted above the road. At this point, take the main road to the left that goes down to a roundabout (the bus station is near by) and turn right into avenida 5ta, the main street.

Guanabo has a large beach – a little quieter than the one in Santa María del Mar – but otherwise nothing particularly special, and the village itself is of limited charm. It sprawls out on either side of avenida 5ta, which is quite noisy and just behind the beach. Guanabo seems to be popular with Italian holidaymakers, and so most of its eateries have menus in Italian offering pasta and pizza. There are several small, budget hotels, but nothing special and somewhat lacking in charm, plus dozens of rental rooms in private homes.

An interesting system has been used to number the roads – the ones parallel to the sea mainly have single digit numbers (5, 6, 7, 8 . . .) plus a letter (A or B), while those at right angles to the sea are given much higher numbers (472, 474 . . .). This was obviously an interesting project for some sharp-thinking technocrat!

USEFUL ADDRESSES

Bus station: at the roundabout, right at the beginning of avenida 5ta.

CUPET service station: on the way into the village.

WHERE TO STAY

⚑ **Villa Playa Hermosa**: avenida 5ta, between 472 and 474. ☎ 96-27-74. A double room costs $22, including breakfast. Chalets in a little garden with swimming pool, with the beach on the other side of the road. Cool rooms, if a little tired-looking, with kitchen and large bathroom. There is one Creole and one Italian restaurant.

⚑ **Hotel Miramar**: calle 7B, between 478 and 476. ☎ 96-25-07. Three blocks from the high street, therefore further from the beach than the others. A double room costs $20–22. An ugly concrete block like all the rest, with a dirty swimming pool and lots of comings and goings. The rooms are fairly clean with rather narrow bathrooms. Only if you really can't find anything else.

Casas Particulares

These are a much cheaper, more authentic and nicer alternative to the local hotels, which are state-run, ugly and lacking in hospitality.

At Guanabo, those who rent out rooms do so legally (they pay tax). They can often be recognized by the multilingual sign outside: 'Se alquila', 'Rent a room', or 'Stanze affitasi'. The nicest houses are not by the sea (due to the soft, wet soil), but on the side of the hill, on the other side of the main street. Below is a selection of addresses, but there are dozens available.

☖ Bertha y Tony: 902 calle 472, on the corner with calle 9. ☎ 96-64-74. A double room is $30–35 and the price includes a night security guard. A wooden house with red-and-white walls and a large veranda, reminiscent of houses in Louisiana. The three rooms are not in the main house, but in the neighbouring one, and have air-conditioning, two bathrooms (hot water) and kitchenette. The room on the first floor has a balcony. This is one of the best-maintained places around and all very pleasant, although the owner has a tendency to inflate the prices without warning.

☖ Barranco y Miriam: 48412 avenida 7B, between 484 and 486. ☎ 96-44-03. A double room costs around $25. A blue house with a large, airy balcony on the first floor, and three rooms. Not particularly charming, but it's clean and tidy as a maid cleans the house daily.

☖ Roberto y Yojaida: 486 calle 7B02, between calle 7B and calle 9. ☎ 96-47-42. A double room costs $25. The owner is a handyman who is nice and trustworthy. Security is a priority and there are no problems on that front. There are

two rooms, with communal kitchen and bathroom. Quiet and clean.

☖ Carlos y Nery: 701 calle 492, on the corner with calle 7. ☎ 96-20-36. This large house is only suitable for groups of six people as it's rented out as a whole for $90. There are three rooms with bathroom and kitchen. Away from the centre, but with much more space than elsewhere, surrounded by lawns and young fruit trees. Very quiet and clean.

☖ Alejandro y Sonia: 7B08 calle 472, between calle 7B and calle 9. ☎ 96-36-38. A double room costs $25. Two modest rooms with shared bathroom, plus a kitchen, small dining room and air-conditioning. Fairly clean. Fan in the lounge and small terrace. Try as a last resort.

☖ Tere y Saúl: 7B08 calle 482, between calle 7 and calle 9. ☎ 96-52-79. A room for two or three costs around $20 in this bright little house at the back of a small courtyard where clothes are hung out to dry. There are three tiny air-conditioned rooms, a small kitchen and shared bathroom.

WHERE TO EAT

✕ Paladar El Piccoli: avenida 7, 48410, between calle 484 and 486. ☎ 96-26-63. A meal costs around $10 in this good place to eat, run by the friendly Adalberto Abelas Duran. This *paladar*, with its small

shady flower garden, is close to 5th Avenue, yet very quiet, and only serves fresh market produce. Very varied menu, exquisite cuisine and large portions, mostly based on pasta.

✕ **Restaurante El Brocal**: avenida 5ta, on the corner with calle 500. ☎ 96-28-92. This looks like the sort of old house found on Martinique or Guadeloupe. Now restored, it houses a good little restaurant. There are two set menus, at $8 and $12, featuring Cuban cooking with red meat and chicken. Diners eat on the covered terrace. Also cheap snacks.

✕ **Pizzeria Piccolo Italiana**: avenida 5ta, between 502 and 504. ☎ 96-43-00. Open noon–midnight. Large garden in the front, small house behind. Great efforts have been made with the decor of this Italian restaurant, which serves all sorts of pizzas and pasta for $6–8. The small vegetable garden attests to the freshness of the ingredients. It gets very busy, as the pizzas are good and the prices reasonable.

PLAYA JIBACOA — DIALLING CODE: 0692

Around 30 kilometres (19 miles) after Guanabo the road leads to Santa Cruz del Norte, which has no real beach (contrary to what you might have seen on the postcards) but a pebbly coastline. The industrial reality of this part of the coast soon becomes clear from the numerous pump heads and oil refineries. As you leave Santa Cruz, you will see the factory where the famous Habana Club rum is made (not open to the public).

After the desert-like landscape there are some gently sloping hills and unremarkable vegetation, somewhat subdued in this highly populated region. You then reach Playa Jibacoa, a small seaside resort that is calm and has several coves that are excellent spots for swimming.

There is very little in the way of accommodation here. As in many other places, there are lots of people in summer and it is difficult to find anywhere to stay, even in the less salubrious areas. Out of season, however, it is practically deserted and the whole area seems completely lifeless. Despite the beach, the absence of a village does not make it somewhere you would want to stay for long. At most it is worth spending one night here so you can enjoy a nice swim.

GETTING THERE

There is no direct bus from Havana: either change at Guanabo for a bus to Matanzas or take the No. 669 from Havana for Santa Cruz. Then ask the driver to drop you at the stop for the campsite on via Blanca. It is well signposted and a short walk from the bus stop.

WHERE TO STAY

☆ Budget

⚓ **El Abra**: on the coast road. ☎ 851-20. A chalet costs around $14 for two people. This is a large tourist complex of around 100 tiny, but inexpensive, *cabañas* (huts) with shower and fan. Even so, the *cabañas* don't have much shade and the heat can be unbearable in August. The upkeep is fairly mediocre but the staff are helpful. The Olympic-size swimming pool is as dirty as it is big. Four-wheel-drive vehicles are available for hire, and there's also a grocery.

There are some other similar holiday accommodation complexes along the coast, but they are mostly reserved for Cubans.

♠ **Villa Camping**: via Blanca. On the way into Jibacoa, just under the bridge. A pitch costs around $12 for two. It is still called the 'camping des Français', because it was here that the French Communist youth spent their holidays many years ago. There are around 30 very dilapidated chalets, as the site has not been well maintained and a number have almost fallen into ruin.

☆☆ Moderate

♠ **Villa Loma**: just beyond Villa Camping (if travelling by car). ☎ 833-16. A double room costs about $40. There are around 40 rooms in a dozen big chalets (the rooms are spotless but a touch unwelcoming), sprawling for several hundred metres along the sea. Each has a lounge, bedroom and kitchenette. There's a beach on either side and a swimming pool, disco and two restaurants, one of which is a grill/bar at the top of an old stone tower. Snorkelling is possible: the seabed here is rich in coral and crustaceans. There are plans for a big hotel here, so check before travelling, otherwise you might find nothing but a massive building site.

☆☆☆ Expensive

♠ **Ventaclub Villa Trópico**: on Jibacoa beach. ☎ 852-05/06/07. Fax: 852-08. Obligatory full board costs a good $180. This is a very well-maintained club hotel in front of a superb beach. The complex comprises the big main building and high-quality chalets. It has a swimming pool, diving and catamarans – a real holiday centre – and attracts a predominantly Italian clientele.

MATANZAS   DIALLING CODE: 052

After Jibacoa, the road passes over the Bacunayagua bridge, the highest in the country (116 metres/380 feet), which acts as the border between the provinces of Havana and Matanzas. On one side the view plunges down to the sea, on the other side it extends over the valley.

In the distance you can see Matanzas Bay, one of the largest on the island. Matanzas, which is an important industrial city and crossroads for oil tankers, stretches out around it. The city was founded at the end of the 17th century and spans two rivers, the result being that there are several bridges. There is even a beach under one of them. The town is laid out around the main street, calle Medio.

Stop here to visit the historic city centre (hidden behind the fire station), the famous opera house and an amazing cave. In the 19th century, Matanzas became the largest cultural centre on the island (before being overtaken by Havana) and was nicknamed (rather generously) the 'Athens of Cuba'. Some interesting testimonies to this glorious past have been preserved, in particular, the beautiful colonial houses. This is the birthplace of the *danzón* dance (ancestor of the mambo and the cha-cha). It is also the capital of the *paleteros*, the holy singers of the Afro-Cuban religion.

Strangely enough, the town only has one hotel. Having said this, there is not much reason to stop for long, so you probably won't want to stay the night. However, the hotel in question does have its own delightful old-fashioned charm.

USEFUL ADDRESSES

■ **Banco Financiero Internacional**: calle Medio (calle 85), on the corner with 2 de Mayo (also known as calle 298). ☎ 253-400. Open Monday to Friday 8am to 3pm. Exchanges cash and travellers' cheques, and dollars may be withdrawn in cash using Visa.

☎ **Ectesa telephone centre**: calle 83, on the corner with calle 228.
■ **CUPET service station**: 2 kilometres (1 mile) outside the city towards Varadero, on the left.
🚌 **Bus station**: right at the end of calle 272, around 1 kilometre (half a mile) from the centre in the old railway station.

WHERE TO STAY AND EAT

🛏 **Hotel Louvre**: Parque de la Libertad. ☎ 24-40-78. All 20 or so rooms cost $18 for two or three people in this old colonial establishment, reminiscent of a dilapidated palace, overlooking one of the town's nicest squares. But only four rooms enjoy this view (Nos. 1, 2, 3 and 4). The others overlook the patio and are darker and not as pleasant. The peeling paintwork, the attractive staircase, the wooden furniture in the big hall, the table surmounted by a small crocodile and the large stone bar all serve to give the whole a certain cachet.

The big dining room, as old-fashioned as the rest of the hotel, offers a sparse menu. While you await your food, you can admire the stained-glass windows, the ancient chandeliers and the impressive dresser.

🛏 **Hotel Canimao**: ☎ 26-10-14. 7 kilometres (4 miles) outside Matanzas towards Varadero on the motorway. Take the small road to the right just before the bridge across the river. A double room costs $30 (excluding breakfast). Large, modern hotel with 120 clean and functional rooms and air-conditioning. This very pleasant establishment also boasts a nice clean pool. Just below the hotel, the Canimar river offers scope for a variety of excursions (ask at reception).
✕ **Café Atenas**: Plaza Vigia, opposite the Sauto theatre. Open 24 hours a day. Pleasant terrace covered with bougainvillaea, overlooking the corner of the square between the museum and the theatre. Chicken, sandwiches and pizzas at bargain prices. The food could be classed as the least bad in the town.

WHAT TO SEE

★ **The Sauto Theatre**: in the pretty little plaza Vigia. It's generally open for visits in the morning during the week, but nothing seems to be actually organized and the welcome is dreadful. It's a fine example of neo-classical architecture, however, and was designed by the Italian Daniel Dall'Aglio. Built in 1862, the theatre was called Estebán until 1899, when it took the name of an extremely rich doctor and patron, Sauto. This has long been the most renowned theatre in Cuba: Caruso and Sarah Bernhardt (in *La Dame aux Camélias*) performed here. Inside are frescoes depicting the Muses.

★ **El Museo Histórico Provincial**: next to the theatre. Open Tuesday to Saturday 9.30am–noon, 1–5pm. Sunday 8.30am–noon. Admission $2. This neo-colonial style former mansion of Don Vicente de Unco y Sardinas contains all sorts of things: an exhibition on slavery, old weapons, religious artefacts, copies of old engravings, a mock-up of a sugar factory, the history of the native Indians in the area, etc. On the first floor is the archaeological room, and a reconstruction of a 19th century bourgeois salon, including paintings, porcelain, colonial furniture, rocking chair, etc. And, of course (as in almost all the museums in Cuba), there is a summary of the heroes of the Wars of Independence and of the Revolution.

★ **Museo Farmacéutico**: Parque de la Libertad, the square with the statue of Martí as liberator with a chained woman beneath him at its centre. Open Tuesday to Saturday 8am–5pm. Sunday 8am–2pm. Admission $2. On the charming former Plaza de Armas (the old parade ground). Established in 1882 jointly by the Frenchman Ernest Triolet and the Cuban Juan Fermin Figueroa, this is one of the oldest chemists' on the island and the best preserved; all the medicines are genuine. The nice guide will tell you (in Spanish) that this beautiful shop, which was in operation until 1 May 1964, has become the top pharmaceutical museum in Latin America. There are seven rooms to visit in all – all very interesting.

Magnificent shelves made from valuable wood are covered with porcelain pots made in France. On the counter there are Bohemian crystal medicine bottles and a pair of scales in marble and bronze. One of the most amusing exhibits is a suppository mould! The enormous table with drawers won the bronze medal at the World Exhibition in 1900. The dispensary at the back of the shop is full of magic potions, comical elixirs and Cuban medicinal plants. In the laboratory there is a copper still, a cauldron used for distillation and sterilization, a press and thousands of old phials.

Next to the museum, the house belonging to the pharmacist, Triolet, is undergoing restoration and is not yet open to the public.

★ **The Hotel Louvre**: Parque de la Libertad, next to the chemist's. Even if you're not staying here, it is worth going in for a quick look (*see* 'Where to Stay'). Built in 1894, this little colonial-style mansion is full of character. The decor and furniture are worthy of a museum and haven't been moved for years. Visitors can enjoy a drink on the delightful patio.

★ **San Carlos cathedral**: between Plaza de Armas and Plaza Vigia where calle 83 meets calle 282. Open daily 8am–noon for services. This was erected in 1730 in the Spanish style.

★ **La Cueva de Vellamar**: at Finca La Alcancia, 6 kilometres (4 miles) southeast of the city. Open daily 9am–5pm (last admission 4.15pm). Obligatory guided tours last about 45 minutes. Admission $3, plus a surcharge for taking photographs or video footage. The cave, discovered in 1861, is the major attraction in the village and is believed to have been formed more than 300,000 years ago. It is characterized by vast galleries, a wide range of corridors and passageways, lovely colours and enormous stalactites. It is very humid inside, and the lighting design is excellent. Guides take you into the superb caverns that stretch for over 2 kilometres (1 mile). They are not very deep, yet there are interesting underground streams flowing into unbelievably clear subterranean lakes.

VARADERO   DIALLING CODE: 535

Varadero is situated 40 kilometres (25 miles) from Matanzas. The coastal road leads in a straight line to the long Hicacos peninsula, bordered by 20 kilometres (12 miles) of white-sand beaches and the azur sea.

This superb location, indulged by nature, has made the village of Varadero the best-known holiday resort in Cuba, and it was here that the island's first seaside holiday hotel was built in 1949. Today Varadero is by far the most touristy place on the island, visited mainly by Germans, Italians, Canadians, Spaniards and Mexicans. Since the opening of the international airport, investments have transformed the place into an organized resort on a grand scale, with Pharaonic hotel complexes, luxury cars, roads lined with palm trees, pizzerias and huge advertising hoardings. Another anomaly is the toll point on the approach to town (coming from Matanzas by the motorway) – $2 to come in and $2 for the pleasure of leaving (free if you come by bus). In fact, you could be mistaken for thinking you were in Florida rather than a Cuban town.

Opinions are divided on Varadero. According to the holiday brochures, this is Cuban paradise, indeed some tourists may see Varadero as paradise, although for the government it is a major money-spinner. The beauty of the beach and the water justifies spending at least two or three days here, but strictly speaking there is no real village and the only Cubans you will meet are the ones serving your *mojito* next to the swimming pool. This is tourist-central, you have been warned, and not the best place to discover the 'real' Cuba.

Architecturally speaking, Varadero is a long string of hotel establishments, and guests tend not to venture far from their own particular base. The further east you get, the grander and more luxurious the hotels become. For those who want to relax in total peace and quiet, there are also some small and far more tranquil islands.

GETTING AROUND

Varadero has a childlike simplicity: its roads are all parallel and numbered in order from 1 to 69, starting from the beginning of town. They cross five large avenues, with avenida Primera and avenida Playa acting as the main arteries, as they run along the beach where all the hotels are concentrated.

Minibus: minibuses provide a shuttle service from one end of town to the other at regular intervals. Tickets cost $1.

Bicycle or scooter: you can hire bikes by the hour or day, and scooters by the day. *See* 'Useful Addresses' *below*.

USEFUL ADDRESSES

Tourist Information

■ **'Rumbos' tourist office** (map II): corner of avenida Primera and calle 23. ☎ 66-66-66. Open until 8pm. Little information available, in fact no more than in any of the hotel information offices.

■ **Cubatur** (map II, 6): calle 32 and avenida Primera. ☎ 66-72-17 or 61-44-05. Fax: 61-44-04. Open daily 8.30am to 8.30pm. They can deal with any accommodation problems, find you a car and book excursions (without commission). There's also an office at the airport.

■ **Havanatur** (map II, 7): avenida Playa 3606 (between calle 36 and calle 37, near the Hotel Herradura). Open daily 8am to 6pm (shorter hours out of season). ☎ 66-70-27. Fax: 66-70-26. Useful for transfers to the airports (Varadero and Havana) and excursions.

■ **Sol y Son**: avenida Primera, between calle 54 and calle 55. ☎ 66-75-93. Travel agency that sells air tickets and provides a wide range of information.

Post and Telecommunications

✉ **Main post office** (map II): corner of calle 36 and avenida Primera. Open Monday to Saturday, 8am to 8pm.

■ **Centro Telefónico** (map II, 5): avenida Primera, corner of calle 30, opposite the Villa Caribe hotel. Open 24 hours a day. Sells telephone cards. Also possible to send faxes.

■ **Banco Financiero Internacional** (map II, **9**): 3202 calle 32, on the corner with Primera avenida, close to Villa Caribe. ☎ 66-70-02. Open daily 9am to 7pm. Tourists can change money or withdraw cash with a credit card. Don't forget to take your passport when withdrawing money.

Health and Safety

■ **Hospital** (Clinica Internacional; map II, **8**): avenida Primera and calle 61, opposite the Hotel Cuatro Palmas. ☎ 66-77-10. Reserved for tourists, therefore fees are charged. There is a 24-hour service.

■ **Pharmacy**: in the Cliníca Internacional. Open 24 hours a day.

■ **Life guards**: little tents on the beach every 700 metres. There is a training school for first-aiders on the site.

Transport

🚌 **Bus terminal** (map II): corner of calle 36 and Autopista Sur. On the opposite side to the beach, level with the centre. There are few buses, and you must book as early as possible (*see* 'Leaving Varadero' *below*).

➊ **J.G. Gómez International Airport**: 12 kilometres (7 miles) from Varadero on the Havana road, then turn left. If you are arriving by plane, you will find taxis for Varadero. If travelling from Varadero, take a cab from the bus station.

■ **Cubana**: avenida Primera, between 54 and 55. ☎ 61-18-23. Confirms flights and sells tickets, among other services.

■ **Aero-taxi** (map II, **13**): avenida Primera and calle 24. ☎ 66-75-40 or 61-29-29. This aerial taxi company has six-seater planes for trips over the peninsula or round trips to Key Largo. Departures are from a small airfield 1 kilometre from Varadero. Expensive.

■ **Mica Rent-a-Car** (map II, **15**): corner of calle 20 and avenida Primera. ☎ 61-18-08. Fax: 61-10-84. Certainly some of the best prices around.

■ **Transautos** (map II, **10**): several outlets, including at the airport, at calle 21 and on avenida Primera, opposite the Hotel Tropical. ☎ 66-73-32. Note that rates are on a sliding scale (half as much from the second day).

■ **Havanautos** (map II, **11**): two outlets on the way into the town – the main office on the corner of avenida Primera and calle 31, and another on the corner of avenida Primera and calle 8. ☎ 61-44-09.

■ **CUPET service station** (map II, **12**): on the way into the town, open 24 hours a day, but with just one fuel pump.

■ **FM 17**: corner of avenida Primera and calle 17. You can hire bikes by the hour or the day ($15), or small scooters by the day ($24).

■ **Scooter hire**: available all along avenida Primera for $25–30 per day. Hire places take the form of a table and parasol on the pavement and a few scooters parked in front. Almost all the big hotels also hire out scooters, and prices tend to be much the same everywhere.

Shopping

🔒 **Hanoi bookshop** (map II, **14**): avenida Primera and calle 44. Open daily until quite late. Books on Cuba, postcards and CDs.

WHERE TO STAY

> **TIP** You are advised to book a hotel in high season (July and August, and from December to March). It's worth knowing that prices fall by 20 to 30 per cent in low season. It is better to go out of season, particularly as there are no rental rooms in private homes – they are prohibited to ensure the big hotels have no competition. There are no real budget hotels in Varadero, so it's best to settle for one near the beach in the 'moderate' price bracket.

☆☆ Moderate

⚓ **Hotel Dos Mares** (map II, **21**): avenida Primera and Calle 5. ☎ 61-27-02. Fax: 66-74-99. A double room costs $56, including breakfast. You are in luck as this is one of the few hotels in Varadero with any character, and it's also one of the cheapest! This former two-storey mansion, with a strange internal layout, even has marble in the corridors. Around 30 spacious rooms that are clean, air-conditioned and have beautiful bathrooms. At this price you'll probably think you're dreaming. Plus you can be sure of receiving a genuinely warm welcome. Bar and restaurant. Undoubtedly a favourite.

🛏 **Villa Caribe** (map II, **23**): avenida Primera and Calle 30. ☎ 61-33-10. Fax: 66-64-88. A double room (without breakfast) costs $47. Very central. The U-shaped, three-storey building has more than 100 rooms and tacky furnishings from the 70s. Very cheap considering that there is a nice clean swimming pool and a beach, but don't expect luxury.

Apartments are clean and have two rooms and shared bathroom. Air-conditioning, TV and cable. Breakfast is nothing to write home about. Avoid rooms overlooking the road if possible. The atmosphere is fairly friendly.

🛏 **Hotel Tropical** (map II, **20**): corner of avenida Primera and calle 21. ☎ 61-39-15. Fax: 61-46-76. A double room costs around $50, buffet breakfast included. This big structure next to the beach consists of several buildings on both sides of the road. It has no particular charm

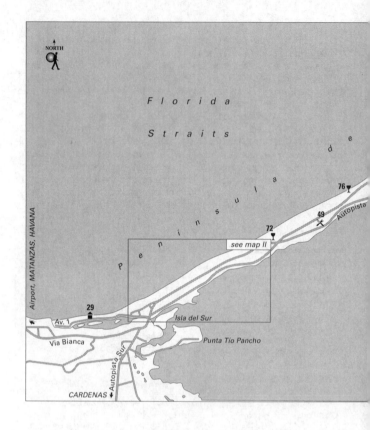

but the rooms have good facilities (air-conditioning, TV, bathroom) and the reasonable prices make it a good choice. Faultless service. Note that most rooms are let on a full-board basis, but there are always a few available just for the night – unfortunately these do not tend to be in prime locations.

☆☆☆ Expensive

≜ **Villa Caleta** (map II, **24**): corner of avenida Primera and calle 20. ☎ 66-70-80. Fax: 61-32-91. A double room costs around $65, excluding breakfast. Small, modern hotel

centred around a swimming pool and a flower garden. Delightful hospitality. Around 50 smart, well-maintained rooms, either in the main building or chalets on the beach. Air-conditioning, TV, and minibar. Table tennis available. A good, cheerful place – and only 20 metres from the beach.

≜ **Hotel Herradura** (map II, **22**): avenida Playa, between 35 and 36. ☎ 61-37-03. Fax: 66-74-96. A double room with breakfast costs $65–70 in this large, charmless building, painted in orange and cream, next to the sea. Large terrace overlooking

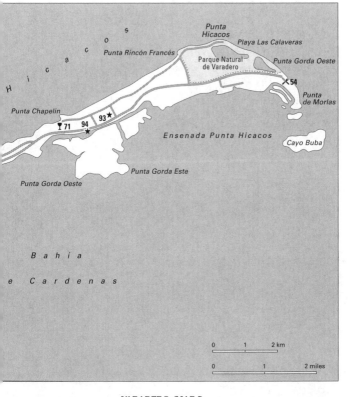

VARADERO (MAP I)

the sea. Well maintained two- to four-bedroom apartments, most with private bathroom and minibar. Public lounge with sea views and a TV. The rooms themselves overlook the street. Staff are very friendly.

≜ **Hotel Pullman** (map II, **26**): avenida Primera and calle 49. ☎ 66-71-61. Fax: 66-74-95. A little under $60 for a double room with breakfast. A pretty, old stone house with only around 15 rooms. Some are a bit dark, but all have bathroom and air-conditioning. With its curious square tower, this is a most original hotel, even if its rooms are more run-of-

the-mill. Lots of character with its little garden and fine wooden bar. There is a pool table on the terrace and some comfy armchairs for relaxing afterwards. Good value for money, although not as good as the Dos Mares (see above).

≜ **Delfines** (map II, **27**): avenida Primera, between calle 38 and calle 39. ☎ 66-77-20. Fax: 66-77-27. Half board only at around $110 for two people. It is often block-booked by an Italian agency so there aren't always rooms available. A fine hotel in two parts, right on the beach. The new building is very big but well laid out and very comfortable. The rooms

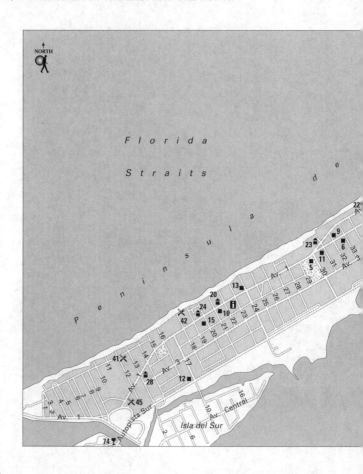

have all mod cons (air-conditioning, TV, safe) and are set round an attractive swimming pool. The old part is also delightful – a freestone building with a courtyard directly overlooking the beach. The two best rooms are definitely Nos. 214 and 215 (slightly more expensive than the others), just above the beach. Excellent value for money. The restaurant on the ground floor of the older building is also worth a visit.

🛏 **Acuazul** (map II, **28**): avenida Primera and calle 13. ☎ 66-71-32.

Fax: 66-72-29. A double room in this huge impersonal hotel costs $72, including buffet breakfast. Rooms have all mod cons, but those at the back are very noisy (the *autopista* is near by). As its name would suggest, blue is the favourite colour here. The annexes (Varazul and Villa Sotavento) consist of chalets on the beach for around the same price.

🛏 **Villas Punta Blanca** (map I, **29**): on the lagoon to the west of the town. If you are coming from the

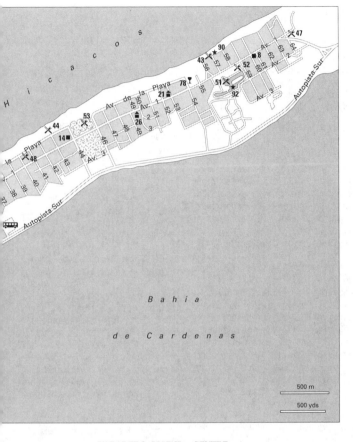

VARADERO (MAP II) – CENTRE

centre, turn right at the first exit as soon as you cross the bridge. The hotel is around 1.5 kilometres (1 mile) further on, by the sea on the right. ☎ 66-80-50. Fax: 66-75-88. Double rooms cost around $100 ($182 for full board); prices drop hugely out of season. This huge tourist establish-

ment is spread over 2 kilometres (1 mile) of beach. Swimming pool, disco, restaurant/grill, etc. The accommodation is in small buildings that are all different. Spotless rooms with all mod cons: air-conditioning, new bathrooms, cable TV, telephone, safety deposit box, etc.

WHERE TO EAT

☆ Budget

✕ **Casa del Chef** (map II, **41**): avenida Primera and calle 12. Open daily until 11pm but the terrace closes at around 6pm. One of the cheapest Cuban restaurants in Varadero, attracting very few tourists. The simple decor isn't much to look at, but the atmosphere is good and the service is very friendly. Full menu at an unbeatable price (around $3–6) includes grilled meat (choose from chicken *asado*, pork or other meat), rice, French fries, *plátanos*, salad, dessert and a Cuban coffee.

✕ **El Bodegón Criollo** (map II, **48**): corner of avenida Playa and calle 40, facing the sea. Open daily noon to midnight. Dishes cost $5–8. This old stone house with graffiti-covered walls is a copy of the famous Bodeguita del Medio in Havana. The difference is that this one has a nice outdoor eating area on the street. Very well known in Varadero and extremely pleasant. Good portions of Creole cooking: *pierna de cerdo asada en cazuela, camarones a la plancha, picadillos a la criolla*, etc. The lobster is expensive, however.

✕ **El Criollo** (map II, **42**): corner of avenida Primera and calle 18. Open daily noon–11pm. Basic dishes cost $2–4 (others are $6–8) in this little old house with a veranda. There are also some long wooden tables under a large straw canopy. Good, inexpensive Cuban specialities, including *ropa vieja, cerdo asado, pollo frito*, etc., but portions are on the small side. The *mojitos* and *cuba libre* are reasonably priced. An ideal setting for a romantic tête-à-tête.

✕ **El Caney** (map II, **44**): at the end of calle 43, on the beach. A tiny straw-roofed eatery, one of the few actually set on the beach. Snacks for less than $5. A handy place for a quick bite before going back to your beach-towel and the turquoise waters, but the food is nothing special. Best to stick to something simple like *pollo congris con papas* and a small salad with a refreshing beer.

✕ **Ranchón Mediterráneo** (map II, **43**): at the end of calle 57. Open daily 9am–5pm. An unpretentious, straw-covered hut on the beach, just behind the municipal museum, serves tasty little lobsters for around $13 or perfectly grilled fish for around $10. Highly recommended.

☆☆ Moderate

✕ **El Aljibe** (map II, **46**): corner of avenida Primera and calle 36. ☎ 61-40-19. The speciality costs $12. Under a superb straw-covered roof, this restaurant basically offers the dish that has made it famous – '*pollo al Aljibe*'. This serves as a meal in itself and was invented more than 50 years ago – it consists of chicken with rice, salad and black haricot beans. An excellent meal that is better still when grilled. Highly recommended.

✕ **Castel Nuovo** (map II, **45**): corner of avenida Primera and calle 11. Open daily noon–midnight. A meal costs less than $10. The airy dining room is quite smart, and the pizzas are some of the cheapest in Varadero (for once, they are what can be called real pizzas). There are also soups, pasta and meat dishes. The only problem is that it is some distance from the centre, right at the end of the avenue on the way into town.

✕ **La Barbacoa** (map II, **47**): corner of avenida Primera and calle 64, opposite the Hotel Siboney. There are several set menus for $6–13 but for a really satisfying meal allow at least $15. The extensive menu specializes in meat dishes, and every meal comes complete with chicken soup, salad, fruit and dessert. Set in a large, Hispano-colonial style building, with a tastefully furnished covered terrace and an attractive dining room. Unobtrusive background music. More suitable for evening meals.

✗ **El Mesón del Quijote** (map I, **49**): avenida las Américas. A little away from the centre next to a stone water tower. Open noon–midnight. Dishes are around $12–15. A statue of Don Quixote stands proudly outside, but Sancho Panza has disappeared from his donkey. Fairly good Spanish specialities, such as *fabalas* (paella Cuban style). The cuisine is fairly classy, but somewhat overpriced.

✗ **Restaurant Imperial** (Delfines, *see* 'Where to Stay'; map II, **27**): open evenings only. A full meal costs around $15–18. The small dining room and the terrace built of large blocks of stone overlooking the beach and sea make this one of the resort's most charming eateries. A romantic and quiet spot hidden inside the hotel away from the casual passer-by. As well as à la carte dishes, an interesting set menu includes things like soup, spaghetti, half a lobster with shrimps and fillet of fish (generally grilled) and a dessert. Good, if not particularly ambitious, food and a fantastic location.

✗ **Itsmo** (Hotel Dos Mares, *see* 'Where to Stay', map II, **21**): Reasonable prices ($3–6 per dish) and a nice setting. The speciality is a well-prepared *pollo Itsmo*, and there are some reasonable pasta dishes.

☆☆☆ Expensive

✗ **Las Américas** (in Mansión Xanadu; map I, **50**): at the end of the avenida las Américas. ☎ 66-77-50. Turn left at the green sign for Varadero Golf Club and continue to the

end. Not to be confused with the Hotel Melia Las Americas, which is an enormous hotel complex. The finest restaurant in Varadero, in a very luxurious mansion, dating back to the 1930s (*see* 'What to See'). A meal costs at least $30. There are a number of very classy dining rooms, with panelling, chandeliers, paintings and antique furniture. The food makes more than a passing nod to French cuisine and there are a number of more expensive seafood dishes (including lobster) that are perfectly acceptable. The quality of the cooking isn't exceptional, but it is still one of the best in the resort. Good wine list, especially for French and Spanish wines. Those who cannot afford to eat here can make do with the terrace café (open noon–5pm), which serves sandwiches, hot-dogs, omelettes and some set menus for $8–18. You can also just have a drink on the terrace or in the superb upstairs bar.

✗ **El Retiro** (map II, **51**): avenida Primera just after calle 59. To the right of the pond in Josone Park. Open noon–midnight. A meal costs around $30. This international restaurant, set in a fine 1940s house, serves some of the best meat in Varadero, especially *filet mignon*. Excellent, but far too expensive. There are other restaurants in this really pretty park, including a good but very pricey Cuban one (**La Campana**), in a house resembling Zorro's, and a reasonable Italian joint (**Dante**) with a terrace overlooking the lake (lasagne for $6–9).

✗ **Antiguedades** (map II, **52**): avenida Primera and calle 59. Just past Josone park. ☎ 66-73-29. Open 6pm–midnight. As its name suggests, it's somewhat antiquarian, hence the extraordinary decor swamped by rare furniture and antique ornaments. Ideal setting for a romantic dinner based on seafood. It attracts lots of ultra-

BEACHES IN THE EAST & NORTH

rich foreigners and is priced accordingly. It's best to book in advance, as there are only six or seven tables.

Paladares

Privately run restaurants are officially forbidden, but locals often approach visitors on the beach and offer to take them home for a meal of fish or lobster. Do not hesitate, as this is generally an excellent option. Make sure you see the fish before it's cooked to ensure it's not frozen and agree on a price. They almost all offer the same thing for the same price (around $10) – lobster (usually caught that morning), side dishes (rice, black beans, fried bananas, and a cabbage and green tomato salad), dessert and fruit juice. It's simple, the portions are generous and it's generally good. Plus, you get to meet the Cubans for a change. Just follow your instincts.

WHERE TO EAT IN THE AREA

✕ **El Galeón** (map I, **54**): Marina Gaviota, right at the end of the Varadero peninsula, 10 kilometres (6 miles) from the centre. Open daily noon–10pm. ☎ 66-77-55 Dishes range from $8 to $15 (although the lobster is more expensive). A sweet little restaurant in front of the Gaviota group's superb catamarans, among the fishing boats. You choose your own lobster or crab. There aren't many tourists here, as they prefer the hustle and bustle of avenida Primera to this almost deserted, sleepy place.

✝ **Coppelia** (map II, **53**): avenida Primera, between calle 44 and 46. Open daily noon–midnight. A safe bet, being a branch of the large Havana ice-cream parlour, set in an unappealing building that looks a bit like a radiator (see it to believe it). Several flavours are advertised but they are not always available.

WHERE TO HAVE A DRINK

🍷 **Hotel Dos Mares** (map II, **21**): The hotel bar is one of the nicest and is open 24 hours a day. *See* 'Where to Stay'.

🍷 **Las Américas** (Mansión Xanadu restaurant; map I, **62**): *See* 'Where to Eat' *above*. Open until around 11pm. Have a drink on the restaurant's terrace or in the upstairs bar, El Mirador, which has an extraordinary setting with pillars, coffered ceiling and bay window overlooking the sea. The dark wood of the room contrasts superbly with the intense turquoise of the sea.

🍷 **Beer pavilions**: There are several of these inexpensive places in the resort along the main avenues, where Cubans come and sit around their Mexican Tecate beers. Entertainment until late evening.

NIGHTLIFE

Dress codes, such as no T-shirts or shorts, might apply in some places.

🍷 **La Cueva del Pirata** (map I, **71**): avenida las Américas, at the kilometres 11 mark. Open Monday to Saturday from 9pm, with shows at 10pm or 10.30pm. Admission $10 (the cheapest in town). The famous cabaret in a cave takes place in the amusing atmosphere of an old pirates' tavern with characters donning costumes. There's a disco afterwards. Certainly the best value in terms of price, quality and entertainment.

❢ **Cabaret Mediterraneo** (map II, **78**): avenida Playa and Calle 54. Open from 8.30pm. Open-air tropical show at 10. Admission $10 for the show (live band) or $5 afterwards. The dances are typical in a corny sort of way, and it turns into a nightclub after the show.

❢ **Palacio de la Rumba** (map I, **76**): avenida las Américas, at the kilometre 6 mark east of town, just past the Hotel Bella Costa. Open every night until 4am. Admission $10. This is a typical nightclub attracting young, trendy tourists and Cubans. If you've got a real urge to boogie, this is the only place for you – the dance floor is packed every evening. The sheer volume of club-bers can make getting to the bar a stressful experience!

❢ **La Patna** (map II, **74**): a floating nightclub aboard a boat. Cross the Varadero bridge towards Matanzas, turn right then right again and it's at the foot of the bridge. Admission $3. A very popular club but with very few tourists. Taped Cuban and Euro/American pop music. Lots of local colour.

❢ **Cabaret Continental** (map I, **72**): next to the Hotel Internacional Varadero. Closed Monday. Show from 10pm–midnight, followed by a disco. Admission $25. The most expensive cabaret, but the best, equivalent to the Tropicana in Havana (although not necessarily worth the extortionate admission charge). A cabaret extravaganza with scantily clad dancers. You can have dinner here too (not recommended). Bookings may be made in any hotel.

WHAT TO SEE

★ **The Dupont de Nemours mansion** (Mansión Xanadu; map I, **50**): end of avenida Las Américas. Turn left at the green sign for Varadero Golf Club and it is at the end. Open daily. This stunning mansion, built in 1930, was the summer residence of the American multimillionaire Irénée Dupont de Nemours, the first of Varadero's property developers, who abandoned the house due to the political situation in 1958. It has now been transformed into a luxury hotel, and it's possible to wander around its rooms if you are discreet. Built on a 6-metre (19-foot) high headland by two Cuban architects, Govantes and Cavarrocas, it occupies the best location in the resort. From the terrace the sea stretches as far as the eye can see. The view is even more impressive from the Mirador bar on the third floor (*see* 'Where to Eat' and 'Where to Have a Drink'). You wouldn't think that 20 years ago the place was completely surrounded by trees and untouched beaches. The small private harbour to the right of the mansion when facing the sea was built specially for the magnate's yacht.

Take time to admire the hall with its purely decorative chimney, as well as the luxurious dining rooms with vaulted ceilings. The lake in front of the house, next to the golf course, used to belong to the dictator Batista. The Carenas Blancas hotel was built on the site of his house.

★ **Museo Municipal Varadero** (map, II, **90**): calle 57. Right at the end of the road, just before the beach. Open daily 9am–6pm. Admission $1. This modest museum is housed in an attractive blue-and-white wooden building dating from 1921. It is full of artefacts illustrating the resort's recent history –

archaeological finds, reproductions of old maps of the country, photographs of the Dupont mansion and sporting paraphernalia. That's not to mention a section on the Revolution with photos of Che Guevara in Varadero, and Castro in his swimming costume, no less!

★ **Josone Park** (map II, **92**): avenida Primera and calle 59. Admission $1 (includes two drinks). This attractive green space is little more than a simple municipal park, with a lake and swimming pool. Before the Revolution, this property belonged to a Spanish multimillionaire, who had a tunnel built to provide access to the beach without having to cross the road. The park is very well maintained and a haven of peace and tranquillity – perfect for when you've had enough of the beach. You can hire rowing boats, sit and read in a deckchair, listen to orchestras playing in the evening or eat in one of the five restaurants (*see* 'Where to Eat').

★ **Dolphinarium** (map I, **93**): Carretera Las Morlas. Autopista, 11.5 kilo-metres mark. Open daily 9am–5pm; shows at 11am, 2.30 and 4pm (lasting 25 minutes). Admission $10, but reservations made through an agency or hotel are a little cheaper. At the tip of the peninsula, past the big, modern hotels is this aquatic centre in a natural setting beside a mangrove swamp. This centre opened in 1985 with three dolphins and now has eight. The highlight here is swimming with the dolphins – which is pricey ($50), but undoubtedly one of the highlights of a trip to Varadero. It is essential to book in high season through one of the agencies in town (no reductions). There are five organized swimming sessions per day between 9.30am and 4.30pm. The delightful dolphins frolic around you in the mangroves, and will catch the little fish that you hold out for them so you can stroke them. After half an hour of fun you can say good-bye like two old friends – they have been trained to kiss you on the cheek!

WHAT TO DO

Information on all sorts of activities, such as **waterskiing** and **parachuting**, is available in all the hotels.

– **Swimming**: the water temperature is heavenly (average of 27°C/80°F).

– **Sunbathing**: you have 20 kilometres (12 miles) of beach to find some-where to spread your towel. But be careful not to get sunburnt.

– **Swimming with dolphins**: in the Dolphinarium (*see above*).

➥ **Diving**: the underwater world round here is attractive but far from the best in Cuba. There are dive clubs here because there are tourists, not because there is anything exceptional to see. The coral around the neighbouring islands is much more beautiful, but to get there you'll need to pay for a boat trip. There are several diving clubs (*club de buces*), all the same price. One of the best, **Aqua**, is represented in all the hotels or you can contact the club directly (☎ 666-80-6). If you're not a qualified diver (or don't have time to learn) you can have just as much fun snorkelling.

– **Boat trips** (map I, **94**): The *Jolly Roger* catamaran, run by an American, offers day trips from Chapelin marina, Carretera Punta de Hicacos (kilo-metres 12 mark). ☎ 66-75-65. The trip includes stop-offs on deserted islands, cruises to Cayo Blanco and Cayo Piedra, swimming, scuba-diving and fishing. It's very expensive (around $70), but includes transfers and a meal (with lobster). Tickets are on sale in all the hotels and the boat leaves at 9am, returning around 6pm.

– **A glass-bottomed boat**: leaves the Hotel Paradiso at 10am, 11.30 and 2pm. ☎ 66-71-65 for a 2-hour trip to the coral barrier reef. Once again, you can book a place in any of the hotels, but it's fairly pricey at $25. A shuttle bus will collected you from your hotel.

– **Golf**: there's an 18-hole course in front of the Mansion Dupont.

– **Shopping**: calle 12, on the corner of avenida Primera, 9am–7pm. This is where local craftsman spread out their wares and sell clothes, souvenirs, ceramics and maracas in a relaxed atmosphere. There's another small craft market on calle 57, next to avenida Primera selling the same sort of stuff, but often at ludicrously inflated prices.

IN THE AREA

★ **Cueva de Saturno** (the Saturn cave): from Varadero, follow the Havana road for 19 kilometres (12 miles) then turn left towards the airport. It is well signposted a short distance along on the left. Open daily 9am–5pm. Admission $3 ($5 including snorkelling gear). The cave is in the middle of the forest, and tourists hurrying to catch their planes pass by without even realizing it's there. But the local children know it well as it's their favourite place for swimming. It is basically a cave partially open to the sky and partially filled with water. There is a natural swimming pool with warm, crystal-clear water, about 30 metres (100 feet) deep. Don't forget your swimming costume and it is well worth taking snorkelling gear. If you are lucky, you will see Cuban kids climbing the giant stalagmites to dive into the magically coloured waters. The Varadero diving clubs come here regularly and you can dive down to 17 metres (56 feet). There is a restaurant and bar at the entrance.

★ **El Coral beach**: 16 kilometres (10 miles) west of Varadero, not far from the airport. The place is somewhat isolated so it's a good idea to negotiate a return price (including waiting) with a taxi driver. To get there by car, the road splits after the toll point – to the left is the airport, and 2 kilometres (1 mile) to the right is Playa El Coral. It's an exceptional site for snorkelling and admiring the underwater world, with a coral reef and hundreds of tropical fish. The water is translucent to a depth of 2 metres (6 feet) although the beach is often unpleasantly rubbish-strewn. Snorkelling equipment hire is available.

LEAVING VARADERO

By Bus

🚌 **Bus station** (Terminal de Omnibuses Interprovinciales; map II): on the crossroads between Calle 36 and the Autopista Sur. Book as far ahead as possible.

– For **Havana**: Viazul bus company. ☎ 61-48-86. Three times a day in theory, journey time around 3 hours. The ticket must be bought in dollars.

Note that if there aren't any available seats, taxis or private chauffeurs will offer their services to Havana (they wait in front of the bus station). Allow $40–50 for a whole car – fairly reasonable if there are four or five of you.

– For **Santa Clara** and **Trinidad**: Viazul bus company. One bus a day to the two towns.

By Plane

Surprising as it may seem, air travel is not expensive in Cuba. For example, a return flight from Varadero to Havana costs around $30.

– For further information and ticket purchase, contact **Sol y Son**, a travel agency on avenida Primera, between calle 54 and 55. ☎ 66-75-93.

✪ **Juan Gualberto Gómez airport**: on the Havana road (*see* 'Useful Addresses'). Regular departures to Havana, Cayo Coco, Trinidad, Santiago and Holguín.

– For **Cayo Largo**: one flight a day, taking 30 minutes. A single ticket costs $70.

– For **Cayo Coco**: one flight daily, journey time 50 minutes. Single ticket $80.

– For **Trinidad**: two flights a week in the morning with Lacsa. Journey time 40 minutes; single ticket $80.

– For **Havana**: three flights a week with Cubana. The journey takes 30 minutes; single ticket $30.

CARDENAS

The town is around 15 kilometres (9 miles) southeast of Varadero, via the Santa Clara road. As you enter Cardenas you will see three stone sculptures – a crab, a bicycle and a carriage – these celebrate the three products for which the town is known.

This charming little old town was the first to see the Cuban flag fly in 1850. It is therefore revered by Cubans. It is also very proud of its twinning with Dieppe in France. It boasts a broad, attractive main street (calle Real) lined with simple, brightly painted houses, and *barouches* provide the municipal bus service. Apart from that, there is not much to see, but the promenade is pleasant and it makes a change from the beaches.

USEFUL ADDRESSES

■ **CUPET service station**: at the approach to town when coming from Varadero.

■ **Telephone centre**: calle Real, on the corner of No. 12.

WHERE TO STAY AND EAT

If you are staying a few days in the town, you are bound to come across a few illegal *paladares* where the food will almost certainly be better than in the state restaurants.

📶 ✗ **Hotel La Dominica**: calle Real, on the corner of calle 9 (also known as Princesa). There's no sign but it is the building with the pink facade next to the church. ☎ 52-15-02. A double room costs $23. The only hotel in town, built in 1830, is a national monument, for it was here that the famous flag was raised. The building has a certain charm with its typical colonial architecture, but the rooms are not particularly well equipped or well maintained – both toilet and shower facilities are pretty ancient. The paint has disappeared altogether, along with any desire to spend the night here. It's really a last resort, which is a shame because the facade is rather tempting.

On the ground floor of the hotel is the restaurant with a big, vaguely colonial dining room. It serves a limited choice of hamburgers, gammon with rice, etc. The quality is mediocre, but it is cheap.

WHAT TO SEE

★ **The church**: calle Real, opposite the hotel. This large building with hexagonal towers dates from the beginning of the 19th century.

★ **Statue of Christopher Columbus**: in front of the church. This is the oldest statue in Cuba, perhaps even in the whole of South America. Note the globe at his feet.

★ **Oscar-Maria de Rojos Museum**: calle Coronel Verduzo, between Vives and Genes. Open Tuesday to Saturday 10am–5pm. Sunday 8am–noon. Admission $2. Located in the house belonging to the governor of the town in the 19th century, this museum opened in 1959, the year of the Revolution. The main exhibits are a 5,790-year-old skeleton and the *Chancha* – a woman's head, the size of a fist, with long blond hair speared on a pick. She was presented to the town by the country of Ecuador, having been decapitated by the Jivaro Indians. Several other rooms contain collections of coins and medals, butterflies and shells.

Zapata Peninsula

The name of the Península de Zapata region, to the south of the Matanzas province, also known as Cienaga de Zapata, has nothing to do with the great Mexican revolutionary. Rather, the peninsula looks rather like a shoe – just as Italy is like a boot – and *zapata* is Spanish for shoe. The Zapata Peninsula is a deserted, wild and flat swampland, which for eons has been inhospitable.

The Cuban government has declared Cienaga to be a national park, known as the Parque Montemar. The marshland is the most stunning nature reserve in the country. It is a birdwatcher's paradise, home to 190 species – including hummingbirds and blue-headed doves – and, of course, the ubiquitous crocodile, the country's national symbol.

There are also pigs in this area, though you probably won't see any. They were originally brought to the island many years ago by Spanish settlers, and have given their name to a notorious geographical feature: the Bay of Pigs (called 'Girón' by the Cubans). Don't think that this place is just a historical battlefield: there is a series of beaches, inlets and natural swimming pools, where you can swim with more peace of mind than in the swampland.

GETTING THERE

By bus: buses leave Havana on Friday, Saturday and Sunday at lunchtime, arriving in Jagüey Grande at 4.20pm. From Jagüey Grande, there are three buses a day to Playa Girón and Playa Larga. Buses leave at 5am, 6.50am and 1.40pm.

You can also do the journey by truck, which leaves from Jagüey Grande at 11.20am daily.

By car: take the main *autopista* from Havana towards Santa Clara. Around 150 kilometres (95 miles) from Havana, turn off towards Guama and Playa Girón on the minor road on the right.

USEFUL ADDRESSES

Rumbos information kiosk: just before you reach the peninsula proper, 142 kilometres (88 miles) along the motorway – look for a boat bearing a sign saying 'The Zapata Peninsula'. There's not a great deal of information on offer, but you can buy a map of the peninsula listing the different activities available and also reserve guides for trips to Santo Tomás, la Salina and Guama.

WHERE TO EAT

✗ There is a nice little open-air, thatched snack bar selling coffee and sandwiches for around $1 near the information kiosk (*see above*). There is also a small Caracol shop.

ZAPATA PENINSULA

✕ *Parilladas* are the tiny refreshment stands dotted along the main road where you can eat and drink for a few pesos.

✕ **Finca de Los Morales**: at the 73 kilometre marker, between San Nicolas and Nueva Paz. Less local colour but open 24 hours a day.

Diners eat under the straw-covered roof, in sight of their cars (you can never be too careful). A great place to refuel, as chicken pieces or a slice of pizza and a drink cost less than $2. Also French fries and cakes to take away.

FINCA FIESTA CAMPESINA

Take the turn-off to Guama and this little tourist spot is 100 metres along on the right hand-side towards Playa Girón, 142 kilometres (88 miles) from Havana. Run by local farmers, it has a farm and a small zoo (with deer, parrots and other birds, boas and iguanas). Open 8.30am–5pm. Admission is free but you will be asked to buy a lottery ticket (for a token dollar). If the guinea pig scuttles into the house with your number on it, you win a bottle of rum!

WHERE TO STAY

🛏 **Hotel Don Pedro**: at the end of the park. A double room costs around $28, the cheapest on the peninsula. Wooden *cabanas* with thatched roofs, set in a large flower-filled garden. The *cabanas* have fans, fridge, bath, hot water and TV. A bit isolated but very peaceful.

WHERE TO EAT AND DRINK

✕ **Restaurant**: at the far end of the park in a pleasant setting. Good, inexpensive food (around $6 for a meal), including omelettes, chicken and pork dishes. The menu isn't particularly extensive but all the ingredients are products from the farm.

❢ **Bar**: very good coffee and excellent freshly squeezed fruit juice. Musicians occasionally serenade the diners.

WHERE TO EAT IN THE AREA

✕ **Pio Cua**: on the way to Playa Girón, 3 kilometres (2 miles) after leaving the motorway. Another overtly touristy restaurant, although you can escape the canteen-like main dining room by sitting at the tables off to one side. You can try crocodile meat ($10) or lobster (around $15). There is also a cheaper snack bar. The place doubles as a disco at weekends (9.30pm–4am), when crowds gyrate under the carefully designed traditional straw-covered roof (reminiscent of Bali). Near by, a natural swimming pool – really a collapsed cave – is set among dense vegetation. There are many such natural pools (*cenote*) in the area.

WHAT TO SEE

★ The entrance to the **Parque Nacional Cienaga de Zapata** (national park) is 3 kilometres (2 miles) after the Pio Cua restaurant (*see above*), along the Playa Girón road. Look out for the disused tollbooth.

LA BOCA

La Boca ('the mouth') is the boarding point for **Laguna del Tesoro**, a magnificent lake surrounded by mangrove swamps, a paradise for anglers and crocodiles. You can also get to Guama from here. La Boca isn't so much a village as a sort of tourist complex, with restaurants, bars, shops, a ceramics workshop and a crocodile farm.

WHERE TO EAT

✕ **Restaurant La Boca**: on the left of the car-park as you arrive. Open until 4.30pm. Try to get here after 2pm, by which time the tour parties should have left. This large *caney* (house with a roof made from palm leaves) contains the best restaurant in the area. The owner is great fun and a confirmed *bon viveur*. The $10 set menu features large portions of chicken, fish or roast pork, vegetables, dessert and a drink. The $12 set menu includes crocodile. On the à la carte side, the speciality Creole chicken costs $5.50.

✕ **Le Colibri**: next to La Boca. Same prices, virtually identical menu but the interior and terrace are smaller and not as nice. The owner is friendly and a mine of information on the region's ornithological treasures.

WHAT TO DO

★ **Criadero de Cocodrilos** (crocodile farm): just behind La Boca restaurant (*see above*). Open 9am– 6pm, but it's better to go in the middle of the day, and definitely before 5pm in winter as the crocs tend to disappear into their natural environment. Admission $3.

This national reserve was created to protect the species, and part of it is now open to the public. This is a very pleasant park where you can see everything from baby crocodiles only 15 centimetres (6 inches) long, to real monsters measuring 3 or 4 metres (10 or 13 feet) and weighing up to 250 kilograms (551 pounds).The biggest are in an enclosure at the far end of the park. They are only fed once a week, with cows, pigs, goats and sometimes crabs. They haul themselves onto the land for a few hours' rest, and lie motionless in the sun with their mouths wide open. Visitors can watch demonstrations of how crocodiles are captured (using a lasso) and other aspects of their handling and treatment. The keepers will be happy to tell you about the lives of their wards.

GUAMA   DIALLING CODE: 53

This much-visited site is named after a Taino Indian who resisted the Spanish *conquistadores* for 10 years and, according to legend, gave his life for a woman. The only way to reach it is by boat, which follows a long canal lined with mangrove before entering the **Laguna del Tesoro** (Treasure Lagoon). The lagoon, vaguely reminiscent of the Amazon, stretches as far as the eye can see. This 16-kilometre (10-mile) body of water is the largest saltwater lake in Cuba. In the middle is the swampy island of Guama, inhabited in the past by Taino Indians. Legend has it that they threw all their treasures into the water when the *conquistadores* arrived, hence the lagoon's name.

Popular with tourists, it is without question an extraordinary setting, in the heart of a lagoon shrouded in mystery. The impenetrable dark blue of the water only adds to the strangeness of the place – the real treasures of this unspoiled wilderness are natural rather than manmade. It is an ideal spot for travellers in search of a little peace and quiet.

Guama has the most original hotel in Cuba, situated in the middle of a crocodile reserve. Unfortunately for thrill-seekers, it is unusual for the crocodiles to venture up round the chalets – they are seemingly less than keen on tourist flesh. All the same, it would be unwise to swim anywhere except the hotel pool. Make sure you take anti-mosquito precautions.

GETTING THERE

The only way of getting to Guama is by boat from La Boca. At the height of the season these leave daily at 10am, noon and 3pm. Out of season, they leave at 10am with another one leaving subject to demand. A return ticket costs $20. The journey takes 20 minutes. If you miss the boat, there are launches that can take you for the same price between 9am and 6pm depending on the captain's mood. These only take 10 minutes. The return times are fixed at 9.30am and 11.30am. Make sure you are suitably dressed as it is often quite windy.

WHERE TO STAY, EAT AND HAVE A DRINK

🛏 **Villa Guama**: in the middle of the lake. ☎ 55-51. A room costs around $42 per night (breakfast included), plus $10 per person for the boat across and $3 for the car-park. The only hotel in Guama, built on marshy islands transformed into water gardens, this incredible tourist complex was converted into a hotel in 1961 and is reserved in principle for tourists, although it occasionally admits well-off Cubans. Made entirely of wood and palm thatch, the 'village' takes its inspiration from Taino architecture. Guests sleep in *cabanas* on stilts, interconnected by huge, narrow wooden walkways, which are rather rickety. Fortunately, arrivals and their luggage are dropped at their *cabana* from the boat. The rooms have air-conditioning, shower and small lounge with fridge and TV, but cleanliness leaves a lot to be desired. Whatever you do, don't let the mosquitoes in. The view first

thing in the morning as you throw back the shutters is breathtaking – the lagoon completely surrounds the *cabanas*, and you are just a few steps away from frogs, birds and flowers. Hire a boat from the hotel for an early-morning outing ($2 per hour).

✗ The **restaurant**, in a straw hut in the middle of the *cabanas*, is accessed via the walkways or boat. There is a bar on a lovely terrace, and a huge wooden dining room (typical but lacking in warmth). A meal costs around $15 and you can try a crocodile dish for $10.

❡ **Nightclub**: opposite the restaurant, on the other side of a stretch of water. Dancing classes between 8pm and 10pm. Many guests complain that the music spoils the tranquillity of the place, but they should take solace in the fact that it is even more beautiful in the early morning, when all the clubbers are still in bed.

WHAT TO SEE

★ **Taino village**: on the island, behind the hotel. When arriving by boat, this is your first view of the island, and it makes a good photo. This reconstruction of traditional Indian dwellings is brought to life by wooden statues made by the Cuban artist Rita Longa. Among them is the great rebel leader Guama. There's a small museum, bar and inexpensive souvenir shops.

★ **Laguna del Tesoro**: take a boat out into the sound, and bring a pair of binoculars to spot the abundant birdlife and other fauna.

| **PLAYA LARGA** | DIALLING CODE: 59 |

Playa Larga (wide beach) is 8 kilometres (5 miles) from La Boca, on the way to Girón. This beach is huge, as its name suggests, and on the famous Bay of Pigs. Dozens of roadside monuments commemorate the Cuban militiamen who died preventing US mercenaries from invading the island in 1960. One of the main landings of the anti-Castro invasion took place here, the other in Girón, a bit further on.

Playa Larga is a pleasant beach that is quite popular among Cubans in July and August. The sea is at its finest in winter, when it takes on a shimmering hue similar to that seen on the island's north coast. The small tourist office in the hotel arranges excursions into the surrounding area.

WHERE TO STAY AND EAT

♠ ✕ **Villa Horizontes Playa Larga**: the only hotel in the village. ☎ 72-94. Fax: 41-41. A double room costs around $46 in high season. Around 50 functional *cabanas* built in a large garden, a stone's throw from the beach. Clean rooms with a lounge, mosquito nets, bathroom, air-conditioning, hot water and a safe. Pleasant swimming pool and bar. The buffet food in the restaurant costs $10 and lacks variety. Attractive beach.

IN THE AREA

★ **Playa Campismo**: 6 kilometres (4 miles) from Playa Larga. This beach, frequented almost exclusively by Cubans during their July and August holidays, has hardly any sand, but the turquoise water is still inviting. There's music at the weekend, a raised pontoon for diving and a great family atmosphere.

★ **Las Cuevas de los Peces** (Cenote de Ilona): 15 kilometres (9 miles) away, on the way to Girón, on the left coming from Playa Larga. Open 9am–4pm. Admission $1. You can hire snorkelling equipment. This idyllic spot is hidden among the trees just off the road. It is a natural swimming pool (*cenote*) 70 metres (230 feet) deep, with wonderful water teeming with multicoloured fish, which come in from the sea along an underwater passage. It is surrounded by lovely tropical vegetation, and a hammock sways invitingly between two palm trees. There is a bar and small fish restaurant if the swimming has given you an appetite.

Just off the shore is a coral reef that's ideal for diving. There's no sandy beach, and anyone who fancies a dip has to brave a pontoon with steps.

On the other side of the road, a **viewpoint** offers a panorama of the magnificent coastline.

The best beaches in this area have apparently been requisitioned by the army to protect Castro's summer residence on the *cayo* just opposite.

★ **Las Salinas de Brito**: this lagoon, situated more than 20 kilometres (12 miles) southwest of Playa Larga, is used by migrating birds, many of which stop off in the nature reserve between November and May. This ecosystem in the middle of a reserve of 37,000 hectares (91,358 acres) is a bird-watcher's paradise – home to over 65 different species.

Another observation point, the **Corral de Santo Tomás**, is open only to tourists accompanied by a guide, and the tollbooth ensures that this rule is respected.

ZAPATA PENINSULA

In both reserves, hordes of mosquitoes attack any fair and sensitive skin that is not covered in insect repellent.

PLAYA GIRÓN

Although this coast may appear quiet and peaceful it was the setting for one of the major incidents of the Cold War – the Bay of Pigs crisis. *See* 'General Information: History', and find out more by visiting the interesting **museum** here.

The place is a commemorative site, and something of a national symbol, but there are no bunkers and barbed wire, as on the beaches of Normandy. Playa Girón is more of a tourist complex, with shops, pharmacy, post office, car-rental agency and nightclub.

There is an attractive sandy beach in front of the hotel, but the view is marred by a concrete sea wall. **Los Cocos** beach, at the end of the hotel garden, is a much more pleasant spot to swim and sunbathe. The island across the bay is where Fidel Castro's residence is situated, and where he often receives foreign heads of state. When Castro is in residence there is incessant helicopter activity.

USEFUL ADDRESSES

■ **Habanautos**: Villa Playa Girón. ☎ 41-23.

WHERE TO STAY

⌂ **Villa Playa Girón**: at the site entrance. ☎ 41-10. There are 200 *cabanas* – all built in Soviet style but more welcoming than those at Playa Larga. The basic price starts at $50 for two people in season, but prices drop depending on the number of people (up to four per bungalow). There are several restaurants where great efforts have been made to make them attractive to visitors. The hotel arranges excursions (such as potholing, visits to botanical gardens, and local wildlife tours), and hires out diving equipment. There is a club atmosphere round the swimming pool, with dance classes and plenty going on in the evening.

WHAT TO SEE

★ **Bay of Pigs Museum**: on the large central esplanade opposite the hotel. Open daily 9am–5pm. Admission $2 (children and students $1). The museum isn't very big but is bursting with the pride of a small island that managed to stand up to the great American Goliath. Outside is a Cuban army propeller aeroplane and a list of the victims of the invasion. Inside the museum is a collection of weapons (including the machete of the Independence hero Máximo Gómez) and exhibits depicting the origins of the Revolution and the causes of the Bay of Pigs landing.

The first thing you come to is a description of local peasant life and the initial measures enforced by the new regime, including the public reading and writing campaign. Then there was the bombing of the *Coubre*, a French vessel carrying weapons that exploded when it reached Havana – an event captured on film. There are detailed explanations and plans of the American army's different points of attack – the departure of planes from Florida and boats from Nicaragua. The Nicaraguan dictator Somoza is reputed to have asked the leader of the mercenaries to bring him back a hair plucked from Castro's beard . . .

For the Americans, it was vital that only Cuban counter-revolutionaries set foot on the island, so that they would not be accused of meddling. However, of the 800 members of this anti-Castro 'brigade', some were South American, and some were American mercenaries in disguise. The majority, though, were wealthy Cubans and landowners, exiled from Cuba at the beginning of the Revolution. It is said that between them and their families they owned 70 factories, 10 sugar refineries, 5 mines, 2 banks and 666 houses in Cuba. It was wealth that was worth coming back for. When they landed on the island, they were stopped by guards on the beach, who successfully held them back for two hours. The assailants burned a bus and its occupants with napalm, but Castro's artillery arrived in time to stop them from penetrating any further inland.

IN THE AREA

★ **Caleta Buena**: 9 kilometres (5 miles) east of Girón along the coast road. Open 10am–6pm. Admission to site $12 (including a meal and access to the bar), plus $6 to eat at the Parilla de Rey (which offers little more than a simple buffet). This snorkelling and diving complex is owned by the Horizontes chain, and is rather pricey if you just want to enjoy the beach. It is a shame because at this point on the coast the sea enters underwater caves, forming a series of natural swimming pools (*cenotes*). The one on the right is sublime, full of tropical fish. Take some bread to entice them to the surface.

You can sign up with the dive club without paying the admission fee. There is a hire outlet on the beach for snorkelling equipment and fishing gear. You reach the sea via a 25-metre (80-foot) tunnel, and then a 10-metre (32-foot) ascent, so you must be fit and wear flippers. It's an impressive, even sinister, swim for 25 metres in dark and unfamiliar surroundings.

The Centre of the Island

Even though its scenery may not be as stunning as that of the Oriente or the Pinar del Río region, the central region of Cuba is steeped in history. Each city brings its own touch of colonial nostalgia, starting with Trinidad, the most beautiful of them all. If you've got the time, explore the centre a little before moving on to the Oriente. Don't miss the marvellous Los Ingenios valley, designated a UNESCO World Heritage Site, with its fields of sugar cane, untouched traditional villages and attractive landscapes.

CIENFUEGOS

DIALLING CODE: 432

Cienfuegos (nothing to do with Castro's colleague Camilo Cienfuegos) is both a lively, colonial city and a rich, industrial port, in an exceptional geographical position. Set at the back of a deep, well-sheltered bay, the city grew up under French and then Spanish influence. It was first known by the name of Jagua, given to it by the Indians. In the 19th century, the central government of Havana decided that the city was 'too black'. In order to make it a bit whiter, they called in a French émigré, Jean-Louis Laurent de Clouet, originally from Bordeaux. He named it Fernandina de Jagua, coming to a diplomatic compromise between the Indians and the Spanish, and invited numerous white immigrants from New Orleans and his own home town to settle there.

The city of **Cienfuegos** was founded on 22 April 1819, but it was not until 1921 that it was officially given its present name, in honour of General José Cienfuegos, who was its mayor from 1914 to 1920. With some 150,000 inhabitants, this provincial capital is now the fifth-largest city in the country.

Industrial Cienfuegos is proud of its cement works, petrochemical factory and oil refinery, and particularly of its Jaragua nuclear power plant, the only one in Cuba, built by the Russians (and still unfinished).

Don't let all this talk of industry make you think this is a dreary city, suffocating under toxic fumes – the main streets of Cienfuegos are bustling and full of life, and further out it still has a very villagey feel to it. The beautiful **Punta Gorda peninsula** has a number of well-established casinos, and the carefree atmosphere adds to its Caribbean charm. The town is as yet mainly undiscovered by tourists, so it's an excellent place to meet real Cubans. However, you are likely to be hassled by people keen to sell you their services.

GETTING AROUND

Finding your way around is easy, as Cienfuegos is laid out like a giant chessboard. The city is divided into parallel north–south streets numbered alternately (odd numbers); the longest is calle 37 (Prado in the city centre, then Malecón towards Punta Gorda). The east–west avenues are also numbered alternately (even numbers).

USEFUL ADDRESSES

✉ **Post office** (map B1): at the Hotel Jagua and at the corner of avenida 56 and calle 35.

■ **Telephone exchange** (map B1, **1**): avenida 58, between calle 43 and 45, just before the railway station.

� **Railway station** (map B1): avenida 58 and calle 49.

🚌 **Bus station** (map B1): avenida 56 and calle 49, next to the railway station.

■ **Clínica Internacional** (map B3, **2**): Punta Gorda. Opposite the Hotel Jagua and next to the Cueva del Camarón restaurant (good *mojito*, nicer than the clinic waiting room).

Open 24 hours a day. Treats all kinds of injuries, large and small.

■ **Banco Financiero Internacional** (map B1, **3**): corner of avenida 54 and 29, ☎ 45-11-47. Open 8–3pm.

■ **Vehicle hire**: Havanautos (map B2, **4**), avenida Prado (next to CUPET); Transautos (map B3, **15**), at the Hotel Jagua, ☎ 79-82; and at Rancho Luna, ☎ 481-66.

■ **CUPET service stations** (map B2, **4**): Prado and avenida 18, on the left before the Hotel Jagua. Also 12 kilometres (7.5 miles) along the coast towards Trinidad; follow signs for the Hotel Pasacaballo.

WHERE TO STAY

Casas Particulares

It's easy to get your bearings from the town's main streets, so make sure you go to these places unaccompanied, otherwise the owners will be expected to pay a commission to your 'tour guide' or tout.

🏠 **María Nunez Suarez** (map B1, **10**): avenida 58, 3705, between avenida 37 and 39. ☎ 78-67. In a quiet road, just a few blocks from the Parque Martí. A double room costs $15 per night, plus $3 for breakfast. There are two, welcoming, white-painted rooms on the first floor, each with a private bathroom. María is full of delightful banter and her friend and neighbour Violetta can take you in if María's rooms are full. Recommended.

🏠 **Mario Cañisares and Luisa Corcho** (map B1, **11**): calle 35, 4215, between avenida 42 and 44. ☎ 78-64. Halfway between the town's two main areas of interest – Parque José Martí and Punta Gorda, Mario makes his guests feel

instantly at home with his cheerful welcome. There are two clean, airy rooms with shared bathroom for $15 per night (excluding breakfast).

🏠 **Señora Deliz Sierra** (map B2, **12**): calle 37, 3806, between avenida 38 and 40. ☎ 66-38. This pleasant house faces the bay but, unfortunately, the rooms don't have a sea view. There are four rooms at $20 per night, with air-conditioning, TV, fridge and shared bathroom with hot water. The host family is welcoming, helpful and cultured. Parking is generally available.

🏠 **La Perla Cienfuegos** (map B1, **14**): calle 35, 4210, between avenida 42 and 44. ☎ 91-08. Opposite Mario Cañisares's house. Two very clean but otherwise unremarkable rooms

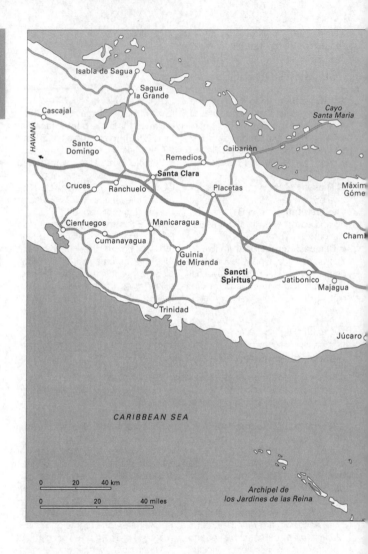

with shared bathroom for \$15 per night. Friendly, understated welcome.

✩✩✩ Expensive

⚐ **Hotel Jagua** (map B3, **15**): 10 calle 37 and 2, Punta Gorda. ☎ 45-12-45. Fax: 45-10-03. A double room costs around \$80 in season and not much less at other times. This large, modern, 'tourist' hotel with full facilities was built in 1950 in the Soviet style, and once belonged to Batista's son. One wing is currently closed for renovation, as is the swimming pool. It is

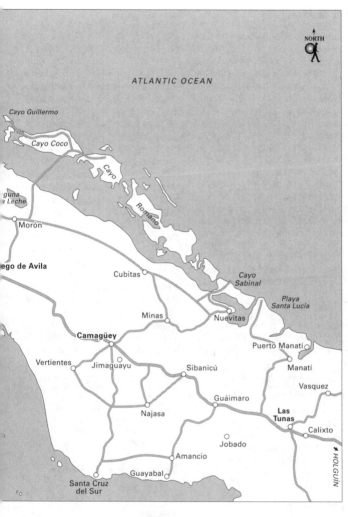

CENTRAL CUBA

the only hotel in the town, ideally located at the end of Punta Gorda, overlooking the sea. The welcome is very impersonal. The hotel is well equipped, with a bar, restaurant (service with a smile an unheard-of concept), a small information office, the Guanaroca nightclub,

post office, shops and so on, as well as marvellous views from some rooms on the higher floors over Punta Gorda and the city. The cafeteria is open 24 hours a day. The nightclub isn't bad, but the noise can make it difficult to get to sleep.

In the Area

Finca Los Colorados: 18 kilometres (11 miles) from Cienfuegos, facing the lighthouse; follow signs for Hotel Pasacaballo, on the Rancho Luna–Pasacaballo road. ☎ (432) 38-08. Fax: (432) 32-65. Email: joma@cfg.jcce.org.cu. A double room costs $20 per night and an apartment for four (two bedrooms, kitchen and bathroom) is $40. Breakfast costs $4. A delightful, rather isolated private property, with children's toys in the garden which make it attractive for families. José, the owner, has worked in hotels across Europe and will ensure that you receive a good welcome and enjoy the highest standards of hospitality. There is access to a peaceful little beach behind the lighthouse.

☆☆ Moderate

Hotel Faro Luna: playa de Rancho Luna, towards Trinidad, 19 kilometres (12 miles) from the city centre. ☎ (53) 481-62, -65 to 68. Fax: (432) 45-11-62. Website: www.cubanacan.cu. Much more expensive but incomparably better than the Pasacaballo. A room costs around $53 including breakfast. Of the 42 rooms in this fairly new hotel, 35 have sea views and have been nicely furnished with rattan. Avoid the rooms that lead off the foyer in the main building as they are very noisy. There's an attractive swimming pool, bar, restaurant and a little beach. The garden, shaded by palm trees, leads down to the sea. There are scuba-diving and snorkelling facilities. This is the most highly recommended hotel as it is much more 'human' than the other two and is spotless. Car hire available.

Hotel Pasacaballo: carretera de Rancho Luna, around 20 kilometres (13 miles) from the town centre. ☎ 096-013. A double room costs around $38 (including breakfast). At the entrance to the bay, opposite

---

■ Useful Addresses

- ✉ Post office
- 🚂 Railway station
- 🚌 Bus station
- 1 Telephone exchange
- 2 International clinic
- 3 Banco Financiero Internacional
- 4 Havanautos

☗ Where to Stay

- 10 Maria Nunez Suarez
- 11 Mario Cañisarez and Luisa Corcho
- 12 Señora Deliz Sierra
- 14 La Perla Cienfuegos
- 15 Hotel Jagua

✕ Where to Eat

- 21 El Palatino

- 22 1819
- 23 Paladar El Criollito
- 24 Paella Cavadonga
- 25 La Cueva del Camarón
- 26 Palacio del Valle

♀ Where to have an Ice-cream

- 20 Coppelia

❦ Nightlife

- 25 La Cueva del Camarón
- 30 La Casa de la UNEAC
- 31 Casa Caribeña

★ What to See

- 40 Palacio Ferrer
- 41 Tomás-Terry Theatre
- 42 Town Provincial Museum

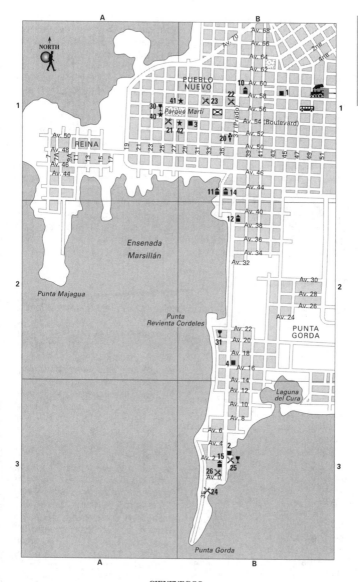

CIENFUEGOS

the village of Perche. The name comes from the fact that, just below the hotel, the Spanish used to take their horses (*caballos*) on a little ferry to the Castillo de Jagua, which guarded the bay of Cienfuegos against pirates. This hotel is built in the Stalinist style also found at Santa María del Mar near Havana, and at Ancón near Trinidad. The 180 rooms have all the usual facilities, but they are not very well sound-proofed and the style has not aged well. The slightly green hue of the swimming pool suggests a less than rigorous attitude towards its up-keep, and it takes a hardened dangerous-sports fan to enjoy a ride in the lift. Cuban guests are fairly numerous, however, and the gentle nonchalance of the staff has a certain charm. There are two reasonably priced restaurants.

â **Hotel Rancho Luna**: playa de Rancho Luna, on the Trinidad road, 17 kilometres (10.5 miles) from the city centre. ☎ 048-120 to 123. Another Soviet-style hotel, with over 220 impersonal rooms costing around $43 a night. Coach-parties tend to take precedence over sole travellers arriving without reservations. There's a post office, information desk, inexpensive restaurant (the Yaina), swimming pool, small beach and (painful) evening entertainment. One good point is that the hotel organizes numerous walks and horse-riding in the Escambray mountains.

WHERE TO EAT

☆ Budget

✕ **El Palatino** (map A1, **21**): José Martí square. An old colonial bar with a gaudy facade serving snacks and sandwiches for around $1. The terrace is an excellent place for watching the world go by in the historic square. It is best to come in the cooler hours of the day.

✕ **1819** (map B1, **22**): avenida Prado, as you enter the city just before the boulevard. The name is the year in which the city was founded. As you enter the city just before the boulevard, the pedestrian street in the city centre. This is one of the locals' favourite restaurants – turquoise panelling in a white, high-ceilinged room with a slightly old-fashioned charm. The menu is in pesos, but you can also pay in dollars ($2 for the chicken, around $5 for a full meal). There's also an outside bar.

☆☆ Moderate

✕ **Paladar El Criollito** (map B1, **23**): calle 33, 5603, between ave-nida 56 and 58. Open 12.30pm to midnight – you need to knock for entry as the door is always closed. Four tables in a cool, dark room. Very reasonably priced and, although the food is not particularly special, the fish, salad and rice are tasty and the portions large. There is a fixed menu for $7 with a choice of main dishes (chicken, pork or fish) a mixed salad and white rice. A friendly welcome and discreet, attentive service.

✕ **Paella Cavadonga** (map B3, **24**): opposite the Palacio del Valle, next to the photo booth. Open noon–3pm, 6–10pm. Despite the name, you don't have to eat paella here. A fish dish costs around $6–7 and lobster is $10. The grilled shrimp at $7 a plate is good. Try them at the bar, in a vast room decorated around a nautical theme.

☆☆☆ Expensive

✕ **La Cueva del Camarón** (map B3, **25**): calle 37, opposite the Hotel Jagua. Open daily 11am–11pm.

This luxurious colonial house offers many different shrimp and seafood dishes for around $10 ($20 for the lobster). The à la carte menu usually includes chicken fricassée, filet mignon, paella and spaghetti. Carefully prepared, excellent food. There's a bar outside and a disco next to the sea – a delightful setting.

✕ **Palacio del Valle** (map B3, **26**): in the gardens of the Hotel Jagua.

Open daily 10am–10.30pm. A restaurant steeped in history (*see* 'What to See'), where you can try Cuban specialities, such as crayfish and shrimps, to piano accompaniment. A meal costs around $15, and lobster is $20. Alternatively, simply have a drink and enjoy the Cuban music on the rooftop bar, reached via a spectacular spiral staircase. There is a lovely view out over the bay and the Punta Gorda area.

WHERE TO HAVE AN ICE-CREAM

🍦 **Coppelia** (map b1, **20**): corner of avenida 52 and Prado. Open Monday to Saturday 11am-11pm. Sunday 9am-11pm. This ice-cream parlour is an institution in Cuba. The big dining room is always busy, with young Cubans noisily chattering and clattering their spoons against the metal plates. There's not a great choice of flavours but the enormous scoops of ice-cream cost 80 pesos and the milkshakes 50.

NIGHTLIFE

🎵 **La Casa de la UNEAC** (National Union of Cuban Writers and Artists; map A1, **30**): west of José Martí park. Open on Sunday and whenever there are concerts during the week – check the programme displayed outside. A pleasant outdoor area where people come to listen to good quality Cuban music.

🎵 **La Cueva del Camarón** (map B3, **25**): calle 37, in the restaurant gardens. Open 11pm–2am. Admission free. A small, open-air disco by the sea, with dancing, bar and barbecue.

🎵 **La Casa Caribeña** (map B2, **31**): at the end of the Malecón, by the sea. Admission free during the day, $1 at night. There are always lots of young Cubans hanging out around this big red building, which has a pleasant outdoor area and a warm, cosmopolitan atmosphere.

WHAT TO SEE

★ **Parque José Martí** (map A–B1): the main square in the city centre. Towards the cathedral, there is a rose window, 2 metres (6.5 feet) in diameter, set in a triumphal arch, depicting Cienfuegos bay. It marks the exact spot where Louis de Clouet set out the boundaries for the French settlement in 1819. You'll also find the following attractions in the square:

– **Catedral de la Purísima Concepción** and its 12 windows depicting the Apostles.

– Further round the square is the neo-classical **San Lorenzo school**, built in 1927 by the Cuban architect Jorge Lafuente. Until 1959, it was a college of arts and crafts.

– **Teatro Tomàs-Terry** (*see below*).

– A remarkable **yellow house** (private), typical of urban Creole style and unique in the historic quarter, built in 1869.

– **Palacio Ferrer** (*see below*).

– Pass in front of the **Palatino** (1842), then visit the **Museo Histórico** (*see below*).

– Before you leave, have a look at **Cienfuegos City Hall**, a grey-and-blue building in Republican style, begun in 1924 and completed in 1954. Finally, the **beige house** on the corner of calle 25 and Parque José Martí is the oldest in the city, and once belonged to Don Louis de Clouet.

When you've finished touring the park, you might like to enjoy a drink on the terrace of the Palatino bar – there's sometimes a salsa band playing here.

★ **Palacio Ferrer** (map A1, **40**): Parque José Martí. Admission $0.50. Built in 1910 for José Ferrer Sires, this eclectic little mansion has been known as the Casa de la Cultura (Cultural Centre) since 1978. It still retains some vestiges of its previous sophistication and contains a beautiful marble staircase, stucco features, and a pigeon loft with a superb panoramic view extending as far as 80 kilometres (50 miles). Unfortunately, it seems to be falling to rack and ruin. Children still play here and there's an occasional musical performance, though most shows now take place elsewhere.

★ **Teatro Tomàs-Terry** (map A–B1, **41**): Parque José Martí. Open daily 9am–6pm. Admission $1. Go to the box office for ballet or concert tickets – they are nearly all $3, although if an artist has a national reputation prices rise to $5. This 950-seat theatre – begun in 1887, completed in 1889 and inaugurated in 1900 – was named after the sugar baron whose statue stands in the foyer. The theatre, which is used for a wide range of events, is a copy of the Matanzas and Santa Clara theatres, themselves copies of a theatre in Milan, Italy. This is one of the three major venues in Cuba and the sloping stage means you can see the feet of the dancers even from the front rows. Look up and admire the ceiling fresco depicting the seven muses, as well as an angel holding a clock showing four o'clock, the time when the painter finished his work.

The great Italian tenor Enrico Caruso (1873–1921) appeared here (as he did in nearly all the theatres in Latin America) and Sarah Bernhardt (1844–1923) gave a performance of *La Dame aux Camélias* here.

★ **Museo Provincial** (map A–B1, **42**): Parque José Martí. Open Tuesday–Saturday 9am–4.30pm. Admission $1. This local museum is great for antiques enthusiasts and includes paintings, porcelain, weaponry and furniture from former French bourgeois families of the 19th century and from some patriots. Free cultural events are staged here some evenings.

★ **Punta Gorda**: southern tip of the city. From the centre, go down the Prado, the main thoroughfare that's known as Malecón at the point where it borders the sea. There are many mansions along the peninsula, former casinos of the American Mafia, who settled here from 1946 until the Revolution.

★ **Palacio del Valle** (map B3): next to the Hotel Jagua. Guided tours (10am–5pm) cost $1 and include a small glass of rum on the terrace. This mansion was built by Asisdo del Valle, a Spaniard from Catalonia. Judging by the mix of styles – Roman, Moorish and Gothic – he had very eclectic taste.

Each of its three towers has particular significance. The one in the centre represents religion, the one on the right (as you face the building) stands for military prowess and the one on the left represents love. The mansion has been converted into a restaurant (see 'Where to Eat'), where the terrace gives fine views of the tip of Punta Gorda.

– Continue your walk past old wooden houses in pretty colours, the last vestiges of the former emigrants from New Orleans. On arriving at the tip, you will find yourself in a little park (admission charge), shaded by a tropical tree, where laughing children bathe on an improvised beach. There is a breathtaking view out over the bay but, in the distance, tall industrial chimneys, an oil terminal and the famous nuclear power plant all create a blot on the horizon.

IN THE AREA

★ **Botanic Garden**: 18 kilometres (11 miles) outside the city towards Trinidad. Open 8am–5pm. Admission $2.5 (children $1). Created in 1901 by rich American sugar baron Edwin F. Atkins, this lovely garden prides itself on being the oldest on the island and, according to some, is one of the most beautiful in the world. It has been run by the Cuban state since 1961, which has ensured that it is managed by professional, scientifically trained staff. It boasts over 2,000 plants and other sub-tropical species across 94 hectares (330 acres), including 23 (impressive) types of bamboo, 400 species of cacti, 69 varieties of orchid, 90 types of *ficus* and 307 palms, including the very rare cork palm (*Microcycas colocona*).

It is a nice place for a walk, but the map for sale in the shop and the few identification labels will leave you wanting to know more. For a more in-depth visit, arrange a tour with one of the three guides (allow about 90 minutes). Watch out for the mosquitoes, which are particularly voracious.

★ **Castillo de Nuestra Señora de los Ángeles de Jagua**: this castle, the oldest monument in Cienfuegos, was built by the Spanish in 1745 to guard the narrow entrance of the bay from pirates. To get there, take the ferry from the foot of the Hotel Pasacaballo – there are departures every hour. Further information is available from the hotel reception. The journey costs $1 and the visit lasts around one hour. As the crow flies, it's really close, but if you're driving it's a good 100 kilometres (60 miles) because of the obligatory detour to avoid the strategically sensitive nuclear power plant near by. You could also try hiring a launch from the Hotel Jagua for the trip, but you need a minimum of six people.

A few years ago, the place was converted into a seafood restaurant. Unfortunately, the site and the village of **Perche** are somewhat dominated by high-rise state-owned housing.

LEAVING CIENFUEGOS

By Train

– For **Havana**: departs Cienfuegos at 10.30am on alternate days, taking around 10 hours.

– For **Santa Clara**: every afternoon. The journey takes 2 hours 30 minutes.

– For **Santiago**: departs daily; no direct train, change either at Santa Clara or at Guayos (20 kilometres/12 miles) from Sancti Spiritus.

By Bus

– For **Havana**: five buses per day. Journey time about 5 hours.

– For **Trinidad**: two buses each morning. Journey time about 2 hours.

– For **Santa Clara**: departures daily at 7am and 9am. Journey time about 1 hour 30 minutes.

– For **Camagüey**: departs at 8am and 2pm (not every day). Journey time about 6 hours.

– For **Santiago**: departs at 5pm (alternate days). Journey time about 10 hours.

TRINIDAD   DIALLING CODE: 419

There is only one way to appreciate Trinidad properly and that's on foot, getting lost in its alleyways, twisting your ankles on its uneven pavements and trying to find your way by using the **Plaza Mayor** as a guide. It's also essential that you take time, something that seems to stand still here. This peaceful city of 60,000 inhabitants (but where are they all?) was cut off from the world for a long time.

Admire the colonial houses and dare to take an indiscreet glance inside the 200- to 300-year-old dwellings. You will be impressed by the ornaments, the numerous portraits of Che Guevara, various keepsakes of sentimental value, family photos, bric-a-brac, glassware and empty bottles of Havana Club, consumed a long time ago. Then you will notice traces of Cuba's glory years – a Baccarat crystal chandelier here, marble furnishings and splendid furniture there. The greatest extravagances are found in the imposing structure of the buildings themselves. Like the mansions in the Plaza Mayor and in the old city centre, they bear witness to a past rivalry between rich, aristocratic families, keen to assert their power. Nowadays, the doorsteps are witness to a more carefree approach to life, that moves in time with the gentle rhythm of rocking chairs.

Mira! ('Look!') . . . In Trinidad it's difficult not to start each sentence with this word. Certainly, your first impression is likely to be a negative one – tricksters, beggars and street urchins congregate on every corner awaiting tourists – but you'll soon realize that this is the most beautiful city in the country. Spend a few days here and soak up the atmosphere. Take a stroll around the city, early in the morning or in the late afternoon.

History

Villa Santísima Trinidad, the third Spanish settlement in Cuba, was founded on 23 December 1514 on the spot known as Manzanilla. Spanish *conquistador* Diego Velázquez had discovered gold here, along with an already well-organized indigenous population. In the 17th and 18th centuries the town came under repeated attack from pirates, but continued to flourish on the profits from smuggling – an occupation that was rife despite the numerous counter-measures taken by the Spanish government. At the end of the 18th century, the use of slaves led to soaring profits from sugar production. The town became rich and superb palaces sprang up, built by the Brunets, Canteros, Iznagas and Borrels – families who had made their money in the rich valley plantations where they lived during harvest time.

■ **Useful Addresses**

🚌 Bus station
✈ Alberto Delgado airport (map I)
🚂 Railway station (map I)
✉ Post office and telephone (map II)
4 Cubatur (map I)
5 CUPET service station (map I)
6 Secure parking (map II)
7 Cubanacan tourist office (map II)

🛏 **Where to Stay**

10 Isis Camargo Echeverria (map II)
11 Casa Colonial Muñoz (map II)
12 Hostal La Rioja, Teresa Leria Echerri's house (map II)
13 La Yolanda (map II)
14 Sara Sanjuán Alvarez (map II)
15 Mariene Ruiz Tápanes (map II)
16 Marisela and Gustavo Canedo (map II)
17 Luis Grau Monedero (map II)
18 Pedro Aliz Peña (map II)
19 Manuel Meyer (map II)
20 Pipo Santander (map II)
21 Rosa Diez Giroud (map II)
22 Manuel Lagunilla Martinez (map II)
23 Carlos Sotolongo Peña (map II)
24 Rogelio Inchauspi Bastida (map II)
25 Hotel Las Cuevas (map I)

✕ **Where to Eat**

30 Don Antonio (map II)
31 El Jigue (map II)
32 Via Real (map II)
33 El Mesón del Recogidor (map II)
34 Plaza Major (map II)
36 Sol y Son (map II)
37 Comida Estela (map II)
38 El Colonial (map II)

🍸 **Where to Have a Drink, Nightlife**

40 La Canchanchara (map II)
41 La Casa de la Música (map II)
42 La Casa de la Trova
43 La Casa Artex or La Casa Fisher (map II)
44 Las Ruinas de Segarte (map II)
45 Las Cuevas disco (map II)

★ **What to See**

61 Museum of Romantic Art (map II)
62 Guamuhaya Archaeological Museum (map II)
63 Museum of Architecture (map II)
64 Art gallery (map II)
65 Iglesia de la Santísima Trinidad (map II)
66 Palacio Cantero (map II)
67 Museo Nacional de la Lucha Contra Bandidos (map II)
68 Cigar factory (map II)

Costa Sur and Ancón hotels, 5 ■ ⚓ ⬆

THE CENTRE

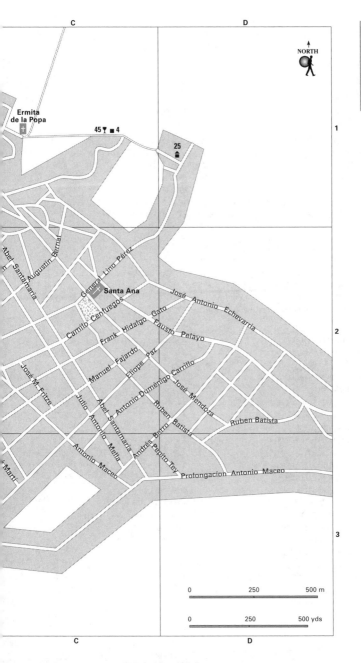

C   D

NORTH

Ermita de la Popa

45   4

25

Abel Santamaría

Augustín Berna

General Lino Pérez

Santa Ana

Camilo Cienfuegos

José Antonio Echevarría

Gato

Frank Hidalgo

Fausto Pelayo

Manuel Fajardo

José M. Fritza

Eliopa Paz

Antonio Dumenrigo Carrillo

José Mendoza

Julio Antonio Mella

Abel Santamaría

Ruben Batista

Ruben Batista

Andrés Berro

Pepito Tey

Antonio Maceo

Prolongación Antonio Maceo

Martí

| 0 | 250 | 500 m |

| 0 | 250 | 500 yds |

C   D

TRINIDAD (MAP I)

This was Trinidad's golden era and, by 1846, it was the island's fourth most successful commercial town. However, it was already showing signs of decline. The depletion of the valley's resources and the mounting demands of the slaves caused people to invest elsewhere on the island or abroad. The social and political crises, the confrontations between land-owners supported by Spain and the *Independentistas* ravaged an economy that was already very weak. The two wars of independence left the town's industry in the hands of foreign enterprises and a population in ruin, suffering from high unemployment.

It was not until 1919 (and the arrival of the railway) and 1950–52 (when the roads to Sancti Spiritus and Cienfuegos were built) that the town began to find its feet again. In 1957 and 1958 some of the town's inhabitants protested against Batista. The revolutionaries and, later, counter-revolutionaries of the nearby Escambray mountains revived the city somewhat. In 1988 UNESCO declared it a World Heritage Site, and today it is a place where visitors can enjoy colonial atmosphere by the bucket-load.

GETTING AROUND

As in most parts of the island, Trinidad's streets were renamed after the Revolution. However, either through laziness or loyalty to the town's golden years, the inhabitants continue to use the old colonial names. So you may have to think twice when asking for directions:

New names	Colonial names
Antonio Maceo	Gutiérrez
Camilo Cienfuegos	Santo Domingo
Ernesto Valdés Muñoz	Media Luna
Fidel Claro	Angarilla
Fernando Hernández Echerri	Cristo
Francisco Gómez Toro	Peña
Francisco Javier Zerquera	Rosario
Francisco Petersen	Coco
Franck País	Carmen
Gustavo Izquierdo	Gloria
Independencia	Nueva
Jesús Menéndez	Alameda
José Martí	Jesús María
José Menoza	Santa Ana
Juan M. Márquez	Amargura
Lino Pérez	San Procopio
Miguel Calzada	Borrell
Piro Guinart	Boca
Rubén Martínez Villena	Real del Jigüe
Santiago Escobar	Olvido
Simón Bolívar	Desengaño

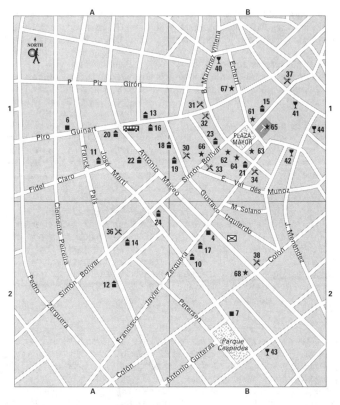

TRINIDAD (MAP II)

USEFUL ADDRESSES

Bus station: corner of Gustavo Izquierdo and calle Piro Guinart, at the top of the street before Plaza Mayor. ☎ 44-48.

Alberto Delgado Airport: carretera de Casilda, on the Playa Ancón road. ☎ 25-47. Domestic flights for Havana, Varadero and Santiago.

Post office and telephone (map B2): opposite the Parque Central Cespedes, Lino Pérez, between José Martí and Francisco Petersen. Otherwise you can make calls from the Las Cuevas Hotel.

International clinic: Lino Pérez, on the corner with Anastacio Cardenas. ☎ 33-91

Car hire: Transautos, Maceo, on the corner with Francisco Javier Zerquera. ☎ 53-14. In the Las Cuevas, Ancón or Costa Sur hotels. Also Transgaviota, Franck País, between Simón Bolívar and Fidel Claro. ☎ 22-82. Also at the airport.

Scooter hire: at the Cubatur office; map I, C1, **4**). ☎ 63-14. Also at the hotel Las Cuevas. Expect to pay around $15 for a half day, including fuel. Avoid steeply sloping roads if you've got someone on the back.

■ **CUPET service station** (map I, off B3, **5**): at the 1-kilometre marker on carretera Casilda, towards the Ancón and Costa Sur hotels, opposite the airport.

■ **Secure parking** (map II, A1, **6**): calle Piro Guinart 243, opposite the bus station. Park your car and it will be watched continuously in exchange for a small, green ticket. Otherwise, you may find your fuel tank being siphoned. If you are staying in a private house, the owner may offer a similar service for the same price.

■ **Banks**: calle Martí 264, between Colón and Francisco J. Zeque. Open Monday to Friday 8am–3pm. It is possible to withdraw dollars here using a credit card (Visa and MasterCard). There is also the CADECA, on Mosé Martí, between Lino Perez and Camillo Cienfuegos. Open Monday to Saturday 8am–noon.

■ **Cubanacan tourist office** (map II, B2, **7**): Hotel Ronda. ☎ 61-42. Carlos the 'King of Spain' will give you a rapturous welcome. There are plenty of interesting things to see in and around Trinidad – special tours on Saturday (including the 'Rambo Tour' in red-painted army jeeps!), horse-riding, diving, visits to the Topes de Collantes waterfalls (Monday and Wednesday, $27), excursions to Cayo Blanco ($25).

■ **La Casa Artex** or **Fischer** (map II, B2, **43**): Principally a bar (*see* 'Where to Have a Drink') but it also offers guided tours of the town ($3), excursions and visits to Trinidad's crafts workshops ($17).

WHERE TO STAY

You will be overwhelmed with propositions for accommodation on the streets of Trinidad, but quality varies considerably – from the grand to the filthy, with all manner of rip-offs in between. You will probably be better off going for one of the addresses below, all of which have some charm. Few are signposted, and you may need to knock on the door to find out whether you are at the right address. Official rooms are usually indicated by a sign on the door (two blue chevrons with the words '*Arrendador Inscripto*'). They are much cheaper than hotels and more convivial, but they will cost you more if you go through a tout.

Casas Particulares

♣ **Isis Camargo Echeverria** (map II, B2, **10**): calle Francisco Javier Zerquera 2. ☎ 31-40. Isis is a dentist, but the lack of antiseptics at the hospital has left him time to spend on his house, which has several spotless rooms for $15–20, with private bathroom. One huge room overlooks a large courtyard garden. An apartment is being built at the end of the garden. Delightful welcome.

♣ **Casa Colonial Muñoz** (map II, A1, **11**): calle José Martí 401, between Fidel Claro and Santiago Escobar. ☎ and fax: 36-73. An attractive house dating from 1800, with a charming patio and antique furniture. Julio is a photographer and is proud to have had some of his work published in the *National Geographic*. There are two rooms with private bathroom for $20 each. There is a lovely roof terrace where guests can sunbathe. The erudite, welcoming owners make very pleasant company. Parking.

♣ **Hostal La Rioja, Teresa Leria Echerri's house** (map II, A2, **12**):

calle Franck País 389, between Simón Bolívar and Francisco Javier Zerquera. ☎ 25-84. Though not as grand as the colonial houses, this is in a good location on the edge of the old town. Three rooms (each with private bathroom) for $15–20. Friends and neighbours are continually at the door to chat with the delightful owner Teresa, who knows the town intimately. The house is always very lively – the whole family lends a hand with the cleaning and cooking, and Teresa often throws impromptu soirées. Big breakfasts. A fine example of Cuban hospitality. You can also arrange for someone to keep an eye on your car.

♠ La Yolanda (map II, B1, **11**): calle Piro Guinart 227, near the bus station. ☎ 30-51. There are two rooms with private bathrooms for $15 and another for $12. The interior of this big, attractive house is typically Cuban, but with a few surprises, such as the striking spiral staircase leading up from the kitchen. Yolanda herself is charming.

♠ Sara Sanjuán Alvarez (map II, A2, **14**): Simón Bolívar 266, between Franck País and José Martí. ☎ 39-97. The green, blue and pastel pink walls of this sumptuous house are typical of Trinidad's facades. The interior is distinctly Cuban, with Louis XVI armchairs, flounced cushions and family photos – reminiscent of 1950s cinema posters. There are three spacious rooms with bathrooms for $20 per night. Sara provides her guests with meals and very large breakfasts. Garage.

♠ Mariene Ruíz Tápanes (map II, B1, **15**): Simón Bolívar 515, between Juan Manual Márquez and Fernando Hernández Echerrí. ☎ 37-73. You cross a huge dining room to get to the heart of this superb house – a delightful courtyard. The three pleasant, spacious rooms (two with private bathroom)

for $15 are ideal for families. Mariene has put some tables on the roof, from where there is an unbeatable view of Trinidad's famous tower. The owners are very welcoming. Garage.

♠ Marisela and Gustavo Canedo (map II, A1, **16**): calle Piro Guinart 216, next to the bus station. ☎ 21-66. Look for the sign. Don't be put off by the ordinary exterior of this place, which hides a superb colonial house. There are two cool, spacious rooms for $15 and a third with air-conditioning for $20. There is a glorious courtyard garden with a mango tree where you can linger over breakfast. Gustavo is a telecommunications engineer and speaks a little English. His wife is a nurse. It may be possible for you to use the garage, but their son will need to move his flamboyant red vehicle.

♠ Luis Grau Monedero (map II, B2, **17**): calle Francisco Javier Zerquera 270, between Maceo and Martí. ☎ 32-53. They like colour here: the walls are bright yellow with green plants and pop art kitsch paintings by the son of the family. Two rooms with crocheted bedcovers and air conditioning. A double room costs $15. Pleasant courtyard and terrace with a grapevine and vast banana tree. Luis and his son speak English. Nilda, the mother, is a hairdresser, in case you need a trim.

♠ Pedro Aliz Peña (map II, A–B1, **18**): calle Gustavo Izquierdo 127, between Piro Guinart and Simón Bolívar. ☎ 30-25. The Peña family is the epitome of hospitality. Pedro and his wife Teresa are unbelievably kind and will help you get the best out of the city. Their house may lack the charm of the large colonial residences, but their welcome more than makes up for it. Two extremely clean rooms for $15, just a stone's throw from Plaza Mayor.

THE CENTRE

â **Manuel Meyer** (map II, B1, **19**): calle Gustavo Izquierdo 111, between Simón Bolívar and Piro Guinart, near the bus station. ☎ 34-44. Time has stood still in this magnificent colonial house. Art-nouveau lamps stand either side of an antique Edison gramophone, glassware is carefully arranged in a display cabinet and a doll (still in its original packaging) lounges on the sofa. However, air conditioning has been installed. You have the choice of two rooms, although the family is only authorized to rent out one of them ($15 per night). Very quiet, with a superb courtyard.

â **Pipo Santander** (map II, B1, **20**): calle Maceo 553. ☎ 33-20. Three clean rooms and two bathrooms in a colonial house for $15–20 (with air-conditioning). Beautiful terrace with views over the red-tiled rooftops and a simple, yet pleasant courtyard. Pleasant welcome.

â **Rosa Diez Giroud** (map II, B1, **21**): calle Francisco Javier Zerquera 403, between Ernesto Valdés Muñoz and Rubén, near Plaza Mayor. ☎ 38-18. Two rooms, each with bathroom, for $10–15. The Girouds are one of the oldest French families in Trinidad. This is an artist's house – Rosa restores murals in the city's museums, and has painted coloured frescoes on the walls. Her work also adorns the two rooms for rent. No courtyard.

â **Dr Manuel Lagunilla Martinez** (map II, A1, **22**): calle Maceo 455 (the house to rent is at calle José Martí 327). ☎ 39-09. Manuel has retrained as a lawyer, and offers a very beautiful colonial house with four spotless rooms ($20 per night), two bathrooms, small courtyard and rooftop terrace. It's nice to be independent amid such luxury.

â **Carlos Sotolongo Peña** (map II, B1, **23**): Plaza Mayor, next to the art gallery. ☎ 41-69. Unbelievably, it is no more expensive to stay right on the Plaza Mayor ($20 per night). Carlos is the curator of the Museum of Romantic Art but is also a scholar/art enthusiast/radio ham/ comic painter. He also speaks English. As you go through the blue door of this 18th-century mansion, you are greeted by two impressive angels and a beautiful collection of antiques. The pink-walled room overlooks a sumptuous courtyard crammed with superb green plants. In the bathroom, the stylish washbasin is from Florence.

â **Rogelio Inchauspi Bastida** (map II, A2, **24**): calle Simón Bolívar 312. ☎ 41-07. This was the first house in Trinidad to open its doors to tourists, even before the arrival of the dollar. There are two big, adjoining rooms for $20, and another for $15 that has been known to sleep up to six. Delightful courtyard.

Hotel

â **Hotel Las Cuevas** (map I, D1, **25**): Finca Santa Ana. ☎ 40-13. The city's largest hotel is situated on the hillside, 20-minutes' walk from the centre. Over 100 rooms in bungalows scattered across the hill, with breathtaking views over Trinidad and the Ancón peninsula. Double rooms have all mod cons and cost $50. Bar, restaurant with a dining room named after the Taïnos Indian Guama, post office, tennis, organized tours and swimming pool with piped music (as always in Cuba). To the left of the swimming pool, the **Maravillosa** cave is far more spectacular than the disco. Admission $7.

IN THE AREA

â **Finca Dolorés**: carretera Circuito Sur. 3 kilometres (2 miles) from Trinidad towards Cienfuegos. ☎ 35-81. Right in the countryside, next to a stream surrounded by a mango orchards and birds, the Finca Dolorés is run by local farmers. It's an extremely pleasant spot. There are around 20 chalets costing only $27 for two people per night, with bathroom. There's the possibility of horse-riding ($4 per hour) and boat trips, as well as a restaurant with a thatched roof, and entertainment in the evening (cock-fighting), plus a bar and swimming pool. It was here, on the banks of the river, that Diego Velázquez first landed on the island. Stylish welcome and the staff speak English. Mosquitoes are a problem in the evening.

â **Hotel Costa Sur**: playa Ancón. 12 kilometres (7.5 miles) from Trinidad. ☎ 61-74. Fax: 61-73. Affordable rates (around $54 including breakfast), but more expensive in high season, when it is best to

book in advance. There are rooms or bungalows; the latter cost a little more. This faces the sea and blends nicely into the countryside, unlike its neighbour, the Hotel Ancón. There is a buffet-style restaurant, an Italian restaurant, four bars and a disco. There's also a nice sandy beach; unfortunately, rocks just break the surface of the water. Diving lessons, mountain bike hire, tennis, horse-riding and billiards. Also car hire.

â **Hotel Ancón** (map I, off B3): Playa Ancón. ☎ 61-74. Fax: 61-73. 14 kilometres (8.5 miles) south of Trinidad. Double rooms in this high-rise block cost $75 in high season, but at least almost all have a sea view – ask for a room in the annexe. There are also well equipped and very comfortable bungalows. Restaurant, bars, swimming pool and disco. Activities include mountain biking, diving (but the equipment is a bit limited) and excursions to Cayo Blanco.

WHERE TO EAT

Trinidad is very touristy and becomes packed with tour coaches during the day – but by early evening it's much quieter. Suddenly, the magnificent restaurants that were so busy at lunchtime are either closed or sad and deserted. So it's probably better to eat out during the day, especially as some places, such as the Plaza Mayor, offer good-value buffets. In the evening try to eat in a private house – you will rarely be disappointed.

Along calle Piro Guinart there are some small stalls selling sandwiches and slices of pizza for a few pesos – ideal for a snack before catching the bus.

☆ Budget

✕ **Don Antonio** (map II, B1, **30**): calle Izquierdo between Piro Guinart and Simón Bolívar. A superb colonial house with an attractive high-ceilinged dining room. The tables are decked with the inevitable plas-

tic roses, but the tablecloths are spotless. Creole specialities and a good Creole set menu for $7.75; also set meals with chicken for $6.75 and with lobster for $20. Unobtrusive, efficient service.

✕ **El Jigue** (map II, B1, **31**): calle Rubén Martinez Villena 69. Open

THE CENTRE

daily 9am–10pm. On a small square next to Plaza Mayor in front of the El Jigue tree planted to commemorate the first Mass celebrated in Trinidad in 1513. Note the cross engraved on the wall and the text bearing testament to this historic event. The setting is delightful, with attractive blue mosaics everywhere, and the menu is very reasonable. Its speciality is *pollo al Jigue* (grilled chicken on a bed of spaghetti and cheese) for $5.95. There are several dishes for $5–6 on the à la carte menu and a meal costs around $8.

✕ **Via Real** (map II, B1, **32**): calle Rubén Martínez Villena 74, opposite El Jigue. Open daily 10am–5pm. Also occasionally in the evening for organized groups. A big dining room and a few tables outside. A meal costs around $10; there's pasta and a Cuban version of pizza (heavier than the Italian original) on the menu, otherwise there's always chicken.

✕ **El Mesón del Recogidor** (map II, B1, **33**): calle Simón Bolívar, near Plaza Mayor. Open daily 11am–10pm. There is a pleasant outdoor bar and a delightful restaurant. Set menus cost $8–20 (the higher end of the scale includes lobster). The speciality is grilled pork.

✕ **Plaza Major** (map II, B1, **34**): corner of Francisco J. Zerquera and Ruben Martínez Villena. A big restaurant close to the square, with two dining rooms and a few tables outside. It's a favourite with organized groups during the day, but deserted in the evening. It's notable for its good-value ($9) lunchtime buffet, with big portions and a wide choice – vegetables, fish and even dessert. Such variety is unusual in Cuba. In the evening only the à la carte menu is on offer, so it's more expensive.

Paladares

In Trinidad, the touts selling 'private tourism' are particularly tenacious. The advantage of this is that by casually following them, you will often find yourself in a favourable negotiating position, and sometimes you will be lucky, and come across some really special places. The list below is not exhaustive and only covers official *paladares* (private restaurants), all of which have some character.

There are many unofficial *paladares*. Consider having a meal in a private home, and staying there too, setting the price (around $7) beforehand. Think about including drinks. The portions are usually plentiful and the food is pretty good.

✕ **Sol y Son** (map II, A2, **36**): calle Simón Bolívar 283, between Franck País and José Martí. This establishment offers an excellent combination of quality, quantity, presentation and friendliness. After waiting in the superb hall of a colonial house, you are invited into the romantic courtyard. Take your time when choosing your meal, as the selection on offer here actually resembles a proper menu. Pasta dishes for $6 make a nice change from rice, otherwise there are fish and chicken dishes for around $8. Finally, enjoy a delicious piña colada or a *mojito* at the bar before wandering back towards Plaza Mayor.

✕ **Comida Estela** (map II, B1, **37**): calle Simón Bolívar 557, just down from Plaza Mayor. Open 6–11pm. Go through a heavy blue door into the impressive dining room. Don't be put off by the *Pietá* in the entrance hall, head through to the peaceful courtyard. A full meal, including a drink and coffee, costs $8. A very good welcome, and good-quality cuisine.

✗ **El Colonial** (map II, B2, **38**): Maceo 402 and Colón. Open daily until 10pm. This bar-restaurant is an institution. Its decor is worthy of this beautiful city – spotlessly painted walls, impressive chandeliers, antique furniture and old pictures. It specializes in fish (generally Creole-style or grilled) for $6–7. Slightly lukewarm welcome.

WHERE TO HAVE A DRINK, NIGHTLIFE

❣ **La Canchanchara** (map II, B1, **40**): calle Rubén Martinez Villena 76. Open from early morning until the last customer leaves (but generally closed in the evening). It is becoming more and more touristy, but it's difficult to resist the lure of the pergola at siesta time. Relax in the wooden armchairs, lulled by the background music and slowly sip a *Canchanchara*. This is the house cocktail, served in small earthenware bowls, and comprising honey, lime, rum, water, ice and a secret plant that gives it its unique taste. It is very sugary, and some may still prefer a *mojito*.

❣ **La Casa de la Música** (map II, B1, **41**): two entrances – one is to the right of the church at the top of the steps, where there's a terrace bar and salsa at all hours of the day. The other leads to the stage area, where there are all sorts of performances, including dancing, fashion shows and, above all, some excellent evening concerts. A great place for dance classes, with Cubans and tourists rubbing shoulders on the dance floors. Note, however, that some of the locals may not be there just for the dancing . . .

❣ **La Casa de la Trova** (map II, B1, **42**): Plaza de Segante. Open from 9pm; music from 9.30 or 10pm. In a blue house perched on the hill, to the right of the Santísima Trinidad church (Plaza Mayor). With superb salsa concerts and excellent *mojitos*, the bar is very popular in the evening.

❣ **La Casa Artex** or **Casa Fisher** (map II, B2, **43**): calle Lino Perez 312, between José Martí and Cadahía. Open 10am–1am. Admission $3 (including a drink). This is a colonial house with a pleasant outdoor area where you can sit with a drink. It becomes a nightclub in the evening, and the programme varies each night – traditional music, salsa, bolero, Afro-Cuban, etc. – so you'd need to stay a week to hear all the Cuban sounds. Popular with the young people of the town.

❣ **Ruina de Segarte** (map II, B1, **44**): a stone's throw from La Casa de la Trova (*see above*). Open 24 hours a day. A lovely courtyard where you can enjoy a drink in the shade or strut your stuff in the evening: bands play from 9pm onwards. Snacks are available all day.

❣ **Las Cuevas disco** (map I, C1, **45**): Hotel Las Cuevas, Finca Santa Ana. A 20-minute walk from the town centre. At the entrance, take the road to the left, then turn left into the car-park. Open daily 10pm–3am. Admission $7, but includes as many drinks as you like. Not many discos give you the chance to dance amid stalactites and stalagmites, but this one is located in a natural cave. There are potential hazards: you may get lost in the maze of corridors, so make sure you stick with company. And be careful, because the walls and ceilings are wet, which means that the dance floor is often slippery. There's Cuban and international music, and the atmosphere and temperature are hot. Note that cameras and videos are banned, apparently because a tourist secretly filmed a porn film here.

WHAT TO SEE

★ **Museum of Romantic Art** (map II, B1, **61**): Plaza Mayor, on the corner of calle Bolívar and Echerri. Closed for restoration at time of publication, for an unspecified period. Before the works began it was open Tuesday to Sunday 9am–5pm. The construction of this mansion, where several very wealthy families have made their mark, is a touch dramatic. It was begun in 1740 by the Albarez Traviezo family, who handed it over in 1807 to the Marianno Borrell family, who added the first floor. The mansion emerged in its final form in 1808.

The paths of the Borell and Brunet families later crossed, led by Cupid's arrow. In 1830, Marianno's daughter married Count Nicolas de la Cruz y Brunet (born in Trinidad to a Spanish father), a member of one of the richest families in the city. They spent some happy times in the house until 1857. Since 1974, the mansion has been the home of a superb, atmospheric museum. Unfortunately, photography is not allowed.

The rooms are expensively, but tastefully, decorated in 18th- and 19th-century style. There is a cedar ceiling in the main salon, paintings of Paris, an English porcelain spittoon, an 18th-century Viennese enamelled writing desk, silk paintings from Córdoba and much more. The whole is a mixture of styles in which Austria, Bohemia, Spain, France and America play at *entente cordiale . . .*

★ **Guamuhaya Archaeological Museum** (map II, B2, **62**): Plaza Mayor, calle Simón Bolívar 457. Open Monday–Friday 9am–5pm, Saturday 9am–noon. The German explorer and naturalist Alexander Humboldt (1769–1859) spent a large part of his life exploring Latin America. He stopped off for two days in Trinidad on 14 March 1801, before heading for South America. He is remembered in this fine museum, which displays a whole range of curiosities.

Several rooms house an eclectic jumble of exhibits: stuffed iguanas, tortoises and crabs sit alongside Stone-Age relics in joyful, chronological disarray, while Taïno and other pre-Columbian remains enjoy the company of 19th-century pistols. Lots of the exhibits attest to the influence of the Spanish occupation and the years of slavery. Don't miss the fossilized *manjuari*, a fish species still to be found in the **Laguna del Tesoro** (*see* 'Zapata Peninsula').

★ **Museum of Architecture** (map II, B2, **63**): Plaza Mayor. Open Saturday to Thursday 9am–5pm. This colonial house is very well known among Cubans, not for its wonderful architecture, but simply because it was the set for one of the most famous local TV soap operas. It houses an attractive museum that may give you a different slant on the colonial house where you are staying. Explanations and photos illustrate how ancient techniques were used during the colonial era, such as the construction of wooden frameworks, but with the use of better-quality materials, and with the addition of frescoes, canopies and other embellishments. To make their residences stand out, the rich proprietors affixed the road name and the number of the house to the outside of their property.

★ **Art Gallery** (map II, B2, **64**): Plaza Mayor. Open daily 8am–5pm. Entry free. The gallery is in a large, yellow-painted colonial house also known as Casa Ortíz. The Trinidad School of Painting is known throughout the country and further afield, and includes artists such as Benito Ortiz (who died in 1978). Work by some of his pupils is displayed around the gallery, together with sculptures, furniture, pottery, paintings and contemporary works – all of it for sale. The school of painting is on the first floor, which is worth visiting not just for the embroidery on sale or the Renoir, Van Gogh and Toulouse-Lautrec copies, but also for the view over the square.

★ **Iglesia de la Santísima Trinidad** (map II, B1, **65**): Plaza Mayor. Open for visits from 11am, reserved for worship prior to this time, but the interior is really of little interest. The building was begun at the end of the 19th century, but was never finished due to lack of money following a sugar crisis. Even so, there are some beautiful paintings and an impressive wooden altar. For some reason, at one time there was a car actually parked inside the church.

★ **Palacio Canterro** (Trinidad Municipal Museum; map II, B2, **66**): calle Simón Bolívar 42, 30 metres down from Plaza Mayor. ☎ 44-60. Open Monday to Friday 9am–5pm. Admission $2 (under 13s free). This splendid colonial house was built between 1827 and 1830 and converted into a museum in 1980. On display is the family tree of the Canterro family, one of whom was the first to introduce the steam engine to Cuba and develop the railways in the early 1800s. There is a small room with an exhibition about the treatment of slaves in Trinidad – always an edifying subject. Paved with Carrara marble and with a lovely brick patio, the museum also offers a superb view of the town from its watchtower. You need to be fit to get up the steps, but it's a good spot for photos of Plaza Mayor.

★ **Museo Nacional de la Lucha Contra Bandidos** (National Museum of the Struggle against the Bandits; map II, B1, **67**): Echerri and Boca, to the left of Plaza Mayor, as you face the Museum of Romantic Art. Open Tuesday to Sunday 9am–5pm. Admission $1. Inside the 18th-century former convent of St Francis of Assisi is Trinidad's museum of the Revolution, inevitable in all Cuban cities. But this is more interesting than many of the others, since for a long time the Escambray mountains on the outskirts of town were home to revolutionary and (later) counter-revolutionary rebels. These so-called 'bandits' controlled the area until 1965. The last one came down from the hills in October 1966; everyone had forgotten he was still up there.

Revolutionary fetishism is very much in evidence, with Che Guevara's hammock, copies of Castro's speeches ('Morale and Discipline', made at the first Party Conference in 1966, and 'Guantánamo the Cancer'), and a plan of the battle of the Bay of Pigs. There are lots of photos (including Castro aged 20 and Che, the most photogenic of the *barbudos*) and various objects relating to local heroes. The star exhibit is a piece of metal from an American U2 reconnaissance aircraft brought down on 27 October 1962. The short film on the victory at the Bay of Pigs is, not surprisingly, very pro-Castro. On the upper floor is a display cabinet containing 3-peso notes with Che Guevara's head on them.

★ **Cigar factory** (map II, B2, **68**): Maceo and Colón, opposite the Colonial restaurant. Open daily 7am–5pm. Admission is free but tips are welcome. If you haven't yet been to one of these factories, you might want to take a look inside this little one, which makes inexpensive cigars. It's a bit disappointing as you can't go into the workshops where 70 people spend the day rolling cigars intended for the Cuban market. As you come out, you are likely to be hustled, as this is where all the tourist coaches stop.

WHAT TO DO

– **Cerro de la Vigía**: this is a superb viewpoint looking out over the Valle de los Ingenios that gives a different perspective over the colonial town. Allow 20 minutes for the walk to the top of the hill. To get there, go up one of the little streets behind the church towards the Ermita de la Popa (a ruined hermitage), keeping it to your right where the road divides. Continue straight up, along a small stone track.

– **Beaches**: the beaches of the Ancón peninsula lie 15 kilometres (9 miles) from the city. Avoid Playa La Boca, where the city's sewers empty out. A better bet is Playa María Aguilar, next to the Hotel Costa Sur. María Aguilar is the name of the fishing village that was destroyed to build the hotel. The 'deported' inhabitants now live in a high-rise block on the outskirts of Trinidad – an example of zealous socialism in favour of tourists!

– **Cayo Blanco**: is an island 2 kilometres (1 mile) long and 400m wide, half of which is sandy beach. It may not be as impressive as the *cayos* to the north of the island, but it's a good alternative to Trinidad. A full-day excursion departs from the marina at the hotel Ancón at around 9am, returning between 3 and 4pm. The Cubanacan office at the La Ronda hotel organizes transport from Trinidad for $2 per person. A 45-minute boat ride (expect lots of spray) goes as far as the coral reef, which is great for snorkelling. It's much nicer when the sea is calm, as it can become very tiring when the wind gets up (life-jackets and buoys are available). Groups are limited to 15 and there's a good atmosphere, and a bar. After the snorkelling, lunch consists of a kind of paella containing lobster, rice, fruit and raw vegetables. Any leftovers can be fed to the domesticated iguana that lives behind the straw-roofed hut where lunch is prepared.

Sierra del Escambray waterfalls: *see below* 'In the Area'.

El Cubano: carretera Circuito Sur, 2.5 kilometres (2 miles) from Trinidad towards Cienfuegos, just before Finca Dolores. Here you can combine a walk through a conservation area with a spot of trout-fishing, horse-riding or boating. The fish restaurant naturally serves fish fresh out of the water.

– **Carnival**: between 24 and 29 June each year, all the locals take part in this traditional event, which features a colourful procession of masks and allegorical floats, dancing and horse-racing through the streets.

SHOPPING

🔒 **Craft market**: calle Francisco Gómez Soto, just below Plaza Mayor. Open daily. This sells embroidery and woodcraft for tourists. You may find something you like amongst the kitsch – look out for wooden dominoes, 3-peso notes showing Che's image, and collections of cigar bands. Music courtesy of a real old-timers' orchestra.

🔋 **Pottery workshop**: Oscar Santander Rodriguez, calle Concordia. Not very easy to find – continue along the extension of calle Maceo, turn left next to the school, then ask for Casa Santander. The family here have been potters since 1860, and Oscar demonstrates his skills to visitors. There are some nice, cheap souvenir items for sale that make a change from cigars.

LEAVING TRINIDAD

By Bus

🚌 The **bus station** is in calle Piro Guinart, in the town centre. Buy tickets here between 8 and 11.30am. ☎ 44-48. The air-conditioned Viazul buses are more comfortable than the train, and seats are readily available.

– For **Havana** (5 hours 30 mins): one bus per day at 3pm, arriving in Havana at 8.30pm. Cost $25. The bus from Havana arrives at 1.50pm.

– For **Cienfuegos** (2 hours): two buses a day, at 9am and 2pm; fare $3.

– For **Santa Clara** (3 hours): departs at 3pm daily; $6 per person.

– For **Sancti Spiritus** (2 hours): daily at 6am, noon and 8pm; tickets $2.

By Plane

Aerotaxi: is a small company that organizes excursions and offers flights between Trinidad and Havana for $50 per adult. The aircraft is a 12-seater Antonov. You'll be on the edge of your seat!

Daily flights are also available with **Lacsa**:

– For **Havana**: one flight daily. Flight time: 50 mins. $50 for a single ticket.

– For **Varadero**: one flight daily. Flight time: 40 mins. $45 a single ticket.

– For **Cayo Coco**: one flight daily. Flight time: 50 mins. $50 one way.

IN THE AREA

★ **The Escambray Mountains**: for some fresh air and a bit of altitude, drive into these mountains, 10 kilometres (6 miles) from Trinidad. The road which leads to Topes de Collantes offers a superb view over the Ancón peninsula and Cailda bay which you can admire from the Bar Mirador, a short way off the Cienfuegos road. Note, however, that this steep and very tortuous road should be avoided in rainy weather.

The massif is 90 kilometres (56 miles) long and 40 kilometres (25 miles) wide, and is one of the three most extensive mountainous areas on the island. The range was first a refuge for Che's guerrillas, then, after 1959, it became a base for counter-revolutionary activities. Today, you'll only come across walkers and anglers fishing for trout. The clouds are quite low here in the tropics, and it rains frequently in the Escambray range, where the average altitude is 700 metres (3,000 feet). As a result the vegetation, comprising mainly of bamboo, eucalyptus and pine, is extraordinarily lush. This curious microclimate, unique in the Caribbean, has therapeutic benefits, making it a well-known place for health cures.

WHERE TO STAY IN TOPES DE COLLANTES

☆☆ Moderate

♠ **Villa Caburni**: ☎ 401-80 to 89. Some distance from the tourist complex, this is very quiet and next to the start of the main walks – perfect for real mountain lovers. Light, spacious chalets cost $38 and are ideal for three to four people. Rattan furniture, bathroom and kitchen – cutlery and crockery are available from reception.

♠ **Hotel Los Helechos**: ☎ 401-80 to 89, ext. 22-44. Fax: 403-01. A rare hotel for tourists, where a double room costs $50 in season, $40 at other times of the year. The rooms are a pleasant contrast to the building's thoroughly Soviet-style exterior. They are spacious and have all mod cons – hot water, air-condition-

ing, TV, telephone. There's a restaurant, bar, video room, bowling area and a covered swimming pool. The hotel organizes lots of guided tours in the surrounding area.

♠ **Kur Hotel Escambray**: ☎ 401-80 to 89. This enormous concrete tower block dominates the whole village, but it can't be blamed on a Socialist architect, as the building was finished in 1954 under the Batista government. After the Revolution, Castro turned it into a school, but in 1976 it was transformed into a tourist complex for state employees. There are 210 rooms and a double costs $60 in summer, $42 in low season. The hotel also houses a hospital specializing in the treatment of cancer.

WHERE TO EAT

✗ **Torre Iznaga**: Around 15 kilometres (10 miles) from Trinidad, towards Sancti Spiritus. ☎ 72-41. This restaurant is in the beautiful residence of the Iznaga family – a sumptuous house with big blue doors where you eat amid souvenirs of the glorious days of yesteryear. There's a superb terrace and you'll receive a delightful welcome. The house speciality is grilled pork and pepper kebabs served with vegetables, rice and banana fritters, and there are also chicken, spaghetti, steak and other pork dishes. Cocktails and fruit juice are $1.50.

WHAT TO SEE

★ Stop off at the **mirador-bar** – 4 kilometres (2.5 miles) outside Trinidad, on the left on the Sancti Spiritus road – for a lovely view over the valley.

★ **Torre Iznaga**: next to the Torre Iznaga restaurant (*see above*), this seven-storey tower – 45 metres (147 feet) high, with 136 pillars – was put up by the wealthy sugar baron Alejo María del Carmen Iznaga. Admission $1 (plus $1 parking). It's classed as a World Heritage Site by UNESCO and has been the subject of numerous legends. Was it constructed to imprison the sugar baron's unfaithful wife, who was suspected of having fallen in love with her slave master? Or was it meant to be as high as the well in front of his brother's house was deep? The official version (and probably the most plausible) is that the tower was a lookout from where the owner could keep an eye on the slaves in his fields. It's also worth taking a look around the house, which has been converted into a restaurant and bar (*see above*).

★ On the road, past the tower on the right, is the only **sugar production plant** in the region. To the left of it there's a paper mill. Wood pulp mills are often next to sugar refineries, as the paper is made from the waste from the cane harvest.

★ **Casa Guachinango**: from Torre Iznaga, cross the village, avoiding the Sancti Spiritus road, and continue along the road for 3 kilometres (1.5 miles). On the right, after passing an old, rusty bridge, there's a sign for the hacienda. Continue for a few metres and turn off shortly at Guachinango station. Continue on foot for around 10 metres. This place is a paradise, set in the middle of sugar-cane fields, disturbed only by the singing of birds and the mooing of the odd cow. The hacienda used to belong to sugar barons, and some old murals have been discovered in the house. It caters mainly for groups arriving by the steam train, and it's worth making the trip if you want to visit an authentic hacienda.

WHAT TO DO

Walks

You can do some of these hikes easily yourself, but for others you will need a guide, or even a four-wheel-drive! You can book them at **Gaviota Tours** at Topes de Collantes. ☎ 22-76-70. You can also book some hikes in the hotels in Trinidad or Ancón.

– **Caburni Falls**: 3 kilometres (1.5 miles) from Topes de Collantes. Turn off just 500 metres before you get to the Kur Hotel. It is short walk but you need good waterproof footwear and it's worth taking some water as the stuff sold next to the lake is not distilled. Admission $2. If you'd like to bathe in the pinewood setting, there is a superb little lake with a 62-metre (200-foot) high waterfall/shower. It doesn't take long to get down there, but it does require a lot more effort to get back (it's virtually rock-climbing). Allow a good 3 hours for the round trip. Take a guide, otherwise you might get lost. Other waterfalls in the area include **Vegas Grandes**, **Batata**, **Guanayara** and **Cudina** – one of the caves where Che hid.

– **Casa de la Gallega**: Access is by four-wheel-drive only and the track is marked from behind the Kur Hotel. Those who make the effort are rewarded with a meal in the dining room and, for the rest of the day, can walk about and swim in the lakes or under the waterfalls.

– **Trout fishing**: is available at two well-stocked lakes, **Hanabilla** and **Zaza**; the latter is the closest to Sancti Spiritus.

– **The Sugar Valley**: leaving Trinidad on the road to Sancti Spiritus, travel for 60 kilometres (37 miles) along the **San Luis Valley**, more commonly known as Valle de Los Ingenios, or Valley of the Sugar Mills. Designated part of the World Heritage Site in 1988, this valley was a vital economic centre for a long time. It had over 70 mills until 1850 – the fateful year when the price of sugar dropped dramatically. Up to 11,600 slaves sweated body and soul in this region around the bay.

Endless fields of sugar cane, half-naked men with machetes, oxen pulling carts – the images and clichés of the past are still there. During the harvest, in November, the atmosphere gears up a little. Since the beginning of the 'Special Period', the lack of transportation and fuel have meant that the harvest can take weeks.

Visiting this valley is like dipping into a history book and finding out about the slave trade, wealthy landowners, the Spanish influence and the beginnings of the class struggle. It's also like flicking through a book on the Cuban economy and seeing the influence of the sugar-cane harvest on Fidel's moods, and its consequences for everyday life in this country.

– **The steam train**: it's very touristy, but this old train, that dates back to 1890, provides a good view of the valley. It runs from Trinidad to Torre Iznaga and operates only if a minimum of 12 people have reserved places (reservations can be made at the hotels in Trinidad and Playa Ancón). The journey takes 2–4 hours, depending on whether you've chosen the option that includes lunch.

SANCTI SPIRITUS   DIALLING CODE: 41

Between Santa Clara and Trinidad, on the Ciego de Avila road, Sancti Spiritus is the capital of the province that takes its name.

With around 90,000 inhabitants today, Sancti Spiritus was one of the seven colonial townships founded by the Spanish. It was created initially on the banks of the Tunicu river but, following the massacre of a number of indigenous people, it was transferred eight years later to its current location on the Yayabo river.

Sancti Spiritus, target of several attacks from pirates, still retains many vestiges of war. It has a colonial atmosphere similar to that of Trinidad, with its colourful facades and wrought-iron gates. But the town makes little effort to attract tourists, who are often disappointed to find everything closed. This is set to change, however, as the Cuban state declared it a tourist centre in 2001.

USEFUL ADDRESSES

Bus station: circumvalente and carretera Central, 2 kilometres (1 mile) outside town, on the road towards Ciego de Avila. ☎ 241-42.

CUPET service station: on the outskirts of the town towards Santa Clara. There is another one 50 kilometres (30 miles) from the town on the motorway towards Ciego de Avila, at Majagua.

Banco Financiero Internacional: calle Independencia, No. 2, esquina Cervantes. A stone's throw from the Hotel Plaza. Open Monday to Friday 8am–3pm, closes 12 noon on the last day of the month. You may withdraw dollars here using a Visa card.

Transautos: Hotel Plaza (☎ 271-02) and Hotel Zaza (☎ 253-34). The main agencies have outlets on Central Park.

Havanatur: on the first floor above the El Rapido restaurant. Staff can help with reservations and will provide limited information about the town.

WHERE TO STAY

☆ Budget

⬩ **Ricardo Rodriguez**: Independencia Norte 28, Parque Central, on the main square. Ricardo is the town's taxi operator and rents out rooms for two or three people for $15–20. They are very clean, with hot water, air-conditioning and separate entrances. A very friendly, family welcome.

⬩ **Estrella González Obregon**: Maximo Gomez Norte 26, opposite the Hotel Colonial. Don't be put off by the somewhat dingy-looking ground floor – all the work has been put into the light, spacious rooms above. There is no air-conditioning but there is hot water and a fridge. A double room costs $15 per night. If she has no space, Estrella will take you to her son's house where there are also rooms to rent.

☆☆ Moderate

⬩ **Hotel Plaza**: Independencia 1. ☎ 271-02. A well-kept establishment in the main square, and the only hotel in the town centre that accepts tourist dollars. The comfortable double rooms, with TV, fridge, air-conditioning and radio-alarm clock, cost around $28. There's an outside bar – officially open until midnight, but the music tends to go on until the early hours. If you're an early-riser it's best to request a room over the road where there is less noise. Inexpensive restaurant, plus sculptures and a *trompe l'oeil* on the wall in the courtyard.

⬩ **Hotel Los Laureles**: Carretera Central, on the outskirts of town towards Santa Clara. ☎ 270-15. A double room costs $30 in comfortable pastel pink-and-blue bungalows, each with bathroom, air-conditioning and TV. A little off the beaten track, but it's good value and the setting is nice and quiet (except for round the swimming pool where Ricky Martin is played at top volume).

⬩ ✗ **Hotel Zaza**: take the road to Ciego de Avila for 5 kilometres (3 miles), then turn off at the sign for the hotel and continue for another 5 kilometres (3 miles). ☎ 28-12. Fax: 283-59. A double room costs around $36. Very quiet and the setting is rather nice – the plants and fountain in the hall soon compensate for the concrete facade. The rooms are decent enough – not very spacious but most have balconies. It's a meeting place for anglers, who come here for the trout (or 'black bass' to connoisseurs), and duck hunters. Breathtaking view over the lake, plus swimming pool, games room, restaurant, bar, disco, boat-trips and horse-riding.

WHERE TO EAT

This is not really the place for gourmet diners. The *paladares* tend not to be around long enough to appear in any guidebook and the state restaurants, the 1514 and the Colonial (payment in pesos) are certainly nothing to write home about. Take a chance with the Mesón, in calle Máximo Gómez , which was being refurbished at the time of writing.

✕ **El Rápido**: Independencia Parque Central. Cuban fast food, as its name suggests – chips and cakes, sandwiches and pizza for only $1.50 if you get there at siesta time – otherwise it's best avoided.

✕ **El Conquistador**: calle Agramonte. Open noon–2pm, 6–9pm. A pleasant dining room, a friendly welcome and decent food from $5 – you won't find better elsewhere.

WHERE TO HAVE A DRINK

♪ **Casa de la Trova**: Máximo Gómez 26. There's a nice outdoor area where bands play Monday to Saturday at 9pm and at 7pm on Sunday. Check the notice-board on the right for the full programme.

♪ **La Hermina**: Enjoy a drink on board this boat, moored under the Yayabo bridge. Normal Cuban opening hours.

WHAT TO SEE

★ **Museum of Natural History**: calle Máximo Gómez. Open Tuesday to Saturday 9am–5pm. In a blue house close to the main square, this has nothing of particular interest, other than a huge shark's jawbone. Plenty of stuffed animals and examples of local flora and fauna.

★ **The Old Town**: before you get to the Museum of Colonial Art. The pleasant and peaceful colonial town centre has been restored, but is not frequently visited by tourists. The old chemist's shop at calle Máximo Gómez 40 has a superb counter.

★ **Museum of Colonial Art**: Placido 74, to the right of the parish church (see below), temporarily closed for restoration at the time of writing. Otherwise, open Tuesday to Friday 8am–5pm; Saturday 1–8pm; Sunday 8am–12pm. Built in 1744, this eclectically styled mansion (the largest in town) belonged to the Valle-Iznaga family until 1961. Despite successive inheritances, the property has remained intact. The powerful Iznaga family contributed to the development of the town, both artistically (putting together great collections) and in economic terms (by opening the railway). The family also knew how to maintain the kind of tyrannical image that only very wealthy families were able to cultivate. The daughter on a whim decided that she wanted to play the piano, and persuaded her father to have her one built at Trinidad, which was then carried on the backs of slaves to Sancti Spiritus. On seeing it, she sighed and decided that she didn't feel like playing after all . . .

★ **Iglesia Parroquial Mayor del Espíritu Santo** (parish church): in the old town. Open 9.30am–noon, then from 2pm. Built in 1522, destroyed by pirates and rebuilt in the 17th century, the church contains beautiful woodcarvings. The tower dates back to the 18th century and the cupola to the 19th century.

IN THE AREA

★ **Lake Zaza**: located 10 kilometres (6 miles) from Sancti Spiritus towards Ciego de Avila, this 127-kilometre (79-mile) lake is ideal for trout fishing and duck hunting. Bizarrely, in the middle once stood a bridge and a condensed milk factory, which were swamped when the dam was built. You can take a boat trip from the Hotel Zaza (*see above*), whose third floor offers distant views of the remains of the factory.

LEAVING SANCTI SPIRITUS

By Bus

For information ☎ 221-62.

– For **Trinidad** : three services a day. Journey time 1 hour.

– For **Santa Clara** (2 hours), **Havana** (5 hours 40 mins) and **Santiago** (12 hours): one bus a day.

– For **Camagüey**: no regular service, so check times in advance. Journey time 3 hours.

By Train

There is no station at Sancti Spiritus, so the train goes to **Guayos**, 20 kilometres (12 miles) away. This station serves Santiago and Havana on alternate days.

CIEGO DE AVILA   DIALLING CODE: 033

The capital of the province of the same name is an industrial town with some 80,000 inhabitants. Founded in the middle of the 19th century, the town is not particularly noteworthy, and doesn't offer much for tourists to see or do. However, it's a useful place to stop off on the way from Santa Clara to Camagüey if you need petrol or a break. The local speciality, apart from sugar cane, is pineapple.

USEFUL ADDRESSES

■ **Banco Financiero Internacional**: calle Onorato del Castillo and Joaquin Agüero. ☎ 55-53. Open Monday–Friday 8am–3pm (until noon on the last day of the month) for cash withdrawals in dollars using a Visa card.

■ **Post office**: corner of Chicho Valdés and Marcial Gómez, two blocks south of the Parque Martí.

☎ **Telephone**: Salón de Llamadas Nacionales y Internacionales, on the Parque Martí, next to the Rumbos agency. Open daily 9.15am–9.15pm.

■ **CUPET service station**: on the outskirts of the town towards Morón, just next to the School of Medicine.

■ **Havanautos**: in front of the Hotel Ciego de Avila. ☎ 26-63-45. Open 8am–noon, 1 or 2–7pm. English spoken.

WHERE TO STAY AND EAT

🛏 ✕ **Hotel Santiago Habana**: carretera Central and Honorato del Castillo. ☎ 257-03. This hotel still bears the name of a pre-Revolution hotel chain, but it now belongs to the Iztazul chain. Good value, with a double room for $22. Sombre 1950s decor and large, welcoming leather sofas in the reception area. The restaurant is as gloomy as the lobby. A bar/disco makes the hotel fairly noisy, and not ideal for early risers.

🛏 ✕ **Hotel Sevilla**: calle Independencia 57, on the corner with the Parque Martí. ☎ 256-03 or 256-47. Although the Spanish-inspired foyer of this recently opened state-run establishment is delightful, the rooms themselves are rabbit hutches ($28 per night). The restaurant is recommended – it is clean and pleasant and, although the menu is not extensive, you can get a good meal for less than $6. Very well-trained staff.

🛏 ✕ **Hotel Ciego de Avila**: carretera de Ceballos. ☎ 280-13. Huge, Soviet-style budget hotel, 2.5 kilometres (1 mile) outside town. The rooms are more welcoming than you would except – on the whole they are comfortable and clean, with air-conditioning, TV and fridge. A double costs around $36. Bar, restaurant and swimming pool. Probably worth a try, given the lack of choice in Ciego de Avila

✕ **Restaurant La Romagnola**: two blocks from the Parque Martí, on the intersection of Chico Valdés and Marcia Gómez, opposite the post office. Open 6–10pm (it acts as a factory restaurant at lunchtime). Decent, inexpensive, Italian-based cooking with more than a hint of a Cuban influence at around $6 for a main meal.

MORÓN
DIALLING CODE: 335

Morón is a pleasantly lively town with 45,000 friendly inhabitants and charming surroundings. It's also a good jumping off point for visitors heading for Cayo Coco and Cayo Guillermo. The town's symbol is the rooster, and there is a bronze statue of one outside the entrance to the Hotel Morón, in the park – which is, of course, called the Rooster.

USEFUL ADDRESSES

■ **CUPET service station**: just as you come into town on the Ciego de Avila road, not far from the Hotel Morón.

■ **Transautos**: Hotel Morón. ☎ 30-76.

WHERE TO STAY AND EAT

☆ Budget

🛏 **Juan Pérez Oquendo**: calle Castillo 189, parallel to the main street, between San José and Serafin Sanchez. ☎ 38-23. The friendly owner currently offers one room for $20 (although he will sometimes drop the price to $15) and there are two other rooms under construction. If Juan can't accommodate you he will always find a neighbour willing to do so.

🔒 **Mileidy Almenares Blanco**: calle San José north 18, between Martí and Castillo. ☎ 31-53. From the main street (Martí), turn left at the CADECA. There's just one room (with shared bathroom) for $15 in this light, clean house where you'll be put at ease by Mileidy's smiling welcome.

🔒 **Plácido Sardiñas Balboa**: Sordo 14, between calle 6 and Patria. From the rooster at the entrance to the village, take the fifth turn on the right, then the second on the left. Two rooms for $15–20, one of which is on the first floor with a separate front door and balcony.

Air-conditioning and fridge. Moderate welcome.

☆☆ Moderate

🔒 ✕ **Hotel Morón**: avenida Tarafa, on the way into Morón. ☎ 39-01. Fax: 30-13-47. A double room costs $45. The only hotel in town open to tourists is of the type fairly common in Cuba, neither ugly nor beautiful, but modern and comfortable. The 144 rooms have air-conditioning, bathroom, TV and phone. The courtyard is pleasant and cool, and there's a very good restaurant. Also massage, swimming pool and disco open every evening from 10pm.

WHERE TO HAVE AN ICE-CREAM OR A DRINK

🍦 **Coppelia**: calle Martí 213. Open 9am–9pm. Cuba's ubiquitous ice-cream parlour.

🍹 **Jardin del Appolo**: calle Martí, on the corner with S Antuña. This ter-

race bar has an entrance on the main street.

🍹 **La Fuente**: Izlazul restaurant, calle Martí. Open noon–midnight.

IN THE AREA

★ **Lake Redonda**: 20 kilometres (12 miles) north of Morón, on the road to the Cayos. At the angling centre, you can spend the afternoon with Fello, one of the most famous Cuban anglers. Fly-fishing for enthusiasts (perch, bass and trout), and boat trips are available. You can book at the bar for $12 per person (not per hour), which is quite expensive, as are the drinks ($2.5 for a beer). There's also a restaurant. Take note that there are clouds of mosquitoes and, more particularly, avoid hooking a crocodile.

★ **Laguna de la Leche** (Milk Lake): north of Morón, between the sea and the land. Not a lot is known about it, but the lake gets its name from its milky-white water caused by lime deposits. Admire the countryside and listen to the silence and the birds, or take a boat trip and fish for pike and tarpon. Watersports are also available.

★ **Isla Turiguano**: despite its name, Turiguano is not an island, but a peninsula just above Laguna de la Leche. The little village of the same name, to the left towards the Cayos, is unusual in that the houses are Dutch-style – the Dutch cattle grazing in the surrounding area must feel quite at home. The cows were imported here by Celia Sánchez, the *pasionaria* (passion flower) of the Revolution.

★ **Cayo Coco and Cayo Guillermo**: *see* 'The Cuban Islands'.

REMEDIOS

DIALLING CODE: 42

Situated 45 kilometres (30 miles) northeast of Santa Clara, on the coastal road to Morón, this colonial town off the beaten track was founded in 1514, and has been the subject of many attacks by French pirates. Today, it still has plenty of charm, with 20,000 inhabitants who have a seemingly carefree approach to life. Go for a walk and lose yourself in the streets, where cars are rare, and where the horse and cart or bicycle is still the preferred mode of transport. The central Martí square becomes a lovely place to be in the cooler hours of the day, and the tables outside the El Louvre bar are excellent for people-watching. However, Remedios is mainly known throughout Cuba for its *Parrandas* (*see below*).

The *Parrandas* Christmas Carnival

Remedios's *Parrandas* tradition dates back to the end of the 19th century. Legend has it that the custom began one Christmas Eve, when the inhabitants of one district wanted to wake the neighbouring district with music to summon them to midnight Mass. The following year, the neighbouring district took its revenge, and thereafter, on the Saturday prior to 25 December, the districts tried to outdo one another. The annual disturbance of the peace expanded to include floats, costumes and fireworks, and the winners were those who could draw the most attention to themselves till dawn. Throughout the carnival, Remedios rocked to the sound of the polka, its own special music.

However, since the economic deprivations, as with many carnivals in Cuba, the Remedios festival has become a quieter affair. There are still a few small, low-key processions between 24 and 26 December, as the districts uphold the tradition and conduct a fiercely loyal yet amicable battle to be voted best float. Console yourself for its relative demise with a visit to the Museum of the Parrandas Remedianas (*see* 'What to See').

WHERE TO STAY AND EAT

♠ **Jorge and Gisela Rivero**: Brigadier González 29, between Independencia and José A. Peña. ☎ 39-53-31. Go down Independencia from the El Louvre bar, then take the second on the left to this repainted 1950s house that's so light and airy inside that the locals refer to it as the 'glasshouse'. Jorge and Gisela are very proud of their establishment and keep it absolutely spotless. They offer two pleasant rooms, one for $15, the other for $20. Parking.

♠ **Gladys Aponte Rojas**: Brigadier González 32, between Independencia and Py Margall. ☎ 39-53-98. A few houses down from the previous establishment but a jolly hotchpotch of styles make for a radically different atmosphere. The welcoming decor is cluttered Afro-Cuban, and Gladys and her daughters are very friendly. There are two rooms at $15, one of which (blue-painted) is big enough for four people.

♠ ✕ **Hotel Mascotte**: Plaza Martí. ☎ 39-54-67 and 39-51-44. This hotel has played a modest role in Cuban history. It was here that General Máximo Gómez, commander of the Liberation Army, met the envoy of the American President McKinley in February 1899 to negotiate the discharge of the *mambis*, Cuban independence soldiers who had fought in the Spanish-American war. This historical episode aside, it is a recently renovated, superb colonial hotel. Charm and all mod cons at reasonable prices – a double room costs $30–35. The rooms are spacious and very tastefully fitted out, with high ceilings and yellow-and-blue paintwork. The bar is open from 10am–11pm. The restaurant is nothing particularly special and is on the pricey side ($10 per person), although it may review its prices

given the competition. It's an excellent place to stay, but advance bookings are advisable. Reception sells 'visas' for Cayo Santa Maria and can also reserve you somewhere to stay there, as the hotel has a few chalets on Las Brujas beach.
✕ There are not many places to eat in the town, as it's not a particularly touristy sort of place. As always, your best option is to have a meal in a private home. However, the **El Louvre** snack bar on the main square is a good place, with a nice outside terrace and an attractive colonial setting.

WHAT TO SEE AND DO

★ **Church of San Juan Bautista de Remedios**: to visit the church, you need to go around the back and in through the vestry. Open daily 9.30am–noon, 3.30–5.30pm. If you are in luck, the Mexican priest will show you round. Built between 1545 and 1548, partly destroyed by an earthquake in 1939, then rebuilt, this church hides some real jewels behind its plain facade. These include an impressive cedar altar decorated with gold leaf, a mahogany vault and a richly decorated collection of statues of the saints.

★ **Alejandro García Caturla Museum of Music**: Parque Martí, on the north side of the square. Open 9am–5pm. This splendid 19th-century house is devoted to the works of Caturla (who lived here between 1920 and 1940) – a musician, a judge and a real character. He was one of the first to introduce African rhythms into Cuban music, perhaps influenced by his African wife. A number of instruments are on show, as well as scores, personal effects and recordings of his works. In his work as a judge he was, it seems, merciless, and was eventually assassinated by a former 'client'.

★ **The Parrandas Remedianas Museum**: calle Máximo Gómez 71, close to Plaza Martí. *See* 'The *Parrandas* Christmas Carnival' *above*.

★ **Cayo Santa María**: This is a good place to spend a day at the beach or go diving. You can buy 'visas' from reception in the hotel Mascotte, and the crossing costs around $5. *See* 'The Cuban Islands'.

SANTA CLARA   DIALLING CODE: 422

The capital of the province of Villa Clara is right in the centre of the island, 300 kilometres (185 miles) from Havana, 75 kilometres (45 miles) from Cienfuegos and 135 kilometres (85 miles) from Trinidad. It's a 'must-see' destination for all Che Guevara fans, who will want to visit Plaza de la Revolución and the monument of the armoured train. Santa Clara only retains a few traces of its colonial past. Unlike its sleepy contemporaries, it's a modern, dynamic town that attracts students and offers real employment opportunities in different sectors of industry. It's clearly a rich town and touts and con-merchants are rare. The town is an excellent place to get to grips with a more modern Cuba where tourism plays a fairly unimportant role. Throughout the winter, from November onwards, there is a series of festivals – music, cinema, literature and the like. Although Santa Clara is less photogenic than other places, it is a town worth getting to know.

History

Santa Clara is *the* place to go for Cuban revolutionary history. Imagine the scene: it is 1958; Fidel Castro and his men have seized Santiago; Castro's brother Raúl has taken Guantánamo; Camilo Cienfuegos is fighting in Yaguajay. Finally, on Christmas Eve, Che Guevara enters Sancti Spiritus.

However, on 28 December, when the battle at Santa Clara is in full flow, Che's troops and the city are bombarded by an air attack. Che learns that an armoured train carrying munitions has to cross the city for Santiago. With the help of Molotov cocktails and a bulldozer, Che and his companions succeed in ambushing the train.

This feat was the decisive factor, in that it dealt a serious blow to the army's morale and, more importantly, for the first time the revolutionaries were as well armed as the army itself. Batista's days were numbered. The battle of Santa Clara came to an end during the first hour of the year 1959. On 31 January, Santa Clara surrendered and the dictator fled the country to seek refuge in Santo Domingo.

Following Batista's flight, the way was clear for the Revolution and Che Guevara and Camilo Cienfuegos penetrated Havana on 2 January, followed six days later by Fidel Castro.

USEFUL ADDRESSES

National bus station: carretera Central, between Prolongación de Independencia and General Marino; opposite *Rápido*. ☎ 921-14. For long journeys only.

Municipal bus station: carretera Central, between Virtudes and Ampano. For destinations around Santa Clara only.

Railway station: calle Luis Estevez, in the north of the city.

■ **Telephone**: calle Cuba. Open 7.30am–10.30pm.

■ **CUPET service station**: carretera Central and General Rolof, at the beginning of the motorway to Havana.

■ **Car hire**: Havanautos, at the Hotel Santa Clara. ☎ 275-45.

WHERE TO STAY

☆ Budget

♠ **García Rodriguez**: calle Cuba 209, apt 1, between Serafin Garcia and E.P. Morales. ☎ 223-29. E-mail: garcrodz@civc.inf.cu. Two very

clean, private rooms in a long and narrow apartment for around $15 a night, owned by a very kind couple (a former engineer and a vet) who have given up their professions to try their hand in the tourism industry.

The entrance is not very exciting, but García's smile will win you over. Ask for the room next to the living room, as it is quieter. You can book over the Internet (rare enough to be noteworthy), which is also available for the use of guests. Garage parking for $1 a night.

♠ ✕ **Orlando García Rodriguez**: calle Rolando Pardo 7 (Buenviaje), between Parque and Maceo. ☎ 267-61. Right in the centre of town, 50 metres from Parque Vidal is this surprising house of immense, labyrinthine proportions built in the 1950s. Orlando has built a kind of hut on the roof that would look more at home on the beach than on the Santa Clara skyline. A pleasant spot for breakfast ($6–8) and other meals. Very clean double rooms with air-conditioning and shared bathroom (hot water) for around $15. Good welcome. Secure parking.

♠ **Isolina Delgado Hernández**: calle Nazareno North 75, between Colón and Maceo. ☎ 43-85. Although lacking any particular charm, this spacious establishment is spotless, and it's a safe, peaceful place to stay. Single rooms are $15 a night. Isolina is the archetypal motherly Cuban: her rocking chair and her cheerful chit-chat an invitation to linger longer. Secure parking can be arranged for $1.

♠ **Ana Pérez Martínez**: calle Nazareno North 74, between Colón and Maceo, opposite the previous address. ☎ 264-45. There are two comfortable, self-contained rooms on the first floor – ideal if you are in search of peace and quiet. The rooms cost $15–20 per night, but be prepared to haggle. Small balcony. Reserved but friendly welcome.

♠ ✕ **Hotel Santa Clara**: Parque Vidal 6, in the main square. ☎ 275-48. A double room costs around $28. As the last point of resistance for Batista's troops, this hotel had to paint over the bullet holes that scarred its walls. Noisy and not very well maintained, with small rooms and an old lift. Also a restaurant, disco and solarium.

☆☆ Moderate

♠ ✕ **Hotel Los Caneyes**: carretera de Los Caneyes. ☎ 45-12 to 15. Just 2 kilometres (1 mile) outside the city centre you'll find a fine complex of native Taino Indian style bungalows (91 rooms) set in a pleasant garden for around $45 per night. It's a shame that the interior decor is a bit tatty and the bathrooms nothing to write home about. It's the same for the $10 buffet option in the restaurant, which offers neither quality nor quantity. Swimming pool, bar and disco.

WHERE TO EAT

✕ **The Boulevar**: the pedestrian part of calle Independencia has a series of cafeterias and bars with tables on the pavement – very popular with students. Slices of pizza, ice-cream and the like are available at all times of day and night.

✕ **Casa Cuba**: calle Cuba, close to the Parque Vidal. One of the town's

rare official *paladares* has a cool, pleasant outdoor area, but come early as tables are soon taken. Good set menus include well-prepared fish, chicken and pork dishes for around $8. The *camarones* (a type of large prawn) in sauce are highly recommended ($12). Fast, attentive service.

NIGHTLIFE

❣ La Marquesina: Plaza Vidal. This bar is attached to the theatre and under the same management. It is open 24 hours a day but no longer serves alcohol. Despite this, it's a favourite haunt of the town's artists and intellectuals. With a bit of luck you'll come across a student who will act as your guide around the town in exchange for a coffee and the simple pleasure of chatting to a foreigner.

❣ El Mejunje: the bar's name means 'the mixture' and it is indeed a hotchpotch of all Cuba's cultures and music. Accessible to people of all ages, it's a favourite among the Cubans themselves and offers a different programme of entertainment every evening. Night after night excellent acts take to the stage – many along the same lines as the famous Buena Vista Social Club.

WHAT TO SEE

★ **El Tren Blindido** (armoured train monument): near the railway on the northern outskirts of the city towards Remedios. Open Tuesday to Saturday 8am–5pm; Sunday 8am–12pm. The armoured train (see above) has become a museum, and is now a Mecca for students of the Revolution. This was where Che caused the regular army to falter by seizing an armoured train full of munitions. Inside the carriages you can pore over various documents, weapons and photographs. At the entrance the bulldozer that was used to destroy the rails and derail the train sits imposingly on a concrete pedestal, and the twisted rails can still be seen. The attack on the train happened on 29 December at 3pm. The battle had been raging until the last hour of daylight, and at 6pm, Che's men had the advantage. This was one of the most important military events of the war of liberation, enabling Che Guevara to demonstrate his military talent. Close by, the railway, with its other more anonymous trains, continues to run.

★ **Plaza de la Revolución**: towards the Hotel Los Caneyes. Far from the city centre, this square is virtually deserted, apart from numerous kids who come here to beg. This Revolution Square (they are everywhere in Cuba) is different, for here stands one of the two life-size statues of Che on the island. It's a Soviet-style mausoleum to Guevara, but it was not erected until 1988, on the 20th anniversary of his death. The plinth bears the inscription Hasta la Victoria Siempre ('Forever Until Victory'), and below are the words of the famous letter that Che sent to Castro before departing for Bolivia. Take any photos as soon as you arrive because the guard is quick to insist that you leave your bag and camera in the cloakroom and is not overly cooperative.

At the foot of the statue, you can visit the museum in honour of Che (open Tuesday to Saturday 9am–8pm; Sunday 9am–1pm), containing numerous relics, rifles and unpublished photographs relating to the hero. Che's bones have been housed in a mausoleum in this same square since October 1997, the 30th anniversary of his death (see below).

★ **Che Mausoleum**: Plaza de la Revolución. Open Tuesday to Saturday 9am–8pm; Sunday 9am–1pm. There are 38 tombstones in honour of Che's companions who lost their lives with him in combat in Bolivia. The remains of only seven of them were found. Excavations are continuing in Bolivia and five other bodies are undergoing identification. Che's marble tombstone is surrounded by tropical plants, as the mausoleum's architect, Jorge Cao, tried to re-create the jungle habitat where the national hero lived and died.

Che's remains were repatriated to Santa Clara in October 1997, when there was a rally, larger and more poignant than the January 1998 Mass of Pope John Paul II. Che, who was bold, courageous and charismatic, embodied the ideal of the struggle of the weakest and an unconditional respect for duty. For Cuban people, the three letters of his name stand for *Cubano*, *hermano* ('brother'), and *ejemplo* ('exemplary').

★ **Parque Vidal**: the nerve centre of the city is a pretty, shaded square, with a bandstand in the middle where free concerts are given in the evening. For information contact the community arts centre next door, near the Hotel Santa Clara.

★ **Museum of Decorative Arts**: Parque Vidal 27. Open Monday, Wednesday and Thursday 9am–noon and 2–6pm; Friday and Saturday 1–6pm and 7–10pm; Sunday 7–10pm. Admission $2. Built between 1830 and 1840, this superb 19th-century colonial house contains many exhibits and furniture from the period.

★ **Loma del Capiro**: 20 minutes' walk from the city centre – follow the extension of Carretera Central southwards. It was on this small hill that Che organized the famous battle of Santa Clara. It is a lovely place to look out over the plain – Cubans like to bring their children here to get a different perspective on the town.

LEAVING SANTA CLARA

By Train

🚂 The **station** is not far from the armoured train monument, in calle Luis Estevez to the north of the town.

– For **Havana** (journey time around 5 hours): departures at 2.53am, 8.43am, 11.38pm and 12.25am. Tickets $10 per person.

– For **Santiago** (10 hours): departs at 8.48pm.

– For **Bayamo** (9 hours): departs at 4.18am.

– For **Holguín** (10 hours): departs at 6.08pm.

– For **Sancti Spiritus** (2 hours): departs at 2.37pm.

By Bus

🚌 Note that there are two **bus stations**: one for local destinations and the other for long-distance travel. They are both on Carretera Central, more commonly known as Hotel Caneyes Road.

– For **Havana** (journey time 4 hours 30 mins): at 2pm and 11.50pm.

– For **Trinidad** (3 hours): service at 1.20pm on alternate days.

– For **Cienfuegos** (3 hours 30 mins): at 7.10am and 11.20am.

– For **Varadero** (4 hours): at 9am on alternate days.

– For **Santiago** (11 hours): at 7pm on alternate days.

THE CENTRE

CAMAGÜEY

DIALLING CODE: 322

Halfway between Santiago and Santa Clara, this charming city – Provincial capital and third-largest city on the island – deserves at least a day. If Holguín is known as the 'town of squares and parks', then Camagüey is the 'city of churches', and Pope John Paul II held a Mass here during his visit in January 1998. The colonial city centre is very lively, with narrow streets inviting you to stroll around. The people are very friendly too.

Camagüey's speciality is *tinajones*, large earthenware jars that can be up to 2 metres (6 feet) high and 3 or 4 metres (9 or 12 feet) in circumference. It was potters originally from Catalonia in Spain who discovered the virtues of the local clay back in the 16th century and developed this craft. Designed to store rainwater, oil or grain, the *tinajones* were often buried in the ground to keep the contents cool. You will sometimes catch a glimpse of them in the courtyards of the houses.

Bicycle-taxis are a good way of getting around Camagüey's labyrinthine streets. They are very cheap and less sporty than the ones in Havana. Allow $5 per hour to visit the town's main points of interest.

History

Camagüey is a city steeped in history. Founded in 1514 by Diego Velázquez, it was initially built by the sea, then, due to incessant attacks from pirates, it relocated further inland, to the middle of the island, on the site of an Indian village called Camagüey.

■ **Useful Addresses**

🚂 Railway station
🚌 Alvaro Barba bus station
✉ Post office
1 International telephone
2 Banco Financiero Internacional

🏠 **Where to Stay**

5 Hotel Colón
6 Gran Hotel
7 Hotel Plaza
8 Hotel Puerto Principe
9 Hotel Maraguan
10 Luis Perez Alvarez
11 Casa Manolo
12 El Hostal de Lita
13 Teresa Santana Ortega
14 Alfredo Castillo

✕ **Where to Eat and Have a Drink**

2 Cafeteria Las Ruinas

5 Restaurante Santa María and Hotel Colón bar
20 Panadería Doñaneli
21 Paladar El Califa
22 Paladar El Cardenal
23 Campana de Toledo
5 Bar in the Hotel Colón
24 El Cambio
25 La Terrazza Bar

★ **What to See**

30 Plaza, Juan de Dios and the old hospital
31 Cathedral
32 Galería Alejo Carpentier
33 Casa Jesús Suárez Gayol, or the Museum of the Student Movement
34 Ignacio Agramonte Museum
35 Merced Church
36 Soledad Church
37 Museum of History

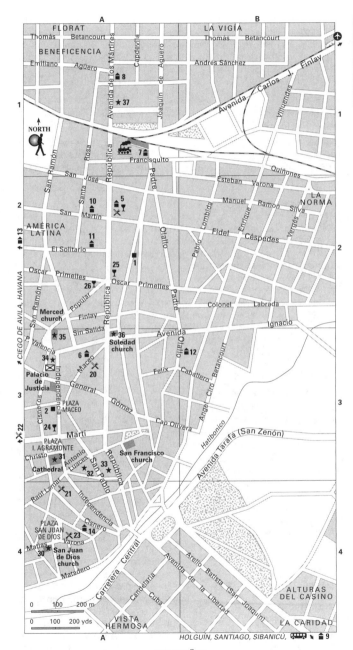

THE CENTRE

FLORAT

LA VIGÍA

Thomás   Betancourt

Thomás   Betancourt

BENEFICENCIA

Andrés Sánchez

Emiliano   Aguero

Avenida de los Mártires

Capdevila

Joaquín de Aguero

Avenida   Carlos J. Finlay

Villuendas

🏛 8

★ 37

NORTH

San Ramón

Santa Rosa

República

Padre

Francisquito

🚂 ♦ 7 🏛

Quiñones

San José

Esteban   Varona

LA NORMA

Manuel   Ramón   Silva

10 🏛

5 🏛 ▼

San Martín

✕

Pablo Lombida

Enrique

Vargas

AMÉRICA LATINA

↑🏛 13

11 🏛

Fidel

Céspedes

El Solitario

25 🏛

1 ■

Oscar   Primelles

▼

Oscar   Primelles

Padre

Otaño

26 ▼

República

Popular

Colonel   Labrada

Merced church

San Ramón

Finlay

Ignacio

★ 35

Sin Salida

★ 36
Soledad church

Avenida

P. Valencia

Otaño

🏛 12

34 ★

6 🏛

Maceo

Independencia

Felix   Caballero

Angel

Cap Olivera

Cisneros

20 ✕

Palacio de Justicia

2 ■

PLAZA MACEO

General   Gómez

Cirilo Betancourt

24 ▼

Martí

Hatibonico

Avenida Tarafá (San Zenón)

✕ 22

PLAZA I. AGRAMONTE

Christo

★ 31

Cathedral

Antonio Luaces

San Pablo

33 ★

San Francisco church

República

32 ★

Raúl Lamar

21 ✕

Independencia

Cisnero

PLAZA SAN JUAN DE DIOS

14 ✕

✕ 23

Matías

Varona

30 ★

San Juan de Dios church

Matadero

Carretera Central

Candelaria

Arello Batista (San Joaquín)

Avenida de la Libertad

ALTURAS DEL CASINO

0   100   200 m

0   100   200 yds

Cuba

VISTA HERMOSA

LA CARIDAD

CIEGO DE AVILA, HAVANA

HOLGUÍN, SANTIAGO, SIBANICÚ, 🚌 ♦ 🏛 9

CAMAGÜEY

Surrounded by rich pasture, the city naturally focused on cattle-breeding and cultivating sugar cane. Already prosperous by the 17th century, it was inevitably the subject of many raids and pillaging, including the 1668 rampage of the infamous Henry Morgan. The narrow network of streets no doubt disorientated attackers and facilitated the work of those defending the city. Several revolts preceded the two great Wars of Independence, in 1868 and 1895.

Ignacio Agramonte, one of the great leaders of the freedom fighters, was born in Camagüey. Jesús Suarez Gayol, hero from the Castro Revolution who died with Che in the Bolivian jungle in 1967, was also from the city.

Today, Camagüey is at the centre of a very important cattle-breeding and milk-producing zone. This is where the Zebu cow (known for its ability to withstand any climate) was successfully crossed with the Holstein (good dairy stock) to produce the famous F1 hybrid – a great milk producer.

USEFUL ADDRESSES

■ **Telephone exchange** (map A2, **1**): Centro de Llamadas, calle Avellaneda 271. Open 6.30am–10.30pm.

■ **Banco Financiero Internacional** (BFI; map A3, **2**): Plaza Maceo, right in the centre, halfway between the cathedral and the law courts. Open Monday to Friday 8am–3pm, and on the last day of the month 8am–noon. You may withdraw dollars using Visa or MasterCard.

🚃 **Railway station** (map A1): corner of avenida de los Mártires and calle República. ☎ 832-14 (reservations), 926-33 (information).

🚌 **Alvaro Barba bus station** (map, off B4): on the Sibanicú road, 2 kilometres (1 mile) southeast of town.

WHERE TO STAY

Casas Particulares

🛏 **Luis Perez Alvarez** (map A2, **10**): San Martín 522, between República and Santa Rosa. The kind owner, a former doctor, speaks fluent English and offers an excellent welcome. The three rooms for rent around a very peaceful, small courtyard cost about $20 a night. The rooms have high ceilings, period furniture, a fan and a bathroom (with hot water). Meals available on request.

🛏 **Casa Manolo** (map A2, **11**): Santa Rita or El Solitario 18, between República and Santa Rosa. ☎ 94-403. A room for two costs $15 per night. Breakfast available. One of the rooms opens onto a small, quiet courtyard to the rear, the other two onto a pinker than pink corridor. The smiling owner, Migdalia, offers a friendly welcome.

🛏 **El Hostal de Lita** (map B3, **12**): calle Padre Olallo (Pobre) 524, between Agramonte and Montera. ☎ 910-65. Two rooms for rent for $15–20 in a lovely colonial house with minimalist decor and a charming courtyard with green plants and white rocking chairs. Guests receive a delightful welcome from Lita and her sister, who are anxious to do all that they can. Garage parking is available for $2 per night.

🛏 **Teresa Santana Ortega** (map off A2, **13**): calle Santa Rita or El Solitario 37, between Santa Rosa and San Ramón. ☎ 95-145. Teresa only rents out one room ($15 per night) so she's always keen to make your stay as pleasant as possible. The family is a model of Cuban hospitality. There is a lovely courtyard.

🛏 **Alfredo Castillo** (map A4, **14**): Cisnero 124, corner of San Clemente. ☎ 97-436. The house itself is modern and uninteresting but the spacious, light rooms are very comfortable and tastefully furnished. Four rooms are available for $15–20 depending on whether they have air-conditioning and private bathroom. Very friendly welcome.

☆–☆☆ Budget to Moderate

♨ **Hotel Colón** (map A2, **5**): calle República 472. ☎ 833-68 and 833-48. A double room costs $22 in this colonial hotel, with a large lobby with traditional wooden bar. The rooms are arranged around a very narrow, internal, covered courtyard and have bathrooms and fans. They are rather monastic but the ones overlooking the courtyard get more light (although they are above the late-opening bar). There's also a very nice restaurant in the courtyard. This is an ideal low budget choice.

♨ **Gran Hotel** (map A3, **6**): Maceo 69, between República and General Gómez. ☎ 920-93, 920-94 and 925-50. Very central, on a pedestrianized street that is lively during the day, but quiet at night. This well-maintained, 1930s, neo-classical style hotel has a degree of charm. Its fairly spacious and clean rooms with bathroom and air-conditioning cost $30–35 for a double. The airy snack bar (open 9–11pm) specializes in cocktails and Creole chicken and the restaurant serves large por-

tions of good food for around $10 per person. There's also a piano-bar with dancing, open daily noon–2am.

♨ **Hotel Plaza** (map A1, **7**): Van Horne 1. ☎ 824-13 and 824-57. Fax: 958-17. Right opposite the station. Not very well soundproofed double rooms cost $28–33. The 1970s decor has dated a little, but the rooms are clean and comfortable with fridge, air-conditioning, TV, bath, etc. Cafeteria, bar and restaurant.

♨ **Hotel Puerto Principe** (map A1, **8**): Avenida de Los Mártires 60. ☎ 824-69, 824-03 and 924-90. Not far from the centre, next to the Museum of History, with a double room costing $28. This hotel is modern and clean, but lacking in charm. There's a cabaret with live music every evening (except Monday), from 9pm–1.30am.

☆☆☆ Expensive

♨ **Hotel Maraguan** (map off B4, **9**): 5 kilometres (3 miles) from Camagüey, on the Holguín road. ☎ 720-17 and 720-27. Fax: 718-54. A double room costs around $55 in this huge hotel complex set in splendid isolation in the countryside. Consequently, it's only really suitable for people with cars in search of a bit of peace and quiet. A series of spacious, comfortable bungalows, plus an attractive swimming pool and restaurant with buffet in the evening.

WHERE TO EAT

✕ Calle República has snacks and ice-creams with pavement seating.

✕ **Cafeteria Las Ruinas** (map A3, **2**): Plaza Maceo. Open 24 hours a day. The ruins create an ideal setting for the tables outside, where you can have a drink or some chicken for next to nothing.

✕ **Panadería Doñaneli** (map A3, **20**): calle Maceo, opposite the Gran

Hotel. Open 7am–7pm. A fairly up-market baker's – for Cuba – where you'll find good rolls and some pastries.

☆–☆☆ Budget to Moderate

✕ **Paladar El Cardenal** (map off A3, **22**): 309 calle Martí, with a sign outside and a freshly painted facade. There are a few tables in an attractive blue dining room. A good, extensive menu for $7–8 includes salad, chicken, meat or fish, rice and banana fritters. Good welcome.

✗ **Paladar El Califa** (map A4, **21**): San Clemente 46, between Cisnero and Lugañero. Open daily 11am–11pm. Allow around $8–9 for a meal in one of the best *paladares* in the city centre, close to Agramonte square and the cathedral. The decor is rather dark with the odd red light bulb, but good, fairly varied cuisine and quite pleasant surroundings.

☆☆ – ☆☆☆ Moderate to Expensive

✗ **Restaurant Santa María** (map A2, **22**): calle República. Right at the back of the Hotel Colón (*see above*), this colonnaded courtyard garden is surrounded by little palm trees. Start off with a relaxing and very cold *Mayabe*. There's open-air dining on the cool patio around 20 or so well-spaced tables. Excellent service and good value for money, at around $6–7 for a meal.

✗ **Campana de Toledo** (map A4, **23**): Plaza San Juan de Dios, in the colonial district. ☎ 95-888. Open daily noon–10pm. A quite elegant restaurant in an old house, with a pleasant dining room and terrace in a green courtyard garden where musicians sometimes play. Fairly varied menu, although the cuisine isn't particularly excellent; specialities include chicken or pork fricassée, *albondiga a la catalana* (meatballs) and grilled fillet of fish. Fairly expensive, at around $15–20 for a meal.

WHERE TO HAVE A DRINK

❢ 🍴 **Hotel Colón bar** (map A2, **5**): calle República. In a pleasant courtyard under a trellis, this gets very lively at night and can be a great place to escape the heat during the day if the music's not too loud.

❢ **El Cambio** (la Casa de la Suerte; map A3, **24**): Parque Agramonte (Cathedral Square). Founded in 1909 and decorated around the theme of the national lottery, it was in this bar that winning ticket number 15922 was sold in 1947.

❢ **La Terrazza Café** (map A2, **25**): calle República, corner of the calle Oscar Primelles. Tables outside in a courtyard are slightly sheltered from the comings and goings on the street. It also sells sandwiches.

❢ **Cafeteria Las Ruinas** (map A3, **2**): Plaza Maceo. Open 24 hours a day. *See* 'Where to Eat'.

WHAT TO SEE

★ **Plaza San Juan de Dios** (map A4, **30**): this is a lovely example of a well-preserved colonial square. Shaded by the church and the former San Juan de Dios hospital, harmonious single-storey buildings have turned-wood or wrought-iron bars in front of their windows, little balconies, colourful facades and tiled roofs in a hundred hues of brown and russet. Some buildings house bars and restaurants with internal courtyards.

★ **San Juan de Dios Church** (map A4, **30**): Plaza San Juan de Dios. Open from 7am for Mass and at apparently random times throughout the day. Built at the beginning of the 18th century, the church has a single nave and a large, dark-wood, pillared retable. The Holy Trinity in the centre is a beautiful piece of polychromatic, gilded woodcarving also from the 18th century.

★ **The Old Hospital** (map A4, **30**): Plaza San Juan de Dios. Open Monday to Saturday 8am–5pm. Admission $1. Guided tours in Spanish and English. This now houses a small museum and is also the place where Camagüey's chamber orchestra rehearses. Workshops are also planned for artisanal pottery makers on the second floor.

The hospital was founded in 1728 by the followers of San Juan de Dios, founder of the first hospital in Granada in 1538. This adventurer became a soldier in Charles V's army fighting the Turks, built the Ceuta fortress in Morocco and sold books in Gibraltar, before turning humanitarian towards the end of his life and devoting himself to public health after a series of personal health problems. In turn, a monk called Brother José Olallo Valdez, began to look after the poor and the sick within these same walls, from 1835 to 1889. He may be the first Cuban to have been beatified.

The entrance is through a green courtyard garden filled with birdsong. In the cloisters are photographs and information boards on colonial Camagüey. And a plaque in a corner marks the spot to where General Ignacio Agramonte's body was transferred in 1873. On 12 May every year, students come here to reflect and deck his tomb with flowers.

★ **Cathedral** (map A3, **31**): Parque Ignacio Agramonte (former military parade ground). Although undergoing complete restoration, features here include three naves with wide arches and the remains of retables at the sides. On one of the walls of the nave there are traces of *mudejar*-style friezes in marble. On the calle Cisneros side (the road running down to San Juan de Dios), stands a stunning blue-and-white building with pilasters, stucco and a baluster roof. On the other side of the square is El Cambio (Casa de la Suerte), a nice bar (*see above*).

★ **Galería Arte Universal** (map A3, **32**): 153 calle Antonio Luaces. Open Monday to Friday 8am–5pm, Saturday 8am–noon. Some 200 metres from Agramonte square (towards calle República) is a very pretty colonial-style house typical of many buildings in the city, with an elegant colonnaded courtyard. The art gallery inside exhibits sculptures, photos and paintings by students or local artists.

★ **La Casa Jesús Suárez Gayol** or the **Museo Estudantil de Camagüey** (museum of the student movement; map A3, **33**): 69 calle de la República. Open Monday to Saturday 9am–5pm. Admission $1. The name of this attraction really says it all, and it served as the centre of the battles for independence and the Castro Revolution. You'll need to speak a bit of Spanish because the guide, Celso, takes his role very seriously and endeavours to strike up a real rapport with visitors. This is a typical Camagüeyan house dating from the early 20th century and where Jesús Suarez Gayol – leader of the student movement against the Batista dictatorship in Camagüey – lived. The revolutionary hero later became vice-minister for sugar, before finally dying by Che's side in Bolivia.

The room devoted to Gayol displays his uniform and appointment to captain by Che. Also here are newspapers, documents, personal accounts and photographs of the fight against Batista, and mementoes of all the unsung heroes who died in combat or were assassinated or tortured. There's an interesting photo of Che in Bolivia with his hair died white by way of disguise. There's also a mini library where students come to consult writings on Gavol, as well as his diaries from Bolivia and the Congo.

★ **La Casa Natal** or **Ignacio Agramonte Museum** (map A3, **34**): on the corner of Independencia and calle Agramonte (opposite Merced Church). Open Tuesday, Wednesday and Saturday 10am–6pm; Thursday and Friday 10am–10pm; Sunday 8am–2pm. Admission $2. This superb late 18th-century building was the birthplace of Ignacio Agramonte, hero of the first War of Independence, who fought in 52 battles before his death on 11 May 1873 in the battle of Jimaguayú.

On the second floor is a very large room with an original cedar ceiling and colonial furniture from the 19th century – but only the bed in the bedroom and the piano belonged to the Agramonte family. Along one wall, some original floral designs are faithfully reproduced.

The dining room overlooking the courtyard contains many souvenirs, personal accounts and family photographs. A series of small rooms is devoted to Agramonte's revolutionary struggle with items such as the red shirt he wore on the first day of the insurrection, and the original blacklist of revolutionaries or suspects compiled by the Spanish authorities (Agramonte's name was second from the top). There are also revolutionary newspapers (*El Tinimo*, *El Mambi*), Agramonte's Colt (36mm) and the original flag belonging to his troops.

Finally, there's a pleasant courtyard with a well and five large local earthenware pots (*tinajones*) from the period.

★ **Merced Church** (map A3, **35**): corner of Independencia and calle Agramonte. Inside are huge pillars and 'heavy' architecture, with traces of frescoes on the ceiling. A silver sarcophagus stands to the right of the choir and opposite is a painting of the *Assumption* from the Cuzco School.

★ **Soledad church** (map A3, **36**): corner of República and Ignacio Agramonte. This brick-built church from the 18th century has the same huge proportions as the other churches in the city, with sturdy pillars and arches. This is the only church that remains in very good condition. It has a dark, gilded, wooden retable, a carved ceiling and some frescoes on the arches of its nave.

★ **Museum of History** (map A1, **37**): Avenida de Los Mártires, the continuation of calle República, after the level crossing. Closed for repairs at the time of writing but generally open Tuesday to Friday 8am–4pm; Saturday 2–9pm; Sunday 10am–2pm. This is housed in an impressive, completely white, pillared building – a former cavalry barracks built in 1848. Two cannon flank the door, but there's no sign to indicate that this is a museum. Inside, in the elegant arched courtyard, a horse trough is the only reminder of the former barracks. There are some beautiful trees, including groves of *Mariposa*, a *Malenga* living as a parasite on a pine tree, a *Siguaralla* with an *Almendra* (a type of orchid) on it, *Ramo de novia*, etc.

Natural history room: here you'll find fossilized trees, insects, shellfish (open the drawers), polymitas (coloured snails), stuffed animals including giant tortoises, sawfish, hammerfish, birds, crocodiles, iguanas. Other rooms display creatures not native to Cuba, such as the anteater, armadillo and duck-billed platypus. There are various slide shows, and one strange exhibit is a prison van that was attacked by the Movement of 26 July.

The **decorative arts rooms** on the first floor contain furniture from the 19th century, including an original type of giant mirror mounted on wooden plinth carved by a French artist. There are also vases from China and France and an impressive dresser standing on tritons and snails, with Poseidon at the top.

Paintings include a large selection of works from the 18th to 20th centuries by a mixture of Cuban academic and avant-garde artists (including Wifredo Lam).

★ **Camagüey Theatre**: Carretera Central Este 331, esquina 4. Home of the Camagüey National Ballet Company.

IN THE AREA

★ **Beaches**: at **Santa Lucía**, near Nuevitas on the north coast is a beautiful stretch of fine sand, almost 20 kilometres (12 miles) long. On the south coast the choice would be **Santa Cruz del Sur** beach, 80 kilometres (50 miles) from Camagüey.

LEAVING CAMAGÜEY

By Train

🚂 **Train station**: corner of avenida de Los Mártires and calle República. ☎ 832-14 (reservations), 926-33 (information). Book your tickets either on the day or, preferably, the day before you leave. Otherwise it's best to buy them from the small office opposite the Hotel Plaza at Independencia 1. Open 8am–noon and 1–7pm. Fast service.

– For **Santiago**: one train daily departs at 1.14pm and arrives at 6.45am.

– For **Santa Clara**: one train daily departs at 10.23pm and arrives at 2.38am.

– For **Morón**: three trains per day. Departures at 8am, 4.05pm and 6.25pm. Journey time 3 hours 45 mins.

– For **Florida**: no special trains, but other services for Santiago, Santa Clara and Morón run through Florida.

– For **Holguín**: the same train as for Santiago.

By Bus

🚌 **Alvaro Barba bus station**: in the southeast of the city, 2 kilometres (1 mile) along the Sibanicú road.

– For **Havana**: two departures daily, book in advance. Journey time 10–11 hours.

– For **Santiago**: one or two departures daily. Journey time 7 hours 30 mins. $1 for a one-way ticket.

– For **Santa Clara**: two departures daily. Journey time 5–6 hours.

– For **Holguín**: change at Las Tunas.

– For **Cienfuegos**: two buses daily. Journey time 6 hours 30 minutes to 7 hours.

– For **Bayamo** and **Manzanillo**: one bus a day.

– For **Nuevitas**, on the north coast, and **Santa Cruz del Sur** in the south: buses leave from the station near the railway station.

Oriente

The large plains, filled with sugar cane or cattle, continue on after Camagüey. In fact, crossing the province of Las Tunas may even seem a little boring. It's not until you get to Holguín and Bayamo that life starts to stir once more. This is the gateway to the Oriente, one of the poorest regions of Cuba, and most tourists visit little more than its magnificent capital. It's an area where memories of the Revolution are overshadowed by a less glorious present. In the distance are the misty mountain peaks of the Sierra Maestra, where the general landscape becomes more hilly.

HOLGUÍN   DIALLING CODE: 24

This large city, with over 200,000 inhabitants, certainly lacks the colonial charm of Camagüey, but it's lively and busy nevertheless. Holguín is known in the province as 'the city of parks' as its centre is a succession of (rectangular) parks and popular, leafy, shady squares where you can take a nice stroll in the evening. Holguín is also the headquarters of the largest brewery on the island.

It was the first place on the island to be visited by Christopher Columbus on discovering Cuba (he landed near Gibara). The city owes its name to the *conquistador* García Holguín, who founded it in 1525. Besides the walks along the north coast, the city also has some interesting museums.

USEFUL ADDRESSES

■ **Banco Cadeca** (map C2, **1**): calle Manduley 205, 50 metres from Calixto García square. Open Monday to Saturday 8.30am–6pm; Sunday 8am–1pm. Cash (dollars) may be withdrawn using Visa or MasterCard.

■ **Banco Financiero Internacional** and **DHL** (map C2): calle Manduley 165. Cash (dollars) may be withdrawn using Visa.

■ **International telephone** (map C2, **2**): Centro de Llamadas Telecorreo y DHL, calle Manduley 183, in Calixto García square. Open daily 10am–6pm.

✚ **Airport**: on the Bayamo road. ☎ 46-25-12 or 46-25-34.

🚂 **Railway station** (map off D2): ☎ 42-23-31.

🚌 **Bus station** (map B3): corner of carretera Central and calle 1 de Mayo.

WHERE TO STAY

There are no hotels worthy of such description in the city centre, but you will find them on the outskirts. However, there are some private lodgings (*casas particulares*) near the *parque* (most are illegal, so be discreet).

Casas Particulares

🏠 **Sonia o Pepe** (map C2, **10**): calle Miró 181, between Martí and Luz Caballero. ☎ 42-32-96. A double room costs $15 (including breakfast) at this good, smart and welcoming place. Three big, clean and pleasant rooms on the first floor (two with shared bathroom) have fans. No. 3, which has two windows, is very quiet as it overlooks the back garden.

🛏 **René Reyes** (map C2, **12**): calle Martí 102, between Narciso López and Morales Lemus. ☎ 46-11-91. Sign outside. Expect to pay $10–15 per room, with or without air-conditioning, in a simple house run by a nice gentleman. Bathroom, and meals also available on request.

Hotels

🛏 **Hotel Pernik**: Avenida G. Dimitrov (and Avenida XX Aniversario), on the outskirts of the city, towards the bus station and the stadium. ☎ 48-10-11 and 48-16-68. Decent rooms with air-conditioning and bathroom for $38. Breakfast is $5. Typical former Eastern-bloc architecture, built by the Bulgarians in a green area of state housing that's not too ugly. Huge foyer. Somewhat Siberian atmosphere in the restaurant, and the service isn't much warmer. Bar and swimming pool, plus disco for $10 per couple. Very popular with package tourists and travel agencies.

🛏 **Hotel El Bosque**: Avenida J. Dimitrov, Reparto Pedro Díaz Coello. Further on than the Pernik. ☎ 48-10-12 and 48-11-40. Pleasant rooms at $20 for one person, $32 for two sharing and $51 for three. Breakfast is extra. Permanent chalets in a tranquil and green park.

WHERE TO EAT

✕ **Cafeteria del chef** (map C3, **20**): Luz Caballero, between Martires and Máximo Gómez. A meal costs less than $5 in this little cafeteria shaped like a canvas-roofed hangar and run by the Provincial Culinary Association of Holguín. You pay for the well-prepared food in pesos and it's excellent value for money.

✕ **La taberna de Pancho** (map off D2, **21**): Avenida J. Dimitrov, Reparto Pedro Díaz Coello. A meal costs under $5, but there's not a great deal of choice unless you've a hankering for a beer and rather paltry hamburgers.

♦ **Cremería Guama** (map C3, **32**): Flore park (Peralta park). This is the best ice-cream parlour in town. When it's well stocked, the queue stretches back to the middle of the square on the other side of the road. There are also pastries for sale by weight – payment in pesos.

WHERE TO HAVE A DRINK

🍷 **La Begonia** (map C2, **30**): Plaza Calixto García, next to the Casa de la Trova (*see below*). Open daily 24 hours. Under trellises covered with foliage and flowers is one of the nicest terraces in the city and a good place for meeting people. 'La Cristal' is particularly recommended here.

🍷 **Cafetería Holguín** (map C3, **31**): corner of calle Luz Caballero and calle Maceo. Open Monday 7am–3pm. Tuesday to Sunday 7am–10.30pm. Large terrace enclosed by a wall, where you will be served fruit juice and simple snacks for around $1.

ORIENTE

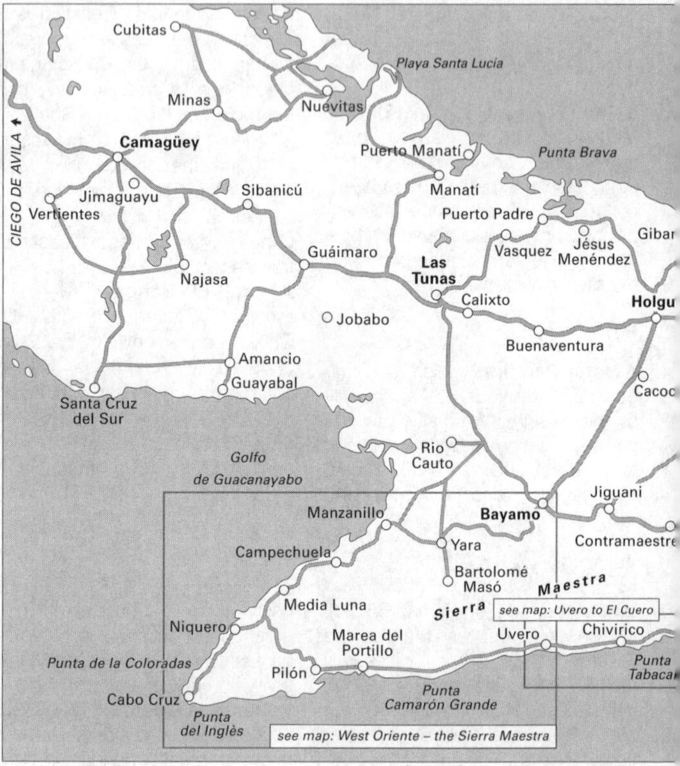

NIGHTLIFE

Casa de la Trova (map C2, **33**): Calixto García square, next to La Begonia café (*see above*). Open 3pm on Wednesday and Sunday and 9pm on other days. Admission 15 pesos for two people. Tourists can pay in pesos too. Performances by both bands and soloists, and you can dance to the music.

Disco Pico Cristal (map C2, **34**): Calixto García square, on the corner of calle Martí and calle Manduley. Open Friday to Wednesday 10pm–4am. Admission $5. On the second floor, this is popular with a young crowd and plays Cuban and disco music.

Club Siboney (map C2, **35**): calle Manduley, Calixto García square, next to the DHL office. Admission $3. On the first floor of a blue, pillared building is a casino and club playing a variety of music, including salsa and merengue, as well as rock and disco.

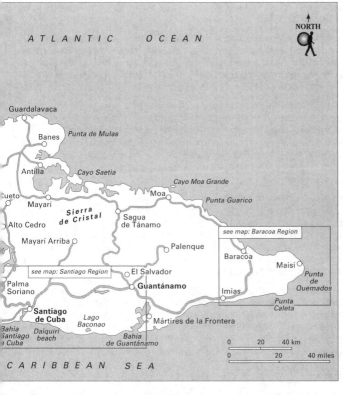

ORIENTE

ORIENTE

WHAT TO SEE

The main places of interest are in the city centre, around the three main squares.

– The first is the Parque de la Flore (Peralta park), which is where you will find the San Isidoro church. Lots of young people in the evenings (no doubt because this is where the best ice-cream parlour is, *see above*). Assembly point for the horse-and-cart taxis and the *bicitaxis*.

– The Parque Calixto García. Very lively here too. Numerous bars.

– Higher up, the third large square (where you will find San José church) is much quieter.

★ **San Isidoro church**: in Flore/Peralta park. Built in 1720, it was recently renovated as a result of aid from a German church. Inside, in the entrance, there is a tomb covered with a pane of glass. It is a relic from the original church. Silver objects belonging to a wealthy person were discovered here. To the right of the choir, there is a chapel with a hand-carved cedar ceiling.

★ **Provincial Museum** (map C2, **40**): calle Frexes 198 (and Libertad). Open Monday to Friday 9am–3pm; Saturday 9am–1pm. Situated in a former mansion, this houses interesting historical collections, particularly relating to aboriginal culture. In the first room you will find the Holguín axe, one of the masterpieces of pre-Hispanic culture (olive-green peridot rock). There's also an aboriginal tomb.

There is a moving letter written in 1845 by a slave to the daughter of one of his masters, together with mementoes of the Wars of Independence and weapons. Other exhibits relate to the martyrs of the Revolution, particularly the 23 victims of the *Pascuas Sangrientas*, including blood-stained shirts, bullets and personal effects. Also on display are war notices issued by the 26 July Movement.

★ **Calixto García Museum** (map C2, **41**): calle Miró, 147. Open Monday to Friday 9am–5pm; Saturday 1–5pm. This is the house of General Calixto García, hero of the Wars of Independence, and contains numerous mementoes and other exhibits. If you want more than a superficial visit, then make the most of the explanations given by the staff. There is a display cabinet devoted to his mother (containing her mantilla), an original flag from his battles, personal effects and photos from the Second War of Independence.

★ **Natural History Museum** (map C3, **42**): calle Maceo 129 and Martí. Open Saturday to Thursday 9am–5pm. Despite the dim lighting and the antiquated appearance, there are some interesting sections, particularly the mammal and bird sections. You will find armadillos, trap-door spiders, crocodiles, tiny frogs and groupers, along with all the exotic migratory birds of prey, including the frigate. There are also amazing polymitas (snail shells) which look as though they have been painted by children. There are also other shells, and a small rock collection.

★ **La casa la más antigua**: calle Morales Lemus 259, between Aricochea and Cables. Open Monday to Friday 8am–4.30pm. The oldest house in Holguín was built at the end of the 18th century and looks like the sort of house you would find in the South of France, with a red pantile roof. The walls, rather than being made of stone, are made from earth mixed with grass, but they're pretty sturdy.

★ **Loma de la Cruz**: situated around 3 kilometres (2 miles) west of the city, a cross was erected on this hill in the 18th century. Go there by car or, if you are really feeling up to it, you can choose to climb the 465 steps for a fine panoramic view over the city and the surrounding area.

LEAVING HOLGUÍN

By Bus

🚌 **Bus station** (map B3): carretera Central, on the corner of calle 1 Mayo. In the southwest of town, this is the interprovincial bus station.

– For **Santiago**, **Las Tunas**, **Bayamo**. Seats must be booked. Most of the buses leave at 5am, except for Santiago (leaves at 9am).

For **Havana**: the night bus (*especial*) is modern and air-conditioned. A single ticket costs $36.

🚌 **Bus station**: Avenida Lénine (opposite the baseball stadium). This terminus serves the east and north of the island, with buses to **Moa**, **Guardalavaca**, etc.

– For **Gibara**: five buses a day. Tickets $2.

– For **Banes**: six buses a day. Tickets $4–5, depending on the route.

– For **Mayarí**: seven buses per day. Tickets $4.

ORIENTE

By Train

This is not the quickest way into and out of Holguín as it's not on the Santiago–Havana line. The nearest station on this line is at Cacocoum.

🚂 **Railway station** (map off D1): ☎ 42-23-31.

There are connections every day to the island's two main cities, **Havana** and **Santiago**.

By Plane

➊ **Airport**: ☎ 46-25-12 or 46-25-34.

– For **Havana**: two flights a day, in the afternoon and evening. A ticket costs $82 with Cubana and Aero Caribbean.

– For **Santiago**: two flights a week. A ticket costs $22 with Aero Gaviota.

■ **Useful Addresses**

  🚂 Railway station
  🚌 Bus station
  1 Banco Cadeca
  2 International telephone and DHL

🛏 **Where to Stay**

  10 Sonia o Pepe's house
  11 René Reyes's house

✕ **Where to Eat**

  20 Cafeteria del Chef
  21 La Taberna de Pancho
  32 Cremería Guama

🍸 **Where to Have a Drink**

  30 La Begonia
  31 Cafetería Holguín

🍸 **Nightlife**

  33 Casa de la Trova
  34 Disco Pico de Cristal
  36 Club Siboney

★ **What to See**

  40 Provincial Museum
  41 Calixto García Museum
  42 Natural History Museum

ORIENTE

ORIENTE

HOLGUÍN

GIBARA

Situated 30 kilometres (19 miles) north of Holguín and reached via a road that crosses the gently rolling countryside, Gibara is a small, colonial port, founded in 1827. At the time it was the most important port in Oriente and there was even a train that went there. Gibara has retained some of its charm and doesn't have the overdone look of Trinidad – it's more natural and rough at the edges. On arriving at the harbour there is little worthy of note, apart from some fine houses on the left.

It is to the west of Gibara, in the bay of Bariay, that Christopher Columbus is said to have landed on Cuba for the first time on 28 October 1492. But this theory is contested by the inhabitants of Baracoa (*see below*), who believe that the explorer in fact landed at the site of their town and not at Gibara. Wherever he landed, 'the Admiral of the Mosquitoes' was convinced that he had reached the kingdom of Mangi, in South China, and that this *terra firma* was just the start of the Indies.

There are a number of cigar factories in Gibara, including the highly renowned Romeo y Julieta. Many of the cigars sold illegally to tourists in Santiago are bought in Gibara, as police checks here are less common than in some other towns. Note, however, that there is a police checkpoint on the way into town, so if you're carrying Cuban hitchhikers you may encounter problems.

WHERE TO STAY

♜ **Hostal Vitral – Nacy Pérez Pozo**: calle Independencia 36, behind the main church in the square. ☎ 34-469. It is next to the only shop in the street to take dollars. There is no *casa particular* sticker, but a small sign on the heavy front door says 'Hostal Vitral'. A double room costs $15, plus $5 for breakfast. The splendour of this typical colonial house is exemplified by the rocking chairs in the spacious lobby. The building is very well preserved – even the art-deco designs on the doors remain. The high-ceilinged rooms all have private bathroom, but not always hot water. The welcoming proprietor ensures every guest is made to feel at home in this highly recommended establishment.

♜ **Los Hermanos**: calle Céspedes 13, between L. Caballero and J. Peraita. ☎ 34-136. The three rooms opening onto an attractive patio may not have the charm of those in the Hostal Vitral, but they are perfectly decent, with shared bathroom and old family furniture. Meals are available if arranged in advance. Guests also receive a particularly warm welcome.

WHAT TO SEE

★ **The Old Town**: everything is situated around calle Independencia, the main street. Right at the end is the main square, where the mid 19th-century **church** (under restoration) has a fairly elegant facade with two bells framing the triangular pediment. Inside there are three naves, a dome and four pillars showing the Disciples. It is here that Fidel Castro and Birta Díaz Balart celebrated their marriage.

– In front of the church is the **Statue of Liberty** and to the side is the old **Governor's mansion**, a long, elegant, pillared building.

– At the bus station is one of the oldest houses in town, the **Miramar** restaurant building (1791) featuring a baroque gate. At the end of the alley is another dining room of the restaurant with a view over the harbour.

– On Donato Marmol you will find the **Casa de la Cultura** and the **Hotel Gibara**. Return to Independencia with its museums, its old, wooden pharmacies and its little snack bars.

★ **Natural History Museum**: Independencia and J. Peralta. Open Tuesday to Saturday 8am–noon and 1–5pm; Sunday 8am–noon. Exhibits include the skeleton of a whale, multicoloured polymitas, beautiful shells, and crustaceans, iguanas and insects. The collection of birds includes herons, spoonbills, ibis and pink flamingos. One strange and unique specimen is the 'cockhen' (*Gallo gallina*).

★ **Municipal Museum**: Independencia, next to the Museum of Art. Open Tuesday to Saturday 8am–noon and 1–5pm; Sunday 8am–noon. The small archaeological section exhibits remains of native Indian culture such as petaloid axes, terracotta, mortars and household objects. Other items include mementoes of old Gibara, photos, colonial banknotes and a map dating back to 1875. There's also a section devoted to the 26 July Movement, the Revolution and internationalist solidarity in Angola. Young people from Gibara fought in Angola against Jonas Savimbi's troops (who were supported both politically and militarily by the CIA and the United States), a conflict in which some Cubans perished.

★ **Museum of Art**: Independencia, next to the Municipal Museum. Open Tuesday to Saturday 8am–noon and 1–5pm; Sunday 8am–noon. The museum is in a large, aristocratic house dating back to 1862, which was General Calixto García's headquarters in 1898. Interesting collections from the 19th and 20th centuries include some fine colonial furniture. There's also the original kitchen (note the carved wooden fridge) and flooring, a dining room with beautiful dinner service (French porcelain, crystal glasses) and a 19th century-style bedroom. Another feature is the beautiful, original *mamparas,* interior doors with engraved glass (showing views of Paris), characteristic of colonial aristocratic homes.

GUARDALAVACA
DIALLING CODE: 24

This seaside resort specifically created on the northeast coast around 60 kilometres (37 miles) from Holguín is supposed to be a second Varadero. It's got the beautiful beaches but it doesn't have Holguín's lively, bustling atmosphere. For now it has settled on being a succession of luxury hotels at international prices. Apart from a discotheque and the usual hotel entertainment, the nightlife is virtually non-existent. There's no village and no real centre, as the Cubans employed in the hospitality industry here live in a large state-owned housing area just behind the hotels and beaches.

ORIENTE

WHERE TO STAY

Hotel rates vary depending on the time of year. High season is between 15 July and 30 August, and from December to March, when prices are high. The hotels are concentrated in the tourist area of town.

☆☆ – ☆☆☆ Moderate to Expensive

⚱ **Hotel Villa Turey**: on the main road. ☎ 301-95 and 301-97. Fax: 302-65. A single room costs $49 and a double $68 in this complex that's part of the Cubanacán chain, offering small, low-rise units situated around the swimming pool. Spacious rooms have air-conditioning, satellite TV, etc., but those closest to the bar can be noisy because of the hotel entertainment. The restaurant serves a good breakfast and a decent buffet-style evening meal. Service is rather slow and staff can be inflexible. No direct access to the beach 300 metres away. Bicycle hire available.

⚱ **Hotel Atlántico**: opposite the Hotel Villa Turey. ☎ 301-80. Fax: 30-200. Email: reserva@guard.gcv. cyt.cu. A large hotel complex, popular with package tours, that charges $46 for a single room and $62 for a double. The bungalows (conveniently located around the swimming pool) are better value at $142 all inclusive. Scooter-hire at reception.

⚱ **Hotel Río de la Luna**: ☎ 300-60. Fax: 300-65. 2 kilometres (1 mile) before Guardalavaca, coming from Holguín. Take a road to the left (surfaced and lit at night), right in the middle of the countryside (sign-posted), which leads to this very large hotel complex, managed by a Spanish company. Traditional in design, but not unpleasant, one night's full board for one person costs $175. Rooms have full facilities including king-size beds. Some overlook the bay of Naranjo and others the swimming pool within the complex. The beautiful beach below is bordered by dense vegetation.

In the Area

⚱ **Hotel Gaviota Bahía de Naranjo**: carretera a Guardalavaca. ☎ (24) 30-132. Fax: (24) 30-126. Allow around $65 for room only, $80 for half board and $100 for full board (all options with bathroom) at this exceptional place. It's a dolphinarium as well as a hotel, and accessible only by sea. Its setting on a tiny island makes it a far cry from places such as Seaworld in Florida. There are nine dolphins and a number of sea-lions. There are two rooms available on the island in a small hut on piles (a replica of the house where Fidel was born) that offer grandstand views of the twice-daily displays. For an extra fee you can even swim with the dolphins, balanced on their noses. Transfers to and from the island are included in the price.

WHERE TO EAT

✕ **Pizza Nova**: ☎ 302-37. Pizzas cost $5–6 and sandwiches $3–4 in this restaurant on a road leading to the disco, 200 metres from the Hotel Turey. The restaurant (signed) is on the right at a large roundabout.

WHAT TO SEE

★ **Chorro de Maita**: well signposted, 7 kilometres (4 miles) from Guarda-lavaca. Open Tuesday to Saturday 9am–5pm; Sunday 9am–1pm. This fascinating Taino Indian burial ground dating back to the 13th and 14th centuries has been restored and left intact, and some bodies in the foetal position indicate burial before the conquest. Those stretched out with their arms crossed demonstrate a clear Christian influence. A small, black cross indicates a Spanish skull. The colours reflect the materials of the jewels and other objects found in the tombs, for example green (copper), red (gold), blue (shell), black (majolica), yellow (quartz) and orange (pottery).

In the display cases around the edge are objects that were found in the tombs, including an idol (bird's head, probably a duck), necklaces made from stones or coral, petaloid axes, mortars and fragments of pottery.

BANES

Banes is the archetypal small, run-down Cuban town. Along its high street, bordered by single-storey colonial dwellings or simple wooden houses with verandas, antiquated little shops are virtually empty. The place has the air of a faded, languid Wild West town. The residents are very pleasant and do not yet take tourists for granted; in general only independent travellers visit the town.

Despite its appearance, little Banes is the archaeological capital of Cuba. There have been around 100 excavations in this area, birthplace of the indigenous people, which is now the site of the remarkable Indo-Cuban Museum. In the main square is an unusual church that's almost post-art deco. And on Saturday and Sunday beer stands open at midday for the workers.

WHERE TO STAY

🛏 **Evelin Feria Dieguez**: calle Bruno Meriño 3401-A, between Delfin Pupo and J.M. Heredia. From the centre of Banes, on the main street (the one ending in a small platform), turn right and head down to a square. It is the third road on the right (ask for Evelin, everyone knows her). ☎ 82-270. The three rooms on offer cost $20 per person (including breakfast if you're prepared to haggle) and come with furnishings and a private bathroom (with showers, although the water is often only lukewarm). Evelin's friendly welcome will soon make you feel at ease. Secure parking is available with the neighbour over the road.

WHERE TO EAT

✗ **Restaurant las Delicias**: Augusto Blanca 1107. ☎ 83-718. A block away from the *casa* Evelin Feria Dieguez, *above*. A meal costs less than $10 per person in this nice little *paladar* serving a few seafood dishes and the traditional *bistec de cerdo* (pork chops). If the owner is in a good mood he will sometimes treat diners to a cigar.

WHAT TO SEE

★ **The Indo-Cuban Museum**: in a road parallel to the high street, just before the main square. Open Tuesday to Saturday 9am–5pm; Sunday 9am–2pm. Admission $1. Extensive collections here relating to the Araucos Indians include shell tools, mortars and stone daggers for burial ceremonies; fine, polished stone axes; Inca-style skulls with flat foreheads; stones for weighing down fishing nets and perfectly formed petaloid axes.

Also on display is a large collection of necklaces (in shell, stone, bone, quartz, etc.), some over 800 years old, including one with a carved talisman. Other items include a replica idol pendant in gold (plus other idols in stone and bone), rings (*anillos*) made from shell and *espátula vómicas* – spoons used by medicine men to make patients vomit.

On the first floor there are carvings showing various aspects of daily life, plus decorative pottery fragments, zoomorphic statues and human figurines, and evidence of the first contact with Indo-Hispanic people, such as metal objects, horseshoes and glazed pottery. The collection is being updated continually with finds from digs still being carried out in the region.

★ **The Museum of History**: in the road leaving the main square (Plaza Martí). Open Monday to Saturday 8am–4pm. While not the best-stocked or most educational museum, this has lots of photos and personal effects belonging to local heroes of the Revolution, plus some colonial furniture.

WHAT TO DO

There are two superb beaches that are always almost completely deserted.

– **Playa Morales**: this is around 15 minutes' drive from the centre of Banes. At the end of the main street, next to the platform, turn right. Go past the old locomotive and head towards the cemetery. Continue straight on for around 12 kilometres (8 miles), crossing four railway lines on the way. The road peters out at a tiny fishing village. There are a few huts perched on the spit of sand with residues of coral.

– **Playa Porto Rico**: from Playa Morales, take the narrow sandy track to the left and follow the coastline for a good 5 minutes. Just beyond a small, disused hotel is another lovely beach as yet untouched by mass tourism, where palm trees bend to almost touch the calm water. The beach is enclosed by a coral reef and swimmers can safely touch the bottom for several metres out from the shore. You can buy seafood from the fishermen in pesos.

Granma Province

The province owes its name to the yacht that transported Che Guevara, Fidel Castro and their followers from Mexico on 2 December 1956. It includes part of the Sierra Maestra from where Castro's guerrillas originated. There are two large national parks in the province: Desembarco del Granma and Pico Turquino.

The capital of Granma Province was founded in 1513 by the activist Diego Velázquez and is steeped in history. With a population of around 150,000, it's not that touristy, and has no particular attractions. But it does have a certain charm, and its centre is quite pleasant and welcoming. For those who have the time, this would be a nice stopping-off place.

A Brief History

The second oldest town in Cuba is largely a cattle-rearing and sugar-producing centre. Due to its good position in the middle of the country, Bayamo managed to escape pirate raids for a long time, but it did not escape the dramatic consequences of the Wars of Independence.

Carlos Manuel de Céspedes, the greatest Cuban revolutionary leader, known as the 'Father of the Nation', was born here. On 10 October 1868, the insurrection against Spanish colonial power began. Bayamo was the first town to rise up. As the Freemasons were very powerful here, this was a place where the ideas of the independence movement naturally found favour. Carlos Manuel de Céspedes freed all his slaves, setting an example to his compatriots. Bayamo symbolized the first battles of the Ten Year War of Independence, becoming the capital of the rebel republic. Around 20 generals came from the area.

In 1869, the town, which was on the point of being recaptured by Spanish colonial troops, suffered a 'revolutionary fire' – the rebels voluntarily set fire to the place, rather than let it fall into Spanish hands. As a result, the town of Bayamo was awarded the title of 'national monument'. A local patriot, Pedro Figueredo, composed *La Bayamesa*, which then became the Cuban national anthem.

USEFUL ADDRESSES

✉ **Correos de Cuba** (map A1, **1**): between General Maceo and Libertad. Open daily 8am–8pm.

■ **Telephone** (map A1, **2**): Centro de Llamadas, calle Libertad 10, on the left of the cafetería Rápido. Open Monday to Friday 8am–4pm; Saturday 9am–1pm.

■ **El Boulevar de los Capuchinos** (map A1, **4**): Main square. This is a popular film centre, frequented at the end of the week.

■ **Banco de Crédito y de Comercio** (map off B1, **7**): General Fuente Díaz. You can withdraw money using Visa and MasterCard.

WHERE TO STAY

⌂ **Gladys's** (map off B1, **10**): Zenea 216, between calle Guama and Saco. From the Plaza Céspedes, take calle Maceo, the fourth road on the right. Two spartan rooms with shared bathroom (no running water) each cost $20.

Only recommended for a short stopover.

⌂ **Hotel Sierra Maestra** (map off B1, **11**): carretera Principal (Santiago–Bayamo) road. ☎ 450-13. A double room without breakfast costs $30 in this Soviet-style hotel

- ■ **Useful Address**

  1 CUPET service station

- ♨ **Where to Stay**

  10 Hotel Punta Piedra
  11 El Farallón del Caribe

Primary roads
Secondary roads
Tracks

SIERRA MAESTRA

Golfo de Guacanayabo

Cayos Manza

Campechuela
Ceiba Hueca
San Ramon

Troya
Israel Li
Dem
L

Nogue

Media Luna
Los Guayos
San Antonio

Cayo Antonia
Cayo Piragua

San Diego
Punta Alegre
Alto de Jo
El Porveni
La Gloria

Las Delicias

Niquero

Guanito
Ricardo
Piloncito
Sevilla Arriba
El Guáimaro
Cinco Palmas
Guairajal
Las Cric

Belic
Los Chorros
Durán
La Alegría
Mare Port

Las Coloradas
Las Guásimas
Siguanea
Pilón
10
Punta Piedra

Alegria de Pio
Pozo Empalado
Caoba
Cayo Blanco
Playa Hicacos

Monte Gordo

Cabo Cruz
Ens. El Real
Ensenada Ojo del Toro
Punta Monje
Punta Brava

NORTH

Punto Nuevo

(huge foyer and corridors) with over 200 rooms but little charm. Plain rooms, but clean and with air-conditioning. Average restaurant and a very noisy disco.

♨ **Hotel Royalton** (map A1, **12**): corner of calle General Maceo and Libertad, in the main square. ☎ 42-22-90. Expect to pay $32 for a double room with breakfast, $28 without in this very beautiful colonial house, with light-blue pillars at the front and decent standards all round.

WHERE TO EAT

✕ **Paladar Sagittario** (map B1, **20**): calle Marmol 107. ☎ 42-24-49. Central, welcoming and with good food, served in the little shady and tranquil internal courtyard. A meal costs $3–4.

✕ **Paladar Polinesio** (map off B1, **21**): calle Parada 125, between Pio Rosado and Cisnero. With meals at less than $10 (payable in pesos), this nice little establishment offers good value for money. Large por-

WEST ORIENTE: THE SIERRA MAESTRA

tions and dishes to share served on the terrace of the owner's home. Small groups sometimes encourage everyone to join in the singing.

✗ **Pizzeria La Casona** (map A1, **22**): Plaza del Himno, behind San Salvador church (cathedral). Simply a pleasant restaurant where a meal costs less than $7.

✗ ❢ **Tropicrema** (map A2, **33**): corner of calle Libertad and calle Figuerado. This unexceptional small bar and cafeteria enclosed by a brick wall is very popular with the Cubans. Beer is sold for pesos: you must pay for your order at the counter on the way in and a waitress will bring your drink. Very noisy but a strategic spot from which to enjoy the play of light and shadow through the acacia trees.

BAYAMO – TOWN CENTRE

■ Useful Addresses	✕ Where to Eat
🚂 Railway station	**20** Paladar Sagittario
✉ **1** Correos de Cuba (post office)	**21** Paladar Polinesio
2 Telephone	**22** Pizzería La Casona
3 Cinema	**33** Tropicrema
4 El Boulevar de los Capuchinos	
5 Casa de la Cultura	♪ **Nightlife**
6 Bookshop	**30** Bar Pedrito
7 Banco de Crédito y de Comercio	**31** La Bodega de Atocha
	32 Casa de la Trova
🏛 **Where to Stay**	
10 Gladys's	★ **What to See**
11 Hotel Sierra Maestra	**40** Provincial Museum
12 Hotel Royalton	**41** Birthplace of Carlos Manuel Céspedes

NIGHTLIFE

♪ **Bar Pedrito** (map B1, **30**): corner of General Maceo and General García. This rather nice little bar is well kept and a favourite with the young in-crowd in Bayamo.

♪ **La Bodegua de Atocha** (map A1, **31**): Plaza del Himno 34, near San Salvador church. ☎ 42-51-09. This colonial house has a shady courtyard that ends with a terrace overlooking the Bayamo river. Strangely, the bar sells wine and beer, but no rum. In the evenings, snacks are provided with the drinks.

♪ **Casa de la Trova** (map B1, **32**): calle Maceo 111, on the corner of calle Martí. ☎ 42-56-73. Open Monday to Friday 9am–5pm. Saturday and Sunday there is music until 2 or 3am. You can drink and eat snacks to traditional music, including *son*, salsa, merengue, cha-cha and *guarija*.

WHAT TO SEE

★ **La Iglesia San Salvador**: built in 1766, this is one of the rare buildings that partially escaped the great fire of 1869. A plaque outside commemorates the place where the Cuban national anthem was first sung, on 8 November 1868. The interior is relatively plain but has been totally renovated. However, the *capilla de Dolorés* escaped the flames and is perhaps the best retable in the country, made from carved and gilded cedar. The Virgin of Bayamo and Christ's sarcophagus are carried around the town on Good Friday. The original ceiling and chancel are made from precious wood. There are some paintings of Cuban flora and fauna on some parts of the ceiling, but they are a little blurred. One picture of Christ dates from 1600, and at the entrance to the chapel is another *Christ* in a violet robe that came from one of the town's 14 churches that were burned down. The one in the baptistry dates back to the beginning of the 18th century.

★ Around the church there are several architecturally interesting buildings, notably the **casa de la Nacionalidad Cubana**, which has been very well restored with fine colonial furniture. It houses the Centro de Estudio de la Nación Cubana, which is not unusual, for Bayamo – former capital of the rebel republic, and home of the national anthem – is also proud of having produced *Espejo de Paciencia*, the first literary work in Cuba. The centre cannot be visited in the same way as a museum, but a member of staff will be happy to provide you with information.

★ Not far from the church is **Plaza de la Revolución**, the main square and epicentre of Bayamese life. Its centre is planted with trees, and there are statues of Carlos de Céspedes and Pedro Figueredo. You will find the birthplace of the Father of the Nation here, as well as the Provincial Museum, the Town Hall and several other interesting colonial buildings. Philatelists will appreciate the little shop that sells collectors' stamps (sometimes in pesos).

Calle A. García, the town's main shopping street, starts from here. At No. 174 is the house that General Calixto García Iñiguez used as his headquarters and where he received the message from US President McKinley on 1 May 1898.

★ **Granma Provincial Museum** (map A1, **40**): Plaza de la Revolución, to the right of the Hotel Royalton. Open Tuesday to Sunday 8am–5pm. Renovated in 1998, the museum's historical section includes aboriginal documents and testimonies to slavery. One part is dedicated to the Bayamo fire, another to the life of the conductor Manuel Muñoz Cedeño (1813–95), born in this house. Note the amazing 'artistic guitar', together with its case (20th century), and the scores.

A modern section (from the Wars of Independence to today) includes the history of the trade union movement, the great revolutionaries, the attack on the Cuartel army barracks of the Guarda rural in Bayamo in 1953, and the work of the literacy campaigners.

★ **The birthplace of Carlos Manuel de Céspedes** (map B1, **41**): Plaza de la Revolución. Open Tuesday to Friday 9am–5pm; Saturday 9am–8pm; Sunday 9am–3pm. This fine, aristocratic house that escaped the fire is where Céspedes (Father of the Nation) was born on 18 April 1819. Large rooms on the ground floor (overlooking the patio) are dotted with mementoes, testimonies and personal effects. On the first floor is the main living room with contemporary furniture, and a pretty view over the square. Then there is a dining room and a bedroom containing his original bed, made from two oval panels encrusted with mother-of-pearl. 'I did what I had to do. I sacrificed myself on the altar of the Nation in the temple of the Law', declared Céspedes.

★ In calle Amando Estevez, next to the monument of Francisco Vicente Aguilera, are the ruins of Bayamo' first **church** – built in 1702 and destroyed during the revolutionary fire of 1869. Its tower served as a portico to the first urban cemetery in Cuba (which was moved when the town was extended).

WHAT TO DO

– **Fiesta de Cubania**: this very lively local event takes place in the main square every Saturday and continues until 2 or 3am. Pigs are roasted in each corner of the square, and music is played.

LEAVING BAYAMO

By Train

The station is right at the end of Avenida General Maceo.

– For **Santiago**: every morning at 10.30am. Tickets cost $4.50.

– For **Havana**: trains every evening, arriving the following morning.

– For **Manzanillo**: four trains a day. Tickets cost $1.50 (fast train) or $1.70 (slow train).

THE SIERRA MAESTRA

Cuba has three mountain ranges: one in the west and another in the centre (the Escambray mountains). The third, and largest, is the Sierra Maestra – a small cordillera 150 kilometres (93 miles) long by approximately 50 kilometres (30 miles) wide – the backbone of the Oriente, east of Santiago de Cuba. 'The last forested highland' before the Caribbean Sea reaches almost 2,000 metres (6,500 feet) at Pico Turquino, which is by no means an easy mountain to traverse. It is full of sheer canyons, wild valleys, steep gorges, hidden caves and windswept ridges. The mountainsides are covered with *monte*, a sort of woodland jungle which makes access even more difficult. There are very few villages and few inhabitants. There are a few roads and some tracks that are often in poor condition.

However, this was the ideal setting for the revolutionary guerrillas to hide themselves and continually harass their adversaries. 'Each point of access to the Sierra Maestra is like the Thermopylae pass, each defile becomes a death trap', declared Fidel Castro, when talking about the time when he hid in these impenetrable mountains from December 1956 to November 1958. It was here that he set up the centre for the Cuban revolutionary guerrillas and, with barely 300 men, he succeeded in standing up to (and finally defeating) Batista's troops, estimated to be around 10,000 men.

Flora of the Sierra Maestra

The vegetation is concentrated on the mountain slopes and includes banana trees, coffee trees and some marijuana (which is now disappearing). Higher up there are also pine trees, and lower down are majestic royal palms, noted by Christopher Columbus and recognizable by the lofty plume crowning their tall, slender trunks. Their brown, supple bark is used in cigar cases and for the walls of the peasants' *bohíos* (huts).

GETTING THERE

Note that there are no petrol stations in the region. The last garages are in either Bayamo or in Manzanillo. If you do run out, you can always buy petrol on the black market.

– From **Bayamo** to **Yara**: 42 kilometres (26 miles). Allow 1 hour 15 mins by bus.

– From **Yara** to **Bartolomé Masó**: 15 kilometres (9 miles). Lorries go there daily if fuel is available, or you could share a taxi (20 minutes' ride) or hitchhike if necessary (less reliable).

– From **Bartolomé Masó** to **Santo Domingo**: 18 kilometres (11 miles) along a concrete road. There are some attractive slopes and sharp bends at the bottom of the small valleys in the last third of this road, before Santo Domingo. Normally, this road is only used by lorries (when they go there). The shortage of fuel means that there are no longer any buses. In actual fact, Cubans make the journey on foot. And there is nothing stopping you from doing the same. Give them a lift if you are in a hire car.

– From **Santo Domingo** to **Altos del Naranjos**: difficult road (*see below*).

USEFUL ADDRESSES

■ **Mountain guides' office**: in Santo Domingo. Adjacent to the Hotel Santo Domingo, next to the road. Open daily 6am to 3pm. Ask for the manager, Luis Angel Segura or Ruben, the guide. Information and advice on walks in the Sierra Maestra, hikes to the Comandancia de la Plata and on climbing Pico Turquino. Note that you must be accompanied by a Cuban guide for all these walks. Make sure you arrange the price for the day before you set out. You can also book the same guides through the Hotel Santo Domingo.

Note: The Sierra Maestra park was closed at the time of writing. Several reasons given include that an ornithological survey is under way, and that revolutionaries have hidden a supply of arms here and don't want walkers stumbling across them. A more likely explanation is that the coffee plantations are being treated with insecticide. Check details before visiting.

■ **Ulises Ramirez Junco**: Ulises is the headmaster for several little schools scattered over the mountain, and is officially responsible for the village of Santo Domingo, so everyone here knows him. His house is on the riverbank opposite the Hotel Santo Domingo, accessible only by tiptoeing over the huge stones in the gushing riverbed. A bit of an adventure! If you decide to go and see him, don't disturb him without good reason. Take some exercise books and pencils for his pupils, as schools in the sierra are short of everything. And be careful not to fall into the river.

WHERE TO STAY AND EAT

🛏 ✕ **Hotel Villa Balcón de la Sierra** (Hotel El Mirador): around 1.5 kilometres (1 mile) outside Bartolomé Masó, on the right-hand side of the road towards Santo Domingo. ☎ 59-51-80. Rooms cost $18–24, depending on size in this renovated hotel on a hill overlooking the vast landscape. It's well maintained, with a swimming pool, restaurant, bar (open until midnight) and two types of permanent cabins: *cabañas familial* (with two bedrooms) and *cabañas matrimonial*, which are clean and tidy. No view from the bedrooms, but there is a view from the pool.

🛏 **Campísimo Popular La Sierrita**: halfway between Yara and Santo Domingo, before the terrain becomes really mountainous. The well laid-out little huts in the middle of nowhere cost only $5. Each hut has two pull-out beds and a small kitchen. Take your own food and drink. Very popular with young people, so get there early to reserve a place.

🛏 ✕ **Villa Santo Domingo**: ☎ 375. On the left when arriving in Santo Domingo. A double room costs $24, and a single $17. Note that it's sometimes closed in low season. Situated between the road (which is empty and quiet) and the gushing river in a very nice, shady site. There are around 20 cabins among the vegetation. The rooms are well equipped (air conditioning and shower), clean and quiet. There is also a bar and restaurant (average prices). One of the nicest mountain hotels in the area (even though it is only at 245 metres/800 feet, you would think you were higher). The hotel organizes walks in the Sierra Maestra in conjunction with the mountain guides' office. During the revolutionary warfare, this was a guerrilla encampment.

WHAT TO SEE

★ **Yara**: 42 kilometres (26 miles) from Bayamo and about 20 kilometres (12 miles) from Manzanillo, this is where the last battle between the native Cubans and the Spanish colonists was fought in 1512. Their chief, Hatuey, died at the stake and became the symbol of their resistance. Near Masó, around 10 kilometres (6 miles) to the south, you can cool down with a swim in the lake of the **Paso Malo** dam (*embalse*).

★ **Santo Domingo**: this pretty area, with banana and coffee plantations, 18 kilometres (11 miles) south of Bartolomé Masó, is the departure point for excursions to Pico Turquino.

HIKING IN THE SIERRA MAESTRA

> **TIP** The best time for hiking in the Sierra Maestra is between November and April. You will need to be fit and to have received some basic training. Take your sleeping bag and a torch (night falls at around 6.30pm).

You will find coffee and tea at the Aguada del Joachín refuge, and you can light a fire. As you will not be able to get fresh supplies from Santo Domingo itself, you will have to buy food before leaving, either at Masó, or in the towns of Manzanillo or Bayamo, which seem to be the best stocked.

The cost of entry to the Sierra Maestra national park depends on the length of the hike: $7.50 for the Comandancia de la Plata; $12.50 for Pico Turquino. You can pay these fees at the mountain guides' office in Santo Domingo. If there is no one there, you can pay the fee to any of the guides you come across en route, but don't forget to ask for a signed receipt.

– **Accompanying guide service**: see their office at Santo Domingo. The rates for guides for hikes range from $7.50 to $15 per person, depending on the weather and the level of difficulty.

The Road from Santo Domingo to Alto Del Naranjo

From Santo Domingo, a fairly well-surfaced road (concrete), leads to the **Alto del Naranjo** panoramic viewpoint, around 5 kilometres (3 miles) to the south. However, the road is on a very steep incline, with difficult bends.

Private cars may use the road, but take great care, especially if it is raining. Use first gear and engine braking, as the slopes are quite nasty. There is a lorry that takes this road, but most people prefer to walk – it's less frightening!

– From Alto del Naranjo there are two possibilities: a path leads to the **Comandancia de la Plata** (3 kilometres/2 miles), another leads to **Pico Turquino**, about 14 kilometres (8 miles) away.

Hike to the Comandancia de la Plata

Allow at least a good two hours from the Alto del Naranjo viewpoint for this good hike, over stony but not particularly difficult paths. Cost: $7.50 per person. Photography is not allowed, and take some water with you.

– From Alto del Naranjo, a mountain path (1 kilometre, 20-minute walk) leads to the **Mesón de Medina** – the *posta de entrada* (entry post) looked after by the peasants. There are a few chairs inside a large hut, from where there is a beautiful view over the valley. Walkers stop here for a rest en route to and from La Plata.

– **La Plata** is around 3 kilometres (2 miles) further on from the Mesón de Medina (allow a 20-minute walk to the museum). This was where Fidel Castro and his men camped at the beginning of the guerrilla war: 'This place was the most familiar to us and the most well-loved. It was where we encountered the first and the last battles of the Sierra Maestra.'

The guide will first of all take you to a little museum containing photos, weapons, a plan of the site and even a sewing machine.

– It's another 10 minutes' walk from the museum before you will finally reach the very heart of the **Comandancia de la Plata**, Fidel Casto's head-quarters. This consists of a series of huts scattered over a steep mountain slope, buried under the thick, tropical vegetation to avoid detection by the enemy. In this poor, hostile and wild corner of the earth the guerrillas built a mini-village that was to be the seed for the new society of which Fidel and Che had dreamt. Each hut had a particular role: kitchen, canteen, joinery, field hospital, grocery and the people's court (where the first verdicts of the Cuban revolution were pronounced), and not forgetting the *invitados* (guests') hut and the one belonging to *radio Rebelde*.

– **La casita de Fidel**: the hut belonging to Fidel Castro, the guerrilla leader, is still standing and has been well preserved. Made of wood, it has a secret trap door for making a quick escape from the enemy during a surprise attack. Inside, Fidel slept in a room with three exits, on a large double bed, built specially for him (a luxury). The large, oil-burning fridge in the kitchenette was carried here by eight men. You will see a hole in his door, which was made by a bullet. To provide light in the hut, there was a generator that produced electricity. Note as well the balcony area where Fidel drank his coffee whilst smoking cigars. Fidel lived in this hut from May to November 1958.

Turquino National Park

Created in 1995, under the auspices of the Ministry of Agriculture, this large, mountainous and wild park, extending over 17,450 hectares (43,000 acres), is home to flora and fauna that are still little known, and poorly documented. Among the animals that a hiker might expect to come across are *capronis*, *jutillas*, iguanas and *amphibios* (endemic). There are also reptiles and numerous birds.

Hunting is forbidden, of course. The regulations on protection are very strict; hikers must be accompanied by a local guide (even though a guide is unnecessary, as the paths are well marked). The peasants who live here are allowed to cultivate the land, but only up to heights of 900 metres (3,000 feet). Alto de Naranjo is at 950 metres (3,000 feet), the Comandancia de la Plata at 1,000 metres (3,200 feet), and Pico Turquino reaches 1,972 metres (6,469 feet).

– **Turquino Peak**: less than 20 kilometres (12 miles) from Santo Domingo, this is a superb but difficult hike amid nature at its wildest. You should allow two days in all to make the trip with Cuban guides, who will explain the flora and fauna. You will leave Santo Domingo around 5.30am, then make the journey from Santo Domingo to the Alto del Naranjo viewpoint (950 metres/3,000 feet), on foot (for small numbers of hikers) or by lorry (for groups). It is 13.5 kilometres (8 miles) from Alto del Naranjo to the summit of Pico Turquino.

The path is well kept and signposted, so it's difficult to get lost. Safety equipment such as steps, guardrails and wooden ladders, have been constructed at critical points. About 9 kilometres (5 miles) from Alto del Naranjo, and after a good three hours of walking, you will reach the Joachín encampment, where the five park rangers live, connected by radio to the valley. The **refuge Aguada del Joaquín** welcomes hikers and there is a water source nearby.

From the Joachín encampment to the Pico Turquino summit is another 3.5 kilometres (2 miles) along a very steep path (2-hour walk). Pico Turquino, the highest point in the country at 1,972 metres (6,469 feet), is often covered by cloud, and bushes hide the panorama. However, 40 metres from the summit is a natural lookout with a beautiful view of the area.

– **From Turquino Peak to the sea**: you can descend Pico Turquino (9 kilometres/5 miles) to La Plata, a village on the coast. The path on the south slope is steeper than the one on the north slope, but well kept. It is difficult, but well worth it. Take a tent and provisions with you.

WHAT TO SEE

★ **The 'Che' Museum**: in Las Mercedes. From Bartolomé head in the Las Mercedes direction. At a junction take the uphill road to the left. After the bridge on the way into the small village of Las Mercedes, take a little dirt track to the left. Open Monday to Saturday 6.30am–5.30pm. Sunday 8am–noon. Admission $1. There is no sign but the little green house is perched on a bend in the road before it wends its way back downhill towards a cross-roads. It is from here that Che commanded Column 8 in 1958 in a hut given over to him by the local peasants. The items on display include the first edition of *Cubano Libre*, of which Ernesto Guevara was the political editor. During the war in question, the rapid dissemination of news was one of the priorities. This small, badly reproduced paper got past the censors and was important in obtaining the support of the peasants.

★ When you've finished in the museum, you can take a quick look at the **Tanqueta del Che** – continue along the street and turn right at the first crossroads along a stone track up the hill. In reality, this small American tank was never actually in Che's possession. It was simply captured by the revolutionaries in the Comandante's pay.

There is another building near the Salto de Jibacoa campsite that may be of interest to Guevara fans. When you come out of the campsite, turn left and go down the road to the lookout point. Continue up the road (for a good 15 minutes) overlooking the bottom of the Jibacoa falls until you get to a crossroads at the top of the hill. Then turn right and with the school behind you and the cloud-capped peaks of the Sierra Maestra ahead, continue along the road until you reach a small, blue hut. It is currently inhabited by country people but they still worship the cult of the Comandante and there are a number of explanations for the bullet-holes in the walls.

MANZANILLO

Situated 67 kilometres (41 miles) to the west of Bayamo, Manzanillo is the second largest city in the province of Granma. From an economic point of view, its main activity is the exportation of sugar (from the neighbouring sugar terminal). The residential districts are located on the peaceful hills bordering the city in the east, down as far as Malecón by the waterfront. The city has a feeling of being cleaner and tidier overall than other cities in Oriente. There are also fewer people and practically no traffic. Anachronistic *coches* (carriages) pulled by horses act as public transport.

This is a port still trapped in the past, enveloped by the *circunvalación Camilo Cienfuegos*, the large ring road south of the city. Built in the 1960s, the ring road is more likely to see pedestrians than cars or lorries. All in all, Manzanillo does not have much of interest to entice visitors to stop.

From a historical point of view, the city has a long tradition of war. Manzanillo was very much involved in the two Wars of Independence (1868 and 1895), and during the 1940s it was presided over by one of just two communist mayors elected in the history of Cuba.

Manzanillo is also famous for its music and the distinctive *son* rhythm. Alsatian organists came here from around 1870. The famous '*órgano oriental*' (the basis of a whole branch of Cuban music) is still made here today. On carnival days, organists play out in the streets until late into the night. They also meet up to play in the small villages in the countryside, like the travelling musicians of old.

USEFUL ADDRESSES

■ **Doctor Juan Alberto Frutos Dominguez**: avenida 6, 121, between calle 7 and 8, Caymari district. This friendly and extremely kind young Cuban doctor knows addresses for private lodgings, and can tell you a great deal about the city.

■ **CUPET Service station**: on the crossroads above avenida Camilo Cienfuegos (the *circunvalación* ring road).

■ **Cubana de Aviación** (map, **1**): calle Maceo, on the corner with Merchán.

WHERE TO STAY

Due to the lack of visitors, there's little choice of accommodation. There are four hotels, but they are not particularly exciting, so you would be better looking for private lodgings. Go and see Doctor Dominguez (*see* 'Useful Addresses') or ask someone in the street.

â **Hotel Guacanayabo** (off map, **10**): avenida Camilo Cienfuegos (the *circunvalación* ring road) on the outskirts of the city. ☎ 54-12. A double room costs from $30. A large building lacking in any charm, but nevertheless functional, with around 100 clean rooms. Air conditioning, hot water and most rooms have a balcony. Swimming pool, bar and cafeteria, all popular among the 'rich' Cubans.

WHERE TO EAT

There are several reasonably priced restaurants around the main square (Parque Céspedes) where foreigners may still pay in local currency (or in convertible pesos).

SIERRA MAESTRA

MANZANILLO

✕ **1800** (map, **20**): on the Merchán. Open noon–3pm, 6–10pm. A meal costs less than 20 pesos ($1). A tiny place with panelled walls and leather chairs. There is a never-changing casserole, fried pigs' trotters and sometimes even tinned spaghetti. Incredibly low prices and laid-back service.

✕ **Las Américas** (map, **21**): Parque Céspedes, on the corner of Martí and Maceo. ☎ 530-43. Open daily noon–2pm and 7–10pm. Very pleasant place with large French windows covered by small, wooden pillars, opening onto the street. Traditional Cuban cuisine at less than $5.

✕ **El Yang Tse** (map, **22**): Parque Céspedes, on the corner of calle Merchán and Maceo. This is where the Cuban flag was flown for the first time in 1898. Fans, mauve table-cloths, red shutters, some Chinese screens, but only one Chinese dish. The same food is served here as elsewhere. Just about OK. A meal costs less than $5 and you can also pay in pesos.

WHERE TO HAVE A DRINK

Under the arches all around the main square are numerous little kiosks offering a typical 'man's drink' known as *cóctel d'ostiones*. This consists of tomato juice, tabasco and a kind of shellfish that is extracted from its shell for the occasion. The cocktail slips down very nicely and is said to have two benefits – the first is that it im-proves the memory, and you'd better ask the locals about the second . . .

❦ **Cafetería La Fuente** (map, **23**): Parque Céspedes, on the corner of calle Maceo and calle Merchán. Open 24 hours. Central, airy and spacious with a large terrace with tables and blue parasols. Good for a drink and inexpensive snacks.

NIGHTLIFE

El Balcón (off map, **10**): Avenida Camilo Cienfuegos, before the Hotel Guacanayabo. Also known as the Mirador del Caribe, this is a motel with a cabaret. Reasonable prices payable in local currency.

Cabaret Costa Azul (off map, **24**): On the Malecón, opposite the sea. Open Thursday to Sunday 8pm–2am. Admission 10 pesos.

The liveliest establishment in the city at the end of the week, you can drink and eat (desserts) here, as well as dance and take part in the dancing shows. Outside, there is a large terrace benefiting from the sea breezes. Inside, there is a bar, Las Cuevas de los Piratas. Another bar is situated in a concrete boat on the waterfront.

WHAT TO SEE AND DO

★ **Parque Céspedes**: the pretty main square square is famous for its Moorish-style gazebo, known as 'La Glorietta'. Otherwise, it's just a nice area, with nothing of particular note.

★ There are some fine, Moorish-style houses around the port and a pretty view over the city from the hills (you can see the sea).

– **Carnaval**: takes place each year in the last week of August, and lasts for four days. It's the most popular celebration in the city.

IN THE AREA

★ Less than 10 kilometres (6 miles) away, is **Demajagua**, the hacienda that belonged to Carlos Manuel de Céspedes where, in October 1868, the 'Father of the Nation' rang a bell to free all his slaves, marking the start of the first War of Independence. In so doing, he showed that there couldn't be emancipation of one set of people if he himself was oppressing another. Today it is a little **Historical and Archaeological Museum** that complements a visit to his birthplace at Bayamo.

LEAVING MANZANILLO

By Bus

🚌 The bus terminal is 2 kilometres (1 mile) to the east of the city, on the road to Bayamo. Services are erratic, as there isn't enough fuel.

– For **Yara** (twice a day, 23 km), **Bayamo** (twice a day, 65 km), **Pilón** (83 km) and **Santiago de Cuba** (192 km).

By Train

🚆 This is the better option. The railway station is in the north of the city. Foreign visitors must pay for tickets in dollars.

– For **Bayamo**, **Santiago**, **Guamo** and **Havana**: one train a day, journey time 16 hours to Havana.

PLAYA LAS COLORADAS

You'll find this beach 18 kilometres (11 miles) south of Niquero, 73 kilometres (45 miles) from Manzanillo and just 12 kilometres (7 miles) from Cabo Cruz, the westernmost point of Oriente. On the way you pass through the strange little village of Campechuela, where all the houses are painted yellow and pink. You then cross a great expanse of uninteresting sugar plains before emerging at the beach.

Even though it's beautiful, it's not really a place for bathing. Instead it's steeped in Cuban history: this is where Fidel Castro, Che Guevara and their 80 followers landed from the *Granma* yacht in December 1956 after a turbulent voyage. If you want to see where the Cuban Revolution began and understand it better, then this is where you should come before heading into the Sierra Maestra.

SIERRA
MAESTRA

A Brief History

A total of 82 men (not the 25 for which the yacht was designed) left for Mexico aboard the *Granma* (the shortened form of 'grandma') with weapons, luggage and ammunition. Their average age was 27; Che Guevara was 28.

The crossing was a nightmare – the boat was overloaded and the crew suffered from seasickness. There were not enough supplies and a violent storm led to one man falling overboard. The voyage should have taken five days but took seven, which upset the plans of the terrestrial branch of the M-26, the rebel movement founded by Fidel Castro.

Celia Sánchez, a member of the movement (and future wife of Castro) waited in vain for their landing on the beaches of Niquero, with jeeps and lorries at the ready. On the specified date, as there was no sight of them on the horizon, she left. In Santiago the young Frank País, believing that the *Granma* had already landed, embarked upon an armed insurrection, which ended in failure.

At dawn on 2 December 1956, Castro, who was impatient for war (and also as a result of an incorrect map), decided to head straight for the coast – a mistake that was to cost him dearly. The *Granma* ran aground on a mud bank near Los Cayuelos, 2 kilometres (1 mile) from Playa Las Coloradas (where Celia Sánchez was still keeping watch). Apparently, there was no one there to greet the expedition. The men therefore set sail in the *Granma*'s lifeboat. They were out of luck though, as the lifeboat sank beneath their weight and that of their equipment. The heavy armaments also disappeared. They ended up throwing themselves into the water with their individual weapons and scant equipment.

At Los Cayuelos they waded through mud up to their waists, working their way painfully through the mangrove. They had to push through spiny bushes and thorny plants and tread on a maze of mangrove roots. They were surrounded by clouds of mosquitoes. 'It wasn't so much a landing as a shipwreck,' wrote Che Guevara later. The men were weak, exhausted, starving and demoralized, plus they had already been bombarded by Batista's air force. They finally reached dry land, but the results were far from glorious. Having scattered due to attack, barely a dozen of the guerrillas reached the Sierra Maestra.

Yet this 'army of shadows and ghosts' was to succeed in resisting and in reorganizing itself, as a result of the extraordinary solidarity of the *guarijos*, the peasants in the area. From the Sierra Maestra, Fidel and his guerrillas, who were determined to win, set out for Havana. They finally came away victorious, overturning Batista two years later.

WHAT TO SEE

★ **The *Granma*'s landing site**: coming from Niquero, you will first arrive at the entrance to the site. Admission $1. On the right of the road is a replica of the *Granma* in a hangar. There is a little museum and *bohío* (peasant hut) further on. The museum visit is conducted by a guide, but you have free access via the path to the landing site. The actual site of the landing is about 1.5 kilometres from the museum, at the end of a path that leads to the sea – which is more like a mangrove swamp than a great ocean.

★ **Replica of the *Granma***: externally, this does look like an authentic yacht, but it's a very clever copy. The boat is set on a lorry frame which cannot be seen from the outside. The guide will show you the inside if you want to see it. The original *Granma* is in Havana.

★ **Portada museum**: open daily until 5pm. This could be a lot better presented and thus more interesting – probably only worth a visit if you're in no hurry. There's a large map of the area detailing the first movements of the revolutionary guerrillas. Another room contains 21 portraits of the first guerrillas to die in combat.

★ **The peasant hut**: contains photos of the *campesinos* who gave their support to the guerrillas immediately after the landing.

★ Further south, at **Cabo Cruz**, there are beautiful cliffs with lots of birds at a protected site that's part of the National Park of the *Granma* Landing.

The Coastal Road from Pilón to Santiago

> **TIP** Allow at least 2 to 2 hours 30 minutes (each way) for this 175-kilometre (108-mile) trip between Pilón and Santiago de Cuba. However, faced with such a landscape, you will want to take your time. Ideally, you should try to stop off overnight at somewhere like Chivirico. Note that there's no fuel station between Pilón and Santiago, so fill up before leaving. Note also that the absence of road signs can make the road dangerous at night.

Pilón, a sugar town with 12,000 inhabitants, 91 kilometres (56 miles) south of Manzanillo, has nothing of particular interest other than a huge, rather ugly, factory.

As the road meanders to the Caribbean coast, it crosses a col in Sevilla Arriba. From there on the landscape gradually becomes more broken, but the sierra itself is not really in evidence, other than in a slight change of vegetation. Then suddenly the horizon opens onto the sea and you find yourself on one of the most beautiful coastal roads in Cuba, with virtually no traffic. Apart from a few carriages, *guarijos* on horseback and pedestrians waiting desperately for an unlikely bus, there isn't a soul around. However, this part of the coast is definitely inhabited, with modest villages dotted along the ocean in the most outlying region of the island.

Up until around 1996, the area's only connection to the rest of the Oriente was a single road that was full of potholes, scattered with stones and cut into by river beds. Today, the now surfaced road (except for one or two longish strips around La Plata and Las Cuevas) is in good condition and accessible to all tourist vehicles. Drivers just need to slow down to navigate them without problem.

The road hugs the contours of the land, passing around the foot of the high mountains of the Sierra Maestra and running along the Caribbean Sea, almost without interruption, from Pilón until about 16 kilometres (10 miles) before Santiago. There really is no comparison. From time to time some indentations reveal little beaches of every description – white, golden or black sand or shingle. And this is a surfer's paradise on the days when the wind whips up good waves. All the same, note that there are some fairly treacherous currents on this coast. Out at sea, the water reaches awesome depths of over 7,000 metres (23,000 feet). This wild, remote, virgin part of Cuba will attract those with a spirit of adventure. Note that there's very little to buy in the villages in these parts.

The road winds along the wave-washed coastline and, after La Palmita, it is just one stunning beach after another. After the baseball pitch and the La Palmita bridge there is an attractive black, sandy beach on the right before the road starts to make its way back inland.

USEFUL ADDRESS

■ **CUPET service station**: on the road going down from Sevilla Arriba, on the way into Pilón. Generally open daily 24 hours.

WHERE TO STAY AND EAT

▲ ✕ **Hotel Punta Piedra**: around 10 kilometres (6 miles) from Pilón. A room costs $25, breakfast not included. A small motel in the Cubanacan chain. The rooms are nothing special but perfectly decent if you discount the noise of the air-conditioning generators. A fair few tourists on cycling tours stop here as it is the cheapest in the region. The uninteresting food is slightly on the expensive side.

▲ **Hotel Marea del Portillo**: around 20 kilometres (13 miles)

from Pilón is an attractive half-moon beach, protected from the wind by a ring of mountains. So tempting were these conditions to investors that they managed to persuade the government to authorize the Canadians to build two concrete hotel blocks here.

▲ **Hotel El Farallón del Caribe**: ☎ (23) 59-70-81/82/83. Rooms cost $35–50 per person per day for full board depending on season. It is a large W-shaped building nestled against the mountain specially dug

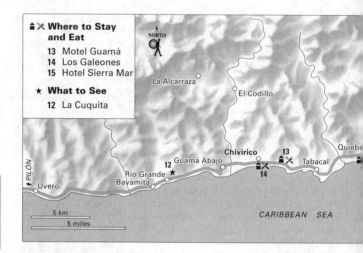

Where to Stay and Eat
13 Motel Guamá
14 Los Galeones
15 Hotel Sierra Mar

★ What to See
12 La Cuquita

out for the purpose. Pale blue bathrooms and gigantic, well-equipped bedrooms. It soon becomes packed in season and the overspill is passed on to the Hotel Marea del Portillo, *above*. These hotels have three advantages – first, everything is included, and they're good places to enjoy some fine food if you are beginning to tire of the lack of gastronomic delights on the island. Second, you can hire scooters to explore the region – a good option as there's only one bus per day to Santiago. Finally, the del Caribe is the only hotel to organize trips to the tiny paradise islet of Cayo Blanco. A 5-minute boat trip and you can enjoy the gorgeous white sandy beach and go scuba-diving.

≜ Private lodgings: as ever this is the cheapest and nicest option. Officially there are no rooms for rent in the region but, as always, you are sure to find somewhere if you ask discreetly in the little villages along the coast (La Plata, La Mula, Uvero, Río Grande, etc.).

≜ Motel Guamá (map, **13**): on a hill 7 kilometres (5 miles) east of Chivirico, on the Santiago road. There is a nice area of tables outside where diners can enjoy some good grilled fish, among other things. Note that prices tend to be set according to how rich the customer looks, so don't hesitate to bargain. In theory, a meal shouldn't cost more than $4, and $2 is reasonable for a plate of fish and vegetables. The motel also rents out rooms, but they leave so much to be desired that they can't really be recommended (in case of emergency they're around $10).

≜ The other establishments, **Hotel Los Galeones** (map, **14**) at Chivirico, ☎ 26-435 and **Hotel Sierra Mar** (map, **15**) at Playa Sevilla (10 kilometres/6 miles east of Chivirico), ☎ 26-213, are a lot more expensive. They have nothing available for less than $106 for a double (although this includes everything from breakfast to dinner and all drinks).

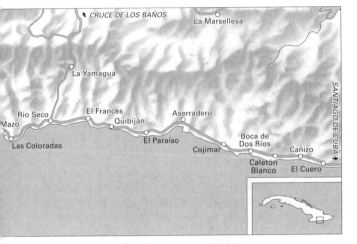

UVERO TO EL CUERO

WHAT TO SEE

★ **La Plata**: 50 kilometres (31 miles) from Pilón, just before Pico Turquino. This is where the revolutionaries experienced their first victory over Batista's troops in January 1957. It is not possible to get to the historic site of **El Jigüe** by car – access is on foot or horseback.

– Just after the bridge across the river Palma Mocha is another beach in the **Las Cuevas** cove. It is pebbly but the surf is good and the waves ideal for body-boarding. Note that the seabed drops away rapidly and you are soon out of your depth.

– Before you reach **El Ocujal**, after the bridge and the old road (now submerged under a riverbed), there is a small white-sand cove.

– Shortly before Mula another river emerges at the sea. On the right is a small pool filled from time to time by waves – ideal for kids.

★ You will pass through **Uvero**, the site of another victorious battle for the *guérilleros* in 1957. Opposite an apple-green bus shelter, before the hamlet of Papayo Playa and before you get to Uvero, a battered, salt-encrusted sign to the left reads a **Cuquita** (map, **12**). This is a small thermal spa in the middle of nowhere. For the nominal one peso admission fee you can swim in the 38°C (100°F) water that is naturally rich in potassium, magnesium and other sulphides and is said to make the skin softer. There is apparently a team of doctors on hand to apply the mud. There is also a small bar with a straw-covered roof.

★ **Chivirico**: situated 107 kilometres (66 miles) to the east of Pilón and 68 kilometres (42 miles) to the west of Santiago de Cuba, on the Pilón–Santiago road. A small, laid-back town (around 4,000 inhabitants), full of local colour, wedged between the mountains and the sea. The climate here is drier than elsewhere, due to low rainfall. There are some beaches near the village. You can make an overnight stop here.

SANTIAGO DE CUBA   DIALLING CODE: 226

The second largest city in Cuba, capital of the Oriente and the 'Cradle of the Revolution', is a delightful colonial city. There are no high-rise buildings here, and the city has a mainly horizontal profile. Buildings have at most one or two storeys, and there's a forest of red-tiled roofs, a profusion of balconies, wrought-iron grilles, long verandas and windows in turned wood. The districts slope gently down to the bay, giving a nice perspective on the architectural unity of the city. The centre is on a pocket handkerchief scale and is organized around three squares – Parque Ajedrez, Parque Céspedes and Plaza Dolores, which everyone refers to as El Búlevar.

The population is the product of a mix of races, including Spanish, Caribbean, Indian, black African, French and Asian. The city is also rich in cultural traditions – music, poetry, the Festival of the Caribbean, and the famous July Carnival, the wildest in the country.

A Brief History

Founded in 1514, Santiago holds the title of oldest city in the Americas. It had a regrettably famous mayor, Hernán Cortés, who, finding his role too routine, left to conquer Mexico. The city thus served as a base camp for the colonization of the continent, and as the first landing port for African slaves. It lost this position at the end of the 16th century to Havana. As it was attacked on numerous occasions by pirates and other sailors, the city built a number of forts. In 1662, an English squadron seized it and many monuments were burned.

Between 1791 and 1804 people from the French colony of Haiti, who were fleeing the slaves' revolts, sought refuge in Santiago, which is why there is such a significant French influence here.

The French colonists from Haiti brought the coffee culture to the region. The planter Victor Constantin established himself on the Gran Piedra mountain with 700 slaves, where he produced coffee in Cuba for the first time, in 13 haciendas (including the famous La Isabélica plantation that you can visit today). The Tivoli district, above calle Padre Pico (the oldest street in Santiago), was the home of colonial families who had become wealthy through this trade. At the time, Tivoli was the French district. There is other evidence of the colonists' cultural contribution in surnames, names of buildings, troubadour songs and the *tumba francesa,* a dance inspired by the minuet and re-interpreted by the Haitian slaves of the French colonists. Napoleon Bonaparte's doctor, Francesco Antommarchi, a fellow Corsican, went into exile in Santiago. He died here in 1838 and was buried in the Santa Ifigenia cemetery.

In the 19th century, Santiago was, of course, one of the main centres of the revolt against Spanish rule, and was very active in the two Wars of Independence.

26 July 1953

On that day, when the carnival was in full swing, a young lawyer, Fidel Castro, led around 100 men in an assault on the Moncada barracks, a symbol of Batista's dictatorship. The aim of the operation was to seize weapons (while the soldiers were tipsy) for the revolutionary war, and to administer a decisive blow to the dictatorship by attacking the second fortified city in the country.

Unfortunately, despite the diversionary attacks led by Abel Santamaría on the hospital and by Raúl Castro on the law courts, the military force was overpowering. Over 1,000 of Batista's men retaliated in a bloody manner. There were summary executions of the wounded and atrocious torture of the survivors. In total, there were 61 deaths. One of the women in the command (the sister of Abel Santamaría), who refused to speak, found herself carrying her fiancé's eye to prison; he had also been involved in the assault.

Castro conducted his own legal defence, concluding with the famous words, 'History will absolve me!'. Despite the failure of the operation in military terms, the Cuban Revolution had begun, with the formation of the 26 July Movement.

Carnival

The Santiago carnival is the most popular and the wildest in Cuba. After a gap of many years, it is now celebrated again in the streets at the end of July (roughly 18–27 to coincide with the national holiday).

As with the Brazilian carnivals, preparations are made long in advance, including the making of costumes and orchestra rehearsals. There is a fantastic procession of floats covered with flowers and young women. Music is played everywhere. Groups of musicians and dancers, *comparsas,* take to the streets, unleashing an atmosphere that defies description. Neighbourhood groups from the Santiago district *(cabildos)* naturally have a large part to play in the carnival. They are formed of around 30 participants (the queen and her cortege) and of around a 100 subjects.

For those who aren't lucky enough to be in Santiago at carnival time, the neighbourhood groups put on shows throughout the year and rehearse frequently, thus providing a glimpse of the festival. In contrast with the Rio carnival, there is no violence, and you won't find corpses in the streets of Santiago after the euphoria of the celebrations has died down.

The most well known of the neighbourhood groups are the Karabali Izvama and Olugo. The Karabali, recognizable by their costumes of 19th-century Spanish courtiers, have their headquarters in calle Pio Rosado (and Maceos). They usually rehearse on Tuesday and Friday evenings.

The Birthplace of *Son*

'Like me, *son* was born in the province of Oriente, in the east of Cuba,' declared Compay Segundo, a 90-year-old musician representing the famous Cuban traditional music (Afro-Cuban).

It all began with the combination of Spanish romantic music with African rhythms. One theory is that it all started at the end of the 19th century with an

English photographer, Walter Huma and a Cuban, Pepe Sánchez. Huma lived in Santiago, and could not understand why the musicians in this city were happy to play compositions that were exclusively of Spanish origin, rather than letting the Cuban genius flourish. He complained to local singers about the lack of any Cuban musical identity. His reproach came to the attention of Pepe Sánchez. As a result, the latter began to compose new pieces in a revolutionary style. He created the bolero '*Tristeza*', and invented the song with two quatrains instead of the stereotypical tunes articulated around two syllables. Thus *son* was born.

As for the instruments, this type of music would not exist without the *tres* guitar, with three double strings. In 1890 a peasant called Nene Manfugas used a *tres* for the first time, creating the *changüí*, the basic *son*. This instrument, from Guantánamo, made its appearance at Santiago at one of the carnivals. A few years later, musicians from this city combined the *tres* with the traditional Spanish guitar, thus inventing the *son maracaibo*, a new musical form.

Then, as now, this type of music was interpreted and sustained by *trovadores* (singers) in the Santiago music halls, particularly in the Casa de la Trova on calle Heredia, the best place for music in Santiago.

Among these *trovadores* was the young Máximo Francisco Repilado (the future Compay Segundo). Born in 1907 at Siboney, and influenced by the music of Santiago and the Oriente, he left for Havana in 1934 to pursue a career as a musician, alongside his job as a cigar roller. Compay, who was the maestro and torchbearer of *son*, was forgotten for decades before being rediscovered in Cuba at the end of the 1990s, and he has been applauded in Europe. This recognition late in life was something of a triumph. Compay plays an *armónico*, a guitar that he made himself. It is a traditional *tres* guitar with seven strings, with the third double-strung.

His musical style, which had long been considered peasant and provincial, won over the Cuban public. Along with him, a whole generation of *son* musicians, who had been abandoned in favour of salsa groups, made a reappearance centre stage. According to Compay Segundo, 'salsa has no heart. Whereas *son* is just the opposite, tender and romantic'.

Musicians will more often than not be playing *Chan Chan*, the most popular of his songs, virtually every evening in Santiago, to packed rooms. Prestigious line-ups from Santiago such as Eliadés Ochoa and the Familia Valera Miranda recognize Compay as their master. Elsewhere on the island other groups – Los Guanchés, the Septeto Turquino group (with the French musician Cyrius), the Septeto Habanero, or Típico Oriental – perpetuate in their own way the spirit of this musical genre.

La Tumba Francesa

It all began at the time of the French Revolution. In 1790, Toussaint Louverture headed up an army of slaves and succeeded in chasing the French colonists out of Haiti. These landowners sought refuge in large numbers in Santiago de Cuba. They maintained their interest in the dances that existed in their royal court in France, such as minuets and rigadoons. Today, as a result of this migration, Santiago retains the last trace of these forgotten dances: minuets that are danced to the rhythm of African drums – the *Tumba francesa* (*tumba* means drum in Bantu). The songs are sung in French dialect.

An association, the *Sociedad de la Tumba Francesa*, founded in 1862, upholds the tradition and organizes shows. It is run by the *Reina*, the queen of the *tumba*, who lives in Havana. In Santiago, Sarah Quiala Venet, sister of the *Reina*, ensures the smooth running of the association and deals with the choreography. On the evenings of the shows, the 24 members of the association dance the minuet, in 18th-century costume with a Caribbean twist, in a large hall with walls bedecked with old photos.

– **La Tumba Francesa** (map I, B2): calle Los Maceos, on the corner of San Bartolomé. Open Monday to Saturday 8am–4pm. Every Thursday the show starts at 8pm and lasts for 1–2 hours.

GETTING THERE

By Air

➊ There's a small **Havanatour** office at the **Aeropuerto Internacional Antonio Maceo** that can provide some rudimentary information on the town. It's next to the customs office and is open 24 hours a day.

By Taxi

The only means of getting to the centre is by official taxi, which costs around $5–7. There are no private taxis as all Cubans driving taxis without official licences are prevented from entering the confines of the airport.

ORIENTATION

– **Road names**: many roads running from the centre of Santiago have two different names. The oldest name pre-dates the Cuban Revolution and is often the name of one of the saints of the Catholic Church. The second name is more recent, but many people are still not used to them. For example, calle San Basilio is called Bartolomé Masó, but the people of Santiago still call it San Basilio. The addresses in the listings use the name by which they are most commonly called, followed by their equivalent. So be careful when you are asking the way or for an address.

GETTING AROUND

– **On foot**: even though the city is very spread out, the old town is not all that big. Allow 10 minutes to walk from the main square to the port, along calle Heredia.

– **By bicycle**: is practical and inexpensive, but not all that easy due to the many hills. For bicycle hire, *see* 'Useful Addresses'. Watch out for theft. You can sometimes get someone to keep your bike safe in their house for a few pesos an hour.

– **By taxi**: many official taxis park near the Hotel Casa Grande in Parque Céspedes. Expect to pay $2 for a trip between the cathedral and the Hotel Santiago. A taxi for the day will cost around $15. A cheaper option (as long as you are discreet) would be to take a private *taxi particular*.

– **Horse-drawn carriages**: these only go along the port and provide a regular shuttle from one end of Paseo Alameda to the other. They are pulled by tired old nags and the most sophisticated are covered in a kind of plastic sheet. They can carry up to 10 people, with passengers sitting facing each other on wooden benches. This mode of public transport was in existence well before the Revolution, and has persisted due to the lack of fuel. Each carriage has a licence plate and is obliged to undergo regular technical checks – the horses are theoretically also given regular veterinary check-ups, although this seems to depend on the goodwill of the owner.

USEFUL ADDRESSES

Tourism and Culture

🆋 **Office of cultural information** (map II, D1, **1**): Patio de los Dos Abuelos. ☎ 23-267. It's not a tourist information office, but a small office (in a pretty courtyard) that issues a bulletin every Tuesday giving cultural information, including listings of shows, exhibitions and concerts in and around Santiago.

■ **Rumbos agency**: corner of calle Heredia and General Lacret (San Pedro), opposite the Hotel Casa Grande. Has a little official information on the city and organizes excursions to places around Santiago.

■ **Havanatur**: calle 8, 54, between Avenida 1 and 3. ☎ 861-52. Open daily 8am–6pm.

■ **Roots Travel** (map II, C1, **2**): calle San Gerónimo (Sánchez Hechevarrí) 569, between Reloj (Mayía Rodríguez) and calle San Agustín (Donato Mármol). ☎ 86-119. This branch of the agency in Havana offers the same sort of information – hotels, private lodgings, car hire, details of the *Carnaval* and the Festival of the Caribbean. It is run by Elsa who has extensive knowledge of the town and region. If you are a beach lover, she can organize day trips to the Hotel Bucanero (south of Santiago) for a reasonable price. It's best to phone in advance rather than just turn up.

Banks and Currency Exchange

■ **Banco Nacional de Cuba** (BNC; map II, B1, **3**): Plaza Céspedes, next to the Hotel Casa Grande. Open Monday to Friday 8am–4pm. Changes travellers' cheques and you can withdraw dollars using Visa or MasterCard. You must show your passport.

■ **Banco Casa Cadeca** (map II, C1, **4**): calle Aguilera 508, between Reloj (Mayía Rodríguez) and Clarín. Open Monday to Saturday 8.30am–6pm; Sunday 8.30am–12.30pm. You can withdraw dollars using Visa or MasterCard. Minimum withdrawal is $100, maximum $5,000 (in theory). You must show your passport.

■ **Banco Internacional de Comercio** (map II, C1, **5**): corner of calle Felix Peña (Santo Tomás) and calle José Antonio Saco (Entremada). Open Monday to Friday 9am–5pm. Cash withdrawals with Visa and MasterCard. Again, you must show your passport.

Telephone

■ **Centro de Llamadas** (international telephone exchange; map II, B2, **6**): calle Heredia, in Plaza Céspedes. Open daily 24 hours. Fax service (in the morning) and telephone service using official rates, and therefore expensive.

Transport

🚆 **Terminal de Ferrocarril** (railway station; map I, A–B1): Paseo Alameda north of the port, level with calle Santa Isabel. Enquiries office open daily 24 hours (see 'Leaving Santiago').

🚌 **Terminal de omnibus interprovincial** (intercity bus station; map I, off D1): almost 4 kilometres (2 miles) from Parque Céspedes, on Avenida de Los Libertadores, at the junction with the *Circunvalación* ring road (see 'Leaving Santiago').

◐ **Cubana de Aviación** (map II, B1, **7**): corner of José Antonio Saco (Enremada) and San Pedro (General Lacret).

■ **Bicycle hire**: (map II, A–B1, **8**): Mariano Corona, 512, between calle José Antonio Saco and calle Roben. Open daily. Fees are $3 for a bicycle for a day (7am–7pm).

■ **Car hire**: most companies have offices at the airport and in the city.

You are advised to book a car in advance, particularly in high season.
– **Havanautos** The main office is in the grounds of the Hotel Las Américas (map III, A1, **25**. ☎ 420-11), and there's another at the airport, ☎ 910-14.

– **Transautos** has an office under the Hotel Casa Grande (Heredia; map II, B1, **24**), ☎ 861-07. Other offices are in the Hotel Santiago (corner of Avenida de las Américas and Plaza Ferreiro; map III, A1, **26**), ☎ 411-21; the Hotel Las Américas (corner of Las Américas and General Cebreco; map III, A1, **25**) and at the airport (☎ 922-45).

– **Micar** (map I, B3, **9**): corner of calle Trocha and calle Morro. ☎ 86-001. The office is in a service station to the south of the town. The easiest way of getting there is to ask for the Oro Negro service station (see below).

Service Stations

■ **CUPET Bujia service station** (map I, B3, **9**); corner of Avenida de los Libertadores and Avenida de Céspedes. The nearest to the town centre – less than 1 kilometre to the north of the Moncada

---

■ **Useful Addresses**

🚆 Railway station
🚌 Bus station
9 Service station and car hire

🏠 **Where to Stay and Eat**

12 Rafael Silva Gonzales
13 Dra Zaida Moraleza Infante
17 Evangelina Portuondo

🍸 **Nightlife**

57 Cabaret San Pedro del Mar
58 Tropicana

★ **What to See**

65 Moncada Barracks museum
67 Antonio Maceo
68 Abel Santamaría Museum
69 Birthplace of Frank País
70 Santa Ifigenia cemetery

SANTIAGO
DE CUBA

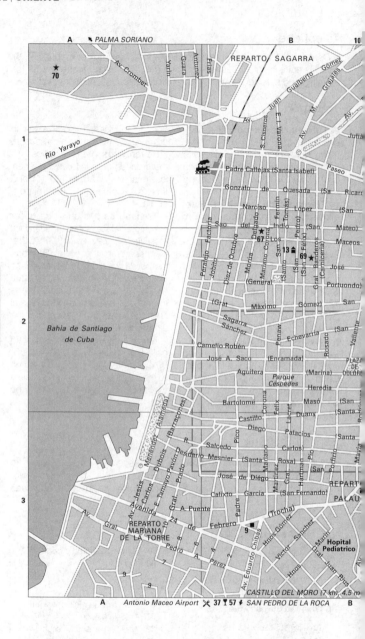

A ↖ PALMA SORIANO   B   10

REPARTO SAGARRA

★ 70

Río Yarayo

Bahía de Santiago
de Cuba

REPARTO S.
MARIANA
DE LA TORRE

1

2

3

Padre Callejas (Santa Isabel)

Gonzalo de Quesada

Narciso López

★ 67   13 🏛
       69 ★

(General

Máximo Gómez)

Sagarra
Sánchez

Camelio Robén

José A. Saco (Enramada)

Aguitera

Parque
Céspedes

Heredia

Bartolomé

Castillo
Diego

R. Salcedo

Desiderio Mesnier

José de Diego

Calixto García (San Fernando)

(Trocha)

9 ■

REPART
PALAU

Hopital
Pediatrico

CASTILLO DEL MORO (7 km, 4.5 m

A   Antonio Maceo Airport ✈ 37 ⚓ 57 ↓ SAN PEDRO DE LA ROCA   B

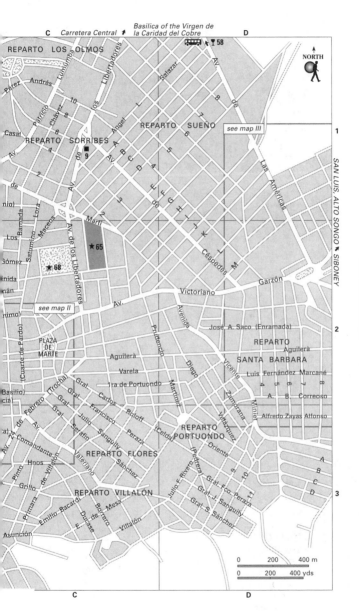

SANTIAGO (MAP I)

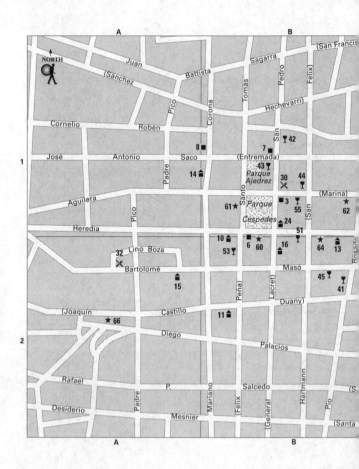

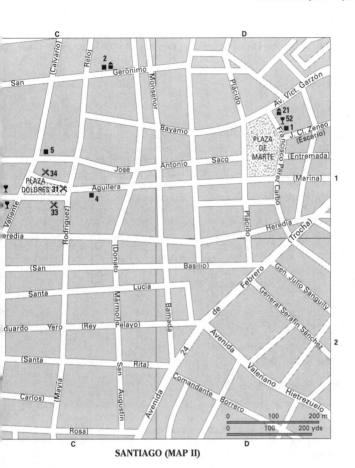

SANTIAGO (MAP II)

33	La Taberna de Dolores	**51**	Casa de Trova
34	Casa Don Antonio	**52**	Patio de los Abuelos
		53	La Claqueta
Y Where to Have a Drink		**54**	Discoteca la Iris
		55	Le Club 300
33	La Taberna de Dolores		
40	La Isabelica	**★ What to See**	
41	La Taberna del Ron		
42	Licorería-Bombonería Universo	**60**	The Cathedral
43	La Fontana	**61**	Diego Veláquez museum
44	El Baturro	**62**	Emilio Bacardí museum
45	1900	**63**	Carnaval Museum
51	La Casa de la Trova	**64**	José María Heredía's house
		66	Museum of the Clandestine
Y Nightlife			Struggle
50	Casa Artex		

barracks. Open daily 24 hours.

■ **CUPET service station** (map I, B3, **9**): corner of 24 Febrero (Trocha) and Avenida Eduardo Chibas (carretera del Morro).

■ **Oro Negro CUPET service station** (map I, off B3): carretera Central. About 2km (just over 1 mile) north of Plaza de la Revolución, on the road out towards the cement works.

Shopping

■ **Librería La Escalera** (map II, B2, **13**): calle Herdia 265, between San Félix (Hartmann) and Pío Rosado (Carnicería). This is a nice little second-hand bookshop in a country where the production of literature has been reduced to a mere trickle. It's full of books (in Spanish and published by the government) on the Revolution and music, etc. Sometimes musicians sit themselves down on the stairway and sing of their troubles – so

it's worth a quick look for this alone.

■ **Farmers' market** (map III, A2, **11**): a lovely little market on the corner of calle 10 and . . . calle 10, near the Hotel Santiago roundabout. When you arrive at the roundabout (coming from the town centre), turn right at the service station for Cubans. The tiny market is hidden behind the adobe walls to the left. Needless to say, any purchases should be paid for in Cuban pesos.

WHERE TO STAY

In the City Centre

Casas Particulares

Santiago has many rooms for rent, at prices ranging from $15 to $25 for a double room for a night. Facilities are gradually improving, even by Cuban standards. Most rooms for rent are indicated by a small blue sign in the street. Things change fast and places come and go, so the establishments listed below are ones that look most likely to stay the course.

♠ **Elsa Vandramme** (map II, C1, **2**): calle San Gerónimo (Sánchez Hechevarría) 569, between Reloj (Mayía Rodriguez) and calle San Augustín (Donato Mármol). ☎ 86-119. Fax: 26-357. A double room costs $20, breakfast included. Halfway up a small, steep street, guests receive a warm welcome from Elsa and an even better one from Campbell, her dog. Elsa has a small, attractive colonial house in which she hires out a room that is practically up to European standards (air-conditioning), painted in retro pastel shades. Shared bathroom.

♠ **Ydania Lardoet Creach** (map II, B1–2, **10**): Heredia 104, between Mariano Corona and Santo Tomás (Felix Peñal). ☎ 26-879. Around $15 for rooms in this little house (negotiable) right in the centre of town. The unmatched furniture is distinctly second-hand and the two rooms have a very flimsy partition between them. There isn't much light but at least this keeps it cool. Only really for emergencies.

♠ **Iris and Felipe's** (map II, B2, **11**): calle Santa Lucia (Joaquín Castillo Duany) 206, between Santo Tomás (Felix Peña) and Mariano Corona.

SANTIAGO (MAP III)

■ **Useful Address**

11 Farmers' market

🛏 **Where to Stay**

18 Sr Angel Luis Silveira Hernández
19 Margarita Gachassin, Lafite N
20 Isidro Fonseca Sosa
21 Margarita Roca
24 Hotel Villa Gaviota Santiago
25 Hotel las Américas
26 Hotel Santiago

✕ **Where to Eat**

35 Paladar Salón Tropical
36 Panadería Cubalse
37 Cafetería Cubalse

🍸 **Where to Have a Drink, Nightlife**

26 Espantasueños
46 El Traylor or El Chorrito
47 Bar de la Casa del Caribe
56 La Maison

☎ 22-713 (the neighbour Georgina's number). The two small rooms leading off a little patio cost $20–25. Decent but nothing special although Felipe's welcome goes some way to compensate for this.

🛏 **Rafael Silva Gonzales** (map I, C2 **12**): calle Reloj (Mayía Rodríguez) 201, between Trinida (General Portuondo) and San Germán (General Máximo Gómez). ☎ 24-440. The attractive double room on the top floor of house costs $25, including orange juice and coffee (and garage). There is a nice, plant-covered terrace area. Recommended, especially since Rafael is so friendly.

🏠 **Dra Zaida Moralez Infante** (map I, B2, **13**): calle San Pedro (General Lacret) 265, between Habana (G.M. Gómez) and Maceo. ☎ 22-190. Zaida is a retired surgeon and her daughter is a journalist. Three spotless rooms on the ground floor of a house with only limited appeal, with shared bathroom with lukewarm water. A double costs $20. A good place to stay, even if the rooms don't look particularly inviting.

🏠 **Ana Castillo Enamorado** (map II, A-B1, **14**): calle Mariano Corona 564, between calle Enrramada (José A Saco) and Aguilera. A double room costs $20 in this large, very central and very well maintained apartment. Three decent bedrooms with air-conditioning or fan open onto a long, cool and pleasant room good for lounging in the rocking chairs. Clean, shared bathroom. Breakfast and other meals available on request.

🏠 **Nieves's** (map II, A2, **15**): calle Bartolomé Masó (San Basilio) 167, between Padre Pico and Mariano Corona. ☎ 542-08. A room for two costs $15–20, depending on size. In a popular, very central part of town, this has several small rooms in a pleasant courtyard, in some kind of small huts used for meteorological readings. One room is off the dining room. The others are quieter. Shared bathroom, except for one en-suite. A small kitchen for the use of guests makes this very good value for money.

🏠 **Norma Arias Puentes** (map II, B2, **16**): calle Lacret 703 (altos), between calle Heredia (Plaza Céspedes) and calle Bartolomé Masó (San Basilio). ☎ 53-169. Situated 50 metres from the cathedral, thus very central. On the first floor are two

doors: ring at the one opposite the coloured glass door. Just one double room with a very high ceiling and no window, but clean and spacious, costing $20. The paintwork looks like it dates from pre-Revolutionary times and the panelling on the walls stops halfway up. Cold water. Only in emergencies as it's relatively expensive.

🏠 ✕ **Evangelina Portuondo** (map I, B3, **17**): calle Palau 57, between Trocha (Avenida 24 de Febrero) and Reloj (Mayía Rodríguez), Reparto Palau. ☎ 20-982. Ask for Eva, whom everyone in the area knows. Not the quietest of places due to the neighbour's cockerels and Dobermanns and the noise from nearby radios. Eva is a motherly figure who does all that she can to make her guests feel at home. She is happy to prepare meals for itinerant tourists and her cooking certainly makes a visit worthwhile. The three rooms on the first floor have decent facilities. There is a shared bathroom with a nickel bath and big shower and hot-water taps in the bedrooms (water heater). Highly recommended. If you don't speak Spanish, book via Elsa who works at Roots (see 'Useful Addresses').

Hotels

🏠 **Hotel Rex** (map II, D1, **21**): avenida V. Garzón, virtually on the corner with Plaza Marte. ☎ 535-07. Small, local and one of the cheapest hotels in the city ($15–$22 for a double/twin room) with 25 simple, yet well-kept rooms (eight with hot water). Air-conditioning, telephone and TV in some. Rooms 32–35 have large windows with a superb view over the rooftops to the mountains in the distance.

🏠 **Hotel Casa Grande** (map II, B1, **24**): Heredia 201, between San Pedro (Gal Lacret) and San Félix (Hartmann). ☎ 866-00. Fax: 860-

35. Rooms with breakfast cost $96–112 (plus $20 over Christmas and New Year). This is the jewel in the crown of the Accor group's accommodation on the island – a fine colonial building, very attractively renovated and overlooking Parque Céspedes. Delightful rooms have minibar, air-conditioning, TV, safe, etc. Some overlook the noisy road, while rooms at the back are very quiet but have no view. There are also some more attractive rooms overlooking Parque Céspedes. The restaurant is not particularly good and service tends to be rather slow. Guests can enjoy breakfast in the lovely roof-garden bar overlooking the whole town with the Sierra Maestra in the distance. Non-residents pay $2 for access. The colonnaded terrace area is an excellent spot to watch the comings and goings in the square.

Outside the City Centre

Casas Particulares

♠ **Sr Angel Luis Silveira Hernández** (map III, A2, **18**): calle L 203, between 4 and 5. Reparto Sueño. ☎ 274-77. Opposite a laundry, next to small café and not far from the hotel Santiago. Very well kept – some of the family live in the United States, and others sing in the cabarets staged for tourists. There are two big rooms with air-conditioning: a double costs $20. Good if you have your own transport.

♠ **Margarita Gachassin Lafite N.** (map III, A2, **19**): Luis Fernandez Marcané 352 (altos), on the corner of calle 10, Reparto Santa Barbara. ☎ 418-40. The breeze-block entrance is a bit off-putting. There is just one double room to let at $20 and it's rather dark. Only for people with their own car as not very close to the town centre.

♠ **Isidro Fonseca Sosa** (map III, A1, **20**): calle Luis Fernández Marcané 307, between calle 9 and 10, Reparto Santa Barbara. ☎ 427-79. A double room costs $20. Situated 3 kilometres (2 miles) from Parque Céspedes in a residential district further out, but quiet. The house is run by a portly gentleman and has one room downstairs (with fan) and another upstairs with a separate entrance opening onto the terrace (and external staircase). Again, you really need your own transport.

♠ **Margarita Roca** (map III, B1, **21**): calle 10, 407, between 15 and 17, Reparto Vista Alegre. ☎ 42-142. A double room costs $20 in this attractive little blue house, covered in plants. You will be greeted by Margarita and her husband, both of whom are doctors. There are three rooms to let – the nicest is the first on the right when you go in (more windows as it's in the corner of the house). Shared bathroom. Recommended.

Hotels

♠ **Hotel Villa Gaviota Santiago** (map III, B1, **24**): avenida Manduely 502, Reparto Vista Alegre. ☎ 41-368 or 41-370. Fax: 8-166. A double room costs $50 in low season and $55 in high in this attractive little complex of chalets in the residential area of Santiago. There are also several rooms for rent in the colonial houses. They are often very well equipped – bathrooms with hot water and rattan furniture. The area as a whole has something of the 24-hour pretentiousness of Miami about it, but this hotel is more intimate than the huge neighbouring establishments. Attractive swimming pool.

♠ **Hotel Las Américas** (map III, A1, **25**): corner of avenida de Las Américas and General Cebreco. On the approach to the city, next to the Hotel Santiago. ☎ (537) 33-42-38 or 33-40-90 (reservations office in Havana). Fax: 860-75. Long, white building set amid attractive palms with the look of a 1950s American hotel, mostly frequented by Cubans. A double room with TV, radio, telephone and air-conditioning costs $56. Take earplugs as it's on one of the busiest roads. Bar, swimming pool and disco, plus reasonably professional hospitality.

🛏 **Hotel Santiago** (map III, A1, **26**): avenida de Las Américas and Plaza Ferreiro. ☎ 870-70. Fax: 871-70. A double room costs $115, excluding breakfast. The hotel is the work of a young Cuban architect and the city is very proud of it. This impressive, coloured, metallic structure cost several million dollars and is run by a Spanish hotel group. The facilities and prices are as you would expect, and it's popular with tour groups.

WHERE TO EAT

In the Town Centre

☆ Budget

There are lots of little stalls in the doorways of houses where you can eat very cheaply. Otherwise, if you want to pay in pesos, there's a long row of state eateries on calle José Antonio Saco (Enramada). Some – such as **Las Novedades** (on Enramada between San Felix and San Pedro; map II, B1, **30**) – open 24 hours a day. There are normally very few tourists, but they're perfect if you feel like a late snack.

– *Paladares* are springing up like mushrooms here, but many barely see out the day. Few are official and many take advantage of their guests.

– There are also a number of sandwich stalls, including: on avenida 24 de Febrero (Trocha), before you get to the docks (map I, A3); on avenida Jesús Menendez (Alameda) near the stage (map I, A2–3); and on avenida de los Libertadores towards the railway station, after the CUPET service station (map I, C2).

☆☆ Moderate

✖ **Las Gallegas** (map II, B2, **31**): Bartolomé Masó (San Basilio) 305 (altos), between San Félix (Hart-mann) and San Pedro (Gal Lacret). ☎ 247-00. One of the best places to eat in Santiago, if only because of its two characterful but friendly managers. The tables are wobbly, the flowers imitation and the TV permanently tuned to a soap opera. The usual dishes are available for $8–12: *pollo frito* (fried chicken), *bistec de cerdo* (pork chops) or *pierna de cerdo asado* (roast pigs' trotters) with the traditional *frijoles, morros y cristianos* (black and white beans) on the side.

✖ **Doña Cristy** (map II, A2, **32**): Lino Boza 8, between Padre Pico and Bartolomé Masó (San Basilio). Open for lunch and dinner. Not far from cathedral square, a nice district during the day, but not so safe at night. Excellent hospitality and good cooking thanks to the enthusiastic and impressive hostess. Cosy surroundings, if a little tacky (collection of glasses). A main meal with drink costs around $10. Good meat dishes and an excellent house lobster with rice, black beans and salad. Very good desserts such as homemade crème caramel. If you come by car, ask the manager if someone can keep an eye on it while you are eating.

✗ **La Taberna de Dolores** (map II, C1, **33**): Plaza Dolores, on the corner of calle Reloj (Mayia Rodríguez). This former rum distillery is as popular with Cubans as it is with tourists. It's more a bar than a restaurant as there's often no food available. However, on a good day, you can enjoy some chicken between a cou-ple of beers. *See* 'Where to Have a Drink'.

✗ **Casa Don Antonio** (map II, C1, **34**): Plaza Dolores. Large, Spanish-style dining room with a high ceiling and quiet atmosphere. Good food at less than $15 per head for a meal and sometimes there's even a choice of local standards on the menu. Check your bill carefully.

Outside the Town Centre

✗ **Paladar Salón Tropical** (map III, A2, **35**): Fernández Marcané 310 (altos), between 9 and 10, Reparto Santa Barbara. Open noon–midnight. The atmosphere is slightly subdued, the air-conditioning as high as it will go and there's irritating supermarket-style muzak. A meal costs around $10 for food that's much the same as everywhere else with a few slightly original dishes – pasta and *buñuelos de chatino* (cassava fritters). Good welcome and very pleasant despite the slow service.

✗ **Panadería Cubalse** (map III, B1, **36**): corner of calle 4 and calle 15. A meal costs less than $5 at this state bakery offering the best chicken in town at lunchtime, freshly fried in front of you for 90 centavos. Everything is ultra-fresh, it's often well stocked and payment is in pesos. Sandwiches are also available. The tables outside on the veranda are a good place to sit and watch the world go by.

✗ **Cafetería Cubalse** (map III, B1, **37**): avenida General Cebreco, between 13 and 15. Meals cost $5–7. This big cafeteria was formerly a restaurant strictly reserved for Santiago's diplomatic personnel. It has been redecorated and now the walls provide an almost Andy Warhol-type pop-art backdrop. Large and surprisingly tasty pizzas make a change from the usual Cuban attempt at the Italian staple. This is a flashy joint for Cubans with spending power to demonstrate their kudos. As a result there are often private taxis waiting near by.

WHERE TO HAVE A DRINK

There are several places where visitors can quench their thirst, as you would expect given the strong Caribbean influence. You can choose your drinking hole on the basis of whether you prefer the sound of the guitar, the maracas, the *tres* or the salsa.

♼ **La Taberna de Dolores** (map II, C1, **33**): Plaza Dolores, on the corner of calle Reloj (Mayia Rodríguez). A popular old rum distillery on two levels. The ground floor is very smoky and the first floor has an attractive patio where a band of old men often serenade the drinkers. The beer here is fresh, but only comes in bottles. Payment can be made in pesos.

♼ **La Isabélica** (map II, C1, **40**): corner of Aguilera and Calvario (Porfirio Valiente). Open daily 24 hours. Old house where you can drink the best coffee in the city – unsurprising since it comes from several local plantations. The *café con ron* (café with rum) is absolutely delicious. Lots of Cuban regulars come here for their morning *cafecito* as payment is accepted in pesos. The waitress is quick to refill your cup. The dining room is rather small with old furnishings, including dark wooden beams, heavy chairs and an old painting on the wall. If you'd like to know more about the place, then ask for Julio (César) who's friendly, very bright and speaks good English. He's here every day from 2–4pm and from 8–11pm.

La Taverna del Ron (map II, B2, **41**): calle Pio Rosado (Carnicería) 358 between Bartolomé Masó (San Bailio) and Santa Lucía (Joaquín Castillo Duany). Open 9am–9pm. A nice cool drinkery under the rum museum where a glass of rum costs less than $1; *mojitos* and *canchacharras* are slightly more expensive. Entrance is via the museum itself or through a small door on calle Pio Rosado. It doesn't tend to serve Havana Club, preferring Matusalem Añejo, Legendario and Ron Caney, which are more aromatic and less common on the black-market.

Licorecía-Bombonería Universo (map II, B1, **42**): calle San Pedro (General Lacret) and José Antonio Saco (Entramada). Halfway down the street to the right of the Cubana de Aviación office. The entrance is not very obvious from the road, and this grocery hides itself timidly behind curtains. If you can't find it, there is always a local policeman on the beat who you can ask. It's one of the only places in Santiago serving draught beer, generously poured with a slight head for 40 centavos. There's also a small selection of rums at lower prices than the shops that take foreign currency. Note that it closes relatively early.

La Fontana (map II, B1, **43**): calle San Pedro (Gal Lacret) and José Antonio Saco (Entramada). Almost opposite the Cubana de Aviación office. This bar is for professional tourists and the first impression is

that it's frequented by prostitutes. However, it's simply a place where Cubans bring their 'girlfriends'. Despite this, it's an interesting place – you very much get the impression than deals are being done among small-time black-marketeers. It's not the place for foreign women to wear miniskirts.

El Baturro (map II, B1, **44**): corner of Aguilera and San Felix. One of the oldest establishments in the city, and very dark and dusty. Note the heavy counter in varnished, carved wood. Little choice of drinks, extremely primitive food and a working-class clientele, so it's basically for those who like propping up the bar.

La Casa de la Trova (map II, B2, **51**): calle José María Heredia, between San Félix (Hartmann) and San Pedro (Gal Lacret). Relatively touristy during the day, since it's among the local crafts shops. The bar on the patio is a nice place for writing postcards and getting to know the locals. It's quite often a venue for bands (see 'Nightlife').

1900 (map II, B2, **45**): calle Bartolomé Masó (San Basilio), between Pio Rosado (Carnicería) and San Félix (Hartmann). Generally open 1pm–midnight. Closed Tuesday. This old, aristocratic mansion looks as if it has come straight out of a 1950s film. It has been under renovation for a long time and is periodically closed for further work. There are tall arches, a marble floor, colonial furniture in dark wood, antique chandeliers and some paintings. It is unclear whether the old-timers in the orchestra are holding up their instruments or vice-versa. There are a couple of things available to eat (such as fried eggs) but they seem to find serving two or three customers as exhausting as a wedding party of 500. You can pay in pesos, so prices are much lower than elsewhere.

Outside the Town Centre

♥ El Traylor or **El Chorrito** (map III, A1, **46**): avenida de las Américas, opposite the Las Américas hotel. A nice little bar with painted walls open onto the avenue attracting an unusual cross-section of Cuban society – the bubbly young customers show a predilection for what they think of as trendy Western clothing. A few *jineteras*, closely watched by the police, make regular rounds.

Don't go early as it doesn't really get busy until after midnight.

♥ Bar de la Casa del Caribe (map III, B1, **47**): calle 8. The cheapest in town, with payment in pesos. This smashing little bar (attached to a pleasant little park) is ideal for an 11am aperitif. Rum is particularly cheap. The ancient jukebox still plays some pre-Revolutionary tunes.

NIGHTLIFE

♥ Espantasueños (map III, A1, **26**): Hotel Santiago, avenida de Las Américas and Plaza Ferreiro. Admission $10 per couple. As this is the hotel disco, the clientele are predominantly tourists. The only real attraction is perhaps its open roof.

♥ Casa Artex (map II, C2, **50**): El Patio Colonial 304, calle Heredia, between Calvario (Porfirio Valiente) and Pio Rosado (Carnicería). ☎ 548-14. Open Wednesday to Monday 9am–1am. Admission $3–5. Beer is $1. Entrance is via a souvenir shop where Cuban girls often lurk to find someone to pay them in. No visit to Santiago is complete without calling in to the Casa Artex, a highly recommended place to enjoy a drink and *moverse la cintura* (literally, to 'shake your belt'). Try not to mind the plastic furniture. It has a very good reputation for decent bands and musicians (*salseros* and *soneros)* to get everyone dancing.

♥ La Casa de la Trova (map II, B2, **51**): calle José María Heredia, between San Félix (Hartmann) and San Pedro (Gal Lacret). Near the cathedral and Parque Céspedes, to the right of the Casa Grande hotel. Open Tuesday to Sunday to 1am. This is the home of *son* with a full, rich musical history. Anyone who is

anyone has played here – just take a look at the series of portraits. Depending on the time of day, the bands play in the lounge, bar or courtyard (after 10pm). If you're short of cash you can join the locals watching through the bars of the window. Otherwise there's an admission fee (the amount depends on who's playing) to watch comfortably from a goatskin-covered chair.

♥ Patio de los Abuelos (map II, D1, **52**): Pérez Carbó in Plaza de Marte. ☎ 232-67. Admission $2. Up some stairs is a shady, narrow terrace with yellow walls. From 9.30pm there are concerts, traditional songs and poetry. There isn't the same throbbing entertainment as at other venues, rather a more family atmosphere. Also temporary exhibitions of work by local artists.

♥ La Claqueta (map II, B2, **53**): calle Santo Tomás (Felix Peña), between Heredia and Bartolomé Masó (San Basilio). Just after the Rialto cinema. Another popular place with Cubans that looks strangely like a children's playground. On some evenings you have to fight your way in. Dancing to live groups. Don't take any valuables with you as there are often pickpockets around.

♥ Discoteca La Iris (map II, C1, **54**): Aguilera 618, between Calvario

(Porfirio Valiant) and Pio Rosado (Carnicería); near Plaza Dolores. Admission $5. Downstairs is a relatively uninteresting bar, and on the floor above a disco plays Cuban music (records and live bands). It has not been open long and is centrally located, two facts that should assure its popularity with both Cubans and switched-on tourists.

☙ **Club 300** (map II, B1, **55**): Aguilera, between San Pedro (General Lacret) and San Felix (Hartmann). Admission $2 (obligatory cloakroom for handbags). A strange kind of nightclub were the DJ plays music from cassettes lined up on racks like dominoes and people sometimes get onto the bar to dance. The big sofas scattered around give it the air of an office foyer – but it's a top

place to be seen for the ultra-rich clientele of the Casa Grande, catwalk models and local wannabes. Lots of people but the atmosphere isn't too suffocating. Unsurprisingly it's very popular with Cubans themselves.

☙ **La Maison** (map III, A1, **56**): avenida Mandulay 52, between 3 and 1, Reparto Vista Alegre. Admission $5. A superb colonial mansion linked to the famous cabaret in Havana, full of green plants and a lot more cosy than its cousin in the capital. The upper echelons of Santiago society come here to watch the turgid fashion shows. These are not particularly exciting in themselves but the setting is pleasant enough to warrant popping in for a drink.

In the Area

☙ **Cabaret San Pedro del Mar** (map I, off B3, **57**): Carretera del Morro, next to the Hotel Balcón del Caribe, 7 kilometres (4 miles) southwest of Santiago. Admission $5. Less touristy and more traditional Cuban, this cabaret extends onto a pretty, open-air terrace overhanging the Caribbean Sea. Very pleasant spot in the evening where you can eat (adequate main courses for around $7) while listening to a live group. Guests dance during the concert, as well as afterwards (to records).

☙ **Tropicana** (map I, off D1, **58**): Autopista Nacional, at the 1.5-kilo-

metre mark via the *Circunvalación*, exit 5. Situated around 6 kilometres (just under 4 miles) northeast of the city centre. ☎ 430-36. As a rule there's one show at 10pm and another at 1am. Admission $2 and two seating areas with prices of $30 and $45 per person respectively (with a bottle of rum for four). Gigantic, open-air cabaret seating around 1,000, similar to the Tropicana in Havana, with tables set out in a semicircle around the stage. Impressive lighting effects and flashy decor that must have cost a fortune. Very touristy, but the shows are of a high quality.

WHAT TO SEE

★ **Parque Céspedes**: sometimes just known as Cathedral Square, this is at the very heart (*el corazón*) of Santiago and is the centre of activity in the city. The shady square is surrounded by old, interesting buildings – the Hotel Casa Grande, the cathedral, the Velázquez Museum, banks and the international telephone exchange – and is so charming you could while away hours here.

Cubans stroll around and arrange to meet people at the end of the day, or simply watch the world go by from benches in the shade. On Saturday evenings, the *Santiagueros* like to make the effort to go into town. Dressed in their finest, they will walk round the square again and again in order to see and be seen – a leisure activity for hard times.

Parking is usually fairly difficult as there's only one side where you may park. Don't hesitate to part with a dollar for the car patrolmen who are always there, day and night.

This square is also a favourite with pimps and *jineteros* and *jineteras* (prostitutes), who wait for the tourists. Likewise, there are increasing numbers of uniformed and plain-clothed policemen to keep an eye on them, particularly at the entrance to the Hotel Casa Grande.

★ **The cathedral** (map II, B1–2, **60**): Parque Céspedes, south side. The original building dates back to the 16th century, but it has been destroyed so many times that there is very little left of it to see. The latest reconstruction dates back to 1932 in neo-classical style – not very ethereal. The building is surrounded by a raised platform that gives it a stunning appearance. Inside, the atmosphere and the decor (in grey and blue) is a little depressing. This is a far cry from the splendour and gold of colonial baroque architecture. Some of the altar panels are in embossed silver. The choir stalls date from the beginning of the 19th century.

★ **Museo de Ambiente Histórico Cubano** (Museum of Colonial Art; map II, B1, **61**): calle Félix Peña 612, Parque Céspedes west side. Open Monday to Saturday 8am–6pm; Sunday 9am–1pm. Built in 1516, this is the oldest colonial mansion in Latin America – a massive construction built around a courtyard, with a long, Moorish-style balcony with a wooden grille. It was originally the home of Diego Velázquez (1599–1660) who lived on the first floor, while the ground floor housed the first gold-smelting centre in the colonies.

– The **ground floor** contains carved furniture and four-poster beds. In the dining room there's a fine dresser, French carvings and objets d'art, a superb screen inlaid with birds in mother-of-pearl and ivory, and some paintings from the 18th and 19th centuries.

Some steps lead to a courtyard in blue and white, from where you can enter a room containing fine engravings of Havana, and the kitchen. Another room also has pretty engravings of Santiago and rich, Spanish colonial furniture.

– The **first floor** features an original carved, cedar ceiling, a vast bedroom with balcony overlooking the square and an interesting Flemish painting called *La Danse Villageoise* (The Village Dance). In a corner there's a view of the original foundations of the house, and at the back is a wooden door also dating back to the original construction.

★ **The Emilio Bacardí Museum** (Municipal Museum; map II, B1, **62**): corner of calle Pio Rosado (Carnicería) and Aguilera. Open Tuesday to Saturday 9am–8.30pm; Sunday and Monday 2–8.30pm. Admission charge. The museum was set up by the great rum producer Emilio Bacardí in a colossal, neo-classical mansion fronted by Corinthian pillars. This is *the* great museum of art and history in the province of Oriente.

– On the **ground floor** are bronze amphorae from the *conquistadors*, memorabilia and testimonies to colonization, torture instruments, a colonial 'chopping block', a santería throne and drum, weaponry and much more. The many display cases contain mementoes, personal effects and clothes worn by leaders and general freedom fighters, as well as documents and newspapers. There's access to a paved alleyway where the facades of 18th and 19th century houses were reconstructed.

– The **first floor** houses a section of paintings, including four interesting panels – *El alegoría de las estaciones*, a pretty work on hangings and gauze. Another painting worthy of note is the *Interior de la casa de Juan Bautista Sagarra*, from 1864. This portrait of a 19th-century bourgeois family shows each individual and each object in its proper place according to social rank and hierarchy – the son is studying with his father, the daughter is embroidering with her mother, the children are playing, there's the dog and cat, and the black nanny right at the back. Canvases by José J. Tejada Revilla show portraits of peasants and drunkards. Another famous portrait artist is Federico Martinez Matos, whose works include a fine self-portrait and interesting *Garibaldino and American Ballerina*.

Along to the right of the museum is the yellow facade, decorated with pink stucco, of an elegant colonial mansion. On the left-hand side is the impressive neo-classical facade of the **Palacio Municipal**.

★ **The Carnival Museum** (map II, C1, **63**): corner of Pio Rosado (Carnicería) and Heredia. To the right of the Bacardí Museum along Pio Rosado alleyway. Open Tuesday to Sunday 9am–5pm (Saturday to 9pm). Housed in a superb late 18th-century colonial mansion complete with traditional long veranda, this tells the story of the Santiago carnival during the great periods of history – when Cuba was a colony, a republic and after the Revolution.

The colonial period details the start and evolution of the carnival in old photos. In the republican period there are beautiful carnival capes, some painted or embroidered by hand, others showing political slogans. There's also the front page newspaper announcement of the attack on the Moncada barracks (*see* 'A Brief History', *above*). Representing the post-Revolutionary period is a room with the *tumba francesa* percussion instruments and the *conga santaguiera*. There are also huge papier-mâché carnival heads and model floats, as well as party costumes. Sometimes there is traditional music playing in the courtyard.

★ **Calle Heredia** is lined with picturesque colonial mansions that now house schools, public libraries and some administration offices. The street contains a brilliant display of ironwork and elegant windows. As you walk along, look through the open doors into the beautiful courtyards and admire the huge, attractively furnished rooms that exude coolness and comfort. Sometimes, on a Saturday evening, there may be a street festival.

★ **The house of José María Heredia** (map II, B1–2, **64**): calle Heredia 1260. Open Tuesday to Sunday 9am–9pm (closed Sunday afternoon). The great Cuban poet was born here on 31 December 1803 and died in Mexico in 1839. He was driven out of Cuba by the Spanish for conspiracy and only came back once to the country in 1836.

The first room contains his writing desk, original furniture belonging to his family and a watercolour of the poet by the artist Bofill, as well as letters and documents. The former bedroom has an exhibition of old porcelain.

A visit to this house is not only interesting from a literary point of view, but is also a moving experience. The place still has the feeling of being 'lived in'. Nowadays, it is the permanent headquarters for literary activities in the city, and a meeting place for international poets.

★ **The old quarters**: from Parque Céspedes, follow (in no particular order) the streets and alleyways that run down to the port to encounter the real day-to-day life of Santiago. **Calle Padre Pico**, with its steps, is one of the most picturesque. Right at the top of the steps there is a very good view over the forest of red-tiled roofs of the old city.

The **port area** along avenida Jesús Menéndez (also known as Paseo Alameda) features numerous buildings and warehouses dating back to colonial times or to the republic. These include the port authorities building, the ferry terminal, the customs house and the old cigar factory with its ochre facade. You can take a slow ride in a trap along the avenue as far as the Santa Ifigenia cemetery.

★ **The Moncada Barracks Museum** (map I, C2, **65**): calle General Portuondo (between G. Moncada and avenida de Los Libertadores). Open Monday to Saturday 9am–5pm; Sunday 9am–1pm. The barracks have been transformed into a secondary school, but some rooms have been preserved as a museum. At the entrance on the left (as you face the barracks) you will see bullet holes in the facade from the attack. The guided tour is quite moving, as you might expect. Rooms in chronological order:

– **Room 1**: exhibits on the slave uprisings.

– **Room 2**: the great Wars of Independence 1868–78 and 1895 against the United States. Photographs of concentration camps in 1898 (for Cuban peasants in the areas of uprising) include ones that look just like Nazi concentration camps. Other periods covered are the founding of the Cuban Communist Party and the overturning of the Machado dictatorship.

There are moving photos of the attack on the Moncada barracks, and a model. Uniforms stained with blood, but with no bullet holes suggest that most of the prisoners were tortured and assassinated. You can also see the lorry that took Castro to prison.

– The **Repression Room** contains torture instruments and photos. Highlights are the first weapons used in the revolutionary war, including Che's (a type of mortar), Raúl Castro's uniform and Fidel's woollen waistcoat (for the chilly nights in the Sierra Maestra), secret newspapers and rare photos of Che.

– In the **Victory Room** are photos and testimonies of the entries into Santiago, Havana and the Bay of Pigs, plus a model of the *Granma*.

★ **The Museum of the Secret Struggle** (map II, A2, **66**): calle G.-J. Rabi, south of calle Padre Pico. Open Tuesday to Sunday 9am–5pm. This museum, which complements the Moncada Barracks Museum, is situated in a former police station which was attacked by revolutionaries on 30 November 1956 (if the photos are anything to go by, they must have used dynamite). Originally a fine, 19th-century mansion, the museum is really for specialists or those interested in the Cuban revolution as there are lots of photos and detailed descriptions of the events.

On the ground floor is Frank País's submachine gun and the original flag of the 26 July Movement. On the first floor much space is devoted to Frank País, the city's hero. Exhibits include various objects (camera, small printing press, etc.) for the secret newspapers, letters from Che, medicines from the maquis, fragments of homemade bombs, etc.

★ **The birthplace of Antonio Maceo** (map I, B1–2, **67**): A. Maceo 207 (and Elena). Open Monday to Saturday 9am–5pm. This modest mansion in a working-class district is steeped in history. General Maceo was born here on 14 June 1845 and died in the battle of Punta Brava, on 7 December 1896. In the first room there are numerous testimonies, including the speech of General Gómez on the death of Maceo, plans for the 1895 military campaign and one of the original flags, as well as front pages from newspapers, memorabilia and personal effects.

– Other heroes' mansions and museums that you can visit include:

★ **The Abel Santamaría Museum** (map I, C2, **68**): in the old Saturnino Lora hospital (next to the Moncada barracks). Closed Sunday. Abel Santamaría was one of those who organized the attack on Moncada with Fidel Castro.

★ **The birthplace of Frank País** (map I, B2, **69**): calle General Banderas 226, between José Gómez and Los Maceos. Open Monday to Saturday 9am–5pm. ☎ 527-10. The son of a Protestant minister, brought up on the Bible and Christian ethics, País was an excellent artist and a precocious young man. Nothing from his school days would suggest that he was destined to become one of the urban leaders of the rebel 26 July Movement. A great organizer and military leader, País was Fidel Castro's right-hand man on the plain. He was assassinated by Batista's henchmen when the guerrillas were slowly progressing towards victory. He was only 23. His funeral at Santiago was attended by a huge crowd. His mother, a widow with three children, died of grief.

His birthplace is now a museum where you can see his bedroom, his school desk and a small internal courtyard. His death mask is in one room (with some strands of his hair) along with photos taken after his death.

★ **The Santa Ifigenia cemetery** (map I, A1, **70**): end of avenida Crombet. Open daily 7am–6pm. Admission charge. If you come here on foot, beware of pickpockets in the district around avenida Crombet. This is the great cemetery of the colonial aristocracy and the republican bourgeoisie. There are grandiloquent mausoleums and tombs, from a time when they were designed to perpetuate the image of the deceased after death, and serve as an indication of the status and wealth of the great families. In particular, you will find the burial places of the great heroes of the Wars of Independence (recognizable by the national flag) and those of the Revolution (with the black-and-red flag of the 26 July Movement).

To the left of the colossal entrance is the mausoleum of José Martí. Next to it is the memorial to the hero of 26 July. To the right of the central walkway, on the path that runs across at right angles and is a continuation of that of José

Martí, is the tomb of Antonio Maceo. In the central walkway, on the left, is the tomb of Carlos Manuel de Céspedes. You will also find graves of Frank País, General Moncada and those who fell in the attack on the Moncada barracks. Also in the central walkway, a commemorative stone encloses the remains of Moreau Bacardí, founder of the rum factory. In the first walkway on the right of the entrance is the unusual tomb of Francisco Antommarchi (Mattei), who was Napoleon's last doctor on St Helena. He died in Santiago in 1838.

★ **The Antonio Maceo Monument**: on the outskirts of the city, towards Guantánamo. This is an impressive tribute to a great general of the 1895 war. In an open space, around 20 *machetes* surround the statue of the General on his horse and pierce the sky, symbolizing pride and rebellion (huge steel rails).

– **Festival**: just as interesting, although less well known than the Carnival, is the Festival of the Caribbean. This takes place every year in the first week of July. It is an opportunity for the people of all the region's different islands to meet up, and is a celebration of all the different art forms – cinema and video, poetry, sculpture and, of course, music. For information ☎ 42-285. Email: caribe@cultstgo.cult.cu.

Around Santiago

Northwest of Santiago

★ **Basilica of the Virgen de la Caridad del Cobre**: around 20 kilometres (12 miles) west of Santiago, on the Bayamo road. There's a signpost on the left. You can't miss it. Open daily 6.30am–6pm. Mass is held on Sunday at 8am, 10am and 4.30pm.

This is one of the most popular places of pilgrimage in the Oriente (and on the island). In santería, the Virgin appears in the image of Ochún, the goddess of love, sensuality, motherhood, fresh water and gold. 'The Virgin of Charity' is the subject of special worship and each year, on 8 September, Cubans flock to the sacred hill to pay homage to the Vierge del Cobre, the patron saint of Cuba.

Built in 1927, the basilica takes its name from a copper mine (*cobre* means copper in Spanish), still in use and visible from the south side of the hill.

There is a car-park behind the church, near the buildings that are home to the sisters of the Order of the Hermanas Sociales and the missionaries of Mother Theresa of Calcutta. Next to the car-park is a secondary entrance to the building that leads to a small chapel with an altar decorated with a gold statue of the Virgin. The main entrance to the church is on the other side of the building.

Inside the basilica are numerous votive offerings brought by the many pilgrims. The American writer Ernest Hemingway left the medal he received when he won the Nobel Prize for Literature. As the medal was later stolen (though subsequently recovered), it is now housed in a secure vault and is no longer on display in the basilica.

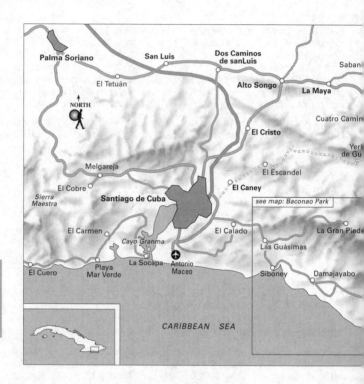

South, Towards Castillo del Morro

The drive along the **Santiago bay** makes for a lovely afternoon's outing.
Rather than taking the quickest route, follow the road to the cement works.
You will pass lots of lorries kicking up clouds of dust, and the works
themselves are a clear indication of the Soviet over-expansion to which Cuba
has been subjected. Opposite the cement works the vast, ugly factory looks
as if it has come straight out of a science-fiction cartoon. Once you have left
these eyesores behind, the road snakes along the coast through some lovely
hills, with glimpses here and there of small bays and secret coves.

More adventurous travellers might like to take a trip to the fishing village of
Cayo Granma. Not many tourists make it this far, and with good reason –
there are no hotels or private lodgings. But it's in an idyllic spot that's also
accessible by boat from the marina in Punta Gorda ($3 for the return journey,
departure times negotiable). For information ☎ 86-314 or 91-446. Fax: 86-
308. This is where sailors stop to replenish their water supplies and take a
shower. Once a year, the national jet-ski championships take place at the
marina. At other times, it's extremely quiet and there are rarely more than 10
boats to squabble over moorings.

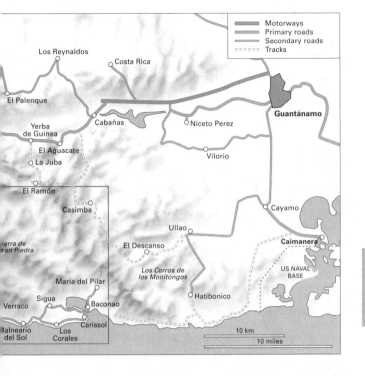

Motorways
Primary roads
Secondary roads
Tracks

Los Reynaldos
Costa Rica
El Palenque
Yerba
de Guinea
Cabañas
Niceto Perez
Guantánamo
El Aguacate
La Juba
Vilorio
El Ramón
Casimba
Cayamo
Ullao
ierra de
ran Piedra
El Descanso
Caimanera
Los Cerros de
los Monitongos
US NAVAL
BASE
María del Pilar
Sigua
Verraco
Baconao
Hatibonico
Balneario
del Sol
Los
Corales
Carissol
10 km
10 miles

SANTIAGO
DE CUBA

SANTIAGO REGION

If you continue along the coast you come to **Laguna de Estrella**, an excellent spot for a swim and more popular with Cubans than tourists. It's effectively the nearest beach to Santiago. There's a risk from pickpockets, so don't carry any valuables here.

★ **Castillo del Morro**: 7 kilometres (4 miles) south of Santiago. Admission $1.50. This impressive fortress guarding the bay was built by the Spanish in 1663 to protect Santiago from pirate attacks and from other sailors. It is said that every evening a chain was drawn across from one bank to the other, barring access to the capital of the Orient over night. It also served as a prison for freedom fighters. Today it's known as the Piracy Museum, although this gives rather an exalted view of its contents as the collections are pretty small – some weapons and explanatory placards in old glass cases. Note the ramp that was used to raise the cannonballs onto the bastions. Next door is a chapel offering a fine view over the bay from the highest level; you can see Cayo Granma and its fishing village. In front of the fort are two beautiful bronze cannon from 1748. Made in France, they bear the coat of arms of Louis XV and came from two ships: the *Pourvoyeur* and the *Comte de Provence*. The lighthouse was also made in France in 1846. It turns on a mercury bath almost 3 metres (9 feet) in diameter.

WHERE TO STAY

♠ Danilo Romeo Vazquez and Carmen Sanchez Roque: avenida Caribe 2, Reparto Ciudamar. ☎ 91-430. Email: carmen@cmar.scu.sld.cu. A double room costs $25, breakfast included. Note that it is quite difficult to get to. Take the Castillo del Morro road until well after the cement works, then turn off down the road leading to the sea. Follow it as far as Bahia de Estrella then turn left. Continue along the road that snakes under a big blue-and-white house with red blinds where Castro stays when he comes to Santiago (the area is then crawling with security men). Follow the road uphill for a short distance to a 'give-way' sign. Turn left down towards the bay as if heading towards the factory on the other bank. On a bend with two small dirt tracks follow the one straight ahead for 50 metres and you should arrive at Orieta's house (if you get lost ask for La Casa de Orieta). There are four little chalets that look like gnome homes, laid out with such care and attention it is hard to believe that you are still in Cuba, with old family furniture, satellite TV and a big paved terrace. Added to this, Orieta's cooking is renowned to guests and Cubans themselves. It's ideal if you're after the peace and quiet of the countryside but with home comforts. The ugly factory and its smoking chimneys can be seen from the house, but are soon forgotten. Naturally, it's very popular, so advisable to book in advance.

♠ Balcón del Caribe: 7 kilometres (5 miles) south of Santiago, just before Castillo del Morro. ☎ 915-06 and 910-11. Pleasant rooms for $32, *cabañas* for $28. An excellent seaside location, near a cliff. It's worth reserving a room if you want a sea view. You need your own transport.

WHERE TO EAT

A few local fishermen have a sideline in preparing grilled fish or some sort of red shellfish. They are probably illegal so no addresses are given, but you will find them (or vice versa) easily enough. Generally a meal will cost somewhere around $7–8 (for a main dish and sometimes dessert).

✗ **El Morro** (map I, off B3, **37**): around 9 kilometres (6 miles) south of Santiago, next to the fortress. ☎ 915-76. Open daily for lunch (and until 11pm November to March). There is a dark wood bar at the entrance and a shady, panoramic terraced area – an excellent place to relax. The setting is delightful, although you are obviously paying for the view. Traditional cuisine: soup, salad, *tortilla de queso* (cheese omelette), *arroz con mariscos* (shellfish and rice), *camarones* (a type of large prawn), *langosta* (lobster), fillet of fish, chicken, pork, etc. A plate of fish costs around $15. Service is a little on the slow side. Major credit cards accepted (except American Express, of course).

South, Along the Coast

Those with a car and the time might make an interesting trip to Baconao Park – a return journey of around 100 kilometres (62 miles) that includes several museums, sites of interest, beaches and a CUPET service station.

★ **Siboney beach**: 10 kilometres (6 miles) southeast of Santiago by bus or lorry. Siboney is the large village where the musician Compay Segundo was born in 1907. It's a definite favourite, at the foot of a rocky peak in a lush spot with lots of palm trees, and is busy at weekends and in July and August. You can drink coconut milk, rum and beer, etc. on the beach. There aren't any hotels, but you can stay and eat in private lodgings. The beach is patrolled discreetly by police who check the papers of Cubans walking with foreign visitors.

★ **Granjita Siboney** (map Baconao Park, **20**): open daily 9am–5pm. On the road there you will notice around 20 memorials recalling the martyrdom of the first patriots to die at the beginning of the Revolution. They take the form of monuments bearing two or three names, dotted along the roadside. It's like a sacred way leading to the Granjita. At the edge of the road, there is a modest mansion of great importance to Cubans, for it was here on the night before the Moncada attack that the guerrillas met for a final, historic gathering. The place has barely changed and still has the power to arouse strong emotions. In the rooms of the small house at the end of the garden there are documents, statements, weapons, clothes and memorabilia from 26 July on display.

★ **Valley of Prehistory** (map Baconao Park, **21**): admission charge. The Parque Baconao road forks at one point. One of the roads goes directly to the park, while the other goes across a little valley filled with life-size dinosaurs and prehistoric mammals made from concrete. Children will love it (and don't forget your camera). Although it's a bizarre place, the setting in the middle of the lush hills is superb.

★ **Daïquiri beach**: 70 kilometres (43 miles) east of Santiago. The name will no doubt be familiar to cocktail drinkers. The famous drink was apparently invented here during celebrations by US troops after a victory over Spain in the 1895 war. This beach is now officially a military zone so tourists are not advised to try swimming here.

★ **Baconao Park**: this is the national park that Fidel Castro dreamed of when his revolutionaries took this route in 1953. It's the largest natural park in Cuba and has been designated a Biosphere Reserve by UNESCO. On the eastern side is Laguna Baconao, a large lake surrounded by arid hills. *Jaibas* (blue crabs) and *agujas* fish live in its waters, and on its banks, near the car-park, are some breeding pools for crocodiles. All along the road, natural caverns house various sculptures amid the cacti. Don't bother with the marine park where visitors pay an expensive admission fee to watch bored dolphins swim morosely in circles.

At the far end of the park the main road comes to an end at a barrier guarded by a Cuban soldier. A Cuban military base is stationed here and, contrary to the road map, it is impossible to continue along the road to María del Pilar. The US base at Guantánamo Bay is not very far away, to the east. Officially, the soldiers are here to keep an eye on the border. Unofficially, they are watching for the numerous Cubans who make a break for Guantánamo via the sea in lorry tyres. Some have managed to reach the port and demand political asylum from the Americans. Others have tried more radical methods – in 1996, Lieutenant-Colonel José Fernández Pupo landed a Cubana aeroplane at the base and asked for asylum. The United States have now agreed to cooperate with the Castro government and systematically hand over any escapees to the military.

Other nice beaches are **Juragua** and **Sigua Verraco**, with its tranquil, little bay and beach shaded by the *uva caleta*.

East of Santiago

★ **La Gran Piedra**: around 25 kilometres (15.5 miles) from Santiago. Take the Siboney road for 13 kilometres (8 miles) and turn left at the village of Las Guásimas – it's signposted. An empty, winding road climbs up to the Gran Piedra, a large rock peaking at 1,220 metres (4,002 feet). The road ends at the Hotel Villa Gran Piedra (with restaurant), whose *cabañas* are scattered amid the pine trees on the mountainside. This is a really pleasant place, as the air is cool. A path from the adjoining car-park leads to the summit (452 steps) where there is a telecommunications tower.

The 'Big Rock' is believed to be the remnant of an ancient volcano that was eroded with the passage of time. It can be reached on foot and you can climb up it via an attached long metal ladder (easy and safe, except if it's raining). From the top, there is a fantastic view – on a clear day you can see Haiti and Jamaica. The best time to go up is at the end of the afternoon. In the evening and at nightfall, you may still go up there as long as you have a torch. The view of the coastal lights and Santiago in the distance is superb. Throughout this region it's easy to pick up Jamaican radio stations – the sound of reggae makes a change from what you become used to elsewhere in Cuba. Along the road, country people sell coffee, bananas and oranges.

★ **Cafetal Isabélica** (map Baconao Park, **22**): 2 kilometres (1 mile) from La Gran Piedra along a poor road; you will need a good car, or even a four-wheel-drive. Open Tuesday to Sunday 8am–4pm. Closed when it's raining. Admission $1; guided tour $5. This is a former coffee plantation founded by Victor Constantin, a French immigrant from Haiti, who came to Cuba after the French Revolution (at the beginning of the 19th century). On the ground floor of the house instruments and objects relating to the early coffee industry are on display. In the 19th century Cuba became the first country to export coffee, but a century later Brazil completely eclipsed the island. The Isabelica plantation was more or less forgotten. It was burned down during the War of Independence, then became a museum in 1959. It was not really until 1971, however – when all the objects from the 60 *cafetaleros* in the surrounding region were collected together – that visitors really began to arrive. UNESCO experts are carrying out an inventory with a view to possibly awarding it the status of Heritage Site.

Coffee has played an important part in the island's industrial development, as methods of processing sugar were developed from those used for coffee. The whole process was carried out in this building. The coffee beans were brought in by mules from the 60-hectare (148-acre) plantation surrounding La Isabélica, which is a small, fortress-like, south-facing structure. In front of the building stand the numerous cement drying-towers where the beans were dried. The coffee was processed on the ground floor (the walls of which were originally whitewashed to avoid humidity) – in the 18th century this stage would have been carried out by slaves.

The first floor contains the master's living quarters with some well-restored rooms. Their simple but comfortable splendour allows you to appreciate the

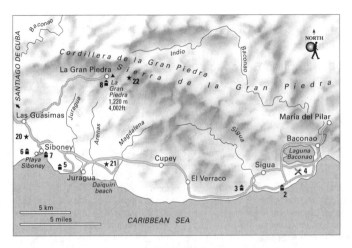

BACONAO PARK

⌂ ✕ **Where to Stay and Eat**	**7** Elpidio Mancebo Pérez
	8 Villa Gran Piedra
2 Hotel Carissol	
3 Costa Morena	★ **What to See**
4 Restaurant Casa Rolando	
5 Hotel Bucanero	**20** Granjita Siboney
6 Casa Particular Terraza Mar Azul	**21** Valley of Prehistory
	22 Cafetal Isabélica

living conditions of the slaves. On the left, the former kitchen – built separately to avoid fire risks – is now the guards' office.

WHERE TO STAY AND EAT

Between Santiago and Baconao Park there are five large beach hotels where Cubans are not allowed – unless, of course, they are working there. On the way, however, are numerous chalets for Cuban holidaymakers. In theory, these chalets do not accept tourists, but if you're passing in a slack period and call in on the off-chance, you may well find them prepared to bend the rules. Camping on unofficial sites is not recommended (even if it is possible). The best plan is probably to rent a room in a private house in Siboney, the only real coastal village.

Visitors who really like their comforts should head straight to the chain hotels. With little architectural originality and very traditional in design, they were initially built for Canadian (package) tourists in particular. Most of them have sandy beaches, even though most of the coastline is rocky. You can now stay here as an independent traveller. A bus generally serves the hotels and goes to Santiago once a day. The one good thing about these hotels is that most offer 'all-inclusive' packages with the price including limitless food (meals are often buffets) and Cuban drinks.

Near Laguna Baconao

â **Carissol** (map Baconao Park, **2**): west of Los Corales. ☎ (22) 356-115. Fax: (22) 356-106. Open only in high season (December to April). $50 per person per day, all-inclusive. Owned by the Scandinavian group LTI, this is a kind of holiday club resort with 144 rooms in five buildings set around a swimming pool and bar. Disco, games room and occasional evening entertainment. Good welcome.

â **Costa Morena** (map Baconao Park, **3**): between Sigua and El Veraco. ☎ (0226) 35-61-27. $55 for a double, all-inclusive. Another package-tour place in long, one-storey buildings only 5 metres from the beach. Exceptionally spacious rooms for two have king-size beds. Small swimming pool.

✕ **Restaurant Casa Rolando** (map Baconao Park, **4**): very close to the lake and the crocodile pools, within the park boundaries. Open daily 9am–11pm. A dish of Creole-style food costs less than $7. A few metres away, in a shady corner next to the lake is the Bar de la Laguna where visitors can enjoy a snack and a drink. Open daily 8am–5pm. Note that the mosquitoes come out in force at nightfall.

In and Around Siboney

â **Hotel Bucanero** (map Baconao Park, **5**): Arroyo La Costa, at the 4-kilometre (2.5-mile) mark, between the sea and the mountains. ☎ (0226) 86-363. Fax: (0226) 86-070. $60 per person, all inclusive. A big hotel complex of 193 rooms, recently given an overhaul by the Accor group.

â **Casa Particular Terraza Mar Azul** (map Baconao Park, **6**): avenida Serrano, Siboney beach. ☎ (22) 393-40. A double room with bathroom and hot water costs $20 ($15 without hot water) in this small house above the pharmacy, furnished like a traditional fisherman's cottage: white-and-blue painted panelling, fishing nets, etc. Very good welcome from the owner.

â **Elpidio Mancebo Pérez** (map Baconao Park, **7**): La Marina 13, opposite the Terraza Mar Azul, *above*. If you get lost ask for '*la casa del campeón de beïsbol*' (the baseball champion's house). ☎ (22) 039-91. A double room costs $40, excluding breakfast. The owner is both a personal friend of Fidel and a former member of the national baseball team. The house is perched on the heights of Siboney and has several terraced areas. This excellent athlete is obviously a softy at heart – he has model animals all over the house. The big, well-equipped rooms are pleasantly kitsch in style. There is a mini-gym available for guests' use, an attractive dining room for the buffet breakfast and even a bar-cum-disco. A nice place to stay, if rather on the expensive side.

In Gran Piedra

⚑ ✕ **Villa Gran Piedra** (map Baconao Park, **8**): 26 kilometres (16 miles) from Santiago and 13 kilometres (8 miles) from Las Guásimas. ☎ 80-143. Fax: 86-147. At the summit of the Gran Piedra mountain, but at the foot of the rock of the same name, is this series of *cabañas* scattered among the pine trees on the mountainside. *Cabañas* cost $38–40 depending on season, breakfast included. The facilities are excellent: good beds, hot and cold water, satellite TV and sometimes even a small kitchen and open fire. Stock up on provisions before you arrive as there are no supermarkets nearby, although meals are available on-site. Highly recommended for the view, the peace and quiet and the location. In season arrive early before it gets full up. There are some nice guided walks along nearby footpaths ($2 for the day, irrespective of the route).

LEAVING SANTIAGO

By Bus

🚌 **Bus station** (terminal de omnibus interprovincial; map I, off D1): avenida de los Libertadores, at the crossroads with the *Circunvalación* ring road and near Plaza de la Revolución. Around 4 kilometres (2.5 miles) from Parque Céspedes. Daily buses depart for the major towns in Oriente. Buy your tickets in advance.

– For **Havana**: two buses a day, one ordinary bus in the afternoon and a Viazul in the evening. A ticket costs $42.

– For **Baracoa**: the journey takes around 5 hours by bus and 3 hours 30 minutes by car (sometimes less). The bus leaves at 6am. A ticket on the Viazul costs $13, or $9 for the ordinary bus.

– For **Holguín**: one bus a day before noon, but the evening Viazul service to Havana also stops at Holguín. A ticket on the Viazul costs $9, or $7 for the ordinary bus.

– For **Bayamo**: three buses a day. Tickets cost $5 and $6.

– For **Matanzas**: one bus every afternoon, but the evening Viazul to Havana also stops here. Tickets cost $37.50 and $30.50.

– For **Camagüey**: one bus in the late afternoon. The Havana Viazul also stops here. Tickets cost $15 and $12.

– For **Trinidad**: no direct bus – take the Havana Viazul to Sancti Spiritus and change. A ticket costs $28.

– For **Pilón**: one bus early morning (before 8am). A ticket costs $10.

By Train

🚆 **Railway station** (terminal de ferrocarril; map I, B1): 800 metres west of Parque Céspedes, after the port area, on Paseo Alameda, level with calle Padre Callejas (ex-Santa Isabel). A large counter at the entrance outside the building serves as an information desk. Open 24 hours a day. ☎ 228-36.

– For **Havana**: two trains a day. The first leaves Santiago at 5pm and should arrive at 7.10am; the other leaves at 9.35pm and should arrive at 11.10am. Tickets cost $43 and are best booked three or four days in advance. The Rumbos agency will make bookings. Refreshments available on the train. No couchettes, but there are reclining seats.

– For **Bayamo**, **Camagüey**, **Ciego de Avila** and **Santa Clara**: the train for Havana stops in these towns.

By Plane

✪ **Aeropuerto Internacional Antonio Maceo**: 11 kilometres (7 miles) south of Santiago, on the Carreterra del Morro. ☎ 910-14. Weekly flights from Madrid, Cologne and Rome.

– For **Havana**: several flights daily with Cubana de Aviación and Aero Caribbean.

– For **Baracoa**: just one flight a week (on Sunday) with Cubana. There is also a small taxi-plane daily to Santiago–Baracoa–Holguín–Santiago. Ticket $28. Flight time Santiago–Baracoa 40 minutes. A little plane often stops at Guantánamo.

GUANTÁNAMO
DIALLING CODE: 21

It's a name that no doubt sounds familiar, due to the most played Cuban song ever. It's also a reminder of the presence of the famous US naval base. Situated 86 kilometres (53 miles) east of Santiago, Guantánamo is the sort of place that you drive through, as it has little of any real interest.

The province of Guantánamo, the furthest east in the country, contains a very pretty road from San Antonio del Sur to Baracoa, an intimate and charming town that's a wonderful, relaxing place to stop.

WHAT TO SEE

★ **The Municipal Museum**: calle José Martí, parallel to the high street. Open Tuesday to Saturday 8am–noon and 1.30–6pm; Sunday 8am–noon. Located in the former town prison, you'll find prehistoric remains, a native Cuban tomb, Indian jewels, etc. Exhibits from the colonial period include a dentist's case, slaves' chains and weapons. There is also an exhibition on the struggle during the dictatorship, local heroes, their history, clothes and personal effects. In the courtyard are the former cells.

★ In calle A. Pérez (the road with the fire station) look out for the unusual **Palace of Baroque Art**, surmounted by a beautiful statue of the *Trumpet of Fame* dating from the beginning of the 20th century. There's also a row of elegant colonial mansions comprising lawyers' and doctors' practices. The pleasant **main square** has a church in the middle. Take a look at the original architecture of the **market** in the high street.

★ **The US naval base**: this huge base, 117 kilometres (72 miles) long, is one of the strangest political and strategic installations in the world. 'Gitmo

Bay', the nickname given to it by the US troops, is an enclosed world surrounded by a ring of watchtowers, mines and barbed wire. It is a heavily guarded camp – a mini US territory on Cuban land, and home to almost 7,000 people. You can usually only get there by plane or by boat; the road is very rarely used. This is a real example of a self-sufficient community, with schools, supermarkets, cinemas, nightclubs, places of worship, golf courses, tennis courts and even a yacht club for the troops and their families. There are several runways and even a desalination plant for drinking water.

Now that the Cold War is over, many experts agree that Fidel Castro's regime no longer poses a threat to US security. So, what's the point of the base? In theory, to protect the Panama Canal and the Caribbean zone. But in practice, many think that it serves no purpose at all, other than to cost the United States a small fortune (in maintaining the site, equipment and personnel). Washington pays the Cuban government a very low annual rent of several thousand dollars. Fidel Castro receives the cheques, but has never cashed them, as a matter of principle. Instead, he keeps the cheques in a drawer, which he once revealed to the camera of the former French naval officer and oceanographer Jacques Cousteau when he stopped off here.

Even so, it's rather odd, especially when you consider that the 99-year lease in the Treaty of 1934 between the two countries means that the Guantánamo base cannot close down before 2033. It all began after the war in 1895 and the Treaty of Paris in 1898. The United States made it clear that they wanted to maintain their military presence in Cuba. In 1902, they were forced to acknowledge the country's independence, but they still imposed the Platt Amendment on the new constitution. In its articles, the USA granted themselves the right to intervene in Cuba at any time both in political and military terms. Furthermore, they obtained a naval base at Guantánamo that would allow them to control the Panama Canal and the whole of the Caribbean zone.

Naturally, there is no communication between the Cubans and the GIs, who are separated by barbed wire and an area of no man's land. The base aroused press attention again in 1994, when thousands of *balseros* left Cuba to seek their fortunes elsewhere. Those who remained on land thought that there could be another way of entering the United States, i.e. via the US base at Guantánamo. On 5 August that year, thousands of Cubans rushed here from all over the island following a rumour that the base would be open for emigration applicants. However, there was bitter disappointment, for the information was false. Guantánamo certainly isn't a gateway to the USA. The remains of the refugee camps are still here.

The departure of the Americans is one of the fundamental issues of any negotiations, should the embargo be lifted. Those who have seen the film *A Few Good Men*, with Tom Cruise, Jack Nicholson and Demi Moore (a few scenes were actually shot at the base), will recall the iron rod of discipline that rules the daily life of the Marines stationed here.

– Two roads follow the contours of the bay to the little harbours of **Boquerón** and, on the western side, **Caimanera**. At the latter, near the local hotel, you may look at the US base from a viewpoint (there is a charge), but it's far away and not all that interesting. Another option is to ask for a guide at the Hotel Guantánamo in Guantánamo.

The Road from Guantánamo to Baracoa

★ This itinerary, which is one of the most beautiful in Cuba, starts from the beach at **Yateritas**. At the end of the afternoon, in good weather, the countryside takes on a marvellous luminosity. The coast is mostly rocky. The road winds between the sea and the bare hills that sometimes end in small, abrupt cliffs overhanging picturesque fishing villages such as **Tartuguilla**. Traditional huts with thatched roofs are scattered over the poorly cultivated land. The climate and the vegetation here are dry, with beautiful fields of cacti. Note that some of the villages are not accessible to visitors, as they are in the 'military zone'.

★ Further east are the picturesque towns of **San Antonio del Sur** and **Imías**. José Martí and Máximo Gómez landed in 1895 on the beach at **Cajobabo** at the start of the War of Independence.

★ Then the road climbs into the **sierra del Purial**, offering breathtaking views. This section was built in 1960 and is also known as the Farola viaduct because so many concrete structures and pillars were required to secure the road to the side of the mountain, at places where it was not possible to dig through or to level the land. Along the roadside you will see numerous country people selling clementines or *cocorucho* (a grated coconut sweet wrapped in a banana leaf).

★ The **mirador de Palma Clara**: around 20 kilometres (12 miles) before Baracoa on the right-hand side of the road, on a bend as you descend the mountain. A few hundred metres from the road, you will see a lookout on a mound; it is open to visitors. From the top there is a superb view of the coffee plantations and the hills covered with pine forests. There is a small Rumbos cafeteria if you need a drink. Take appropriate clothing as it can get chilly.

★ **Zabanilla**: around 11–12 kilometres (7 miles) before Baracoa the vegetation becomes more and more luxuriant the closer you get to the sea. At Zabanilla there are coffee plantations along the edge of the road.

BARACOA

DIALLING CODE: 21

Located 160 kilometres (99 miles) northeast of Guantánamo, Baracoa enjoys a wonderful position and a privileged climate (*see below*). In this part of Oriente, the last foothills of the Sierra Maestra die out at the Atlantic Ocean, forming a natural shield of mountains covered with lush, tropical vegetation. The small town stretches out towards the sea at the foot of the mountains, amid coconut palms and orchards.

In some of the villages in the surrounding area, it is believed that the last remaining survivors (several hundred) of the native Indians of Cuba (related to the Tainos) are still living today. But if you ask exactly where they are, the locals reply that the Tainos no longer exist (they have integrated into the local population).

In addition to its charm, you will really appreciate the laid-back pace of life in the town, together with the kindness of its inhabitants, and you will no doubt regret not spending longer here. You should allow at least three days in this area, ideally a whole week.

Part of the Franco-Cuban film *Villa Vanilla* was filmed at Baracoa in 1997, when many of the town's inhabitants appeared in it as extras.

A Brief History

On 28 October 1492, three Spanish caravels led by Christopher Columbus sailed along the Oriente coastline and dropped anchor at Baracoa. The Genoese sailor wrote in his log, 'A square mountain that resembles an island'. For the inhabitants of Baracoa this mountain is El Yunque, shaped like a table and situated a few kilometres from the town. However, for the inhabitants of Gibara on the north coast of Oriente, who still claim that the first landing occurred at their town, this can only be the Silla de Gibara. This quarrel has still not been settled. But it doesn't really matter. Columbus himself thought he had finally discovered South China.

But there were no Chinese people on the horizon, or the court of the Grand Khan. Neither was there any gold or spices. In fact there was virtually nothing at all besides a few miserable huts inhabited by Taino Indians 'smoking firebrands made of herbs'. This was the first time a European had come into contact with a cigar, which was considered an object of prayer.

The Admiral still didn't know that this piece of land was an island announcing the approach of a new continent (America), like a whale swimming through the sea. On landing at Baracoa, Columbus brought a cross with him that was a good 2 metres (6 feet) tall. Over the centuries, fishermen are said to have shortened it with their penknives, keeping the shavings as relics. A piece remains preserved in the church (*see below*).

When the town was founded in 1511, the Spanish called it Nuestra Señora de la Asunción de Baracoa. Cut off from the rest of the island and therefore protected from wars and revolutions, its colonial character has remained virtually unchanged for over four centuries, as it was only really accessible by boat. As a result of the construction of the Farola viaduct on the Guantánamo road, this town at the far end of the world has partially emerged from its solitary confinement.

Microclimate

Those of you who arrive by the Guantánamo road will notice immediately that the countryside around the south coast of the province of Guantánamo is arid and bare on the Caribbean Sea side, while the Atlantic-facing north coast (the Baracoa region) has lush, tropical vegetation.

This difference is due to climatic conditions. Baracoa, which faces the sea and is protected by a shield of mountains, enjoys an Atlantic microclimate: lots of sun and warmth, but also coolness due to the winds, and sufficient humidity due to torrential rain falling at certain times of the year. As a result, everything grows here, including coconut palms and banana, mango and guava trees. Not forgetting coffee and cocoa, the two main products cultivated in this part of Oriente. It's also the only place on the island where the cacao tree is grown.

– **The rainy season**: between November and December the temperature becomes cooler. It rains almost every morning, then the temperature rises and the sun comes out until the end of the day.

– **The hottest months**: in July and August the temperature rises above 30°C (86°F).

– **May and June**: the spring season is very pleasant and the trees bear fruit at this time.

La Rusa, the Legend of Baracoa

Along the Malecón, facing the sea, is a small hotel called La Rusa (The Russian Woman). On the face of it, it is an ordinary seaside hotel that you might find close to a European beach. But the freshness of the exterior paintwork contrasts with the numerous peeling facades in the area. It is no coincidence that this hotel has such an attractive appearance. The Cuban government maintains it as an historic monument. Why? Because Fidel and Raúl Castro, who led the rebels in the Sierra Maestra, have never forgotten that it was run by an exceptional woman – an exiled Russian singer who became the first person to support them in Baracoa.

Alejo Carpentier, one of the greatest Cuban authors, was inspired by this woman's life to write his book *La Consegración de la Primavera*. In this novel, she appears under the name of Vera. She was as beautiful as a goddess, spoke five languages perfectly, had a pretty soprano voice and played the piano. Magdalena Romanoski (her real name) was born in St Petersburg into the Russian aristocracy. She left her country during the Revolution of 1917 and sought refuge in Paris with her husband, Albert Ménassé Baruch. To earn a living they sold ironmongery and then emigrated to Cuba in 1930, where Albert's wealthy business family had an office in Havana. The young couple lived there for a while before moving to Baracoa, which was quieter, where they built a hotel in 1948.

As a hotelier, Magdalena provided accommodation for many tourists. She also received some strange visitors with beards and olive-green uniforms that were rarely washed – namely, the leaders of the revolutionary guerrillas. Fidel Castro stayed there twice, Che Guevara three times. The hotel, which was called the Miramar at the time, thus became the *casa de confianza* for the *barbudos*. Meeting these charismatic rebel leaders, and the resulting friendship, was as much a human revelation as a political one for this diva with a heart of gold, who was more familiar with grand pianos than guerrilla warfare. One day Raúl, Fidel's brother, offered Magdalena a revolver as a safety measure.

The irony is that as an adolescent in St Petersburg, she had fled the Russian Revolution. Almost 40 years later, at Baracoa, she embraced the Cuban Revolution (which had not yet converted to Communism). She abhorred the *Bolsheviks* but adored the *barbudos*. La Rusa supported and helped the rebels as much as she could. She gave them a lot of money (over $25,000), medicines, equipment and also moral support. Thus her outward appearance of an opera singer in exile belied a woman of courage and conviction. La Rusa died in 1978.

Her adopted son, the painter René Frometa, is still alive. His house/museum is open to the public and contains some mementoes of his mother (*see* 'What to See').

USEFUL ADDRESSES

■ **ETECSA public telephones** (map C2): on the main square, through the door on the right. Open 7am–8.30pm. International calls are payable in US dollars, local calls in pesos. It is also possible to buy prepaid phonecards. Modern and efficient service.

■ **Banco Nacional de Cuba** (map C2, **3**): calle Maceo, on the corner of Callito García. Open Monday to Friday 7.40am–2.30pm. Accepts traveller's cheques, but no withdrawal facilities using credit cards.

🚌 **Bus station**: The *terminal de Omnibus* is at the end of calle Martí, near La Punta fort. The other station (map B1) is on calle Coroneles Galana (and Ruber López) and only serves Guantánamo.

■ **Cubana de Aviación** (map C2, **1**): calle José Martí 181. ☎ 421-71. Around three flights a week from Havana and one from Santiago.

■ **CUPET service station** (map, off D3, **4**): a long way from the centre, on the Guantánamo road before the Yumuri turning. Open 24 hours a day. Also the place to go if you have a puncture.

AROUND BARACOA

■ **Useful Addresses**

✉	Post office
🚌	Bus station
✈	Airport
1	Cubana de Aviación
2	Farmacia Piloto
3	Banco Nacional de Cuba
4	CUPET service station

🛏 **Where to Stay**

10	Clara Carratalá
11	Nancy Borges Gallego
12	Casa Tropical
13	Yolando Quintero
14	Nancy and Noel's
15	Ibrahim Lobaina Cisnero
16	Ana Elibis
17	Neyda Cuenca Prada
18	Hotel La Rusa
19	Hotel Plaza
20	Hotel El Castillo
21	Hotel Porto Santo

✕ **Where to Eat**

20	Hotel El Castillo restaurant
30	Pizza stand
31	Restaurant Walter
32	Restaurant-bar La Colonial

🍸 **Where to Have a Drink**

33	La Casa de la Trova
34	La Casa de Chocolate
35	Cafeteria Rumbos

★ **What to See**

40	Catedral de Nuestra Señora de la Asunción
41	Cathedral Square and Hatuey statue
42	Municipal Museum of History

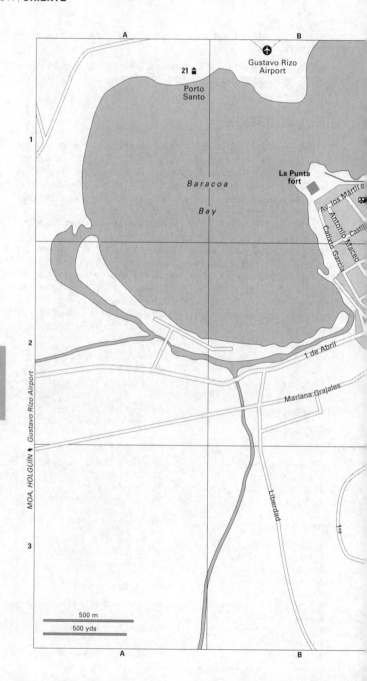

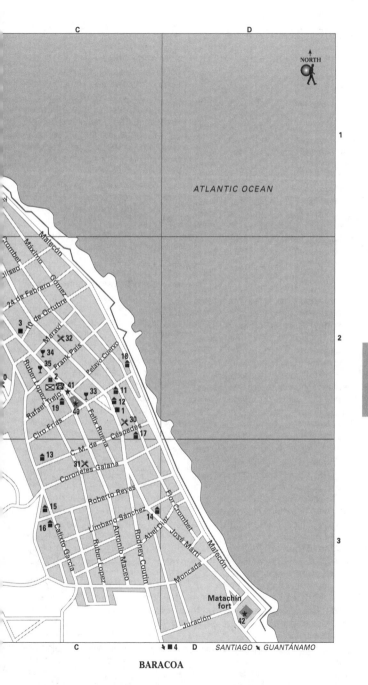

NORTH

ATLANTIC OCEAN

Matachín
fort

SANTIAGO ↘ *GUANTÁNAMO*

BARACOA

WHERE TO STAY

Casas Particulares

⊜ **Clara Carratalá** (map B2, **10**): calle Mariana Grajales 30. ☎ 433-61. Fairly central, with four rooms at reasonable prices ($12–15). The nicest is the blue room with two windows overlooking the courtyard. It's simple, clean and quiet. Half board is available. Clara, a former doctor, can talk to you about her island for hours. She is a very good hostess and maintains her house remarkably well. She will also prepare meals ($7–10). Even if you are not staying here, pop by a few hours in advance to reserve a place at the table. Dishes include *pescado a la ranchona* (spicy fish in coconut milk) served with *achote* (a rust-coloured sauce), and also a few freshwater prawns. Recommended.

⊜ **Nancy Borges Gallego** (map C2, **11**): Ciro Frías 3, on the corner of calle Flor Crombet. ☎ 421-00. This house belongs to René Frometa, the adopted son of La Rusa and a painter from the naive school. René is both courteous and thoughtful, and has lots of stories to tell. He will take you round the room which he has dedicated as a museum to his legendary mother (*see* 'La Rusa' *above* and 'What to See'). He also rents out two rooms that are clean and decent, one overlooking the street and the other at the rear. Individual hot-water taps. A double costs $12, plus $2 for breakfast. Dinner costs $5.

⊜ **Casa Tropical** (map C2, **12**): calle Martí 175. ☎ 43-688. A small, central and safe boarding house run by two friendly brothers, Frank and Arnoldo. Three simple, clean rooms, overlooking a quiet courtyard, with air-conditioning or fan cost $15–20, excluding breakfast. Other meals available on request. Recommended.

⊜ **Yolanda Quintero** (map C2, **13**): calle Céspedes 44, between Ruber Lopez and Calixto García. ☎ 42-392. A double room costs $15 in this attractive house with a wooden porch roof. The inside is reasonable as well. There is a large, cool patio area. The rooms and the welcome are nothing out of the ordinary and although it doesn't offer much in the way of mod cons, it is undeniably good value for money.

⊜ **Nancy and Noel's** (map D3, **14**): calle Marti 304. A double room costs $20. An attractive house that is being renovated little by little by Noel, a Frenchman who has relocated to Cuba.

⊜ **Ibrahim Lovaina Cisnero** (map C3, **15**): calle Calixto Garcia 170, between Coroneles Galano and Roberto Reyes. ☎ 43-205. The small room behind Ibrahim's house with its own front door costs $15. For that you get some very distinctive decor – heart-shaped cushions, kitsch four-poster bed. Shower but no hot water.

⊜ **Ana Elibis** (map C3, **16**): Calixto Garcia 162, between Céspedes and Coroneles Galana. ☎ 42-754. A double room costs $10–15 in this lovely colonial house with welcoming lounge and rocking chairs where guests can enjoy coffee. Ana and her sister have several rooms, notably one on the roof, reached via a white, wrought-iron stairway. Hot water. There are a few signs of good taste here and there in the decor. Quite popular so best to book in advance.

⊜ **Neyda Cuenca Prada** (map C3, **17**): Flor Crombet 194, between Céspedes and Coroneles Galana. ☎ 431-78. Three reasonably comfortable rooms (a double is $13–15), reached via a strange miniature staircase. The rooms are not overly luxurious and can get rather muggy. Only for emergencies.

Hotels

⌂ **Hotel La Rusa** (map C2, **18**): on the Malecón, at the junction with Ciro Frías. ☎ 430-11. This small, cosy hotel, steeped in history, was opened in 1949 by Magdalena Romanoski, a Russian artiste who ran it until 1978. Her adopted son, the painter René Frometa, lives near by (*see* 'What to See'). Former guests include Errol Flynn, Alejo Carpentier, Fidel and Raúl Castro and Che Guevara (their names are in the hotel register in the Municipal Museum). Re-opened in 1993 following what seems to be an as yet uncompleted renovation, it offers a few rooms that, despite everything, are good value for money at $20 for a double (no hot water). Restaurant with terrace and bar.

⌂ **Hotel Plaza** (map C2, **19**): A. Maceo, above the cinema opposite the cathedral. ☎ 422-83. A single room costs $14, a double $17 and a triple $20 in this old-fashioned yellow-and-green establishment. The sponge-painted rooms could almost be described as elegant, and overlook the church square or the back of the building (dark and gloomy). No. 103 or No. 4 have nice views. The bathrooms are unfortunately very basic. The hotel is subject to a water restriction so there are no showers, just a bucket with which guests are expected to perform their ablutions. If there are several of you, however, it can work out cheaply.

⌂ **Hotel El Castillo** (map C2, **20**): calle Calixto García. ☎ 421-47 or 421-03. A fine, single-storey hotel managed by Gaviota. Perched on the top of a hill, it is inside the old Seboruco fort and has the best view of the town. The architecture is really nice with a superb swimming pool in the courtyard. Comfortable air-conditioned rooms ($45 a double), but a little dark and no balcony. There is a bar and restaurant.

⌂ **Hotel Porto Santo** (map A1, **21**): on the other side of the bay near the airport (there are barely three planes a week). ☎ 435-90 and 435-81. Another good hotel in the Horizontes chain with pleasant bungalows facing the sea and the town, in the middle of a vast garden planted with coconut palms. In high season singles cost $26 and doubles $35. Nice swimming pool with a bar in the centre overlooks the sea.

AROUND
BARACOA

WHERE TO EAT

Make sure you try the local dishes such as fish in coconut milk, *calalú* or *bacán* and those funny little fish that are caught from July to December at the mouths of the local rivers. Chocolate lovers: find some Baracoa chocolate, a delicious local speciality.

☆ Budget

Like everywhere else on the island, numerous small **pizzerias** have opened up. The one at calle José Marti 193 next to a photography shop (map C2, **30**) is not particularly remarkable but is nice and cool. A takeaway pizza costs 5 pesos.

☆☆ Moderate

✕ **Hotel El Castillo Restaurant** (map C2, **20**): open daily noon–2.30pm and 7–9.30pm. Large, impersonal room with no real atmosphere and unspectacular cooking. But there's a good choice of meat and fairly large portions.

✕ **Restaurante Walter** (map C3, **31**): Ruber López 47, between calle Céspedes and Coroneles Galana, a stone's throw from the bus station. ☎ 43-380. Open daily 11am–11pm. Private house with small dining room that seats half a dozen. Excellent traditional cooking – large portions of fresh fish, vegetables and mixed salad at less than $8 for main dishes with a drink.

✕ **Restaurante Bar la Colonial** (map C2, **32**): calle José Marti, between Frank País and Maraví. ☎ 43-161. A meal costs around $8 per person at Baracoa's second official *paladar*, which is less typical than the Walter and a bit more institutionalized. Despite the green china crockery, you get less of an impression of eating at home with the Cubans. The portions aren't huge but the service is friendly.

WHERE TO HAVE A DRINK

♪ **La Casa de la Trova** (map C2, **33**): church square. Admission $1. Small concert hall, very lively in the evenings, where local groups play from 9pm onwards. Not very many seats, but lots of atmosphere and dancing in the fairly confined space. Drinks are available.

♪ **Casa de chocolate** (map C2, **34**): around 150 metres along from police station. Open daily 7am–9.40pm. There are no bars of chocolate or cakes, but rather hot chocolate drinks. The liquid is thick and resembles a smooth chocolate soup. But it's definitely chocolate, barely diluted and hot. It's good and is made with the fine cocoa from the area. Sometimes there are excellent chocolate ice-creams too. Very popular in town.

♪ **Cafeteria Rubmos** (map C2, **35**): main square. This state cafeteria is nothing special but it has a nice outdoor area where you can sit and sip a beer.

WHAT TO SEE

★ **Catedral de Nuestra Señora de la Asunción** (map C2, **40**): Cathedral Square. Generally open daily 8–11am and 1–5pm. Nothing remains of the original church, founded by Bartolomé de Las Casas, the great defender of the Indians in Mexico. The current church dates back to 1805. Inside, in a display cabinet to the left of the choir is the famous *croix de la Parra* that is believed to have been planted here by Christopher Columbus. It was rediscovered when the town was established and has been the subject of popular worship over the centuries. The inhabitants of Gibara, however, refer to it as 'a simple 19th-century toothpick', convinced that Columbus never landed at Baracoa. The old verger is very welcoming.

– The area around the cathedral is the real social and cultural centre of the town. In the square is the **statue of Hatuey** (map C2, **41**), a memorial to the first Indian hero, who opposed colonization, and to the genocide of his people. The town band sometimes rehearses here at midday.

In the evening, the square really comes to life. In the road that runs to the front, on the left-hand side, there is a series of elegant mansions with pretty verandas (just after the Hotel La Habanera). Today, they house the **Musa** workshop where the works of local painters are exhibited. Next door is another *tienda-galerie* in the former *lyceo*. Plaza Martí is just as lively (it contains the statue of the great military activist). The high street runs in front with bookshops, photographers' and the 'big stores'). Right at the end is the square from where the horse-and-traps depart. The **Malecón**, which is much shorter and more intimate that the one in Havana, is a lovely place for a walk in the evening at sunset.

★ **The Municipal Museum of History** (map D3, **42**): at the end of calle Martí. Open Monday to Saturday 8am–6pm; Sunday 8am–noon and 2–6pm. This is located in the former Matachin fort, built (like La Punta fort at the entrance to the bay) in the 18th century to ward off pirate attacks.

There are collections relating to local history, Indian civilization, fortification systems from 1739, local forestry (over 100 species) and local agriculture (cocoa, coffee and bananas).

Baracoa is also the capital of Taino Indian culture and the museum contains items such as *conchas* (shells), ceramics, small pottery heads, necklaces made from the vertebrae of *tiburón* (shark) and mortars. There is also an axe that is over 500 years old. Other items include memorabilia from 100 French families who settled here at the end of the 18th century (and introduced coffee-growing methods). Note the Baracoa insignia (1838) with the *Yunque* (anvil), the symbol of the town. There are also display cabinets relating to the two Wars of Independence and the original flag from the 1895 war, as well as the first flag to fly over the town when it eventually won its independence.

Finally, there are exhibits relating to some famous people from the town, such as La Rusa (Magdalena Romanoski), who ran the hotel of the same name. You can see the hotel register that Castro and Che Guevara filled in. Another local figure, the singer Ayamba, has a hat here decorated with the multicoloured polymitas.

★ **The House/Museum of René Frometa** (map C2, **11**): Ciro Frías 3. ☎ 421-00. No sign outside. Ring the bell and René Frometa will answer in person. This sprightly old man has devoted a small room in his house to his paintings from the naive school and to the life of his adoptive mother, a Russian artiste known as La Rusa. He will give you a guided visit, beginning with Baracoa, whose history he portrays through a series of paintings. Then he will tell you about the extraordinary life of La Rusa (*see* 'La Rusa, the Legend of Baracoa', *above*).

In this unpretentious museum room, René has set out his memorabilia as best he can. It includes his mother's clothes, personal effects, old photo albums and photographs. He has also set about erecting a shared tomb at Baracoa to reunite the bodies of his parents, Albert and Magdalena. At the end of the visit, it's a good idea to leave him a tip or buy one of his little paintings. You may also rent a room in the house, (*see* 'Where to Stay': Nancy Borges Gallego).

– **Cinema**: A. Maceo, next to the Hotel Plaza. A visit here is a good way to meet the Cubans and hear a bit of their language. Showings at 2pm, 4pm, 6pm and 8pm. Tickets are ultra-cheap at 8 centavos.

Around Baracoa

The Beaches in the North

★ **Playa de Duaba**: situated 6 kilometres (4 miles) northwest of Baracoa, bordered by coconut palms, is this very popular (but not very clean) beach where General Antonio Maceo, the great hero of the 1895 war, landed.

★ **Playa de Maguana**: this is some 20 kilometres (13 miles) north of Baracoa so hire a car for the day to get there. Take the road towards Moa, after the fifth bridge turn right, then continue straight on. The road first crosses the river Duaba, then the river Toa (the warmest in Cuba). The rivers in the Baracoa region have the clearest waters on the island. Maguana is an attractive white-sand beach lined with palm trees stretching for some distance. A small Rumbos stall on the beach sells snacks.

WHERE TO STAY IN MAGUANA

🛏 **Hotel Villa Maguana**: Follow the same directions for the beach but before you get there turn right along a small track rutted with tree roots. Bookings should be made via the Hotel Castillo in Baracoa. ☎ 42-147. The Villa Maguana is basically a big square hut next to the sea made up of four big bedrooms. Good welcome. Check with the hotel for prices.

The Southeast Coast

Take the Baracoa road out of Baracoa and turn left before you get to the service station. This area gets much more rain than the rest of the island and the results are obvious in the rich diversity of landscape. Although the vegetation is very lush, the level of poverty is clear from the state of the huts and *cabañas* that you will see along the way.

★ **Bahía de Miel**: about 10 kilometres (6 miles) east of Baracoa. The mouth of the Río Miel is a very popular place for bathing; when you look down from the road bridge at the children having fun below, it will make you want to join them. A local saying sums it up: 'Once you have bathed in the Río Miel, you will never be able to leave Baracoa . . .'. There are also several little bays where the water is calm and free of tourists.

★ **Bahía de Mata**: you'll find this around 20 kilometres (12 miles) east of Baracoa, via the village of Jamal. This is a gorgeous place where peace and quiet reign. On the right is the little local school, an adorable Baptist church and a tiny fishing harbour.

★ **Playa Mangolito**: a little further east from Bahía de Mata, this is very quiet and ideal for a picnic. Take everything you need as there's no supermarket around. It's a nice bike-ride from Baracoa as the route doesn't present any major difficulties. Allow a good two hours.

★ **Bariguá**: this is another pretty beach halfway between Bahía de Mata and Boca de Yumurí.

★ **Boca de Yumurí**: this beautiful enclosed valley is 30 kilometres (19 miles) east of Baracoa, and you can catch a bus from Baracoa for a day trip

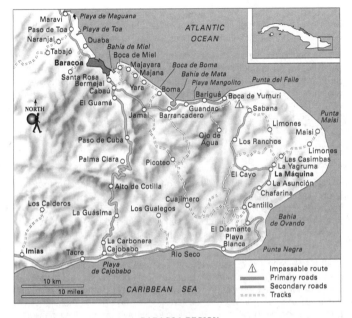

BARACOA REGION

to Yumurí. The first bus leaves at 8am and the last one returns from Yumurí at 5pm. The best option (a little more expensive) is to hire a private car (allow around $15 for the day). Vehicles take the coast road to Yumurí. Avoid visiting at the weekend when it becomes packed with families from Baracoa.

At Yumurí you can then take a boat across the river, then follow the road that leads into Boca de Yumurí, a sort of tropical canyon planted with coconut palms and banana trees. It makes a lovely, easy walk, which you can also do with a guide from Baracoa.

Hikes

★ **The Río Duaba estuary**: north of Baracoa. Head in the direction of Moa and, just after the chocolate factory, turn left towards Finca Duaba (signposted). A few metres from the main road take the turning to the left. After around 2 kilometres (1 mile) you reach a very pretty dirt track that runs alongside the river. Near the source are the **Cascadas del Pellicazo** (waterfalls) where it is possible to swim.

★ **The Yunque**: this is the nickname of the strange, almost table-shaped mountain that protects Baracoa. Meaning 'the anvil', it is a well-known landmark for navigators and even Christopher Columbus remarked upon it in 1492. Some hotels (including the Castillo in Baracoa) organize hikes here. The Yunque is part of a strategic zone watched over by the Cuban army and so it's advisable to be accompanied by a guide. Having said that, this walk has been done without a guide, and without any problems either with the police or with the route. Note that there's a river to ford along the way.

On the northern exit from Baracoa, at the sign 'Campismo del Yunque', turn left onto a road in poor condition and follow it for around 3.5 kilometres (2 miles) past coffee and cocoa plantations. Go past the Yunque campsite and cross the river on foot. Then climb up to the summit – allow 3 hours, and 2 hours for the descent, but there are no particular difficulties. You will pass through fields planted with tropical trees, such as banana, coconut palms, coffee, cacao and pineapple.

Punta Maisi

★ **Maisi**: situated around 70 kilometres (43 miles) southeast of Baracoa, this large village at the end of the world is the easternmost town in Cuba. Due to its extreme geographical position and its location at the junction of two seas (the Caribbean Sea and Atlantic Ocean), Maisi is the only place on Cuba where the four prevailing winds meet. Most of the coffee plantations are in this area, where the climate is more favourable than elsewhere.

Note that this area is currently closed to tourists as the coffee beans have been affected by some sort of disease. Consequently the authorities are carrying out a vast fumigation programme. However, there is also a large camp on the site hosting refugees from Haiti, and the authorities would prefer to keep visitors out (a few have been known to have their passports confiscated by the Popular Revolutionary Police). In any case, the road into Maisi is in very poor condition and becomes almost impassable after Boca del Yumuri.

LEAVING BARACOA

By Car

– For **Santiago de Cuba**: 234 kilometres (145 miles), journey time around 4 hours.

– For **Cayo Saetia** (near Mayarí): 169 kilometres (105 miles), around 2 hours 30 minutes.

– For **Playa Guardalavaca** (north coast): 248 kilometres (154 miles), around 5 hours 30 minutes.

– For **Holguín**: 250 kilometres (155 miles), around 5 hours 30 minutes.

– There are also some **lorries** that go in the morning (very basic travelling conditions, but the countryside is particularly beautiful).

By Bus

🚌 The **Terminal de Omnibus** (bus station) is at the end of calle Martí, near La Punta fort.

– For **Havana**: three departures a week.

– For **Santiago de Cuba**: allow 5 hours. One departure a day, usually leaving at 1.50pm. Ticket $9.

– For **Yumurí**, **Moa**, **Barigua** and **Imias**. One departure per day, at around 7am or 8am (check in advance).

– For **Guantánamo**: one bus a day (early afternoon) from the terminal on calle Coronales Galana.

By Plane

✪ **Aeropuerto Gustavo Rizo**: near the Hotel Porto Santo, on the western side of Baracoa bay. ☎ 422-16.

– For **Santiago**: a small taxi-plane flies daily between Santiago, Baracoa, Holguín and Santiago, and often stops at Guantánamo. Ticket $28. Flight time Santiago–Baracoa: 40 minutes.

– For **Havana**: three flights a week, on Tuesday, Friday and Sunday, with Cubana de Aviación. Ticket $80 single booked in advance, otherwise $108.

From Baracoa to Holguín via Moa

This road, which is accessible to vehicles, is not particularly difficult. There's a short stretch just out of Baracoa where the road isn't surfaced, and just before Moa, a few kilometres of stony road eventually return to asphalt.

Allow 90 minutes (at average speed) from Baracoa to Moa. The road traverses superb coastal scenery that is still wild and untouched, where the wooded hills descend into the Atlantic Ocean, but less abruptly than at Baracoa. The road also crosses numerous clear rivers; this is your chance to stop off and sample the *ríos* of Oriente.

The Moa region is an example of the huge economic effort in which the country is engaged. It is here that the 'Che Guevara' nickel factory is located. Cuba is in fact the fourth largest producer of nickel in the world. This mineral is an essential source of revenue and the means for extracting it have therefore evidently been supplied.

– Along the 15 kilometres (9 miles) of seafront en route to Moa, you cross an apocalyptic landscape of disembowelled mountains, monstrous machinery, huge lengths of pipeline expelling vapour at their joints, beaches transformed into blackened dumps, suppressed vegetation that has sometimes disappeared altogether and treatment plants belching acrid, yellow smoke.

In this maelstrom of red-and-black earth there is sometimes an incongruous palm tree or a green clump. On the edge of the road, a gigantic picture of Che exhorts Cubans to work for the future of the Revolution. The poignancy of this large-scale industry is that the US embargo and the ossified Cuban political system between them prevent any real economic development in the country. Closed in 1990 due to the lack of fuel, this factory, with its capacity to produce 30,000 tonnes of nickel per year, is set to reopen with 'a few technological improvements' – hopefully ones to stem the flow of red water spilling from the factory and marring the coastline. Many of the local inhabitants have been poisoned by the drinking water. Photography is strictly forbidden.

– You will shortly arrive in **Moa**, a working-class town with state-owned housing eroded by the humidity and pollution. After passing through this region, where there is little nickel, you return to the calmness of the straight roads, flirting once more with a crystal-clear sea, running through the middle of cane fields, with the Sierra de Cristal on the horizon. You then pass through **Cayo Mambí**, **Levisa** and **Mayarí**, small, hard-working, agricultural towns.

– To get to **Cayo Saetia** (nature reserve) take a road on the right, 2 kilometres (1 mile) after Levisa. Having said this, the trip isn't really worth the effort unless you're staying in the hotel as the $10 admission fee to the natural park is enough to put most people off.

MAYARÍ   DIALLING CODE: 24

The road continues through a sensual landscape of sugar cane fields. This region between Cueto and Mayarí inspired some of the words in Compay Segundo's famous song, *Chan Chan*. If Mayarí itself doesn't grab you – it's not one of Cuba's most lively towns – follow in the footsteps of the revolutionaries and continue on into the mountain ranges.

The lovely region wedged between the Sierra de Cristal and the legendary Sierra Maestra is a big coffee-growing area. It is rather reminiscent of Kenya with its scattering of small plantations, its blood red paths and native species of orchid.

WHERE TO STAY AND EAT

Villa Pinares de Mayarí: loma la Mensura, Pinares de Mayarí. ☎ 53-308. Fax: 30-126. From the centre of Mayarí, take the only road up into the mountains. Certain stretches are not well maintained and a four-wheel-drive vehicle might be the best option. This is a small 'resort' consisting of big log-cabin style chalets in an isolated spot in the mountains. A big double room costs around $40, but if you book from Europe it's substantially cheaper. There's a $10 set menu for meals. Tiny swimming pool. Guided hikes in the surrounding area available.

Walks

Salto de Guanabo (waterfalls): 5 minutes from the Villa Pinares de Mayarí. As the diggers moved in to attack the foothills of the Sierra de Cristal in search of nickel, the Empresa Forestal Integral embarked upon its project to protect 577 hectares (1,425 acres) of forest. For an insight into the situation, try and get hold of Ermelino Napoles, a friendly guide who will accompany you to the 200-metre (656-foot) high falls. Ermelino is very knowledgeable and can give you in-depth information about the interesting sights en route, such as the strange kinds of tree dating from the Carboniferous period (about 363–290 million years ago). The walk comes out on the lip of the falls and takes you over large blocks of stone rising out of the foaming waters. It's not for the faint-hearted. The walk takes about 10 minutes by this route. Another path leads to the foot of the falls in about 20 minutes, and suitable footwear is essential.

The Cuban Islands

Cuba is not just one island but actually a vast archipelago of 1,600 islands and a total of 4,000 islets. Needless to say there is not scope in this guide to cover them all. The vast majority of the islands are simply rocky outcrops, or *cayos*, the Cuban equivalent of the Florida Keys. Once the authorities realized the huge potential of the area to profit from tourism, many of the most beautiful *cayos* were quickly snapped up by tour operators, and are no longer deserted. In reality, only a few dozen of the islands are inaccessible, and it would seem that the desire of those in authority to open them up to tourism is tempered by environmental concerns. Given the way in which the Varadero peninsula has been sacrificed, this is certainly a good idea. However, there are still some islands where you can live out the Robinson Crusoe idyll, as long as you can find a boat to take you there . . . and you can put up with the mosquitoes.

Isla de la Juventud

The 'Island of Youth' – for a long time known as the Island of Pines – is the biggest of the Cuban islands after Cuba. Although less than 50 kilometres (30 miles) long, it offers such a diverse landscape that it gives the impression of being much larger. Driving from one end to the other, you will pass through rolling plains, forest and mangrove plantations, before reaching the beach.

It is a fairly pretty island but not stunning. Although it's quite well known, the authorities seem to be doing all they can to hinder its development – the single hotel is being allowed to slide into disrepair, there's little or no transport, and numerous sites are not open to tourists or are subject to very tight restrictions.

More than anything else, this island is renowned for its diving, with some of the most spectacular underwater flora and fauna in the Caribbean. If you're not a diver, you may be disappointed as there's little else to do.

GETTING THERE

There are boat and hydroplane crossings from **Batabanó**, a small town to the south of Havana. These arrive at **Nueva Gerona**, the island's only town, at the end of calle 24, 10 minutes' walk from the centre. Buy your ticket as early as possible as the boats are always fairly full.

By boat: one ferry a day. Cheap, but the crossing takes six hours. It's quite a hassle so the hydroplane is perhaps a better option. Tickets cost $7. To get to Batabanó catch the Astro bus from Havana. However, the return connection back to Havana is by train, which makes the journey even longer.

By hydroplane: three departures a week in both directions (normally Tuesday, Wednesday and Saturday). Tickets $11, journey time two hours.

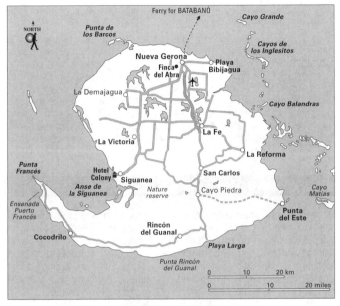

ISLA DE LA JUVENTUD

When you return, the Astro bus is waiting at Batabanó to take you back to Havana, but it's often packed.

By plane: three flights a day and four on Friday and Sunday on Cubana de Aviación, from Havana. The flight takes around 30 minutes. This is by far the best option as it is not very expensive. Book as early as possible as the plane is often full. To get to the airport, you can order a minibus from the Hotel Colony (though this is expensive). If you're staying in Nueva Gerona, there are taxis on the square opposite the Hotel Cubana.

A Brief History

Inhabited long ago by indigenous people, according to cave paintings found in the grottoes, the island was officially 'discovered' by Christopher Columbus on his second voyage. Until the 18th century it served as a port of call for Spanish galleons, but this attracted buccaneers and other pirates. It was the inspiration for Scottish writer Robert Louis Stevenson's adventure story *Treasure Island* (1883).

The Island of Pines managed to escape falling under the control of the colonizers, which explains its lack of development. The first town, Nueva Gerona, was not founded until 1830. The tradition of sending revolutionaries here started early and included José Martí, at the tender age of 17. This tradition was passed from one government to the next and, in 1926, General Machado built a gigantic 'model penitentiary' inspired by the 'Devil Circle of

Atlanta'. Later on, after the Moncada ambush, Batista incarcerated Fidel Castro and his men here.

Once Castro was free and in power himself, he did not forget the Isle of Pines: he renamed it Isla de Juventud, or 'Island of Youth', and decided to dedicate it almost entirely to young people (although there don't seem to be any more here than elsewhere). Many schools were built, as well as youth hostels, holiday camps, free leisure centres . . . and voluntary work camps. Everyone had to take part in the development of the island, and youngsters from everywhere were expected to participate in the building work. New agricultural initiatives were adopted, but lack of experience led to failure, and the island now produces barely nothing except for citrus fruit.

NUEVA GERONA

The capital, to the north of the island, is a small, charming, colourful fishing port on a river, with a very provincial air. The airport is 15 minutes away; a bus (payable in *pesos*) serves the village. Alternatively, there are a few taxis (expensive). There's not a lot to do here, but it's the only stopping-off point besides the Hotel Colony, at the other end of the island. It seems devoid of tourists, perhaps because there's no longer any accommodation available in the town itself, with the exception of a few rooms in private houses.

USEFUL ADDRESSES

All these addresses are in a tiny area in or around calle 39, the town's main street. It's easy to find your way around – the odd-numbered roads run north–south and the even-numbered roads run east–west. There's no tourist office.

✉ **Post office** (Nueva Gerona map): calle 39 (or calle Martí), between calle 18 and 20.
■ **Banco Crédito y Comercio** (Nueva Gerona map, **1**): corner of calle 39 and calle 18. Exchanges traveller's cheques, plus cash withdrawal facilities using a credit card.
■ **Cadeca** (Nueva Gerona map, A1, **2**): corner of calle 39 and calle 20. Same services as above.

■ **Cubana Agency** (Nueva Gerona map, A1, **3**): calle 39, between calle 18 and 16, next to the Hotel Cubana. ☎ 24-29. Open Monday to Friday 8am–noon and 1–4pm; Saturday 8am–noon
■ **Havanautos car hire** (Nueva Gerona map, A2, **5**): corner of calle 32 and calle 39. ☎ 24-432.
■ **CUPET service station** (Nueva Gerona map, A2, **6**): corner of calle 39 and calle 30. Open daily 24 hours.

WHERE TO STAY

There's very limited accommodation on the island, so advance booking is essential during the high season. Children at the airport will tell you about some rooms available in private houses, but make sure you take a look at the room before you reach any agreement.

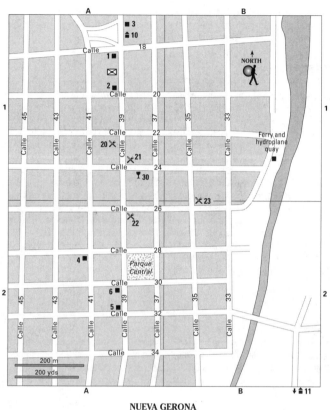

NUEVA GERONA

■ **Useful Addresses**

⊠ Post office
1 and **2** Currency exchange
3 Cubana agency
4 Telephone exchange
5 Car hire
6 CUPET service station

🛏 **Where to Stay**

10 Hotel la Cubana

11 Villa Isla de la Juventud

✕ **Where to Eat**

20 Pandería (bakery)
21 Cochinitos
22 El Dragón
23 Restaurant Delicias Pineras

🍸 **Nightlife**

22 El Dragón
30 El Patio

🛏 **Hotel Villa Isla de la Juventud** (Nueva Gerona map, off B2, **11**): just under 2 kilometres (1 mile) outside town. ☎ 23-290, 23-278 or 23-256. Double rooms in small bungalows, with fridge and air-conditioning, cost around $30, including breakfast. Not too depressing even given that it's owned by the army. A very clean, attractive swimming pool, plus restaurant, bar and boutique. Cuban families come here on holiday.

WHERE TO EAT

✗ **Panadería** (Nueva Gerona map, A1, **20**): calle 39, between calle 22 and 24. Open daily 24 hours – perfect if you've got a hankering for a hot bread roll at four in the morning.

✗ **Cochinitos** (Nueva Gerona map, A1, **21**): corner of calle 39 and calle 24 (Sanchez Amat). Open daily noon–11pm. The name of the town's 'big' restaurant means 'little pigs' so, unsurprisingly, the speciality is pork. Choice of various dishes of a reasonable standard and credit is due for trying so hard to provide a classy service. Payment is in dollars.

✗ **El Dragón** (Nueva Gerona map, A2, **22**): corner of calle 26 and calle 39. Open daily noon–10pm. Cuban influenced Chinese cuisine. Besides the typical gong at the entrance, there's a kitsch tiled patio complete with fountain and little bridge. It is best to come in the evening. It turns into a nightclub from Thursday to Sunday.

✗ **Restaurant Delicias Pineras** (Nueva Gerona map, B1–2, **23**): corner of calle 26 and calle 35. Chicken specials at very reasonable prices.

NIGHTLIFE

❦ **El Patio** (Nueva Gerona map, A1, **30**): calle 24 (Sanchez Armat), between calle 37 and 39. Open Tuesday to Sunday. Shows start at 11pm. In this small, nondescript room the number of people creates a lively atmosphere. Although some evenings it is packed, on others it can be completely empty.

❦ **El Dragón**: see 'Where to Eat'.

WHAT TO SEE AND DO

★ **El Presidio**: 5 kilometres (3 miles) east of Nueva Gerona. Open Monday to Saturday 8am–4pm; Sunday 8am–noon. Museum admission $3. There is an additional charge for taking photos inside, and a prohibitive charge for video cameras. The island's famous prison is very impressive, inspired by American penitentiaries (notably the Joliet in Illinois). The prison, which has been closed since 1967, consists of four enormous circular blocks, each with hundreds of little windows (one per cell) with the bars removed. Now empty, the place has a strange, surrealist atmosphere about it. You can imagine that a month in here would be enough to drive anyone mad.

More than 4,000 detainees were held there before the Revolution. The refectory, where nobody was allowed to speak, was known as the 'canteen of a thousand silences', where 3,000 prisoners ate at one sitting. Walk round one of the open buildings – there are 93 cells on each of five levels, housing two prisoners per cell. There were no doors and the prisoners were forced to remain standing throughout the day. There was no room to sit down, anyway. The single guard would access the central viewing point through an underground passage so he didn't have eye contact with any of the prisoners. The place was designed so that he could keep watch over almost everyone at once.

– There is a museum in block No. 1 containing the cell where Castro lived from 1953 to 1955, after the attack on the Moncada barracks. Judging by the size of the room and the conditions of his detention, in comparison with the norm he was looked after pretty well for a revolutionary. The reason for the difference in treatment is supposedly because he had to be kept separate from the other revolutionaries. The books that he was at leisure to learn by heart, including five volumes of *Das Capital* by Karl Marx (1818–83), are displayed in a cabinet. During his incarceration he wrote his first manifesto 'History will absolve me'. Also displayed is the register in which Fidel and his brother were signed out (under No. 1818).

Further on is a room dedicated to the construction and history of the penitentiary, including a photograph of Machado laying the first stone in 1926. In 1939 the Cuban dictators officially named the prison 'Concentration camp for foreign enemies'. There is a full plan of the initial project and details of a typical day in the life of a prisoner.

In the hospital room there are photographs of the beds of Fidel and of his brother Raúl. On each bed lies a black eye-mask that they used at night, as the lights were never turned off. A small commemorative plaque shows that the *moncadistas* (the name given to the revolutionaries who attacked the Moncada) composed an anti-Batista hymn here.

★ **Bibijagua** (island map): this famous black-sand beach is around 8 kilometres (5 miles) east of Nueva Gerona in the same direction as the prison.

★ **Finca del Abra** (island map): 2 kilometres (1 mile) outside Nueva Gerona. Open Tuesday to Saturday 9am–5pm and Sunday morning. Admission $1. It was on this estate that José Martí spent nine weeks before being deported to Spain. There's a long avenue with attractive vegetation forming an arch overhead leading up to it. Note the amazing tree with gigantic roots in front of the *finca*.

★ **Excursions**: it's possible to visit the areas to the south of the island, but you need to hire a car and guide from Havanautos (either in Nueva Gerona or at the Hotel Colony, *see* 'Useful Addresses'), because this part of the island is off-limits to lone tourists. It's impossible to make your own way there, as you must have a pass (available free from Havanautos), with which you can do the round trip in a day. It's cheaper if there are four of you (five including the guide), but it's probably not really worth the expense.

– The **Criadero de Cocodrilo**, in the southwest of the island, is one of the largest crocodile breeding centres in Cuba. After the village of La Fe, in the wild southeastern part of the island, is a **nature reserve**. Major attractions here are vultures, enormous crabs and, if you're lucky, a boa or a crocodile all in their natural environment.

– **Rincón del Guanal** (island map): in the centre of the southern coast is a beach where turtles lay their eggs in July and August.

– **Punta del Este** (island map): drive 34 kilometres (22 miles) south of Nueva Gerona, then follow a track to the left for 24 kilometres (15 miles). This is a small pre-Columbian cave, swarming with mosquitoes, and decorated with strange pictographs. Near by there's a small, deserted beach with a lot of algae, but the sea is superb. Don't forget to pack a picnic as there's no restaurant out here.

★ **Playa Roja**: this large, palm-fringed beach 40 kilometres (25 miles) southwest of Nueva Gerona is very popular with tourists. A shuttle bus will take you straight there if you're staying at the Hotel Colony (*see below*), but you have to pay (there's no alternative). The beach in front of the hotel is of little interest and the sea is quite rough so there are no fish. The only reason to go would be the scuba-diving excursions arranged by the club.

WHERE TO STAY AND EAT

🛏 ✗ **Hotel Colony** (island map): on the beach. ☎ 981-81. Fax: 26-120. A double costs $46 for bed and breakfast, $70 half board and $94 full board. You're obliged to eat here anyway, since there's nowhere else around. The charmless 1960s building is the only real hotel on the island for tourists, and a meeting place for divers. The drab corridors lead to reasonably comfortable, if somewhat shabby, rooms with air-conditioning and hot showers. The restaurant is decent but nothing special, offering an all-inclusive buffet (although lobster is extra). The swimming pool is pleasant enough and there's also a garden. The best thing is perhaps the *mojito* bar, right on the water at the end of a long jetty. Delightful at sunset but make sure you can find your way back to your room.

WHAT TO DO

Diving is the speciality of the region, and there are at least 56 different spots along the southwest coast discovered over the past 25 years by the inimitable Tony at Club Colony.

🛶 **Club Colony**: in the marina, 2 kilometres (1 mile) from the hotel by minibus shuttle. ☎ 98-181 or 98-282. Fax: 26-120. From the club a boat takes divers beyond **Cabo Francés**, about one hour away. The dive costs $35, plus $20 for equipment hire. If you do a second dive on the same day it costs $30. There are also four-day courses. You can book dives through the main Cuban agencies.

This club is reputed to be the best in Cuba and has about 20 monitors and a dozen boats. The world champion scuba-diver (a Cuban) trains here. The dives basically entail a full-day trip as the sites are some distance away. Aside from the superb black coral reefs, there's plenty to see underwater, such as tunnels and caves. The marine life includes manta rays, barracudas, groupers, lobsters and much more.

You come back to have lunch in a big wooden cabin at the far end of a long pontoon, not far from the dive sites. You can either take your own food (remember the nearest shops are in Nueva Gerona), or buy a meal on site (not recommended). If you're only doing a morning dive you can spend the afternoon on a vast, completely deserted beach. The peace is only occasionally shattered by cruise ships weighing anchor near by.

CAYO LARGO

Over 100 kilometres (62 miles) east of Isla de la Juventud is the last island of the Los Canarreos archipelago. In spite of its name meaning 'Long Island', Cayo Largo is less than 40 kilometres (25 miles) long. However, it has all the ingredients of a tropical Garden of Eden. With great expanses of sand as fine as talcum powder, it's permanently bathed in sunshine with a warm, clear, turquoise sea. It's simply a dream island, normally only found in magazines and travel brochures.

The good thing is that tourist development has not spiralled out of control – only a small proportion of the island has been exploited, and the six adjacent hotels do not cover more than 2 kilometres (1 mile). This still leaves vast expanses of wilderness that are quite difficult to access but well worth the effort.

This is one place that was discovered not by Christopher Columbus, but by Fidel Castro. The story goes that his helicopter broke down and was forced to land here. He was so taken by this paradise isle that he decided to turn it into a holiday camp for Cubans, and so the airport and the first hotel were built. Since then Cayo Largo has been the most overrun with tourists of all Cuba's isles. Here, as in Cayo Coco, the magic formula is the *todo incluido* (all-inclusive). Once you've bought your ticket (not cheap), you can put away your dollars. Meals, all-night bars, diving equipment – everything is included. You won't get to see many Cubans, but on the other hand it's a far cry from the luxury of Cayo Coco and you can enjoy relative peace and quiet (just one disco between the six hotels) as long as you can escape the mosquitoes.

GETTING THERE

By Air

All the travel agencies in Cuba and the tourist offices in the major Havana hotels offer package tours to Cayo Largo, including flight, board and lodging. A bus collects visitors from the main Havana hotels and drops them at a small private airport not far from the national airport. Although the flight itself only lasts 30 minutes, the frequency of flights seems to be completely random, so be prepared for a long wait. There's also a daily morning flight from **Varadero** (returning in the evening) and charter flights from **Isla de la Juventud**. Reservations are essential in all cases. At the end of your trip, check on the noticeboards in reception to make sure you are booked on the return trip, as some people have been stranded.

By Boat

There's no service, but there is a marina full of private yachts.

USEFUL ADDRESSES

■ **Bank**: on the marina. Open Monday to Friday 8am–noon and 2–3.30pm; Saturday and Sunday 9am–noon. Takes Visa and Master-Card. There are also bureaux de change at the hotel receptions, where credit cards and travellers' cheques are accepted.

■ **International telephone**: opposite the Hotel Isla del Sur. Open all

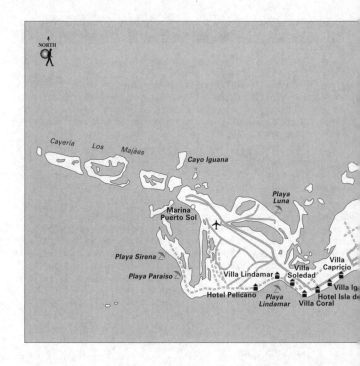

day for telephone cards, stamps, postcards, etc.

■ **Shuttle buses**: free service between the hotels and to Playa Sirena, Playa Paraiso and the marina. Timetables are displayed opposite the Isla del Sur.

■ **Car hire**: on the main road, opposite the hotels. Hiring a car is not that useful given the size of the island. You can also hire buggies with sidecars – quite expensive but very good on the sandy tracks.

■ **Horse-riding**: next door to the car-hire office.

■ **Policínica** (medical centre): emergency service at the marina, 8 kilometres (5 miles) from the hotels. No call-out, so you have to go by taxi. The pharmacy is next door. There's also an emergency doctor on call in the hotels – ask at reception.

■ **Toilets** and **showers**: there are facilities for sailors in the marina.

WHERE TO STAY

There are six big hotels next to each other along Playa Lindamar, the main beach. If you've bought a package holiday in advance it will include accommodation in one of these hotels. However, you won't know which one until you check in at the central reception at the Hotel Isla del Sur. Allow a minimum of $170 per person for one night (less for a longer stay but there's

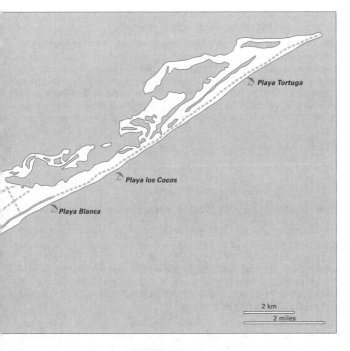

△ Playa Tortuga

△ Playa los Cocos

△ Playa Blanca

2 km
2 miles

CAYO LARGO

not much to warrant a week's visit). Out of season the agencies automatically upgrade you to the Lindamar or the Pelicano if there's room.

– Sailors who want to spend a few days on dry land can rent a house. Check at the port office.

≙ **Villa Coral**: one of the nicest, with bungalows arranged around the pool and bar. Friendly staff, well-kept rooms with bath, mini-bar and air conditioning, and also billiards and table tennis.

≙ **Lindamar**: newly built, comfortable chalets.

≙ **Isla del Sur**: the oldest (built in 1952), and its only interesting feature is that the apartments have a sea view.

≙ **Villa Iguana**: the saddest, though it does have a small swimming pool and a diving club.

≙ **Villa Capricio**: the most original: the bungalows are straw huts. Note that it has fewer mod cons than the others, and watch out for the mosquitoes.

≙ **Pelicano**: this is the biggest and one of the newest.

WHERE TO EAT

Each hotel has buffet meals included in the package. There's an Italian restaurant in Villa Coral if you want a bit of a change (book the day before),

THE CUBAN ISLANDS

and there are *ranchones* (snack bars) all over the place. They're open daily 10am– 5pm and tend to specialize in fried chicken.

✕ **El Criollo**: in the marina. A good, welcoming restaurant – but expensive at $8.50 for grilled chicken, $15 for prawns and $20 for lobster. Only really for the few people who have come by boat or to swim, or those who are desperate to escape the interminable buffets.

✕ There are various bars and snack bars in the marina (opening times vary). The **Taberna del Pirata** snack bar on Playa Sirena is only open at midday, but sometimes it has lobster.

WHAT TO DO

The package deals normally offer a few activities into the bargain, such as an hour's pony trekking, cycle rides and the use of sailing or diving equipment. These should be booked with the relevant clubs.

– To the west are two superb beaches, **Playa Paraiso** and **Playa Sirena**. There are minibuses to take guests out to the beaches, and snacks, drinks and snorkelling gear are available on arrival. If you prefer more isolated beaches, head for the east coast, where no development has taken place – not a single sun-lounger or drinks stall. This tranquillity has its downside, however: there's no road, just a sandy track full of potholes. The best option is to go by bike, otherwise hire a buggy and sidecar. Scooters are not recommended. The beaches on this side are so fabulous, you could almost forget there's anyone else on the island.

– **Turtles**: there are three sorts on Cayo Largo: the greenbacked turtles, the parrot turtle and the *carreta carreta*, which is also found in the Mediterranean. They come to lay their eggs on the seashore between May and September, but it's becoming difficult to see them as they only come out at nightfall and are ever-more nervous at signs of human activity. If you're very lucky you might spot them when swimming behind the coral reef in front of the Villa Capricio and Pelicano hotels.

– Otherwise, you could visit the **Turtle Park**. Although it's not particularly big, you can see all three species here. Octavio, who runs the park, is heavily involved in conservation work – collecting eggs the moment they're laid, burying them in the sand and releasing the hatched turtles back into the wild after a few months. He's very happy for tourists to accompany him.

– **Excursions**: ask the agency representatives at the Hotel Isla del Sur for details. Some of the trips are very expensive, for example $65 to go to **Cayo Iguana** (Iguana Island), which is only 15 minutes by boat from the marina. However, it's a very interesting place, as some of the iguanas are more than a metre (3 feet) long. One option is an excursion to **Cayo Rico** in a glass-bottomed boat, with snorkelling next to the coral reef ($54, including lunch and drinks). There's also a day trip by catamaran, diving and visit to a virgin island ($69).

CAYO SANTA MARÍA

Cayo Santa María is a dream islet for those who love their nature to be almost unspoiled. For several years the only means of access was a causeway over 50 kilometres (30 miles) in length. However, now the government is encouraging mass tourism, the fragile ecosystems of the *cayos* are being put at risk. A 300-bed hotel is already on the drawing-board and a tiny airport has appeared in the middle of nowhere, near Cayo Las Brujas.

Consequently, time is not on Cayo Santa María's side – if you want to enjoy the beaches of white, virgin sand – with little more company than the odd iguana or two – get there as soon as possible.

GETTING THERE

By car: access to the *cayo* is from the port of Caibarién (56 kilometres/35 miles northeast of Santa Clara). However, don't go directly there as you'll have to pay the equivalent of $5 per person for a 'visa' from Café Rumbos, on the main road in Caibarién. This visa entitles you to pass the frontier post of the *cayo*, a few kilometres along the causeway. If you don't have it, you will be sent back. The road is absolutely sublime and crosses more than 50 bridges. Since the sea is very shallow, the water is emerald green and completely clear. On the road you pass the construction workers fishing under the bridges, oblivious of the pink flamingos and pelicans watching them.

WHERE TO STAY AND EAT

≜ ✕ **Villa las Brujas**: hamlet of Las Brujas; at the 38-kilometre marker, turn left towards the airport. It's sign-posted. ☎ 02-41-99. Around 20 chalets, costing $45 per night for two (up to $54 in high season). Most have a sea view (but make sure you specify that you want one when booking). On the edge of a small cliff overlooking a superb bay with little spits of land edged by mangroves. A restaurant with an observation tower (spectacular panorama at sunset) offers good fish and shellfish, even if you do pay a high price for the view. The beach is immense and will please snorkellers. Guests can also hire equipment for catamaran sailing, windsurfing and other activities. The seabed is very rich along the rocks and it's not unusual to see a few barracudas.

≜ ✕ **Barco San Pasquale**: Rumbos, on the *cayo*. No telephone. A double room costs $28, plus $6 per person for the crossing, bookable at Villa las Brujas (*see above*). This is possibly the most isolated place to spend the night in the whole of Cuba – an old petrol tanker 145 metres (467 feet) long, built in 1920 and resting on the sand a few hundred metres from the coast. The *San Pasquale* was converted into a floating hotel in 1960 and offers 10 cabins with amenities, one of which was once occupied by Ernest Hemingway when he used to fish in the area. After a 30-minute crossing in a small boat, you are greeted by the sound of the ship's bell. The extremely verbose manager, a fount of knowledge on the history of the ship, organizes educational visits and day trips ($13 for the visit and a meal, again via Villa las Brujas). The evening entertainment consists of dinner in a mess room with a video presentation of the hull of the ship. Strolling along the ship's decks at night is very romantic.

CAYO COCO AND GUILLERMO DIALLING CODE: 33

Bathed in the Atlantic on the other side of Cuba from Cayo Largo are these other two *cayos*, north of the town of Ciego de Avila.

If you don't like sunbathing, swimming or watersports you won't have much to do on these twin islets.

Cayo Coco has eight beaches spread over 22 kilometres (14 miles), while **Cayo Guillermo**'s three beaches stretch for 5 kilometres (3 miles). Apart from the beaches, these islets are particularly inhospitable, with a not particularly attractive mangrove plantation and a few forgotten palm trees. Then there are the mosquitoes, which are hungry as monsters here.

In spite of the mosquitoes, Cayo Coco is a haven for birdlife of around 159 different species. However, apart from the hotels, there is nothing on the island, not even a village or small café – just a few prefabricated dwellings for the hotel staff.

GETTING THERE

The only way to visit Cayo Coco and Cayo Guillermo is to book a number of nights in hotels through a tour operator before departure, or to take a chance at one of the few cheap establishments listed below. If you're not a real beach lover, a day trip from Morón will be enough for you, since it's no more than 40 kilometres (25 miles) away and there isn't much else to do.

By Car

Incredible as it may seem, these isles can be reached by road, just like the Florida Keys. There's a superb 17-kilometre (11-mile) causeway that links the two isles to the land across the lagoon of **Bahía de Perros**. Here the sky and the sea merge into one, and the lagoon's calm is only disturbed by the pink flamingos or the ducks. There's a superb promenade, but the road is so straight that some people have difficulty keeping awake; try not to go for an unplanned dip in the lagoon!

You pick up this road on leaving Morón (*see* 'The Centre of the Island'), at the village of La Loma, after the lagoon of La Leche – which turns the colour of milk when the wind blows. It takes a good hour. First you arrive at Cayo Coco, which you have to cross to get to Cayo Guillermo.

– Note: You have to pay a toll of $2 per person both ways.

By Air

– For **Cayo Coco**: there are four flights per week with Cubana departing from **Havana**, or flights to **Ciego de Avila** from **Varadero**. Charter flights are also available via travel agencies.

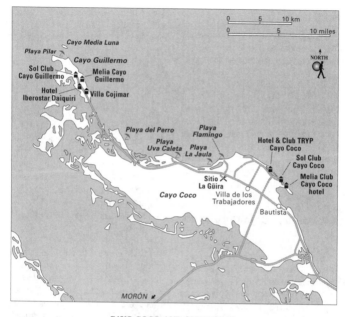

CAYO COCO AND GUILLERMO

WHERE TO STAY AND EAT

In Cayo Coco

There are no top-class hotels in Cayo Coco, but it's still possible to enjoy the super beaches without forking out huge amounts for accommodation.

☆☆ Moderate

⚓ ✕ **Sitio la Güira**: centre of the island, signposted from the main road that leads to the airport. ☎ 30-12-08. La Güira is a model rural farm hamlet – slightly more touristy than the rest of the island with its restaurants, bars and souvenir shops. Once the tour buses leave, however (they generally arrive at lunchtime and leave around 5pm), it lapses back into peace and tranquillity and you find yourself alone among the turkeys, goats, chickens and other farm animals. Children love it. There are two huts where you can sleep for $25 a night, or an apartment with two

bedrooms and shared bathroom for $20 a night. Simple facilities and capricious hot-water supply, but life on a farm more than compensates.

⚓ ✕ **Motel Los Cocos**: on arrival at Cayo Coco on the road from Morón, turn right at the first roundabout, go through the workers' village then take the first on the right. ☎ 30-81-21. Managed by Cubanacan, this is another economic option on the island – spacious and clean double and triple rooms for $25 and $30 respectively. There's a reasonably priced bar and restaurant at the entrance. Advance booking recommended.

☆☆☆ Expensive

– If you book through an agency, all the hotels are run on an all-inclusive basis, so you can relax and eat and drink as much as you like. If you have a choice, the hotels in the Sol y Melia chain are perhaps the most tasteful; the Sol Club hotels offer activities every half-hour. The Melia hotels (even posher) leave you more to your own devices, with a huge array of sports to choose from (cycling, horse-riding, watersports etc.). Non-residents may also make use of these facilities, but check with the hotels.

🛏 ✕ **Sol Club Cayo Coco**: ☎ 30-12-80. Fax: 30-12-85. Email: sol. club.cayo.coco@solmelia.es. Website: www.solmelia.es. Prices vary hugely depending on season and agreements with agencies. There are 266 bedrooms and four suites in comfortable chalets. Copious, varied buffet meals and other à la carte restaurants. On the seafront and offering non-stop activities.

🛏 ✕ **Melia Club Cayo Coco**: ☎ 30-13-00. Fax: 30-13-86. A whacking $134 for a double room with breakfast, mid-season, or $184 all-inclusive. The other hotels are modest by comparison. The swimming pool stretches from the bar to the apartments – very Hollywood. Better guarded than Fidel Castro's office, this vast complex consists of 400 rooms, a buffet, grill and six restaurants, bars everywhere, two swimming pools, a sailing club, masses of entertainers to stave off the boredom, a discotheque, etc.

– There's less choice when it comes to restaurants as most of the hotels include meals in the package. However, non-residents can eat at the **Sol Club Cayo Coco** for $20. Not a bargain, but the portions are big and the menu varied – a nice change from the ubiquitous fried chicken. There are also the restaurants in **Sitio la Güira** (see above), a **snack bar** on Flamingo beach and a **cafeteria** next to the service station.

WHERE TO STAY AND EAT

Cayo Guillermo

This has much the same hotels and range of options as Cayo Coco. There is a **Sol Club** (☎ 30-17-60. Fax: 30-17-48) and a **Melia** under construction.

🛏 ✕ **Villa Cojimar**: ☎ 30-10-12 or 30-17-12. Fax: 33-55-54. The first hotel to open here, now run by an Italian company, and the most affordable if you turn up without a reservation ($135 for a double in season, all-inclusive). Impossible to book through an agency unless you're from Italy or Quebec (no agreement with any British tour operator). Not as luxurious as the other hotels, but the bar and swimming pool are as they ought to be. Pleasant apartments, restaurant and grill. There's a display in the foyer of the construction project for

the *cayo* – a frightening prospect with no part of the coastline left untouched.

In the evening you can put the world to rights at Guillermo's **La Bodeguita**, under the inevitable signatures on the walls, the photograph of Gregorio Fuentes and a model of '*The Old Man and the Sea*'. Deep-sea fishing, windsurfing, dinghy and catamaran sailing available.

🛏 ✕ **Hotel Iberostar Daiquiri**: ☎ 30-16-50. Fax: 30-16-45. Spanish-run luxury complex with more than 300 apartments. A double room costs around $180 in season, all-inclusive. The lobby is vast and full of plants. There are four bars, three restaurants, three swimming pools, a mini club for children, sauna, etc. Also watersports and beginners' diving lessons.

WHAT TO DO

– It's probably best to head straight for the north coast of Cayo Coco before the inevitable development work begins. You can still get to a few beaches that are not overrun by people wearing 'club' bracelets, including **Playa Flamingo**, just west of the big hotels. It's a state-owned beach so there are lifeguards on duty, and it's ideal for snorkelling. You can hire equipment and go out to the coral reef by catamaran. A thatched restaurant/bar is open daily 9am–4pm.

– Further west along the Cayo Guillermo road are the wilder **Playa Uva Caleta** and **Playa del Perro** beaches.

– **Playa Pilar**: right at the end of Cayo Guillermo, after 6 kilometres (4 miles) of track that is suitable for cars. The only signpost on the island points towards the entrance to the car-park. You'll find a lovely white-sand beach lapped by turquoise waters. The bar/restaurant is open daily – with cocktails at $1.50, chicken $2.50, grilled fish $6 and prawns for around $11. You can hire canoes, windsurfers, catamarans and the like.

– Facing Playa Pilar is **Cayo Media Luna**, where Batista had a small retreat built for himself that was subsequently destroyed in a hurricane. There is still a straw hut that you can get to by catamaran if you want to go snorkelling – it's used to store the equipment. The dive site is next to the coral reef, just offshore (around $5 an hour).

Index

Make the most of your mini-break

Great Weekend titles provide all the information you need to ensure that you really get to know a city in just a few days – from advice on what to see, where to stay and where to eat out, to exploring the city's character through its culture and lifestyle. Plus a detailed section on where to do your shopping. Full colour throughout and great value for money.

A GREAT WEEKEND *in* ....

AMSTERDAM	1 84202 002 1
BARCELONA	1 84202 170 2
BERLIN	1 84202 061 7
BRUSSELS	1 84202 017 X
DUBLIN	1 84202 096 X
FLORENCE	1 84202 010 2
LISBON	1 84202 011 0
LONDON	1 84202 168 0
MADRID	1 84202 095 1
NAPLES	1 84202 016 1
NEW YORK	1 84202 004 8
PARIS	1 84202 001 3
PRAGUE	1 84202 000 5
ROME	1 84202 169 9
VENICE	1 84202 018 8
VIENNA	1 84202 026 9

Forthcoming titles:

BUDAPEST	1 84202 160 5
SEVILLE	1 84202 162 1

Titles are available through all good booksellers, or by calling 01903 828800, quoting ref. RT2 (in the UK).

HACHETTE

HACHETTE VACANCES

A unique series of regional guides in colour that focus on the needs of families and those in search of an active holiday. Packed with hundreds of suggestions for places to visit, sights to see and things to do – as well as providing detailed information about the region's culture, heritage and history

Titles currently published:

Brittany	1 84202 007 2
Catalonia	1 84202 099 4
Corsica	1 84202 100 1
Languedoc-Roussillon	1 84202 008 0
Normandy	1 84202 097 8
Perigord & Dordogne	1 84202 098 6
Poitou-Charentes	1 84202 009 9
Provence & The Côte d'Azur	1 84202 006 4
Pyrenees & Gascony	1 84202 015 3
South West France	1 84202 014 5

Forthcoming titles:

Alsace-Vosges	1 84202 167 2
Ardeche	1 84202 161 3
Basque Country	1 84202 159 1
French Alps	1 84202 166 4

Titles are available through all good booksellers, or by calling 01903 828800, quoting ref. RT1 (in the UK).

HACHETTE